Yale Publications in Religion, 4
David Horne, Editor

Published under the direction of the Divinity School

# FAITH AND PREJUDICE

Intergroup Problems in Protestant Curricula

by BERNHARD E. OLSON

New Haven and London, Yale University Press, 1963

To my wife, Frances,
and our children: Sandra Lee, Judith Anne,
and Terese Maria

# Acknowledgments

I am clearly indebted to many persons not directly involved in the process of doing the actual analysis of the lessons and organization of the findings. Special gratitude is due Liston Pope of the Yale Divinity School, whose interest in the study and its importance made it possible in the first place, and who provided the necessary facilities. The original faculty supervisory and administrative committee appointed by Dean Pope consisted of four members. Its continuing and able chairman, Paul H. Vieth, representing the Department of Religious Education, has encouraged the steady completion of the project while showing unusual understanding of the problems the researcher faced in setting up, revising, and carrying out the work.

Hugh Hartshorne, Professor of Psychology of Religion and himself a noted researcher, was indispensable in evaluating the research design. Kenneth W. Underwood, now of Wesleyan University but at the inception of this project an assistant professor in social ethics at Yale, has given valuable guidance and advice at every stage of the undertaking, and from the very beginning has insisted that Protestant curriculum materials be examined within the context of American culture. Franklin W. Young, from the field of New Testament studies, after leaving Yale was succeeded on the committee by Paul W. Meyer, assistant professor of the New Testament. Dr. Hartshorne, upon his retirement, was followed by William A. Christian of the Department of Religion, who served on the committee for a year. His place was filled by Norvin J. Hein, associate professor of comparative religion. Professors Meyer and Hein have both devoted many hours to the evaluation of passages about Jewish and non-Christian religions scored in the distortion-correction category.

I am also deeply grateful to Roland H. Bainton for checking scores of distortions in references to Catholicism in the medieval, Reformation, and post-Reformation periods. Rabbis Morris N.

Kertzer and Marc H. Tanenbaum have been invaluable as resource guides, as have Judith Hershcopf and other officials of The American Jewish Committee, which encouraged this project and was instrumental in securing foundation support for it. Nina Ridenour was extremely helpful with suggestions for limiting the project to manageable proportions. J. Oscar Lee has been *ex officio* a member of the advisory committee and has shared insights into intergroup relations out of a rich background of experience in the fields of religious education and racial relations. Thomas P. Coffey and Theodore Solotaroff were highly instrumental in making the manuscript more readable. Mrs. Margaret Hesser typed the final manuscript.

To the communicators with whose curricula this volume is particularly concerned, and to their editors, there is owed an unusual debt. They have given permission to identify their materials, thereby making the writing easier and the book more valuable than it otherwise would have been had the communicators remained anonymous. Consultations with Arnold C. Mueller, editor-in-chief, and Arthur L. Miller, executive secretary, of the Board for Parish Education, the Lutheran Church—Missouri Synod; Bernice T. Cory, editor-in-chief, and Henry L. Jacobsen, editor of senior and adult publications, Scripture Press; Ernest W. Kuebler, director, Robert L'H. Miller, curriculum editor, and Sophia Lyon Fahs, curriculum consultant, of the Division of Education, Council of Liberal Churches (Unitarian-Universalist); Norman F. Langford, editor-in-chief, and Donald L. Leonard, executive editor, Presbyterian Church U.S.A., have all been helpful in the extreme.

*B.E.O.*

*New Haven, Connecticut*
*February 1962*

# Contents

# Contents

# Preface

This book is a Protestant self-study of church school teachings in the complicated and delicate area of intergroup relations. By analyzing current official lesson materials, it describes and evaluates how four representative Protestant groups portray other racial, ethnic, and—more particularly—religious communities. The following pages provide answers to certain fundamental questions. Is any prejudice, implicit as well as explicit, found in Protestant curricula? What images of other groups, especially religious ones, are provided teachers and pupils? How do Protestants see themselves vis-à-vis the other faiths with which they compete in the free market of a pluralistic culture? Do significant differences exist within Protestantism itself in depicting those who live outside it? If so, what are the relationships between the diverse theological orientations of modern Protestants and the kinds of problems they encounter in teaching about non-Protestants? Finally, at what points, if any, do the deep commitments of the various versions of the Protestant faith promote or impede wholesome intergroup relations?

These questions spring partly from the desire of the Protestant community to continually re-examine its own life, in keeping with its vigorous slogan of self-criticism, "The church must be free to reform itself!" But they also stem from a realization that Jews, Catholics, Negroes, and others are genuinely apprehensive about the attitudes of outsiders toward them. These anxieties are not entirely groundless. If the Protestant legacy of freedom and toleration is impressive, it is also tragically stained. This mixed legacy is not entirely a matter of past history. In the battle for religious liberty from the days of the Reformers to the present, two forces have contended for supremacy—an emerging commitment to freedom of conscience, and a tendency to punish dissent. Not even the democratic ethos of Protestantism in the nineteenth and twentieth centuries was sufficient to check the tide of the "Know-Nothing" and Ku Klux Klan eras. The same ambivalence is no less marked today. Many white Protestants, for example, have spoken and acted bravely to advance the cause of civil rights; yet the disturbing fact remains that the churches are the most segregated institutions in America. Elsewhere, the holocaust that all but destroyed European Jewry raises the same crucial paradox. Why were some Christians staunchly able to resist the anti-Semitism that culminated in the horrors of Buchenwald and Auschwitz? Yet why did the vast majority succumb? These ambiguities deeply disturb conscientious Christians who raise questions about the relevance and import of Christian ideology and commitment, which leads us to inquire whether there are both strengths and liabilities in Protestant teachings that permit these radically disparate responses to the fate of minorities. In sum, do the Protestant faiths contain both sources of and antidotes to prejudice, and, if so, can these contradictory factors be isolated and named?

It is hoped that such an inquiry will prove helpful to Protestant religious educators, clergy and laymen who wish to reassess their teachings about other groups and to draw more fully upon the resources of their own faith for more constructive images of non-Protestants. However, our intent is not so much to stimulate piecemeal changes in this or that type of statement about Jews, Catholics, or Negroes as it is to provide the kind of analysis that will assist all men of faith to clarify and refine the perspectives from which they write or speak about others.

But the issues involved in this study clearly go beyond Sunday School problems, even specifically Protestant ones. Prejudice is a human trait and the perennial problem of all groups—Protestants have no monopoly on it.[1] Like other communities, they may be hostile or sympathetic to outsiders; similarly, they may view other religious, racial, and ethnic groups chiefly through the lenses of their own paramount concerns, and tend to take account of them mainly as they affect their own life for good or ill. As such, their group concepts of what they are and what others are derive in

1. In sociological literature there is little recognition of the existence of anti-Protestant prejudice; there is also a tendency to associate prejudice with the designations "White Protestant" or "white Anglo-Saxon Protestant." This usage makes Protestants appear as the definitive bigots and possibly reflects assumptions typical of an earlier era when Protestantism was a more dominant influence in American society.

good part from the inevitable encounters of diverse groups as they relate and conflict with one another in a pluralistic society. For this reason, Protestant images of "self" and "otherness" shed light on the general social problems of intergroup rivalry and cultural conflict in our time. Further, these images illuminate the peculiar issues with which the religious institutions must struggle as they face—from within their respective faiths—the difficulties of co-existing creatively in our society without undermining each other's freedom and security.

In this connection, it is important to realize that our general religious and cultural heritages in intergroup relations are notoriously ambiguous.[2] Our most common platitudes laud the Judeo-Christian and the American creeds as the twin supports of freedom for all groups. But within both traditions there are powerful forces that oppose the practice of this freedom. The values placed on independence, permissiveness, and diversity of opinion and observance are contradicted by others that promote conformity, restriction, and elimination of dissent. The growing tendency today to impose political and social consensus raises in a new and more subtle form the older questions—such as the nature of liberty—that we assumed had been settled. Thus, though the political structure of America is designed to guarantee freedom to its members, the fact remains that the defamation of certain groups and the threats to their rights receive tacit or active support from various sectors of society, including some that claim they draw their sanction from Christian ideology.[3] Despite the unmistakable trend toward dialogue, understanding, and cooperation, there has also been an increase in inter-religious conflict.[4]

2. An excellent historical account of these ambiguities is given by Roland H. Bainton, *The Travail of Religious Liberty* (Philadelphia, Westminster Press, 1951). The dark side of the struggle in the United States is portrayed by Gustavus Myers in *History of Bigotry in the United States* (New York, Random House, 1943). For a popular version see Everett B. Clinchy, *All in the Name of God* (New York, John Day, 1934).

3. Particularly, the anti-Semitic organizations and publications which use the designation "Christian," or which appeal to proof-texts from the Bible. For a very partial description of some of these groups see Milton Ellerin, "The Hate Groups," *Social Action* (Nov. 1960), pp. 14–21.

4. For a provocative analysis of Catholic-Protestant tension see Kenneth Wilson Underwood, *Protestant and Catholic: Religion and Social Interaction in an Industrial Community* (Boston, Beacon Press, 1957).

Thus the contemporary culture which shapes and is shaped by the American churches provides equivocal implications for the future freedom of our racial and religious communities. As long as there are potent racist mythologies in our midst and widespread approval of institutionalized segregation and discrimination, our national way of life will continue to nourish as well as restrain the would-be oppressors; so, too, it will provide and pinpoint, as well as protect, their potential or actual victims. Whether the churches uncritically reflect these dangerous ambiguities (and whether they create any of their own) becomes an important question, not only for students of our religious institutions, but for each American who cherishes freedom and justice.

It is essential, then, for Protestantism to re-examine the intergroup aspects of its life and teachings in the light of these fateful oppositions within both the culture and the churches, and to see in what specific ways these oppositions are reflected or transcended. But at the same time, the following pages will also raise issues which concern non-Protestant readers, whether general students of society, specialists in intergroup relations, or simply adherents of another faith. For the problems Protestant educators struggle with are, finally, but variants of the problems that all of us face in belonging to groups that must relate themselves to one another in a tense, complex, and heterogeneous social order, while also trying to preserve their own identity and advance their own views.

The complexity of this study and the problems thrown into sharpest relief by its findings led the writer to emphasize certain aspects of the Protestant struggle with prejudice and to subordinate others. Thus Protestant images of religious groups are analyzed almost exclusively, with racial and ethnic ones receiving only general treatment. Similarly, beliefs and attitudes expressed about other Protestants receive less attention than do those which pertain to non-Protestants, particularly Jews and Catholics. In order to characterize the different Protestant conceptions of themselves and of other groups, the writer has chosen to concentrate on data which can be placed within two general types—those of "victims" and "oppressors." This typology, along with the selected analytic categories it involves, should not be taken in a simple or necessarily invidious sense. It does not imply that a tyranny has been let loose in America by or against Protestants, but merely helps to sort out the many kinds of statements that appear in Protestant teaching material concerning the ways in which various groups (including their own) suffer or inflict prejudice, segregation, and persecution in their encounters in the past and within contemporary culture. The system of analysis that follows from this typology is intended to be both precise and yet broad enough to embrace the total scope of victimization and oppression that figures in Protestant teaching —ranging from mild to severe, from mere dislike to hatred, from simple avoidance to segregation, from name-calling to massacre.

Despite the fact that writers of religious textbooks are primarily concerned with nurturing persons in the faith, they inevitably deal with the relations that exist between their faith and others. In doing so, they communicate their attitudes toward other faiths and also indicate what they believe are the attitudes of the other faiths toward their own. While these types of statements do not appear as frequently as do those which describe the moral behavior of Jews, Catholics, or non-Christians or which judge the validity of their beliefs or practices, nonetheless they are crucially important; they isolate the significant problems that Protestants experience in portraying their past and present conflicts with other communities of faith. In fact, Protestant teachings about the moral characteristics and behavior of outsiders are of consequence primarily because of their bearing on the questions raised by the victim-oppressor typology. For example, a positive view of Jewish morality can be used to combat the defamation of Jews; on the other hand, a negative view of Negro or Jewish behavior can be used to justify existing segregation or religious discrimination. If Catholic doctrines and actions are made to seem sufficiently menacing, it may encourage Protestants to conceive of themselves catagorically as victims and Catholics as oppressors and to behave defensively. To deal with the victim-oppressor theme in some depth, then, is to clarify the major Protestant anxieties and resources that impel them to subvert or affirm the full liberties of other racial, ethnic, or religious communities.

In order to analyze an adequate cross-section of Protestant teaching, the curriculum materials of four publishers were compared and contrasted. These publishers represent four basic theological perspectives—conservatism, fundamentalism, naturalistic liberalism, and neo-orthodoxy (the popular designation for the neo-Reformation movement that includes the thought of Barth, Brunner, the Niebuhrs, Tillich, et al.). The materials of other church school publishers (or "communicators," as they are often called), have also been examined for significant variations from the characteristic content found in the four representative ones.

By making a statistical analysis of the lesson materials of these four Protestant groups for their Intermediate (Junior high school), Senior (high school), and Adult programs, the following study provides a more systematic analysis of intergroup attitudes in religious textbooks than has yet been attempted. Little was done in this field until the early 1930s, when a notable increase in anti-Semitism prompted a good deal of research. The most extensive program was one instituted at Drew University in 1933, with the encouragement of the American Jewish Committee, under the direction of the late James V. Thompson. At the outset only the officially approved texts of certain major denominations were examined for their Jewish content. In time, racial attitudes were also included.[5] Ten years later a second study was made of current teaching materials and its findings compared with the earlier ones; the conclusion reached was that "editors and lesson writers today have in large measure eliminated undesirable direct references to minority groups." [6] However, important areas of modern Protestantism were not represented in this survey, particularly the fundamentalists, most conservative groups, and some Lutheran denominations. As recently as 1953, Frank and Mildred Moody Eakin published a joint report of the Drew findings for 1946–51, covering only Elementary textbooks.[7] Despite the limited scope of the Drew studies, the work of both Thompson and the Eakins was influential in increasing the awareness of the importance of the intergroup aspects of religious teaching.

By 1953, when the present study was begun, a number of investigations of group prejudice had given currency to the view that

5. "Jew-Christian Relationships as Found in Official Church School Materials," unpublished manuscript, Drew University (1936).

6. "A Study of Protestant Church School Literature Used in 1946," manuscript, Drew University (1947–48), p. ix. Certain shortcomings were noted, e.g. the "failure to deal directly, frankly, and fearlessly with specific human relations in American everyday living" (p. x).

7. *Sunday School Fights Prejudice* (New York, Macmillan, 1953).

racial, ethnic, and religious bigotry was an interrelated phenom-enon.[8] Many studies of intergroup relations assumed that analyses of racial or ethnic relations were directly applicable to the problems of anti-Semitism, anti-Catholicism, or anti-Protestantism.[9] One of the objectives of this study, therefore, has been to test the widely held belief that religious prejudice implies the existence of other types.

Any study of religious perspectives and intergroup relations requires an explanation of the presuppositions that underlie it and the method used in carrying it out. These are dealt with in the first chapter of the book. The second and third chapters describe the general findings of the research and also provide the context for the following chapters, in which the data is organized according to the victim-oppressor typology. The final chapter evaluates the study as a whole. For the sake of readability and emphasis much of the technical matter of the study has been incorporated into various appendices, which will be of interest primarily to professional students in this field. Such students may wish to consult the full report of the study, originally written as a Ph.D. dissertation at Yale University.

Because the following pages will expose the negative as well as the positive intergroup aspects of Protestant religious education, it is essential to bear in mind that this is a self-study, identified with and friendly to the Protestant point of view.[10] Moreover, it should be made clear that in analyzing Protestant teaching materials we are dealing with only one of many factors that contribute to the formation of social attitudes. Among these are the use which is

8. Notably T. W. Adorno et al., *The Authoritarian Personality* (New York, Harper, 1950), and Robin M. Williams, Jr., *The Reduction of Intergroup Tensions* (New York, Social Science Research Council, 1947).

9. Willard Johnson in the mid-forties expressed the typical opinion—reflected, for example, in the previously mentioned study by Williams—that the causes and cures of anti-Semitism "are fundamentally the same as those of other types of prejudice, such as anti-Negroism, anti-Protestantism or anti-Catholicism": *Humanist, 5* (1945), 30. See remarks by John Harding, "Religious Conflict in the United States," *Journal of Social Issues, 12* (1956), 1–2.

10. This inquiry is but one of several such autonomous studies; Jewish teaching materials are being examined by a Jewish institution, and Catholic publications by a Catholic university. A Jewish survey has been made by Dropsie College with Bernard D. Weinryb as director; Catholic studies have been undertaken under the direction of Father Trafford P. Maher, S.J., of St. Louis University.

made of the material in the classroom by the teacher, as well as other social influences which will be operative in the classroom. There are also other potent formative influences in our culture, not the least important of which are the existing social structures, folkways, traditions, and institutions into which we are born. At the same time, these lesson materials do play a significant role in church school, pulpit, and family instruction; further, they gain additional impact from the "halo effect" of learning within a religious situation. Thus when prejudicial attitudes, ideas, and practices of individuals and society come to be given the implicit blessing of the churches and are endowed with religious overtones and divine sanction, actual or incipient prejudices (regardless of their sources) become more deeply rooted and hence more resistant to treatment. The same is true of antiprejudicial teaching. Because the Protestant publishers share these same insights and concerns, this study was initiated with their approval and cooperation, and most of them have contributed to it materially by way of suggestions, insights, and friendly criticism.

# 1. Intergroup Content of Protestant Textbooks

The sociological and polemical literature of intergroup relations during the past three decades has most frequently and specifically charged that Christian education lays the groundwork for anti-Semitism. Objections have also been raised about instruction pertaining to race, Roman Catholicism, and the non-Christian religions, but the anti-Jewish implications of Protestant teaching materials are generally emphasized.[1] R. A. Schermerhorn, a sociologist, sums up the essence of these indictments:

> Among the chief sources of anti-Semitic indoctrination of the American child are juvenile literature and the educational materials of church and school . . . In attending church school or receiving religious instruction the American child learns that the Jews were responsible for the death of Christ and that they have rejected him ever since. In many cases he is taught that the Jewish "race" has since had to live under a curse for refusing the Gospel or that Cain symbolizes the Jewish people who put the Saviour to death. The place of the Romans in the Crucifixion is omitted and the fact that Jesus was a Jew who was carrying on many of the prophetic ideas of former Jews is never mentioned![2]

More recently, Ephraim Frisch examined hundreds of texts and concluded that while there is "great improvement" in the ways Jews and Judaism are presented in the Christian classroom, "there is still much bad material left in many of these textbooks, some of

1. Statements in recent literature about racial content in religious textbooks are usually echoes of Bruno Lasker's *Race Attitudes in Children* (New York, Holt, 1929).

2. *These Our People: Minorities in American Culture* (Boston, Heath, 1949), p. 419. Schermerhorn has depended greatly for his sources on Sigmund Livingston, *Must Men Hate?* (New York, Harper, 1944).

it quite shocking for the middle of the 20th century." [3] More commonly, writers automatically assume the culpability of Christian instruction in spreading anti-Semitism.[4] Other critics, while careful not to accuse Protestant educational manuals of anti-Semitism, point out that they may inadvertently foster or re-enforce it. Says historian James W. Parkes:

> Though it would be unfair to say that the ordinary Sunday School or the religious teaching given elsewhere to children was intentionally anti-Semitic, yet it remains true that in the immense majority of cases the Jews are simply presented as the people who killed Christ and who opposed and persecuted Paul and the early apostles . . . The result is inevitably to create a dislike of the *modern* Jew in the mind of the child, since it is only with these events that he connects the word "Jew!" [5]

These observations leave us with some bare, factual questions: What do Protestant curriculum materials actually say about Jews? Do they, in fact, teach that the Jews live under a continuing "curse"? Do they place the mark of having rejected Christ upon the Jew and charge him with responsibility for the death of Jesus? Do they fail to observe that Jesus was Jewish? Many such pertinent questions can be framed which lend themselves to objective content research. However, to reach fully meaningful conclusions, some type of quantitative survey is required. Even a relatively precise statistical approach, such as the one adopted in this study, provides a more informative and discriminating description of Protestant attitudes toward other faiths than the previous nonstatistical investigations have been able to supply. All of them are vague in several crucial respects. They give helpful examples of favorable and unfavorable references, of distorted and accurate teachings about other groups, but without indicating how typical these instances

3. "Judaism, Distortion and Reality," *Journal of Bible and Religion* (January 1955), p. 39.

4. One such victim of prejudice, who had been rejected by his classmates, typically suggests the connection: "Surveying this situation, I began to wonder about the kind of Sunday School education these religious Christians had received!" Armond E. Cohen, *All God's Children* (New York, Macmillan, 1945), p. 75.

5. *The Jew and His Neighbor* (London, Student Christian Movement Press, 1930), pp. 99–100.

are—either of a given curriculum or of Protestant teachings as a whole. Further, investigators have not systematically classified statements about other groups into categories which illuminate the persistent controversial questions that historically have plagued the relations of Christian to Jew or of Protestant to Catholic. Little attention has also been paid to the ways in which differing doctrines and perspectives within Protestantism may influence statements about outsiders. Because such information has been unavailable, generalizations about the intergroup teachings of Protestants frequently have been based on isolated and colorful examples of bias or expressions of good will.

## NATURE AND SCOPE OF THE STUDY

While we commonly speak of "prejudice and tolerance," a more precise and objective methodology for describing and evaluating Protestant attitudes about outside groups is made possible by using the concept of ethnocentrism. This concept, along with its opposite, is more specific in meaning than that of prejudice and tolerance and lends itself more readily to the construction of suitable analytic categories. It denotes the well-known tendency to make rigid ingroup-outgroup distinctions, even on matters that are unrelated to these distinctions. Ethnocentrics make their own groups the normative center of all their thinking. Unable to love their own kind without expressing antipathy toward others, they draw sharp lines of exclusion. Insofar as they idolize and remain submissive to and uncritical of their ingroup, they are likely to blame outsiders for their own ills and those of the world and to regard them as both inferior and hostile.[6]

Another and opposite phenomenon is discernible in Protestant curricula, which for want of a better name is termed "anti-ethnocentrism." It denotes more than the mere absence of the above characteristics; it has, rather, a distinct and measurable content of its own. Anti-ethnocentrics support the efforts of other groups to

6. A convenient working definition is given by Daniel J. Levinson: "Ethnocentrism is based on a pervasive and rigid ingroup-outgroup distinction; it involves stereotyped negative imagery and hostile attitudes regarding outgroups, stereotyped positive imagery and submissive attitudes regarding ingroups, and a hierarchical, authoritarian view of group interaction in which ingroups are rightly dominant, outgroups subordinate" (Adorno et al., *The Authoritarian Personality*, p. 150).

achieve and protect their rights and freedoms. They characterize others positively. They are able to accept and criticize their own group and are sensitive about the quality of its relations with outsiders. Between themselves and others they find both similarities and differences; frequently they regard the latter as correctives rather than merely as barriers. They include rather than exclude others, cross group lines frequently, and encourage social intercourse and intellectual dialogue.

Adorno's *The Authoritarian Personality*, from which these concepts have been derived and reformulated,[7] describes other characteristics of ethnocentrism. The first is the generality of outgroup rejection—that is, rejection is not limited to a single outgroup. Thus the tendency of ethnocentrics is to shift their hostility and allegiance from one group context to the next. Thus, where Jews are involved, ethnocentric white Protestants identify with Christianity; in a Christian context, their targets are the Catholics; in a Protestant one, they make the other Protestant denominations into outgroups; in a racial one, Negroes or orientals become suspect. In short, the compulsion to maintain an ingroup identification is so strong that some outgroup must always be located and rejected.

These characteristics, as well as those previously mentioned, provide helpful criteria in determining the presence and degree of ethnocentrism or its opposite in Protestant teaching. However, these criteria cannot be used in the abstract—the realities of American society must be taken into account. It is ethnocentric in most cases for white Americans to feel themselves threatened by Negroes who are struggling for their rights. But Negroes who believe they are being discriminated against, or Jews who are aware of antagonism toward them—like the American who feels that his security is threatened by the behavior of Soviet Russia—cannot be regarded as ethnocentric solely by virtue of these reactions. The criteria

7. These criteria have not been used uncritically. The nature and role of religion is not familiar to the authors of *The Authoritarian Personality*, and their biases in this respect are obvious. This work has also been widely criticized for its fundamental neglect of the problems of a functioning society. See criticisms made in *Studies in the Scope and Method of "The Authoritarian Personality,"* Richard Christie and Marie Jahoda, eds. (Glencoe, Ill., Free Press, 1954). Also Paul Kecskemeti, "Prejudice in the Catastrophic Perspective," *Commentary* (March 1951), pp. 286–92, and Nathan Glazer, "The Authoritarian Personality in Profile," *Commentary* (June 1950), pp. 573–83.

formulated for this study necessarily presuppose the existence of majority groups who have the social, economic, and political power to discriminate effectively against minorities. At the same time, it must be kept in mind that in any complex society minorities and majorities are not mutually exclusive, and minority situations may exist even for majority groups. For example, Negroes belong generally to the religious majority and Jews to the racial one. On the other hand, members of a majority group such as the Protestant can find themselves in a religious minority in New York or in Boston. Accepted minorities in our society influence the welfare of more powerful groups when they hold in their hands the balance of power needed to force or settle an issue. It is the actual power that a group exercises in a given situation that is the decisive social factor. The Negro population in some sections of the South exceeds the white, yet it is the white minority that governs.

Along with the complex problems raised by the distribution of social power in America, there are also those that come from the historical and theological content of Protestant teachings. The problematic nature of this content, particularly as it involves the commitments of a given Protestant faith, will be discussed at length later in this chapter. For now, it should suffice to point out that the assertions a Protestant lesson writer makes about historical events often involve issues about which the facts and their interpretation are still far from being clear and settled, even for skilled historians. Thus what looks to be an ethnocentric reading of the ministry of Jesus or of the causes that led to the death of Mary Tudor may have considerable support from respected scholars. One cannot reasonably expect that disputed areas of history that involve Protestant relations with other groups will be equitably resolved in Sunday school texts or that the failure to do so necessarily arises from ethnocentric motives. On the other hand, the constant reiteration of reasonably factual statements—say, about the sufferings of Protestants—may not be free from ethnocentrism. Moreover, for many Protestants certain areas of history are sacred and their reading of them is rooted in theological commitments. Deeply held religious values and whole theological perspectives can underly statements such as that Roman Catholics teach false doctrines or that references to Israel and Zion in the Bible apply not to the Jews but to the Church. Such judgments cannot be rated as unjustifiable, distorted, or bigoted in a study that seeks to be objective.

Taking these considerations into account, one concludes that the basic criteria for evaluating ethnocentrism in the texts must be controlled by two overarching principles: the *generality* of outgroup rejection or acceptance, and the warranted or unwarranted nature of the *total* portrait. While some groups, then, may be justified by their history, theological position, or present circumstances in making certain negative judgments about certain outsiders, it still must be determined if negative images predominate throughout the outgroup portrait. Similarly, if they unfavorably describe not just one but many racial, ethnic, and religious communities, it is certain that we are dealing with an ethnocentric ideology.

In general, therefore, the teachings about a specific religion or race in *all* lessons of an adequate sample of a textbook series must be rated and incorporated into an over-all descriptive profile in order to appraise accurately a given denomination's tendency to resist or succumb to ethnocentrism. Consequently, the focus of the method employed is not on discrete references in the texts but on clusters of opinion and patterns of attitude. It is quite possible for a Protestant writer repeatedly to point to actual instances of persecution of his people by Catholic authorities and still, in the interpreter's judgment, not to be guilty of a single distortion or untruth. However, if the sum of the references to Catholic treatment of Protestants does not take account of those occasions when Catholics defended Protestant rights, or fails to acknowledge that Protestants have also persecuted Catholics, then this one aspect of the total Catholic portrait is seen to be skewed and unwarranted. Similarly, an assertion that this or that Jewish belief is false or true cannot be judged as ethnocentric or its opposite. It is possible, however, for the analyst to score the first type of statement as negative and the second as positive. In this way, one can discover to what degree a given Protestant educator teaches that Jews hold false doctrines or that they possess both truth and error.

Without this neutral procedure the analyst of the material would be forced to quantify all references on the basis of his own judgments as to their supposed factuality and justification. Thus he would be placed in the unenviable position of having to defend each of his scores against a variety of objections from all sides. As is, the Analytical Categories for this study are used only systematically to classify what the lesson writer says. The quantitative analysis, then, requires a purely information-gathering and sorting technique.[8]

Fourteen Analytical Categories were developed and tested for this study.[9] Every type of reference to an outside group may be classified in one or another of the categories. Each of them has a positive ("for") and negative ("against") pole. Since each lesson is analyzed as a unit, any of its statements which are favorably disposed toward a given outside group are placed in the proper categories and given a plus score. Unfavorable references are similarly distributed and given a minus score. Statements that include both types of attitude are classified with both a plus and a minus.[10] The completed result for all the lessons in a curriculum will therefore inform us of both the content that appears in it as a whole and the proportions that are positive and negative.

The ratios of the positive to the negative proportions are called "imbalance scores." These scores tell us whether favorable or unfavorable statements predominate within any or all of the fourteen analytic categories of a given church school curriculum.[11] If, for example, it holds the Christians responsible for the plight of the Jews in sixty discussions of this issue, and holds the Jews responsible in five such discussions, the imbalance will be positive, but will

8. A description of the research design and procedures is also given in the various appendices.

9. See Appendix II for a breakdown and description. Four Analytical Categories in our research design are concerned with the deprivations and injustices from which other groups suffer and the questions of group status and human rights. Five other categories analyze the ways in which Protestants depict the beliefs, characteristics, and practices of outsiders. The remaining five categories deal with the different types of relationships curriculum writers see as existing between their own and other groups; they measure what kinds of relationships are encouraged, permitted, or forbidden by the writers, and the way they understand the attitudes and actions of outside groups toward their own.

10. For the scoring sheet used see Exhibit 1 in Appendix III.

11. For a fuller discussion see Appendix I. There are two kinds of imbalance scores. The general scores are over-all scores which denote the intergroup orientation of the curriculum as a whole, either for all of the outside groups taken together or for each group considered separately. The profile scores, however, apply to each of the fourteen analytical categories of the total profile for a single group.

raise serious questions about the degree to which Christians can or cannot validly hold the Jews accountable for their own victimization. If a majority of lessons portray Jews as despising Christians and Gentiles, a negative imbalance will be found in this category of information. The imbalances, then, provide a relatively precise index of beliefs and attitudes toward other groups, ranging from +1.00 to −1.00.[12] A zero score means that plus and minus scores are found in equal measure.

Underlying the concept of imbalance is the assumption that negative statements about other groups will necessarily be made. Unless one wishes to entertain imaginary views about human groups, delete the prophetic utterances of scripture, ignore history, and close his eyes to contemporary power and value conflicts, he will expect a certain amount of criticism of Catholic, Jewish, and other faiths. At the same time, one who has a realistic view of humanity and the social scene will expect to find unequivocal examples of good will and fairness toward others and an active concern for their rights. Because it takes into account the legitimacy of certain anxieties and criticisms concerning outsiders, the concept of imbalance offers a sound basis for evaluating by means of the adopted criteria of this study the ethnocentric or anti-ethnocentric tendencies of various religious curricula.

*Scope*

The following chapters will show how seven different groups are portrayed, with primary emphasis upon the religious bodies: Non-Christian, Jewish, Roman Catholic, other-Christian, Negroes, other-ethnic, and national groups. The eighth group category incorporates references to intergroup relations in general. Ideally, materials from all the major and many minor denominations and independent religious publishing houses should be analyzed, for each provides materials that are to some extent unique. However, a selective method was necessary. Seventeen groups of both denom-

12. A general score of +1.00 means that only positive statements are made about another group; a score of −1.00 signifies that only negative references are made; a zero score indicates that favorable and unfavorable references are evenly balanced in the curriculum as a whole. However, the profile scores—for each of the analytic categories—are always relative scores which take into account the comparative distribution of statements among the 14 analytic categories, as well as their positive and negative ratios.

inational and nondenominational religious educators, or "communicators," as they are sometimes called, contributed to the study.[13] Four of them were selected for thorough and detailed examination, and a large sampling (ranging from one-third to one-half of the materials produced by each publisher over a three-year period) was quantified.[14] Inasmuch as a previously published report of intergroup content in Protestant materials had covered the textbooks for the elementary division,[15] research was further limited to the intermediate (junior high school), senior (high school), and adult materials of these four communicators.

The four communicators were selected for several reasons. They represent certain basic variations within Protestantism, though they do not, of course, exhaust the possibilities. Diverse ethnic and class composition, denominational and nondenominational sponsorship, and sociological "sect" and "church" perspectives have been thereby included, as well as major traditions stemming from Calvinism, Lutheranism, Anabaptism, and naturalistic-theistic humanism. The four publishers also represent constituency membership within the National Council of Churches, the National Association of Evangelicals, and the Council of Liberal Churches, although one belongs to none of these groups. The theological range is of major interest: it covers fundamentalism, classical conservatism, naturalistic liberalism, and neo-Reformationism, the last being referred to by its popular name of neo-orthodoxy. Labels are sometimes libels, and it must be remembered that each of these four theological versions is not fully representative of the strains of thought that bear the name. For example, there are many forms of liberalism, some of it pietistic and evangelical, which the liberal group in this study does not represent. Similarly, there are a number of types of conservatism and many variations of fundamentalism. To summarize:

1. The Beacon Press curriculum of The Council of Liberal Churches (Unitarian-Universalist) represents an influential version of *liberalism.*

13. A full list appears in Appendix V.
14. However, the Beacon Press (Unitarian-Universalist) textbooks were analyzed almost in their entirety because they were relatively few in number. See discussion of sampling theory in Appendix V, and Tables 16–19, Appendix VII.
15. Eakin and Eakin, *Sunday School Fights Prejudice.*

2. The neo-Reformation theology, *neo-orthodoxy*, is found in the Christian Faith and Life and other curricula of the Presbyterian Church, U.S.A. (now known as the United Presbyterian Church).

3. The viewpoint of The Lutheran Church-Missouri Synod is classically *conservative*.

4. The *fundamentalist* perspective is represented by the curricula of the Scripture Press: it is one of the largest independent publishing houses serving independent churches as well as churches of all denominations.[16]

This selection gives us an opportunity to test a number of widespread assumptions about the relation of prejudice to theological presuppositions. Liberal theology has been associated with "tolerance" and fundamentalism with anti-Semitism and prosegregation views. One observer claims that certain liberal materials are "free from bias" and anticipates that "all Christian sects, except perhaps a few fundamentalists, will eliminate all biased material in the not far distant future." [17] A research project reports that active anti-Semitism is largely to be found in "the fundamentalist sects," [18] while another study associates intolerance with "conservatism" in theology.[19] On the other hand, Adorno names a number of small sects, including some clearly fundamentalist as well as liberal groups, as being among the tolerant scorers; he shows that the prejudiced tend to come from the larger denominations, in which liberalism has made great inroads.[20] Eckhardt points out that among

16. When this study began, Scripture Press was dispensationalist in its theology; during the interim years its position has shifted midway between right-wing dispensationalism and neo-evangelical thought. Defining its own theological position, the Board of Christian Education of the Presbyterian Church, U.S.A. (now the United Presbyterian Church), says: "If the term 'Reformed theology' is not adequate, then let it be modified by nothing less inclusive than the adjective 'ecumenical'!" ("Theology in the New Curriculum," official statement, Nov. 19, 1953, pp. 7–8).

17. See Ephraim Frisch, "Judaism—Fact and Fiction," *Hibbert Journal*, 5 (1957), 164–65.

18. This unpublished report of the Institute of Social Research, Columbia University, is summarized in part by Roy Eckhardt, *Christianity and the Children of Israel* (New York, King's Crown Press, 1948), p. 79.

19. See *The Drew Gateway*, 27, No. 2 (1957), 59–69.

20. Adorno et al., *The Authoritarian Personality*, pp. 208 ff.

the groups conspicuous on the American scene for their intensive fight against anti-Semitism is a fundamentalist group, The American Prophetic League, and observes that conservatism in Christian theology historically has been associated with anti-Semitism, since the theology of the past has been orthodox.[21] Moreover, in some quarters the spread of "neo-orthodoxy" is suspected of carrying with it the seeds of a recrudescence of prejudice and anti-Semitism. Since political and theological liberalism has done so much for the emancipation of the Jews, neo-orthodox criticism of the "liberal social optimism" of our era seems to presage a return to the social attitudes of an earlier era. In the light of these observations, our choice of these four communicators becomes significant. Questions are raised as to what degree the actual teachings of these Protestant communities, as embodied in their official curricula, support the diverse judgments that are currently being made concerning their intergroup orientation.

## THE CONTEXTUAL APPROACH

This self-study seeks not only to describe the content of the images Protestants communicate in their textbook material but to make available to Protestant educators resources and insights which can be used to strengthen anti-ethnocentric tendencies and eliminate ethnocentric content. Some critics of Christian education clearly believe that past recommendations for doing this have made an insufficient impact upon the Protestant community and the quality of its instruction. For example, they point out that despite the studies of the Pharisees by Herford, Montefiore, Moore, and others, the traditional, negative stereotypes of the Pharisees continue to be drawn. A widespread suspicion exists that Protestants resist the need to reappraise their teachings, particularly about Jews.

On the other hand, Protestant educators often express very different kinds of anxieties about these problems, despite their desire to continually improve the intergroup aspects of their curricula. They are aware that to some degree their religious beliefs are inevitably involved in portraying other faiths—whether these beliefs concern the doctrines of the nature of God, man, and the kingdom of God or such biblical themes as the crucifixion, the Great Commission, or the conflict between Jesus and the Pharisees.

21. Eckhardt, *Christianity*, p. ix.

They insist that in reassessing their portrayals of other groups there must be no compromise with the demands of the Christian faith as they see it. They are understandably wary of certain proposals for revision which imply that prejudice can be overcome only by essentially changing the faith or discarding certain sections of the Bible. Some of their critics have alleged that the belief in a super-natural God promotes authoritarianism and hence prejudice, that certain other articles of faith such as "chosenness" make for ethno-centrism, and that evangelistic efforts must be soft-pedaled in behalf of intergroup comity. These critiques leave some educators with the fear that in such a study as this they are being asked to conform to a program that soft-pedals what is vital and central to their faith and stresses what is marginal and, perhaps, entirely foreign.

The suspicion that Protestants resist making needed changes in their teachings about non-Protestants, and the counter-feeling that some approaches to this problem are characterized by indifference to certain Protestant commitments both suggest that the past scrutiny of education materials has paid inadequate attention to the concrete aspects of the particular educator's religious faith. The result has been that investigators in this field and commentators on intergroup relations have not always made themselves com-pletely aware of what the communicators of a denomination feel is at stake in the relations of their faith to others as they seek to teach that faith. Thus recommendations for improving the inter-group content of religious texts have often had only partial rel-evance and usefulness for most Protestants.

These recommendations have usually fallen into one of three types. Each has its justification and utility; but each also suffers from a degree of externality. These three approaches can be de-scribed as (1) the factual, (2) the concessive—eliminating all state-ments objected to by other groups, and (3) the consensus—pro-viding a common core of acceptable teachings about outside groups.

## The Factual Approach

This widely used method relies on locating and calling attention to unfavorable errors of fact—to inaccuracies, distortions, or omis-sions that create an unwarranted as well as negative image of out-groups. Usually, certain scholarly works are recommended as definitive source material to be used to correct the lesson writer's misinformation—the assumption being that unfamiliarity with these materials led him to make biased judgments about the life and thought of other groups and to depend solely upon his own sectarian traditions.[22]

There is considerable merit in this attempt to eliminate inaccuracies and distortions that mar so many lessons.[23] However, it is not always clear what the facts are. For example, studies made of the Pharisees and Judaism in the first century have been tremendously helpful in improving the treatment of this subject by Protestants.[24] Yet, assuming that all the lesson writers were willing to abide by the scholars' account, they would still be confronted with the problem that many competent Jewish and Christian specialists in this field fail to agree among themselves as to what the facts are in the period of the historical Jesus.[25] There is hardly any view of first-century Judaism and Christianity that is without its scholarly authority.

The difficulty is primarily that of being unable to draw a clear line between reasonably established facts and debatable areas that involve factual questions. Assertions of fact are always interwoven

22. See Frisch, "Judaism," pp. 160–61.

23. This is acknowledged in the present study by the use made of Analytic Category 5; see Appendix II.

24. Notably George Foot Moore, *Judaism in the First Centuries of the Christian Era* (3 vols. Cambridge, Harvard University Press, 1927–30); R. Travis Herford, *Pharisaism: Its Aim and Its Method* (London, Williams & Norgate, 1912) and his *The Pharisees* (London, Allen and Unwin, 1924); James W. Parkes, *The Conflict of the Church and the Synagogue* (London, Soncino Press, 1934) and his *Judaism and Christianity* (Chicago, University of Chicago Press, 1948); and Claude G. Montefiore, *The Synoptic Gospels* (2 vols. London, Macmillan, 1927).

25. For example, Herford writes: "the conclusion is justified that what is found in the extant Haggadah is on the whole much the same as what was believed and taught at least as early as the time of Jesus, and probably earlier still; and that it is legitimate to use the literature, which is in form later but in substance only slightly affected by the lapse of time, to illustrate the contents of Judaism in the New Testament period" (*Judaism in the New Testament Period*, London, Lindsey Press, 1928, p. 85). However, C. A. H. Guignebert warns that "the historical use of anything derived from the Talmud is a delicate matter requiring great caution. . . . [The compilers'] chronology, where they have any, is vague and confused; the attributions of teachings to a particular doctor often seems doubtful; and there are irritating anachronisms by which characters are introduced into scenes far removed in time from the period in which they lived" (*The Jewish World in the Time of Jesus*, London, Kegan Paul, Trench, Trubner, 1939, pp. 28–29).

with interpretation, and, often, data are selected in accord with an over-all point of view. Moore, Parkes, Moehlman, Montefiore, and Herford all approach their scholarly tasks with presuppositions and perspectives which determine the framework from within which facts are selected and interpreted. Thus Herford—a non-trinitarian liberal—portrays the conflict between Jesus and the Pharisees from a liberal point of view: it involved a collision of two "fundamentally irreconcilable" interpretations of how God's will was to be done. According to Herford, the Pharisees held that God's will was to be found revealed in Torah, while Jesus "maintained the individual conscience as the only guide to the right doing of the divine will." [26] Herford contributes much to a clearer understanding of first-century Judaism, but his interpretations of what Jesus, Paul, and the early Church were trying to say to Israel, and his analysis that follows from it of the essential conflicts between Church and Synagogue, are such that they can be accepted without drastic modifications only by those who already share his theological and hermeneutical convictions.[27]

In short, the same facts, even when fairly clear, may be subject to quite different interpretations by opposing parties. Whether writers see in Pharisaic legalism a source of religious strength or deficiency depends greatly upon the value judgments they bring to a consideration of it. Those who make judgments on some passages in Protestant curricula, therefore, may at times be quite unaware that there are also vital theological issues at stake in the intergroup references they intend to judge only as to fact. And, of course, some questions that deal with other faiths are not really factual ones: whether Christianity displaced Judaism in God's economy, for example, is finally a matter of theology and biblical criticism, not of historical scholarship. Thus Jews, Catholics, and Protestants must recognize that not all the issues among them can be understood and solved simply by recourse to history or to studies, however useful, that purport to be authoritative records of accurate information.

26. *Judaism in the New Testament Period*, pp. 206–07.

27. Many present-day Protestant educators, for example, would from their own understanding of Pauline Christianity vigorously dispute the accuracy of Herford's contention that Paul's definition of the function of the Law "was a rather desperate makeshift to get free from Judaism, to set the Church at liberty from the entanglements of its Jewish origin" (*Judaism in the New Testament Period*, p. 236).

*Recommending Elimination of Material*
*to Which Other Groups Object*

This approach, although open to the charge of censorship, has substantial value. Much offside Protestant criticism and unfair characterization of other groups could be prevented if the problems, convictions, sensitivities, and objections of other groups were more clearly understood. It is the obligation of every group to examine seriously the complaints of other faiths about the fashion in which they have been portrayed. It is particularly important that Protestants re-evaluate the traditions of Christian teachings about the Jews, for some of these teachings historically have played a role in imposing disabilities on the "people of the Book," and, conceivably, might do so again.

However, the correctives of persuading editors to delete from their literature everything that another group considers adverse to its interests are negative at best. Even if there were consistent agreement—which there is not—among Catholics, Jews, and Buddhists about what is objectionable to them, any thoroughgoing policy of meeting their demands would leave but a mutilated and all but valueless series of lessons. Protestant teachings that had been reconciled with a given Roman Catholic view of the Reformation or with a Jewish position concerning the New Testament would be in effect an abandonment of the Protestant position. The need still remains to assess the social impact that Protestant teachings may have on outsiders in ways that are constructive to society and which also lead to the internal reform of Protestantism. As such, the practice of making concessions to the objections of the groups portrayed has but limited value.

*Recommending a Common Basis*
*for Anti-Prejudicial Teaching*

This third approach, one frequently found in America, assumes that Protestants will profit from filtering out and accepting a body of anti-prejudicial teaching which is common to other groups yet basic to their own. The advocates of this underlying consensus believe there are ideals, principles, and beliefs which are shared by all groups and which, when acknowledged by them, will provide the dynamic for the positive transformation of intergroup images.

Sometimes this consensus is associated with the chief religious perspectives; other writers visualize it as the informing spirit of a common American heritage.

One result of this approach is that it tends to address Protestants *en masse* and to provide identical analyses and recommendations for all the denominations. The various theological orientations are ignored, sometimes for the sake of a governing stereotype of "the Protestant." [28] There are various ways in which the common approach proceeds. Some analysts, such as the Eakins in their excellent study of elementary religious texts,[29] recommend or criticize intergroup content by an implicit appeal to the values which inhere in American life and which various groups have helped to create. Other students of the problem assume, at one extreme, that religious ideologies are irrelevant to the formation of intergroup attitudes,[30] and, at the other extreme, that there is an essential incongruity between racial, religious, or national bias and all truly religious teaching. They contend that Christianity, for example, is a religion of love and therefore cannot be other than opposed to all forms of bigotry. Carried to its extreme, this view assumes that religion is a universal cure-all for prejudice and that religious bigotry is a violation of the essential faith of the religious person. No distinctive content is attributed to his religion, nor is it acknowledged that a bigoted person may also be deeply religious. Religion is merely recommended indiscriminately. There is considerable evidence of tangible cultural support for this position in the wave of popular piety that has swept America.[31]

The chief embodiment of the consensus approach has come to be the rapidly growing interfaith movement. In its fight against prejudice, certain segments of the interfaith movement have stressed the unity of human brotherhood within the multiplicity

28. An outstanding example is Henry Conrad Moehlman, *The Christian-Jewish Tragedy* (Rochester, Leo Hart, 1933), a study which gives an essentially monolithic view of Protestantism.

29. *Sunday School Fights Prejudice.*

30. A typical instance is found in "A Summary of an Interfaith Seminar," reported in the Columbia *Daily Spectator*, March 1940: "Prejudice against Jews, or any other religious minority for that matter, is not a racial or religious problem. . . . The religious question, if we may call it that, is just a peg upon which the in-group, doing the persecuting or hating, hangs its hat of hate."

31. Roy Eckhardt, *The Surge of Piety in America* (New York, Association Press, 1958), p. 38.

of its religious expressions.[32] Differences, whatever their nature, are considered divisive and unimportant when ranged alongside the common corpus of belief in the essential kinship of humanity and in human worth and equality, which can be shared and used by all religions. However, some religious groups have shown little enthusiasm for this approach, for the following reasons:

In the first place, the "common faith" may actually be a rival faith. This is the source of threat which some communicators anticipate in intergroup content analyses. Most common-ground recommendations for creating more favorable images of other religious groups assume that one need only conform to the tenets of a charitable liberalism, or some other creed, in order to escape the pitfalls of prejudice. This attempt to go beneath the many faiths to shared fundamentals is itself grounded in a faith which sets up its own criteria in rivalry of others. It is therefore bound to be resented by those who cannot share it.

Furthermore, though a common faith may indeed exist, in the sense that all religious groups share certain concepts and values, it does not necessarily have the power to motivate all religious groups equally. Common-ground approaches may stress value perspectives which are off center for some faith groups, even when they are able to assent to specific components of the common faith. The claim that some convictions (such as the brotherhood of man) are basic holds true only to a limited extent. There are some denominations whose centers of value, representing the real dynamic of their faith, lie far outside the boundaries circumscribed by the common faith. In conclusion, then, the common-ground approach fails to motivate those who are addressed, not because its grounds are not always sharable but precisely because they do not always express what is fundamental to the faiths held by the audience. For this reason, more than any other, the interfaith movement has been widely criticized on the grounds that by preserving the comity of vague similarities its activities have become more or less innocuous.[33]

32. It is important to distinguish between different kinds of interfaith movements. For example, the present trend in the National Conference of Christians and Jews is to respect the existence of vital differences between religious movements, and to engage all of them in dialogue on the common and controversial problems all groups encounter in American society.

33. Cf. Paul S. Minear, "The Church and the Jewish People," *Theology Today* (July 1955).

At the same time, the theological differences within Protestantism have also been ignored by those who, like the authors of *The Authoritarian Personality*, believe that "freedom from religious dogmas would go with . . . freedom from prejudice, while acceptance of religion would go with . . . authoritarianism and, hence, probably with ethnocentrism." [34] These differences seem also to have escaped those critics who argue that there is an intimate relation between Christian theology and certain types of religious prejudice. We began this chapter by airing the charge that Christian theology promotes anti-Semitism; some critics who fail to distinguish among its varieties, such as E. H. Wilson, go so far as to question "whether Christians can eradicate the essentially anti-Semitic character of their doctrinal position, without advancing to something that would be quite different from what Christianity has been." [35] Or again, Karl M. Chorowsky, a Protestant minister, asserts that "historically and in its basic doctrine, Christianity . . . has been and is anti-Semitic." [36]

Such massive indictments raise the crucial question of this study. For if all varieties of Protestant doctrine prove to be infected with anti-Semitism, there is little hope for improving teaching materials in this vital area until such time as Christians abandon their faith. Yet, as we examine positions that have been taken on the question of the relation—or lack of relation—of religion to prejudice or good will, we find that an examination of the history of intergroup conflict hardly gives unqualified support to any of these stated judgments. At the same time there are, possibly, truths in each of them which we ignore at the peril of an adequate understanding of the nature of religion and prejudice. The memory of Christians persecuting Jews as well as other Christians is much too vivid to convince us that all expressions of Christianity are fountains of good will. Yet Christianity at various times and in various forms has fought for human liberty and dignity, and many Christians have taken upon themselves the onus which the majorities have placed upon the minorities.

34. Adorno et al., *Authoritarian Personality*, p. 52.

35. E. H. Wilson, "Anti-Semitism: A Political Weapon in Clerical Hands," *Humanist*, 4 (1944), 112, 115. See also Dagobert D. Runes, *Of God, the Devil and the Jews* (New York, Philosophical Library, 1952), pp. 72-73.

36. "Is Protestantism Anti-Semitic?" *Humanist*, 4 (1944), 97, 102.

This ambiguity in religion, including Christianity, has been noted by many scholars. Gordon W. Allport points out that church-goers are both more and less prejudiced than others, and that "re-ligion bears no univocal relationship to prejudice." [37] Concluding his study of the struggle for religious liberty in the West, Roland H. Bainton finds that "Christianity as such cannot be regarded as the panacea for all the ills of the world. It all depends upon what kind of Christianity." [38] At present the pendulum of scholarly opinion appears to be swinging toward a consensus that

> (1) some kinds of religious inclination are associated with bigotry and chauvinism, and that (2) other kinds are an anti-dote against them. A basic challenge to the scientist and the religionist is to describe the differences and to discover the conditions which promote the one and the other.[39]

In general, then, the factor of faith involvement has been the most neglected feature of previous content analysis of intergroup teachings and of the recommendations for their improvement. The controlling evaluative assumption of this study is that the variants of the Protestant faith are specific, that each faith has its own core of doctrine and essential genius, and that little can be accomplished by attempting to impose on any denomination and its publishers those norms and suggested solutions that spring from other and often alien orientations. For those who hold a faith, something vital is at stake which an analyst of intergroup content must respect. Certain movements in American religion during the past half-century illustrate this point. The "social gospel," for example, was characterized by a strong sense of responsibility to society, and its intergroup strength derived from these commitments. Yet its Protestant critics argued that the social gospel, in the process of becoming relevant to the social problems of our era, lost the Gospel by uncritically accommodating to the dominant thought forms and norms of American culture and ceased to be Christian at its core. One cannot, therefore, speak meaningfully to those of conservative and fundamentalist persuasion without understanding the legitimate

37. Gordon W. Allport, *The Nature of Prejudice* (Cambridge, Addison-Wesley, 1954), pp. 444, 455.
38. Bainton, *The Travail of Religious Liberty*, pp. 52–53.
39. *Conference on Group Life in America* (New York, Am. J. Comm., 1957), mimeo. report on Arden House Conference, Nov. 9-12, 1956, pp. b11-13.

anxiety they have concerning the adoption of any perspective to social problems which risks compromising the faith by robbing it of its distinctive features or accommodating it to alien presuppositions. All the branches of Protestantism represented in this study are anxious to remain planted firmly in their own tradition, yet at the same time to relate their theology to the problems that their members face in a pluralistic society.[40] The writer has therefore been led to adopt a contextual rather than a piecemeal approach to the intergroup content of teaching materials, and to frame a pluralistic rather than a monolithic standard of judgment. In so doing, the study seeks to take into account both the theological [41] and social contexts in which Protestants speak about other groups and must make ethical decisions concerning them. Hopefully, then, the following pages will isolate certain basic problems of writing about non-Protestants, encourage an indigenous intergroup policy for each curriculum, and assist in the widespread desire for the Christian faith—as the different denominations hold it—to speak relevantly to our time.

40. See, e.g., Carl F. H. Henry, *The Uneasy Conscience of Modern Fundamentalism* (Grand Rapids, Eerdmans, 1947), and his *Evangelical Responsibility in Contemporary Theology* (Grand Rapids, Eerdmans, 1957). Periodicals such as *Eternity, Christian Life,* and *Christianity Today* show increasing interest in social themes.

41. To ignore this fact is to misread continually what lesson writers say. A statement in the conservative literature in this study—derived from Luther—is "The Law shows us our sin and the wrath of God; the Gospel shows us our Saviour and the grace of God." This definition has been criticized for allegedly representing "the Hebrew God" as "a God of wrath and vengeance, in contrast with the Christian God who is represented as a God of love and mercy and grace" (Frisch, *Fact and Fiction,* p. 163). This misinterpretation would never have occurred had the critic understood the theological context of the Lutheran reference. The critic thinks the statement invidious because he assumes that "the Law" is associated in the lesson writer's mind with the Old Testament and Judaism, while "the Gospel" is linked with the New Testament and Christianity. The truth is, however, that the conservative Lutherans believe that both Law and Gospel are taught in both the Old and New Testaments, and that Law and Gospel must be preached equally in the Church. No denigration of the Law or comparison with Judaism is implied. The lesson merely seeks to define the distinctive functions of Law and Gospel for the Christian. This instance illustrates the need for critical analyses to be faithful to the context of the communicator's teaching.

# 2. The Basic Findings and Their Implications

In order to follow the analyses of Protestant teaching materials in the ensuing chapters—particularly in regard to the victim-oppressor typology—an understanding of the basic findings of our research is necessary.[1] These findings, in themselves, provide some interesting and at a number of points surprising answers to several crucial questions. How frequently do images of other religious and nonreligious groups appear in the four kinds of material studied? Are these images dominantly favorable or unfavorable? How do the representative Protestant groups whose publications were analyzed compare in their ethnocentric and anti-ethnocentric inclinations? Are the tendencies to accept or reject other groups consistent or variable, and general or selective? To what extent are the intergroup orientations of Protestant teaching materials conditioned by or independent of the biblical material used as the base for most Protestant instruction? Finally, are there any preliminary clues in the statistical analysis as to the sources of prejudiced and anti-prejudiced teaching? Since these are leading questions—and in some cases controversial ones—they cannot, of course, be adequately answered purely by statistics; consequently, a certain amount of interpretation is necessary in order to draw out the implications of the general data in an illuminating manner.

*The Extent of Preoccupation with Outside Groups*

First of all, it is perfectly clear that Protestant educators are extensively engaged in struggling with the problems of intergroup relations, whether they realize it or not. Although all the editors approved of this study at its inception and encouraged us to "range

---

1. The reader of this and the following chapters will find it helpful if he constantly keeps in mind the method of gathering, quantifying, and evaluating intergroup data set forth in the preceding chapter.

far, wide, and deep," some also remarked, "You will find that we say very little about other groups in our materials." A few also said, "We have no problems in this area." The basic findings of the quantitative content analysis do not support either claim. In point of fact, Protestant religious textbooks incorporate an astonishingly high percentage of lessons in which other groups are spoken of, incidentally or in detail. While it is true that most of these references may have no other aim than to set forth Christian teaching—being primarily a part of expositional and illustrative passages—they nevertheless supply the student with expressive content that can strongly influence his images of outsiders. About 67 to 88 per cent of the lessons and articles published by the four communicators selected for intensive study were found to contain such references. Surprising as it may seem to some readers, the fundamentalist Scripture Press [2] and the conservative Missouri Synod—who publish very few, if any, lessons that specifically deal with the problems of intergroup relations—are nonetheless preoccupied with outsiders in nearly 67 to 68 per cent of the lessons measured. Further, almost 88 per cent of the Unitarian-Universalist (or liberal) communicator and 79 per cent of the Presbyterian (or neo-orthodox) communicator produce lessons with perceptible intergroup content.[3] Thus the indisputable fact emerges that images of other groups bulk large in religious instruction; nor is it any less clear that these images

2. When the word "fundamentalists" is used hereafter in this report, the Scripture Press communicator is meant. Generalizations about the publications or views of all fundamentalists (occasioned by observations about Scripture Press material) will be attributed to "fundamentalism" or indicated by such phrases as "fundamentalists as a whole." Similarly, the designation "liberals" refers to the liberal (Universalist-Unitarian) writers, and not to liberals in general. The same usage applies also to "conservatives" and "neo-orthodox." The former term signifies the Lutheran—Missouri Synod and the latter the Presbyterian Church U.S.A. (now the United Presbyterian Church).

3. See Table 1, Appendix VII. It is also worth noting that lessons which provide images of outside groups mention on the average more than one group. For example, in the neo-orthodox curricula 858 out of 1,084 lessons have intergroup content; these 858 units are equivalent to 1,758 units which contain references to single outside groups. In short, there is a multiple mention of outsiders in this curriculum to the extent of 162 per cent. It is interesting that the fundamentalist communicator made the greatest number of multiple references (producing a preoccupation score of almost 186 per cent), while the conservatives had the least number of such references (141 per cent). See Tables 1 and 15, Appendix VII.

are so profuse that they inevitably inculcate ideas about and attitudes toward others.

A second significant finding is the marked prominence of the Jew in all four curricula. Forty-four per cent of the lessons and articles produced by the neo-orthodox communicator contained references to the Jewish leaders, people, and religion, and this score is the lowest of the four. The Jewish preoccupation score for the conservative publisher is 56 per cent, for the liberal, 61 per cent, and for the fundamentalist, over 66 per cent. That other religions are mentioned in only 10 to 21 per cent of the lessons that were analyzed serves only to dramatize the high textual visibility of Jews in Protestant teaching materials.

It should be pointed out that the much more frequent preoccupation with the Jews is not an unexpected finding or even an invidious one. Certain historical, theological, and educational characteristics of Protestantism need to be kept in mind in evaluating its import. First of all, Christianity began as a Jewish sect, and present-day lessons will inevitably contain constant reminders that the Church's founders, its earliest followers, and its scriptures all were Jewish. The basic beliefs and practices of Christianity were rooted in one or another of the traditions of Jewish thought, and the earliest ideological conflicts took place within the matrix of first-century Judaism. While the modern Jew may be able to state his faith and set forth his biblical history without any necessary reference to Christians, the Christian is not able to do so without references to the Jews. The basic origins of Christianity compel the lesson writer to elevate Judaism to a prominent place in his own thought.

Closely related to these historical constituents are certain theological convictions. In Protestant texts the Gospel is understood as the ubiquitous challenge of God to Israel. Jesus is believed to be the fulfillment of Jewish history and Jewish eschatological hopes. Judaism is important not merely because Jesus was a Jew but because his message and mission were to Israel. Consequently, Christian theology requires an understanding of Judaism, particularly of its role in God's plan and its relation to the Church. A conception of the spiritual status and role of the Jew becomes essential to the Christian's comprehension of his own mission. For he

cannot know who he is and what his own role consists of until he
understands who the Jew is and what is Israel's role. No two of the
four communicators derive the same conclusions from these questions and their data, but all of necessity must come to grips with
them.

Also contributing to the conspicuousness of Jews and Judaism in
Protestant materials is the biblical nature of the curriculum. For
the Protestant, the biblical text is primary, and his chief educational
method is the exegetical and doctrinal treatment of it. The more
conservative denominations often teach the faith by means of a
chapter-by-chapter and even verse-by-verse exposition of the Bible.
Since scripture deals integrally with Jews and Judaism, this approach makes the Jew unavoidably conspicuous, regardless of how
much a writer may seek to minimize him. Thus the Jews are not
just another minority that happens to get mentioned more than
others in Protestant teaching; they are integral to the biblical-
theological subject matter—the outside group of whom the writer
cannot avoid speaking, whether he intends to do so or not.[4]

While nothing essentially invidious, then, inheres in the marked
prominence of the Jew in Protestant texts, there is in it an ever-
present danger. As a minority which inescapably figures in the
foreground of Christian thought—and remains an accessible minority in a society which contains deep strains of anti-Semitism—the
Jewish community easily becomes a vulnerable target. There are
instances cited in this study where the Jew is used as a convenient
whipping boy for human ills and failings, simply because he is
"there" in the biblical material and therefore was suggested to the
writer as the most relevant object of criticism. That the writers
may have in mind only biblical Jewry does not make the problem
less serious, since this distinction is seldom made. For the Jew to
be under the continual scrutiny of the pupil and teacher with their
open textbook is to expose him to potential hazards; in the Christian
era the Jew has infrequently escaped these dangers unharmed.

If, in consequence, Jewish-Christian relations loom large in this

4. See Table 1. It would be of interest to compare Jewish prominence in
Catholic texts to that in Protestant ones; the teaching method of the Catholic
Church is more catechetical and instructional, because its interests are primarily
doctrinal and ecclesiastical. While studies of the biblical texts are used, they are
more subordinate than in Protestant teachings. Hence the references to Jews
would be expected to be less frequent.

report, it is not because issues which affect other groups are regarded as less vital but because of the very complex and special nature of Jewish-Christian relations and the special questions they address to Christians. Many of the knotty problems of intergroup writing in Protestant texts involve precisely those scriptural themes and motifs which inevitably implicate Jews and Judaism. Some are important for this study—the conflict between Jesus and the Pharisees, the crucifixion, the "rejection of Christ," and the problem of Gentile inclusion. Most of these themes will be dealt with at length in this work, and the general relation of scripture to Protestant teachings about Jews will be discussed later in this chapter.

The third significant finding is that religious groups not only are highly visible in Protestant teaching materials but are considerably more prominent than nonreligious ones. While Negroes and Negro-white relations are referred to in 3 to 9 per cent of the lessons and other-ethnic groups in 3 to 7 per cent of them, both scores are considerably lower than the 10 to 66 per cent of the lessons in which Non-Christians, Jews, Roman Catholics, and other Protestant denominations are depicted. While this higher degree of preoccupation with other religious groups in religious curricula is to be expected, as we have suggested with reference to the findings on Judaism, it does take on considerable significance once we break down the general findings on the ethnocentric and anti-ethnocentric tendencies in the four samples of Protestant teachings.

## The Intergroup Orientation of Protestant Materials

To begin with, the most comprehensive findings for all eight religious and racial-ethnic categories are expressed in general scores which place the conservative, fundamentalist, neo-orthodox, and liberal curricula in distinctive positions on the scale.[5] The liberal and the neo-orthodox materials place high on the upper, or anti-ethnocentric, side of the graph by their scores of +59.2 and +58.2

5. See Fig. 1, Appendix VIII. These are massed imbalance scores, arrived at by combining all the ratings for all intergroup references, regardless of which outgroups are being referred to. For a discussion of the utility and meaning of the general score see Appendix III. The distributions (represented by the shaded areas above and below the zero line) indicate the total plus and minus content, respectively. The score (imbalance) is a product of the difference between the two distributions. For explanations of the importance of the imbalance concept see the previous chapter and Appendix I. For the mathematical rationale see Appendix III.

respectively. The fundamentalist materials score just about zero. The conservatives with a score of $-21.3$ are medium-low on the bottom, or negative, part of the scale.[6] Accordingly, one finds that the total thrust of Protestant teachings about outsiders is by no means in one direction; in some cases it is favorable, in others it is unfavorable. Two publishers are predominantly positive in their depictions, one is ambivalent, and the remaining one is negative.

However, once we break down the general data into more specific classifications, a number of more significant generalizations emerge. First of all, we separate the data into the two categories of religious and nonreligious groups and obtain general scores for each.[7] The scores for religious groups are slightly less positive than are the undifferentiated general scores. In sharp contrast, however, the scores for nonreligious groups show that they are depicted positively by all four communicators. The nonreligious scores for the liberal and neo-orthodox ones rose even higher on the anti-ethnocentric scale, but, even more interesting, the fundamentalist press rose to a $+12.3$ score and that of the conservative publisher —whose over-all score was markedly negative—rose remarkably to a $+42.1$!

Secondly, when we take the next step and factor out the scores made for each specific outside group—Catholics, Jews, Negroes, and so forth—we find that in no instance are any one of the several racial-ethnic-national groups portrayed negatively.[8] On the other hand, the scores for the individual other-religious groups are by no means so favorable. Only the liberal and neo-orthodox portray all other religions positively. The fundamentalists treat only the Jews in a slightly favorable manner. The conservatives depict ad-

6. Two preliminary pilot studies, some subsequent statistical content analysis of 12 other denominational materials, and a reading of several thousand random texts and manuals all indicate that the range of imbalance scores given here for the four representative educators will not be exceeded, on either the negative or the positive sides, by any of the Protestant denominations. These scores, then, provide the maximum anticipated range of scores for Protestant curricula as a whole, with the great bulk of scores grouped at various places on the plus side of the scale.

7. See Fig. 2, Appendix VIII. Here the general score for each communicator is divided into two segments, one for religious groups only, the other for racial, ethnic, and national groups.

8. See Fig. 3, Appendix VIII.

versely all other religious groups but their own. Moreover, the treatment of other religious groups by each communicator is far from uniform. For example, the liberals' rating for non-Christians is more than 43 percentage points higher than it is for Catholics and about 32 percentage points higher than it is for Jews. These marked variations in the general scores and profiles concerning the different religious groups are typical for all the communicators.

These findings, then, suggest three important things about the intergroup tendencies of Protestant teachings:

(1) The controverted relationship of fundamentalism, conservatism, and liberalism to prejudice already referred to remains unclear and somewhat ambiguous. Our general data seems to indicate that a possible connection exists between a very conservative, classical orthodoxy and a negative intergroup orientation; also there seems to be some justification for associating liberal theology with high positive ratings. But contradictions to this conclusion are also disclosed. Not only do fundamentalist educators manage to avoid a negative orientation in their over-all teachings, but they and the conservative ones speak about *all* racial, ethnic, and national groups with a positive impact. There is also the further finding that a neo-orthodox denomination with its Reformation and biblical approach is as capable as is the liberal perspective of taking a strongly anti-ethnocentric position toward all outside groups. Specifically, the fear is undercut that a return to orthodoxy predisposes one to take an unfavorable view of Jews.[9]

On the whole, then, we find partial support for, as well as evidence against, some popular assessments of the intergroup orientation of teaching materials fostered by conservative and liberal theologies. In general the more detailed findings discussed in the latter part of this chapter and in the work as a whole demonstrate that being orthodox in their theology does not necessarily predispose Protestants to being hostile to outside groups. Nor do the scores disclose any generality of outgroup rejection on the part of even the most negative scorer. Analyses of particular themes in

9. It should perhaps be noted that neo-orthodoxy, which represents a sharp revolt against theological liberalism, is also a child of liberalism as well as of orthodoxy, and attempts to conserve the social concerns of the former while preserving the theological insights of the latter.

lessons which yield invidious imagery of other religions will demonstrate that many influences, other than conservative theology, operate to produce these negative results.

(2) As has been suggested earlier, religious groups will have considerably more difficulty with the existence of other religions than with nonreligious groups, because they encounter unique problems of commitment and value conflicts with respect to the former. Thus Protestants are more preoccupied with other religions and picture them less favorably. They are less disposed—as our findings clearly indicate—to make negative judgments about racial and ethnic outsiders and more disposed to identify sympathetically with their problems and aspirations. Some communicators, in fact, handle the problem of race and ethnic relations so commendably that their scores set a ceiling of sorts beyond which it may be impossible to go. The neo-orthodox score for the other-ethnic category, for example, is +87.8, and for the Negro +93.8. The conservative's other-ethnic score is +72.0, and the liberal's Negro category rates a +86.7. This is not to claim that these achievements are ideal, but they are highly commendable, particularly when compared with what the same communicators are able to do when talking about religious beliefs and practices other than their own.[10]

Our findings make clear that the problems of racial and religious relations are separate and distinct, challenging the assumption of some earlier studies—for example, *The Reduction of Intergroup Tensions*—that all intergroup conflict can be understood as a single phenomenon.[11] Although racial prejudice is unquestionably the most immediate and explosive social issue we face today in American society, the problems that Christians have of fostering a positive image of outside groups apparently lie elsewhere. These are impor-

10. On the racial-ethnic side of Fig. 3, teachings about the Negroes for the most part score highest in this all-positive orientation. However, the conservatives have their lowest score in their treatment of Negroes— +33.3 per cent. The fundamentalist scores range from +8.0 per cent (international) to +56.7 per cent for the Negro. These positions for the low-positive scorers reflect a somewhat marginal concern about the depth of the interracial-ethnic problem in the United States, plus a minimum focus upon this problem from a consciously Christian perspective.

11. I.e. when the separation between scores for religious and nonreligious areas is made, the comparability of scores in the two areas is not demonstrated. This finding is significant in the light of the view expressed in *The Authoritarian Personality* that "A *primary* characteristic of ethnocentric ideology is the *generality* of outgroup rejection" (Adorno et al., p. 147; italics added).

tant points to keep in mind because they highlight an area which Protestant thinkers frequently overlook. In innumerable textbooks the characteristic assumption is that prejudice is *ipso facto* racial prejudice, without any serious consideration of the possibility that the readers could be equally or more prejudiced toward a religious group. Even Jewish-Christian relations are sometimes assumed to be fundamentally racial, such as in the typical statement, "We cannot be Christian and be prejudiced against Negroes, Jews, or any other race." Such a formulation not only helps to perpetuate a racial notion of Jews but also permits the Christian to evade the concrete issues which currently confront him in the area of Jewish-Christian relations.

(3) Protestants see each religious group quite differently. Roman Catholics represent to them one kind of problem and Jews another. In our sample, Protestant educators not only react differently to each outside religion but, more significantly, each one of them also apparently has its own distinctive image of the same religion. The liberal conceptions of Buddhism, Confucianism, and the other high non-Christian religions have little in common with those held by the conservatives. The neo-orthodox attitudes toward Catholics do not square with those held by fundamentalists. With these observations in the background, let us examine in detail the more specific findings concerning how Protestants view each of the outside religious groups.

## PROTESTANT VIEWS OF ROMAN CATHOLICISM

It is clear that Protestants in this study have their greatest problems in dealing with Catholics. This conclusion is supported by a host of statistical findings as well as by the textual references themselves. The Roman Catholic Church without exception occupies the lowest position in all the Protestant general scores for religious groups; this finding holds true whether the over-all profile of Roman Catholicism is negative or positive.[12] Moreover, this ranking of Catholics is characteristic not only of the representative curricula but of Protestantism as a whole, judging from an extensive reading of tens of thousands of denominational lessons which are not reported in these pages. The liberals and neo-orthodox, as we have seen, score positively all along the intergroup spectrum; yet the

12. Consult Fig. 3, Appendix VIII.

liberal general score for Catholics is +36.6 per cent, while the scores for all the other religious groups are considerably higher (ranging from +45.9 to +80.0 per cent). The neo-orthodox rating for Catholics is even less favorable (+23.4 per cent), but it ranges from +37.4 to +79.9 per cent for non-Christians, Jews, and other Protestants. Fundamentalists and conservatives, whose approach to religious groups is primarily negative, have a more unfavorable attitude about Catholics than they have about other groups. The spread for fundamentalist interreligious scores (excluding the Catholic) is +7.9 to −33.5 per cent; the Catholic score is −52.8 per cent. The conservatives produce an even more intensely negative image (−66.9 per cent), while the non-Catholics get scores from −15.4 to −58.1 per cent.

It would appear from this evidence that the greatest challenge today to Protestant values comes from the Roman Catholic sector of American society, despite the recent increase in Protestant-Catholic dialogue. The clashes between Protestant and Catholic positions on such questions as birth control, censorship, state aid to parochial schools, and freedom of religious choice in mixed marriages are reflected in these scores, since they are the subject of considerable comment in the lessons. But there is an even more serious conflict to which these scores point, one that concerns questions of belief and value, namely the conflict over questions of civil liberties and religious freedom. Three of the four publishers (liberals being the exception) provide statistical evidence that Protestants have some grave misgivings about the present-day attitude of the Roman Catholic Church toward them and toward traditional American freedoms.[13] Moreover, three of the four publishers (with the liberal one again the exception) question the truth and validity of much Roman Catholic doctrine. Judged as false, unscriptural, or otherwise unacceptable is a broad spectrum of theological dogma, centering prominently around the Roman Catholic interpretation of the nature and authority of the Church.

The misgivings of conservatives and fundamentalists about Roman Catholicism are also evidenced in their negative scores in the different categories of the Catholic portrait other than the ones concerned with rights and plights. They both paint unfavorable

13. See analytical profiles for the Roman Catholic group, Figs. 5–8, Appendix VIII.

portraits of Catholics, Catholicism, and the Catholic Church (some writers make careful distinctions between the three) when discussing their moral roles and characteristics and their social and cultural traits. Both denominations stress differences between their own point of view and that of Catholicism. Both distort Catholic life and thought far more often than they make corrective statements. Both raise barriers against certain types of relations with Catholics (dating, intermarriage, and such interfaith activities as common worship).

The liberals and the neo-orthodox, on the other hand, usually speak of Roman Catholics and Catholicism as possessing valuable moral and godly characteristics. Both stress kinship and common values over admitted differences, provide for avenues of interaction with Catholics (learning about Catholicism through direct contact, etc.), and more frequently correct stereotypes of Catholic life and thought than they create distortions.

Nevertheless, certain concerns about the Catholics are obvious in both negative and positive scorers. The main Protestant apprehensions have to do with the Catholic views of the Church and what these imply for religious freedom and, secondly, with the ability of the Church to rectify itself in its doctrine and curb its own powers. Some of these writers see no clear source of self-correction in the life of the Roman Catholic community, and no effective inner check on its powers. Consequently, Protestants are concerned about what inherent resources the Roman Catholic community does possess to preserve freedom for those who adhere to a different faith. With the two positive scorers, this anxiety takes the form of asking whether Roman Catholics can find unambiguous and compelling grounds for religious tolerance in their own faith, not merely those of expediency or prudence.

However much they oppose or criticize the teachings of Catholics as well as some of the positions their church takes on contemporary social and political questions, all four publishers not only condemn anti-Catholicism and indulge in varying degrees of self-criticism in this regard, but also explicitly or implicitly affirm the inherent right of Catholics to exist and perpetuate themselves. Nonetheless, in discussing Roman Catholicism the conservatives and fundamentalists tend to create a monolithic picture of the religion as a network of evil. The neo-orthodox, however, while contending with their Catholic brethren, inveigh against monolithic views of Catholicism and produce a more diverse and discriminating profile of the Catholic. Subsequent discussion will differentiate between these two approaches.

One firm conclusion that may be reached is that it is quite possible to raise points of fundamental conflict with the Catholic position without presenting it in a derogatory light. In doing so, however, criticism, frank acknowledgment of differences, and other negative statements inevitably appear, as is evident from the minus distributions on the graphs. Unless this is so, the portraits of outside groups may be overly idealized and the real problems between the contending communities never really faced. But it is apparently possible to keep these negative elements of the portrait subordinate enough to make constructive discussion of the problems feasible.

## PROTESTANT VIEWS OF JUDAISM

With few exceptions, Jews are more advantageously presented by the Protestant educators than are all other religious groups. This observation is not meant to detract from the seriousness of low positive and highly negative images of Jews where they occur. For example, the scores for Jewish references made by fundamentalists and conservatives are at the top of their interreligious columns (above that for their references to non-Christians, Catholics, and other Protestants); yet the fundamentalists achieve only a slightly favorable score of +7.9 per cent, while the conservatives in general present Jews unfavorably (−15.4 per cent). Although these scores are either close to being equivocal or are actually negative, they are not so negative as fundamentalist-conservative ratings for other religious groups. The neo-orthodox and liberals picture Jews with greater approbation than they do most other religious communities. Their respective scores for the Jewish category are +44.3 and +48.6 per cent, but their Jewish scores take second rather than first place.[14]

Thus the common conjecture that the Jews would probably be found at the bottom of any scale measuring ethnocentrism and anti-ethnocentrism in Christian publications cannot be supported. Yet

14. Fig. 3. The significance of the fact that the highest scoring religious group among liberals are the non-Christians while other-Christians are the most favorably represented by the neo-orthodox will be discussed in the next chapter.

our findings—most of them the main subject for comment in this book—warn us not to infer that the existence of Jews and Judaism, either in the past or present, offers no difficulties for Christians. As has been pointed out, Protestants struggle with a unique set of problems in this area, inasmuch as Judaism plays a special role in Christian thought, and images of it are formed by a history of dialogue and conflict that has its own disturbing features.

## The New Testament and the Jewish Image

Some of the leading questions about Jewish-Christian relations that Protestant educators confront are raised by the scriptural basis of their curricula. Sometimes an editor is led to claim that the picture their curricula gives of Jews is merely a reflection of what is in the Bible. "If our materials are negative for Jews," an editor will say, "it is because scripture is negative." A problem at this particular point involves intergroup statements which are, presumably, based on certain Bible passages; when the researcher assigns to such references a plus or minus score, is he passing a judgment on scripture? One editor of church school materials expressed the question as follows: "Since the lessons in our [denomination's] current curriculum are actually comments on the Bible, does not your study . . . presume to measure what scripture says rather than the intergroup bias of our lesson writers?" [15] However, there is no consensus among Protestant interpreters on the point. One school of biblical commentators maintains that the Gospel narratives, the Acts of the Apostles, and some epistles contain bitter anti-Jewish polemic deriving from the controversy between the Christian and Pharisaic communities during the first century.[16] Those of this school, whose understanding of scripture is both literal and liberal, see the problem as essentially one of "softening" the New Testament account, largely by omitting or mitigating any comment which appears to be critical of Judaism.[17] While not denying instances of exclusiveness, provincialism, or even bigotry in the Bible, other interpreters insist that the dominant tendency of scripture is anti-ethnocentric

15. Notes of discussion, editors' breakfast meeting, Cincinnati, Ohio, Feb. 8, 1955. Only lesson *commentary* on the Bible is examined for its intergroup content. The mere quotation of scripture itself as a base for commentary is not.

16. E.g. Parkes, *The Conflict of the Church and the Synagogue*, pp. 57–60, 82–85.

17. See Eakin and Eakin, *Sunday School Fights Prejudice*, pp. 36–37. The Eakins regard the issue as a conflict between first-century group antagonisms embodied in scriptural statements and twentieth-century desires for tolerance

and that certain difficult passages about Jews must be understood in this larger context. Still another group looks at any alleged anti-Semitic sentiment in the New Testament as purely a delusion of misguided Gentiles.[18] In sum, Christian thinkers do not agree that scripture contains ethnocentric polemic, nor do those who find both tendencies concur on its dominant orientation toward Jews. On the other hand, many Jews regard the New Testament as a prime source of anti-Semitic teachings.

Specific research on the question was undertaken in an early stage of this study. A comparison was made of the use of scripture for Jewish content in independent self-styled "Christian" magazines commonly regarded as anti-Semitic and in official publications produced by three large Protestant denominations (Methodists, Presbyterians, and Disciples of Christ). The study was based on comparable biblical passages and themes. Between the two types of periodicals there was discovered a profound difference, not only in the ways in which Jews and Judaism were pictured but also in regard to intergroup content in general. In a great many cases the scripture in question elicited some negative comment about Jews from both the anti-Semitic and official Protestant publications. But the denominations sharply distinguished themselves from the anti-Semites by their predominantly high favorable imbalances. The anti-Semites, in contrast, were as negative about Jews as it is possible to get.[19] The denominational publications found scriptural justification for breaking down prejudices as well as other barriers to interaction, and noted positive as well as negative statements

---

(p. 138): "writers still experience a conflict between fidelity to the New Testament sources and an impulse toward present day good will. The sources are often harsh toward Jews. The lesson writers succeed only to a degree in avoiding such harshness. Some do not try."

18. One finds such statements as the following: "Although religious anti-Semitism or anti-Judaism may have formally appealed to certain hard words of the New Testament about the Jews, in fact even in its religious form it has *thoroughly misunderstood* the attitude of the New Testament Church towards the 'People who murdered Christ,' and has *misused* its utterances to the detriment of the Church, too." Karl Heinrich Rengstorf, "The Jewish Problem and the Church's Understanding of Its Own Mission," in Göte Hedenquist, ed., *The Church and the Jewish People* (London, Edinburgh House Press, 1954), pp. 41–42 (italics mine).

19. Scriptural commentary in the anti-Semitic sample for Jews was −97.4, while the denominational scriptural commentary averaged +42.6—a difference of 140 percentage points. Analyzed were copies of *The Defender Magazine* and *Women's Voice* for three months in 1953.

about biblical Judaism. The anti-Semitic journals, on the other hand, denied any historical connection with Judaism, created heavily negative images of the Jews, and used scripture to justify discrimination and persecution.[20]

The findings led to an hypothesis that a publisher would communicate his ethnocentrism or anti-ethnocentrism in his comments *regardless of the nature of scripture as a whole*. It was also conjectured that although scriptural material would figure in the larger research design, the anti-ethnocentric–ethnocentric orientation of the writers would nevertheless show through in the scores of imbalance.[21]

These hypotheses are supported by evidence from the completed study. There proves to be little statistical relation between the New Testament sources and the images of the Jews in the lessons that are commentary on them. For one thing, some of the biblically based curricula create a quite positive and constructive view of Jews and Judaism, both ancient and modern; whereas others devise either an ambiguous or a predominantly negative one. It is necessary to assume that the intergroup content in curriculum materials is not based on the scriptural sources alone: a point of view is brought to scripture as well as derived from it.

That extrascriptural factors are involved in the Jewish images in Protestant materials is graphically highlighted in Figure 4.[22] It reports what results when biblically based lessons were separated

20. Some sample quotes from the anti-Jewish journals: "Did not [Christ] say, 'If ye reject Me, ye reject My Father also?' . . . The Jews reject Jesus Christ; they admit it; a Jewish authority has said, 'Our God is not a God of Love.' Then what is their god? The opposite of love is hate or the devil. Jesus told them so: 'Ye are of your father the devil . . .' When the Jews quote God's promise to Abraham, 'I will curse them that curse thee,'" this writer says, "Ask them how that promise could apply to the Jews whom Jesus Himself condemned." "Jesus in very strong terms denounced the Jews, and pronounced judgment upon them . . . This explains why these judgments are falling upon the Jews, from Jesus' time until today; they are receiving just what they measured out to Christians."

21. For example, even if negative scores in the information-gathering categories are made necessary by the biblical subject matter (showing up in the negative distribution), other scriptural passages and primarily the attitudes of the writers toward the Jews (and their theological understanding of the judgment and mercy of God) will show through either in (a) balancing, self-critical, and corrective statements which would create positive distributions (and make for neutral or positive imbalances), or in (b) selectively one-sided negative statements making for negative imbalances.

22. Appendix VIII.

from nonbiblical ones—that is, scores for the Jewish group category were computed for Old Testament lessons, New Testament lessons, and nonbiblical lessons, thus permitting a quick visual comparison of biblical and nonbiblical scores. Assuming that negative scores for the Jewish group category were due entirely or even largely to scripture, we would expect that biblical lessons would produce a significantly negative Jewish portrait, while lessons based primarily on church history, polity, personal and social problems, and contemporary issues would not. At the very least, we would anticipate that scriptural commentary would depress the over-all scores. The results of this comparison are instructive:

Three of the four communicators (liberal, neo-orthodox, and fundamentalist) show a range of favorably disposed images of Jews in nonbiblical lessons. The conservative lessons, on the other hand, are heavily negative in this same area. Where writers, then, are free of any necessary or direct biblical influence, both positive and negative images of Jews still appear. All four communicators fashion a favorable portrait of Jews and Judaism in Old Testament lessons. In New Testament lessons the liberal and neo-orthodox scores remain positive, but the fundamentalist score becomes equivocal, and the conservative score shifts to a negative one.

In addition, while the liberal, neo-orthodox, and fundamentalist lessons not derived from scripture are more favorable to Jews than their biblical ones in each case, their biblical lessons are, on the whole, quite positive. But again, the conservative materials produce the opposite results. Their nonbiblical lessons, while few, contain significantly more unfavorable statements about Jews and Judaism than do their writings based on the Bible.

Because these communicators differ in their images of Jews when free of biblical subject matter, extrabiblical factors are plainly at work in the creation of the images. And since lessons based on scripture also differ widely in their intergroup orientation, a similar conclusion may be drawn with respect to them. Otherwise the biblical lessons of the four curricula would have scored similarly— in direction if not in intensity. It is clear, then, that the difficulty which some Protestants have in setting forth a positive and constructive view of Jews and Judaism is the result of perspectives that go beyond, and perhaps may be more basic than, scripture as such. These influences are usually compounded of exegetical views, theological commitments, and other teachings about Jews that derive from tradition and from attitudes formed by social and cultural forces. These basic attitudes and perspectives, whatever their origins, determine the intergroup orientation of the materials more significantly than does the scriptural text.

Nonetheless, the fact that most of the Protestant groups produce biblical lessons that are less favorable (or more negative) than those not based on scripture, indicates that scripture which involves Jews and Judaism does indeed present some problems. The conservatives and fundamentalists, for example, have much less difficulty in portraying Jews favorably in their expositions of the Old Testament than of the New Testament. Similarly, the neo-orthodox show a less approving (although still positive) attitude toward Jews in New Testament lessons than in Old Testament lessons. Only the liberal curriculum reverses this tendency; since they tend to think of the first part of the Old Testament as concerned with merely another primitive religion, they therefore take a higher view of Jews in New Testament than in Old Testament lessons. Scripture, then, as well as views about the Bible, can and does affect the degree and kind of Jewish references, imposes certain difficulties upon the writers, and may even set some kind of ceiling on the potential scores. But the fact remains that whether the over-all profile of Jews is favorable, ambiguous, or unfavorable, it has no relation whatever to the scriptural sources.

The extrabiblical factors that help to determine a given Jewish portrait operate on scriptural content in several ways. First of all, writers are selective in their choice of scripture upon which to comment. In the selection made in the early stages of curriculum construction, and later in writing the lessons, the editors and writers are relatively free to ignore or include whatever scripture they wish. The nature of the passages they choose will partly determine whether the curriculum is relevant or irrelevant to intergroup relations, and whether it will or will not lend itself to negative or positive teachings about the Jews.

This selectivity and its relation to the larger faith perspective is demonstrated in Table 2,[23] which shows the degree to which the various publishers appeal to scripture (along with other religious precedent and teachings) to support their various statements about

23. Appendix VII.

other religious and racial-ethnic groups. No explicit appeals to religious authority are made by liberal writers for any negative statement scored in any of the fourteen analytical categories. The neo-orthodox cite scripture or doctrinal sources for only four negative as compared to 346 positive statements. The fundamentalist writers lay a proportionately greater claim to scriptural support for their negative views, but the positive citations still predominate in the ratio of 3 to 1. The conservative curriculum is more ambiguous, with fifty negative as against seventy-seven positive citations. Some writers are apparently able to find authority in the sources of their faith for unfavorable as well as favorable statements about outsiders; others either do not find such warrants or else pass over them.

There are significant differences, then, in the kind and degree of scriptural citations which various Protestant groups invoke in behalf of their interreligious teachings. For example, the conservative publisher quotes scripture at a ratio of 9 to 1 against various forms of religious interaction (cooperation, intermarriage, interfaith activities, etc.); the fundamentalist ratio is 4 against to 3 for. The neo-orthodox reverses this tendency by finding authority for diverse forms of interaction by 6 to 1, while the liberal produces no negative citations at all. From their respective faith-perspectives the communicator selects different passages of scripture and other religious precedent to weight their directives in intergroup relations.

It is also worth noting that the same biblical passages serve lesson writers in differing—and sometimes opposing—ways. Some biblical statements are like intergroup Rorschach ink blots, in that the content they elicit comes not from the text but from the writer. When the Gospels say that after hearing Jesus' words from the cross, *Eloi, Eloi,* "some of the bystanders" cry, "Behold, he is calling Elijah" (Mark 15:35), much is left to the interpretation of the lesson writer; were these "bystanders" Roman soldiers or Jews? Again when one of them said. "Wait, let us see whether Elijah will come to take him down," did he speak in derision, misunderstanding, awed curiosity, or sympathy? One lesson writer, contradicting other interpreters, regards these words as "bitter mockery" spoken by Jews; they are said to have known that *Eloi* meant "My God," but in ridicule they *purposely misinterpreted* his words to refer to Elijah.

The way in which the same scripture sometimes allows contrary interpretations is seen in a passage from the Gospel of John, where "the Jews" are said to have "marveled" at Jesus' teaching in the temple, asking, "How is it that this man has learning when he has never studied?" One lesson regards this passage as expressing Jewish "admiration" for Jesus' knowledge and teaching, despite his lack of training in the rabbinical schools. Another claims that it is a "disdainful taunt" at Jesus' lack of a rabbinical education. Or, to give a further example, Acts 19:33–34 describes the attempt of the Jew Alexander to quiet a rioting mob at Ephesus. Three different lessons based on this incident make diverse judgments about Jewish attitudes toward Christians:

| *The Scripture* | *The Lesson Comment* |
|---|---|
| Some of the crowd prompted Alexander, whom the Jews had put forward. And Alexander motioned with his hand, wishing to make a defense to the people. But when they recognized that he was a Jew, for about two hours they all with one voice cried out, "Great is Artemis of the Ephesians." | EXAMPLE ONE: The Jews tried to take advantage of the situation and stir up a persecution of the Christians, but the crowd would not listen to them.[24] EXAMPLE TWO: Finally the Jews who lived in Ephesus became alarmed for fear they might be blamed for the whole affair, though they were against Paul as much as Demetrius and his friends. Therefore these unbelieving Jews pushed Alexander to the front, as their representative, to explain that they had nothing to do with Paul.[25] EXAMPLE THREE: Why did the assembly refuse to listen to Alexander, the Jew? What does this indicate was the Gentile's attitude towards Jews? [i.e. the riot of idol-worshipers turned out to be as much anti-Jewish as anti-Christian].[26] |

24. *The Early Christian Church According to the Book of Acts* (pupil's book), Missouri Synod, p. 121.

25. Scripture Press, unit 671, p. 28.

26. *Intermediate Bible Guide* (3d Year, Oct.–Dec. quarter, Disciples of Christ), p. 44.

The first commentator sees a Jew intent on attacking the Christian community. The second sees the same person attempting merely to dissociate himself from the Christians so as to avert a possible attack upon the Jewish community. The third interprets the reaction of the crowd as Gentile anti-Semitism. The biblical text determines the theme; but the mind-sets of the different writers to Jews lead them to quite different inferences.

These variant interpretations are sometimes related to hermeneutical and exegetical principles. The parable of the Last Judgment is a good example because it defines judgment versus everlasting beatitude as depending upon the quality of man's response to the needs of "these my brethren." Their principle of literal interpretation leads some fundamentalist writers to take the phrase "my brethren" as signifying Jesus' fellow Jews—those nations who persecute the Jews, the brethren of Christ, shall be cast out. The conservatives think of Israel as displaced by the Church and therefore identify Christ's "brethren" with the Christian. For the neo-orthodox, "these my brethren" signifies anyone or everyone in need, for they believe that man meets Christ in his neighbor. Such differences of interpretation are quite evidently not merely isolated reflections on the text but part of a larger point of view.

Another way in which the image of the Jews is created more or less independently of scripture is to downgrade or upgrade the Jew from the biblical text. Downgrading takes various forms. Sometimes disparaging statements about Jews foreign to the text are injected into the commentary. Or derogatory passages are singled out and enlarged upon, while contradictory passages are ignored. Or a hostile reaction occasioned by a given passage may be fortified by bringing in other unfavorable, though often loosely related, passages from scripture. Other practices are to attribute contemptible hidden motives to Jewish figures or to misstate the facts of their behavior. Often the Jewish personages whose actions are being condemned are labeled "Jews," while the exemplary personages are not. Finally, the lesson writer may resort to stereotypes, verbal tags, and other rhetorical devices of invective. Thus Jews who observe Torah may be spoken of as "slavishly submissive" or as paying "petty attention to trivial detail."

By "upgrading" is meant that the writer does more than simply ignore, reject, or explain negative elements in the text. He assigns valued and distinctively human motives to the Jewish figures; he corrects typical and unfavorable distortions; he warns against prejudice and misunderstanding; he expresses himself in honorific language, such as "devout" or "pious," where the hostile writer uses negatively charged expressions. In controversial areas, such as when discussing the Pharisees, he provides explanatory background material that illuminates the actions of Jesus' critics and those who opposed the message and work of the early Church. Beyond this, he is careful to comment on biblical events in their biblical-historical context.

It is important to recognize that downgrading and upgrading are both observable normative deviations from the specific scripture being discussed, even though sometimes they may be inspired by exegetical and theological understandings of scripture.[27] Regardless of how such statements may be thought to be justified by scripture, faith perspectives, historical fact, hermeneutical principles, or exegetical method, the important fact remains that some writers regard as favorable to Jews and Judaism the same passages that others interpret as unfavorable. Thus, when these differences in judgment between communicators are measured, the results mirror not the content of scripture per se but the views and attitudes of the interpreters.

If it is obvious that the Bible often does nothing more than provide occasions for writers to express their attitudes about Jews and Judaism, it is even more obvious that the Bible provides opportunities for writers to discuss nonbiblical groups, like Roman Catholics, and nonbiblical problems like race relations.[28] Roman Catholicism, of course, is not mentioned in the Bible; but a verse from the epistles may remind the writer of Catholic interpretations of the same passage and thus lead to observations of the helpfulness, danger, or "falseness" of such views. Or the writer may content himself with a free-floating association inspired by the text: the parable of

27. Upgrading and downgrading are not so much calculated devices as by-products of a point of view, i.e. upgrading involves an approach to scripture which is self-critical, which identifies with Israel and/or humanity, which universalizes rather than particularizes scriptural passages, etc.

28. See Table 3, Appendix VII. Considerable mention is made of Negroes, Catholics, and other denominations in lessons devoted largely to commentary on scripture, despite the fact that these groups do not appear in the biblical drama.

the Pharisee and the Publican, for example, prompts one writer to describe Pharisaic legalism, and then to remark, "Romanism teems with this Pharisaic spirit as a filthy kitchen does with vermin."

## The Jewish Profile

Since the word "Jews," when used in scriptural commentary, does not necessarily signify modern Jews, the Jewish portraits that emerge from this study do not inevitably represent Protestant views of contemporary Judaism. The designation "Jews" may at times have a strictly contemporary reference, but mostly such distinctions in the use of the word are not made. As a result, the Jewish portrait is a mixture of past and present. It is frequently not clear to what extent ancient and modern Jews are identified in the minds of the writers or are evoked in the minds of the readers. Nevertheless, it must be noted that the most favorable portraits of the Jews as a whole are made by those communicators who are most aware of the Jews as a continuing people, living among Christians, to whom Christians owe a spiritual debt and are obligated to treat with consideration and fairness.

The Protestant profiles of this conglomerate Jewish image can be roughly described on the basis of our findings as follows. The liberals and neo-orthodox communicators view Jews positively throughout the respective profiles, except that the neo-orthodox stress somewhat the past hostility of Jews to Christians in discussions of the early history of the church.[29] Both liberals and neo-orthodox tend to "correct" distortions of Jewish life and thought or direct the students to Jewish sources in order to discover such facts for themselves. Both express attitudes of kinship and interdependency with Judaism, set forth a relatively high evaluation of Jewish morality, godliness, and wholesome group life, and provide constructive statements of many kinds. The liberal teachings are particularly marked in recommending relations with Jews across all barriers, including marriage.

The fundamentalist Scripture Press predominantly identifies with Jews and Judaism, condemns anti-Semitism, and at times strongly defends the Jews against attack. The fundamentalist writers also stress kinship with Jews, even though some of them regard Israel and the Church as separate communities ordained by God to exist

29. Figs. 9–10, Appendix VIII.

together until the end of time. The social and cultural characteristics attributed to Jews are largely positive, and there are slightly
more corrections than distortions. Fundamentalist educators, however, are more ambiguous in their views of Jews and Judaism than
are those of liberalism and neo-orthodoxy. Their main difficulties
arise in discussing the moral roles and characteristics of Jews as
they find them in scripture, in affirming the truth in Judaism, and
in discussing New Testament hostility of Jews toward Christians.[30]

Whereas the fundamentalist lessons have negative scores in only
four of the fourteen categories that involve Jews, the conservative
ones have negative scores in eleven. A slight expression of kinship
with Jews and approbation of their non-moral cultural characteristics are the sole respects in which the conservative lessons speak
favorably. The two lowest aspects of their profile are in the categories of describing the more ancient Jewish attitudes of hostility
to Christians and evaluating Jewish moral characteristics. Conservative teachings also distort more than correct images of Jewish life
and thought, judge Judaism as a false religion, and experience difficulty in discussing the continued existence of the Jewish people.[31]

## INTER-CHRISTIAN AND NON-CHRISTIAN RELATIONS

Protestant images of other (non-Catholic) Christians and non-
Christians deserve extensive discussion—particularly those in the
liberal and neo-orthodox writings—and further attention will be
paid to this in the next chapter. For now, we can note that while
both liberals and the neo-orthodox see other Christian groups positively, both the conservative and the fundamentalist communicators do not.

Some Protestants, particularly among the fundamentalists and
conservatives, are in fact somewhat more disturbed by Protestant
pluralism than they are by the existence of the Jews as a distinct
religious and cultural group.[32] For the conservatives the main point
of conflict with the sects and denominations lies in the definition of
the true faith and the preservation of the Gospel. This finding is
true to a lesser degree for the fundamentalists. Although their view

30. Fig. 11.
31. Fig. 12.
32. Fig. 3, Appendix VIII. Note that the "other-Christian" group scores lower
than the Jewish.

of other denominations is generally favorable, their curriculum is preoccupied with the teachings of such competing sects as Seventh Day Adventism, Jehovah's Witnesses, and Mormonism. These sects are regarded as threats to the truth of the Gospel, and the Scripture Press devotes considerable space to the errors they are judged to be spreading across the land.

While the fundamentalist educators are willing to engage in dialogue with other Protestant theologies, the conservative ones raise rather strong objections to formal intercourse with the other communions. For this position they claim some biblical support. On the whole, both the fundamentalist and conservative writers are apt to see more evil and ungodliness than goodness and godliness in the mass of sects and denominations.[33]

The fundamentalists are concerned for the liberties of the non-Christian religions, such as Buddhism and Islam, but neither they nor the conservatives see much to commend in these religions.[34] Their attitude again contrasts with that in both the liberal and neo-orthodox curricula, which will provide the basis for some of our later observations.[35]

## AMBIGUITIES AND ANTIDOTES TO PREJUDICE IN PROTESTANT LITERATURE

In assessing the impact on the students of Protestant teaching as a whole, it is necessary to recognize that even denominations which produce the most auspicious portraits of outsiders are also responsible for bits of negative Christian teaching, produce some lessons that are equivocal in tone, and leave room for improvement. The opposite observation is also valid—that even the most negative scorer publishes a considerable body of lessons whose inter-group tendency is constructive, and that there is a decided anti-ethnocentric potential in fundamentalist and conservative lessons. Antidotes to bias may be said to exist in all curricula, if not to the same degree.

This conclusion becomes even clearer when we again focus upon the Jewish portrait. It has already been pointed out that negative

33. Figs. 15–16, Appendix VIII.
34. Figs. 19–20, Appendix VIII.
35. Figs. 17–18, Appendix VIII. For profiles for other Christian denominations see Figs. 13–14.

statements about other groups are not considered invidious in this inquiry. They are significant only if they make for an unwarranted over-all portrait or if the nature of the total teachings is primarily accusatory and unbalanced by a realistic self-critical view of one's own group, and so on. It therefore becomes important to discover the intergroup tendency of the *individual* lessons analyzed in each curriculum (e.g. favorably disposed toward Jews); the question asked of the entire curriculum could be asked of the single lesson, "Is its impact plus or minus?" Our analytic method made it easy to answer this latter question by taking each lesson and subtracting the number of negative scores for Jews in the 14 analytical categories from the positive, or vice versa. For each lesson a plus or minus imbalance, or else an exact balance, was determined. By following this procedure for each lesson and then tabulating the results for the whole curriculum, it was possible to discover the intergroup impact of the sample of lessons analyzed. The question can be put like this: Do conservative scores for Jews, for example, represent a consistent but low negative emphasis, lesson by lesson, for all the lessons across the board? How negative do they become, or, conversely, how positive? Finally, how frequently do negatively disposed lessons occur as compared with their opposite?

One set of results shows that 48 per cent of fundamentalist lessons mentioning Jews are positive in impact (with overages on the plus side ranging from 1 to 6 scores), while more than one-third of the conservative lessons were positive (with overages of 1 to 5 scores). This finding clearly indicates that even the most negatively disposed groups possess indigenous resources for presenting a positive portrait of the Jews.[36] Further, an examination of those lessons that score positively reveals perspectives in fundamentalist and conservative literature which, if adopted by all their writers, would raise the intergroup content of their curricula to the level of high positive-scorers.

As expected from our other basic findings, the liberals and neo-orthodox again come off best. But one notes that 8 to over 11 per cent of their lessons mentioning Jews were negatively oriented, 15 to 17 per cent were equivocal, and the remainder (73 to 75 per cent) ranged on the plus side. So here, too, there are clearly some areas of weakness that editors and writers can strengthen.

36. Fig. 21, Appendix VIII.

Further ambiguities and anti-ethnocentric potentials turn up in the scores for certain variables within the teachings about Catholics, Jews, and non-Christians. A limited number of these have been placed in the Appendixes.[37] The difference, for example, between the −56.8 per cent general score for Jews in conservative material produced for adults and the +9.3 per cent scores in texts produced for Intermediates and Seniors indicates that negative thinking about Jews is not necessarily implicit in the conservative outlook. Here again, the important conclusion is that favorable teachings about Jews are possible.[38]

The crowning result of this investigation of conservative materials came when an attempt was made to identify the source of the most negative materials produced. A single writer (referred to in this study as $X$) was found to be the author of a large segment of lessons. When the productions of $X$ were subtracted from the total scores for the Jewish category, the general score rose from −15.2 to a +0.6 per cent. It was immediately clear that a single prolific writer can strongly influence the over-all orientation of a body of teaching.[39]

In fairness it should be added that the conservative editors have by this time either dropped or completely revised all the texts produced by $X$ (and others as well) since this survey was instituted. The conservative curriculum is a dynamic, not a static, one and undergoes continual revision. Revision, in fact, is a characteristic feature of Protestant curricula, and the tendency of our research method to freeze its findings in a necessarily time-bound perspective is not meant to obscure the fact that the data alters from year to year. Ultimately what these findings signify is that Protestant educators must constantly be vigilant in seeing that the new curricula produced do not lose the intergroup strength of the old or perpetuate their intergroup liabilities.

37. Figs. 36–39, Appendix VIII.
38. Fig. 37, Appendix VIII.
39. Tables 4 and 5, Appendix VII.

# 3. Anti-Ethnocentrism in Two Contrasting Faith Perspectives

The liberal Unitarian-Universalist and the neo-orthodox Presbyterian materials in this study prove to be equally and clearly anti-ethnocentric. Not only do they view all religious as well as nonreligious groups favorably, but they are the only communicators of the four to satisfy the overarching criterion of "generality of other-group acceptance." [1] These findings are of special importance. They demonstrate that a positive intergroup orientation is possible within distinct and opposing faith-perspectives, and also shed light on the question of how significant religious ideas are in visualizing other groups. This chapter will discuss some of these illuminations in detail.

The contrasts between the two faiths are evident in their respective discussions of intergroup relations. The liberals understand reality monistically, the neo-orthodox through the perspective of a radical theism. The first faith is nontrinitarian; it concerns itself exclusively with the humanity of Jesus, it believes that man is potentially good and one with God, and it deplores such concepts as "revelation," "the chosen people," and "uniqueness." The other faith is trinitarian and takes its starting point from the Incarnation; it believes in both the full humanity and the divinity of Christ, declares that man is a sinner, and carefully distinguishes between God and his creation. It accepts the ideas of chosenness, special revelation, the primacy of the "Word of God" in scripture as well as the uniqueness of the Christian claim. Although the liberals and the neo-orthodox share intense concerns about intergroup relations, they approach its problems from radically different presuppositions. Consequently, they emerge with different conclusions about the nature, etiology, manifestations, and cure of intergroup conflict and prejudice.

1. Below, Fig. 3, Appendix VIII.

These preliminary statements, then, have four important implications:

(1) Anti-ethnocentrism is not the exclusive possession of religious liberals.

(2) We are obliged to examine more carefully the role played by a faith perspective in expressing an intergroup point of view.

(3) Questions are raised as to the nature of prejudice, inasmuch as contradictory views exist among the very persons who are looking for ways to improve intergroup relations. There is no unanimous agreement as to what is bigoted and divisive.

(4) Apparently there is more than one type of anti-ethnocentrism. Several kinds of assertions reflected in the positive imbalances for the two communicators often contradict one another.

The last two points are key ones. In formulating their anti-ethnocentric outlook, the liberals consider it essential to judge the similarities between religions as vital and basic; the neo-orthodox think it necessary to understand each specific faith in its fundamental differences as well as in its marginal or basic likenesses. The former, consequently, has a single formula for transcending the barriers that divide the faiths of mankind. The latter has a variety of formulae, each arising from a detailed examination of a specific faith. The liberal educator takes up Christianity, Judaism, and Buddhism in much the same way and engages them in dialogue about their basic and universal truths. The neo-orthodox must relate his faith to Judaism in a fundamentally different way than he does to Buddhism and examine both in a concretely different fashion than he does Christianity: with Judaism, the fact of a basic identity as well as of distinctions must be acknowledged; with Buddhism and Hinduism the challenge to the Christian faith comes primarily at those points of basic differences; while with Christian groups, the loyalty to Christ is stressed and differences are dealt with in a more marginal way. This is not to say that the intergroup content of liberal and neo-orthodox materials will differ at all points; they differ mainly in their general interpretation of the questions of mutual concern.

The respective world-views of these two top scorers provide convenient frameworks for assessing all the other variations, since the liberal and neo-orthodox publishers show a high degree of internal consistency between their intergroup teachings and their theology. Thus the Great Divide of faith between the liberals and neo-orthodox can profitably be examined in its manifold and representative implications for understanding intergroup relations.

## TWO WAYS OF CROSSING GROUP LINES

The similarities in the ways in which these two communicators involve themselves in outside groups are sundry. Both seek to state and implement the anti-ethnocentric genius of their own faith. Both grant to other groups the same rights which they claim for their own. Both can place themselves "inside" other groups, are able to acknowledge and sympathize with their plights and problems and to understand their views. Their concern for people crosses all group lines unconditionally. There are no obligations imposed on members toward their own group which are not also considered obligations toward members of other groups. All peoples are, essentially, looked at in the same ways from the standpoint of their humanity, dignity, rights, and obligations.

Nevertheless, these common ways of universalizing a faith do have their important differences. These are more easily seen once we develop further the background of their respective ideologies.

The liberal's universality is predicted on a "many roads to truth" approach which is consistent with his pervasive monism. Truth is regarded as universal and as discoverable and sharable by all men. Religion becomes a search, rather than a goal. The nature of the truths and of the search for them presuppose the existence of many saviors and many revelations. This practice of universalizing envisions an emerging global religion which the adherents of many faiths participate in discovering, each from within his own inherited tradition. Mankind is bound together by its common search and by the oneness of truth.

Although they also have a respectful, if critical, attitude toward other faiths, the neo-orthodox writers unqualifiedly identify with the Judeo-Christian tradition. In this respect, neo-orthodoxy is particularistic; it places itself in one specific tradition in the world, and not in many. From within this tradition, however, it seeks to establish a firm basis for positive and responsible relations with other religious groups.

*Monistic Inclusiveness and the "Natural"*

Like all monisms, the liberal view has a marked ability to absorb diverse religious standpoints:

> If you exchange ideas with a liberal of the Jewish faith, you will find him close to your own (if your own has the breath of fresh air that the prophet breathes). You will not be surprised if one of your friends calls himself both Christian and Buddhist, if you know something of the essentials of each faith. You will attend the simple service of a Ramakrishna meeting-house in New York City with the feeling that the founder of your own religion is present in this house of God. And you will appreciate the Hindu affirmation that truth shines more brilliantly when it shines from many angles, like the diamond with its many facets.[2]

The liberal curriculum directs the student to share the many answers offered by the world's high religions to humanity's common questions. The theory that reality is one, and that the vital aim of life is served by a realization of our essential oneness with each other and all that exists, places a heavy stress on similitudes. This emphasis in turn provides the liberals with an important anti-ethno-centric principle—viz., religious differences divide and set men against each other, while their similarities, by definition sharable and cohesive, are able to unite a divided mankind. Theoretically, this does not exclude some appreciation of diversity or signify its ultimate elimination. Monism provides for diversity by including diversities within itself; the differences must be seen from the point of view of the essential underlying oneness to place them in the right perspective. Differences per se are not thought "divisive" (the liberal term for "prejudice") unless one makes claims of unique and central validity for a particular tradition or set of symbols. Diversity, then, is regarded as peripheral and as pointing to the deeper universal truths that lie at the center of beliefs and experience.

The liberals' perspective that is intended to eliminate all divisive

2. Unitarian-Universalist, Beacon Press Curriculum, Lesson No. 245 (see below, Appendix V), p. xii, hereafter signified by UN, followed by lesson number and page number.

distinctions may be understood in several ways. Let us approach it here from their understanding of what is natural to the growing person. The author who has most definitively set forth the curriculum philosophy of this communicator first notes the experiences that are natural to the learning child, and then their correspondence with the experiences of the primitive religious man. The underlying assumption is that human history is less basic in religion than are the common human experiences and problems of men as creatures who are bound to nature and to each other.

The author's premise follows that children are not born with a historical sense and cannot experience history. Their apprehension of time permits no concept of history. The natural experiences of the child (as of primitive man) are with the world of nature and people—birth, growth, death, love, fear, trust; time is experienced as night and day, sun, moon, and stars. The natural is prior to the historical, and for the liberal those experiences which antedate others are considered to be controlling in religion as in life. For example the author applies this principle to locate the essential identity and larger meanings in the Jewish Hannukah and the Christian Christmas. Their antecedents are found to be mid-winter festivals, celebrating the yearly cycle of death and rebirth symbolized also in the equinox. Seen in this way, it is recommended that in educating the young child Jews and Christians can unite in stressing those natural similarities which make sense and have value for all children rather than the particular historical meanings which tend to set off these holidays, and Jews and Christians themselves, from each other. It is anticipated that children taught in this way will not develop those premature loyalties to their own groups which determine later attitudes and so foster prejudice.

There is a second reason for the liberal stress on natural experiences. These not only lay the foundations for love, confidence, security, and relatedness to people but also are *universal*. The same natural needs, experiences, and insights are shared by all the world's peoples. Since this universality of human experience provides in the liberal view the basis of all religion, the writers have frequent recourse to doctrines of naturalism. Because the natural is universal, it, in turn, supports the perspective of a common fellowship, a common world understanding, and a global religion in-the-making which will unify mankind.

The historical, then, is distinctly subordinate in the liberal conception of religion. The historical represents a limited experience in the narrow tradition of one people. All history is particular—the history of *my* group, *my* church, *my* nation. Unsharable symbols, ideas, customs, and observances arise within these specific histories. Since these symbols and observances celebrate discrete events, they can have meaning only within the group that shares a given history. One must go beneath this parochial content to tap the universals.

The fundamental unity of mankind is thus seen to lie much deeper than their common human needs, problems, and experiences; in a sense it already exists in the similar values and meanings that men share. The discovery of these underlying similarities is intended to break down barriers and eliminate the sense of being different, unique, and therefore superior—feelings which lead to group conflict, prejudice, and hatred.

Furthermore, this solution to intergroup conflict has another basis beyond a rational analysis of the differences between the natural and historical categories of human experience, and a commitment to the emerging world-consciousness of our own times. It also derives from the monistic pantheism of the Universalist-Unitarian faith. The conviction that the varied symbols and root beliefs of the high religions point to common universal meanings necessarily implies that all reality is one, and the corollary, that mankind is a part of one God. If all reality and man are one, man's varied expressions of this oneness must, in their essentials, be directed to the same basic truths. This position does not deny, however, that there is diversity in the world, or say that it is entirely unimportant; for in diversity there can be error.

This error is described in the liberal literature as consisting either of wrong assumptions about the disunity and disparity in the world (for example, the assumption that there are truths unique to my own group) or of wrong ways of discovering or communicating the universal truths. The latter mistake comes from limiting the search for truth to "our own" group, or authoritatively forcing on the child ready-made truths (rather than arranging for the child to discover the truths that lie in the experiences he shares with human beings everywhere). There are, therefore, ideas which liberals feel they must surrender because they stand in the way of the emergence of a world faith. One is that any group could be a "chosen people," with a divinely appointed task not given to other people. Such a belief is considered divisive—a manifestation of group pride. But it is also considered undesirable because it enables both Judaism and Christianity to regard themselves as proclaiming unique messages, therefore implicitly contradicting the unitary conception of reality and truth.[3] Similarly, historical loyalties and emphases are suspect—not because they are unnecessary but because they tend to cut off the search for truth and to identify truth with the already fixed formulations of the group. From the liberal standpoint, an interest in history comes mainly from the conviction that one is better equipped to deal with modern problems by studying their historical roots. "All things, all problems, have their yesterdays, and to live unaware of these yesterdays is to return to the naivete of primitive peoples." [4]

All this amounts to an anti-ethnocentric thrust in the liberal view of history; its use makes universalizing possible. Growing children are said to need to feel "deeply related to the whole human race," which cannot be accomplished at the start of their study of history by leading them "through the narrow channel of the Hebrew or Christian tradition exclusively." They need to know the history of other great religious personalities, like Buddha, Confucius, Mohammed, Zoroaster, Akhenaten, as well as Jesus and Moses. "To treat the history of man's religious experiences as though it were contained in one sacred book about one religiously superior people is to foster narrowness and intolerance at a time when breadth of appreciations is sorely needed." [5]

*The Primacy of the Historical*

"The God of the Hebrew-Christian tradition is a God who has acted in history. This accounts for the superior quality of Judaism and Christianity over other religions that have worshiped a god

3. Unitarian writers sometimes regard divisiveness as the form that beliefs take, i.e. the way in which beliefs are held—as special, final, superior, etc. At other times it is described as consisting of "beliefs"; in this case, divisive beliefs may be regarded as beliefs about symbols.

4. UN269:258 and UN400:183.

5. UN400:183–84.

who is primarily a nature deity." [6] This is a statement of the neo-orthodox view that Christianity is not only an historical religion but one that proclaims God as actively and uniquely revealing himself in history.

From this doctrine it follows that the Christian is directed by the self-revealing acts of God to pay serious attention to the daily, objective world where he acts, suffers, and enjoys. The consequences which men experience in their relations with this world are the result not solely of their own individual or compounded action but also of the action of God.[7] God is not passive in history, but a participant in it. He discloses himself in history through his acts; in these events man is also disclosed to himself.

Men thus confront a basic reality in the events of history, according to the neo-orthodox view, and they must comprehend and come to terms with its unyielding demands. This understanding of God's reality comes to man through a specific religious history, namely the history of the Jewish people and the church. Though God has acted in the past and acts today, the decisive divine act in history for the redemption of mankind took place in the work of Jesus Christ. In contemporary history the ever-present action of God demands obedience to him in the love of neighbor. But such a view of history is not looked upon solely as providing moral imperatives in the concrete situations of every-day life where Christians confront their fellow men, some of whom are members of other racial, national, and religious communities; these imperatives transcend geographical, national, racial, or any other consideration. This unrestricted ethical requirement leads to what may be termed neo-orthodox universalism.

Another feature of the neo-orthodox way of universalizing is the power of its insights to illuminate the human situation in its broadest as well as most concrete nature. The history of Israel,

6. Presbyterian Church U.S.A. (Christian Faith and Life Curriculum), *Crossroads* (1955), p. 82 (elective based on Herbert Butterfield's *Christianity and History*, New York, Scribner's, 1950). The lesson writer is describing as well as approving Butterfield's thesis. See also PR37,016:27. Here and below, quotations from the Presbyterian curriculum are indicated by PR, followed by lesson number and page number.

7. God's acts are, at the same time, judgment and redemption. Although God's redemptive acts are revealed in the Bible, the divine action must be thought of as a present and continuing constituent of all human history. PR37,542:60 ff.

as reported in scripture, is particular; the knowledge of God as having revealed himself in a concrete manner through his acts belongs to those within a specific tradition. But it is the same God who has acted in the history of all peoples, and whose respective histories must be understood in the light which Israel's history throws upon them. As one writer asserts: "and in understanding the history of Israel, we gain an understanding of mankind." If all men have confronted God in their history, and if all nations can see their own history reflected in the history of Israel, it is still the unique Judeo-Christian insight to know this truth.[8]

From the neo-orthodox viewpoint, to meet God is a shattering, demanding experience, since all persons are called on to acknowledge his sovereignty. Yet, although all men meet God, they refuse to acknowledge his sovereignty in their actual responses to their neighbors. These rejective responses to God's acts everywhere make for dividedness, hatred, ill-feeling, indifference, and prejudice. These prejudices (individual and collective) are indications both of our rebellion against God and of the "judgment" which we choose; yet, in these very events God seeks to remake us. History, then, is regarded as the drama of the real God who seeks and confronts us, despite all our evasions and pretentions, and who challenges all the idols we put in His place.

This view is not meant to exalt one history above other histories. Its purpose is to illuminate *all* history (and all particular histories) through an account of what God has done in *one* history, in which he revealed himself and redeemed all men despite man's universal rejection of him. By understanding this history all people can come to know themselves and God in a corrective and redeeming perspective.

The liberal treatment of history differs in a fundamental respect from the neo-orthodox, and all other differences relate to it. Liberals see history as purely human, man-made, yet within one reality

8. The Bible is unique in that it is the only book written to tell the history of a people with the purpose of showing how God has dealt with his people and has made Himself known despite the unwillingness of the nation to know Him, i.e. history written from the viewpoint of those to whom the meaning of their history in ultimate terms was revealed. Other religions have scripture, but none is a history or interpretation of history. While Indians, Chinese, and Japanese writers have produced a remarkable religious literature, these consist principally of teachings, lyrics, philosophy, manuals of discipline and devotion, and epic narratives. PR37,460:30, PR37,016:27.

which impinges alike on all men; their understanding of deity is therefore quite different from those who understand God as acting concretely in history. The meaning of history for man, the self-disclosure of God in historical events, and the crucial nature of the historical in the human drama are all central questions for the neo-orthodox writer, but are not even marginal ones for the liberal. For instance, the importance of the historical scene is barely evident in the liberal exposition of the lives and message of the Hebrew prophets, where it is indispensable for an understanding of the prophetic message.

## God, Man, and the Oppressor

The differences in ideology of the two anti-ethnocentric communicators are nowhere more vivid than in their debate over God and man. The liberal maintains that Christendom and the Semitic religions, which traditionally have believed in a God external to man, have been characteristically bigoted, cruel, and unfeeling in their relationship to other persons. A transcendent God "rules his subjects by divine command. With such a God, *religion tends to be a matter of external sanctions and obedience to a will other than one's own* . . . Such a general outlook makes religion authoritative, dogmatic and external."

In the liberal view, this kind of God can be used to rationalize any aggression and hatred. A church, institution, or individual may arbitrarily use such a God to sanction despotic purposes by characterizing him as requiring such and such a belief, ritual, or observance; his invoked authority can thus enable the worshiper to hate, vilify, or persecute his neighbor for the latter's nonconformity and lack of faith. In the "Old Story of Salvation," as one liberal writer claims, it was "inevitable that the blessings of the Kingdom of God should have been limited to those whom God should declare righteous, and that the rest of mankind should be regarded as enemies to be defeated and made impotent."

Liberal writers also contend that the concept of a personal God who stands over against man and who speaks through a special revelation nurtures two authoritarian patterns. The first is the appeal to external authority, to which men are asked blindly to submit. The second is the imposition of the content of a given revelation which men must accept. Since neither the source of authority nor the content of the revelation can be validated by the universal experience of mankind, men must take other men's word that the authority is valid and the revelation true. At worst this submission to external authority prepares the way for an "oppressor," inasmuch as the power of the despot depends upon the submissiveness of the people to his power. At best, the authoritarian discipline is able to produce the conformist, who does not make an observance or belief his own, but merely substitutes the external form for the inner reality.

These views of God, according to the liberal critic, foster as well a view of life as a battlefield in which evil and good are contending in people who take sides against each other. One group, it is said, assumes that they have the truth and all others believe in falsehoods. Another group claims to be good and accuses others of evil. A struggle thus develops between the faiths, in which diverse religions engage in "a battle unto the death."

While completely sympathetic to the liberal anxiety about assisting oppression, neo-orthodox writers see a great danger in the idea of God as wholly immanent. When God is identified with nature or man, they claim that there is no objective, external check against the tendency of a subjective apprehension of God which can result in subtle prejudice, or indifference and privileged rationalization in matters of social justice. In order to understand this objection, one must view together the neo-orthodox doctrines of man and God.

One of several neo-orthodox terms for man's condition is "alienation": basically this signifies a separation from God, from oneself, and from one's fellow man. Alienation is manifest in society in its fragmentation, intergroup bitterness, prejudice, and disunity. Man strives in various ways to overcome this separation, but in doing so he only deepens the rift. It is the "good news" of the Gospel that this dividedness has been objectively overcome by an act in history of God in Jesus Christ.

The human condition of alienation relates to intergroup relations by means of a double movement within history. God is seeking man; but man, although he needs God, tries to escape Him. God ubiquitously confronts man in those events of history which intimately and directly involve him. But man evades the self-understanding and ethical responsibility which this objective meeting with God requires and, instead, seeks his own gods in order to embody and advance his own interests and aspirations. These gods are often respectable—idols of man's high ethical ideals and purposes, such as those of justice and love, his exaltation of all he values in human nature, culture, and institutional life. Even the church becomes such an idol.[9]

> This church [at Laodicea] was guilty of idolatry, finding the center of its existence in itself rather than in God, pointing to its own life rather than to Christ.
> This is the ever-present temptation of the Church—idolatry. There always are two sides to idolatry: first, the idol, which is a false god, unworthy of man's ultimate devotion; and secondly, the idolater, who senses that life must find fulfillment, and so worships and serves a false god, because he is seeking to avoid the claims of a true God.[10]

In intergroup matters these substitutes for the real God may be the racial, national, or religious groups with which a man identifies. His idol-worshiping is manifest in action which exalts his own group or in which he divorces himself from responsibility for his neighbor. Consciously or not he may affirm the doctrine of white supremacy in his behavior toward the Negro, elevate the native-born in reacting to the presence of the foreigner, idolize the Christian by his rejection of the Jew, the Hindu, or the Moslem. In so doing, he increases his alienation from self, God, and neighbor, no matter how he may seek to justify or excuse his attitudes and actions. Essentially, then, prejudice and intergroup hostility is a rejection of God through the substitution of personal, cultural, and tribal gods.

9. Idolatry is defined as acknowledging some god in our responses whether or not we are aware of it. "Martin Luther follows the Bible . . . when he defines a god as that which a man serves with his whole heart." PR37,616:49.

10. PR, *Crossroads* (Sept. 1956), p. 77. The same lesson describes "religious idolatry"—by which is meant the idolatry of the religious man—as the "most subtle" and "most reprehensible." Religious people try to "trim God to *our* measure; we bring him down to *our* level; we use him for *our* purposes; he becomes the instrument of *our* ambitions. We tend to pray, 'Father, not thy will, but mine, be done.' This is the continual temptation of the Church: to view itself as the goal of its own existence . . . to think that it has God's blessing on all the petty projects it invents for its own glory; to point to itself rather than to Christ" (ibid., italics in original).

It is only symptomatic of his condition that man is unwilling to acknowledge the idolatrous nature of these acts.

Behind this analysis lie several presuppositions about God and man. The first is that man is a sinner—that is, he stands over against God. God the Creator and man the creature cannot be identified or merged at any point. Man is made in the image of God, but he is not God nor a part of God. Although God transcends his creation, he gives it real existence, so that neither the world nor the self are illusions. It is in his real situations and by his own actions that man alienates himself from deity by his continuous elevation of some subordinate good to the place that only God can occupy. This is what "sin" is: the favorite neo-orthodox term for it is "rebellion against God."

The second assumption is that God is actively redeeming his creation, specifically in all of the experiences in which man meets his neighbor. God's deeds are encountered in every experience in which a man responds to his neighbor's actions, needs, or plight. God is the ever-present third party who, through and beyond man's acts and intentions, both destroys and redeems.

Thirdly, in each such situation man responds to God's action with both obedience and rebellion. He is enjoined to act in faith—that is, in faithfulness to God's call. Faith, in the neo-orthodox view, is an act of the whole person. One lesson defines faith as knowledge, trust, and obedience. Man's proper response of faith is a totally obedient act in a concrete situation where he stands in a triadic relationship to himself, his neighbor, and his God. This triad is inseparable. We obey God in our response to our neighbor. The valid claim of the neighbor upon us is also the claim of God upon us. We are to love the neighbor universally and unconditionally in the situation where we meet him, even as God loves him.

Man, therefore, as sinner does not find God by searching for him; he sins precisely because he is the creature who flees from God's presence. In his searching he looks elsewhere than to those situations of life where God pursues him as the hound of heaven. He places his trust in some abstract "good," or in the values, goals, and institutions of a secular culture, or in a person's creed, affiliations, groups, and desires. He retreats into nature or recoils on the past and these, too, he makes into gods.

The neo-orthodox therefore, unlike the liberal, does not see the solution to man's dividedness in the essential or potential goodness of human nature. He finds it, rather, in the prior and objective action of God: the decisive act at the center of history, in Jesus Christ, and secondly in continuing history, including the emerging events of the present. Human beings are indeed united by nature; they are all creatures of the one God, created in his likeness and with noble potentialities; they have all the same essential needs. But one aspect of this complex of shared traits is central to the neo-orthodox: we are "one in our sinfulness," alike in our common rebellion and in our need for wholeness, forgiveness, and recon-ciliation to God:

> As long as men seek to find unity in our common goodness, they will fail. There are many well-meaning efforts made to bring men together on the basis of moral virtue; but how can we be united by a virtue that we do not really possess? The gospel begins at a different point. It unites people in their common sinfulness by providing in Christ a Savior from these sins.

> Therefore, when we confront the sinfulness of the Chris-tian Church in matters like racial intolerance and prejudice, we are not surprised, dismayed, or disillusioned. We have no illusions about the Church! It is a society of sinners; that is the bold, bold fact we know about ourselves! And we start from there to receive God's judgment and to know his grace in reconciliation . . .[11]

One illuminating aspect of this Judeo-Christian revelation for intergroup relations is the conviction that God has taken the initia-tive in seeking men out; but the God who thus discloses himself is the kind of God man does not want. The God who appears in biblical history is conceived as one who sits in judgment upon *us* and *our groups*, and not only upon outside groups. Man, the neo-orthodox contend, prefers a God who plays favorites and permits him to destroy his enemies, but who will not allow his own groups to be destroyed; he wants no God who refuses to bless his preju-dices and hallow his divisive distinctions; he desires a God who hates those whom he hates, not the God who, in scriptures, is pictured as

11. PR, *Crossroads* (Oct.–Dec. 1958), p. 23.

loving those whom men hate; he yearns for a God who serves the aims of his country, not one who may contradict its aspirations and bring its hopes to nought. In brief, he wants a God who will leave him free to build the kind of world he wants in his own way and on his own terms. At the very heart of racial, ethnic, and religious prejudice, therefore, are the idolatrous propensities of mankind.

The neo-orthodox contend that every man, even the most devout Christian, must understand himself as this person who tends to rebel against God's imperious demands; literally, all men are sinners. Christians as well as others stand with all men impartially under the divine "judgment" and saving "mercy." To men who reject his universal mercy and grace by idolizing their own race, church, or nation, God's response appears as "judgment." Far from being punitive, arbitrary, and anthropomorphic, the neo-orthodox concept of judgment accounts for certain objective and discernible phenomena in history—the shattering of social orders and the necessity for recreating men's relationships to each other. The very exigencies that have forced men to struggle with the problems of intergroup relations are a judgment, since God, through them, forces him to sift his prejudices and hatreds: "The first effect of God's word in history is negative. God says no to his people. He negates all false values, destroys all human securities, and uproots men who comfortably settle down in their status quo. God is the great disturber of the peace."

To the neo-orthodox the judgment of God is always for the purpose of redeeming man: his shattered idols enable him to turn again to the true God who in his grace has destroyed them. Thus the Supreme Court ruling against segregation and the vigorous Negro demand for justice is seen as a judgment on white complacency and racial sinfulness at the same time that it is a call to national repentance and a fresh opportunity for redemptive renewal.

In thus being aware of and open to the action of an objective God, the neo-orthodox believes that he has a multiple check on his own bias and tyranny. He is on guard against his own powerful tendencies to rebel against God; he seeks for evidences of prejudice in himself and his own groups; with the illumination scriptures provide, he seeks to understand the contemporary world. He finds little reason to become defensive in his responses to criticism, since he does not claim that his acts correspond to the action of God, even though in his action he seeks to be obedient to God; he is ever aware that God will overrule or go beyond his action. In contrast, the neo-orthodox say, a religion that begins with man's search for truth concludes with gods shaped to the ends of man's desires, loves, hates, hopes, and ideals. These gods conform to whatever is central in our lives, serving our lust for power, prestige, importance, and even our devotion to some limited good.

The liberal's basic objection to the view of man as sinner is its deep note of pessimism, dooming man to a succession of unsuccessful "crises in the conflicts between good and evil unless he [accepts] God's offer of salvation . . ." The writer quoted believes that the Christian hope of God's "supernatural intervention" in history as a final solution to man's ills is no more than an extension of this pessimistic view of human nature:

> In a period such as ours, when we are constantly reminded of the threat of atom and hydrogen bombs, this theology of unsuccessful crisis is again being preached . . . If, however, such pessimism remains in our concept of human destiny, how can it be absent from our concept of God? Or, if we must believe in God because we cannot believe in ourselves, we are surely in a sorry plight. Humanists and liberals have been accused of being unduly optimistic regarding human capacities; yet, psychologically speaking, clinical experience has shown it wiser to err on the side of self-confidence than to start with a belittling of one's own powers.        [UN398:148–49]

The liberal curriculum also judges the doctrine of man as sinner to denigrate human nature; it leads to a low estimate of humanity and destroys self-respect as well as confidence in the achievement of the good. The doctrine is said to stress the shortcomings of people at the expense of their "virtues or potentialities," to encourage harsh methods of discipline by warring against the evil in the child, and to emphasize guilt rather than growth. The liberals' view of man is intended to provide the basis for human self-respect and positive moral action in the world and to defend against a moralistic condemnation and hatred of mankind.

This view must be understood in the light of the liberal's observation that what a person sees in himself he sees in others. When one thinks of himself as "sinful," he is said to lack true self-knowledge which would allow him to affirm the potential good in his neighbor.

Only when man is aware of himself as divine in his innermost being is he able to love and accept himself fully and so to love others. All persons can make this discovery. The liberal position is that, when one knows himself as potentially good, one can see and acknowledge the divine potentials in one's neighbor, and the breach between man and man can be healed.

However, the neo-orthodox doctrine of the sinfulness of man (and the concept of prejudice as sin) is also intended to curb moralizing and domineering attitudes. The doctrine rejects the notion that men can be neatly divided into good and bad; not only the pupil and child but the teachers and parents sin, so that reconciliation between man, his neighbor, and God is a universal need. In the light of this belief, all men are on the same level before God, and none enjoys a position from which he can look down upon and despise another. At the same time, the doctrine is seen to have a realistic grasp of the despair and evil of human life. Man cannot love himself or others until he can accept himself as God accepts him, in his evil as well as his goodness. In the neo-orthodox view the most saintly anti-ethnocentric Christian must face up to the fact that, though loved and accepted by God, he is tainted to some degree with the blindness of prejudice.

The human concepts of good and bad are quite irrelevant to this neo-orthodox thought of man as sinner. Man's acts are sinful only in the light of God's acts and revealed purposes, not in the light of man's moral ideals. Man is creature, limited, and contingent; God is creator, holy, and infinite. To confuse fallible human judgments of "good" and "bad" with divine righteousness and sin is to identify oneself with God—a tendency which fosters self-justification by claiming for one's actions the sanctions of deity. There are many examples of this distinction in the neo-orthodox curriculum: Man may moralize, legislate, coerce, and dominate his fellows for worthy ends he has in view and with which he identifies God, the good, and the true; he may use his commendable qualities to demonstrate that he is better than others who fail to live up to their potentialities. In fact, it is the noble and the godlike in man which may most strenuously contradict the divine purposes. The neo-orthodox doctrine of human sin does not deny that there is good in man; good as well as evil exists in even the most hardened criminal. Yet the very perpetrators of the most obvious intergroup sins are convinced that what they are doing is good. As one lesson asks the students, after giving an example of prejudice: "Did you notice how many of Mrs. Gregory's prejudiced attitudes were based on what she considered the best of motives? She had always tried to bring her children up 'right'; it was 'wrong' to shop where she found her neighbor, in a store owned by foreigners . . ." In a similar vein, another writer comments:

> From the youngest to the eldest, all of us like to think we are in the right and [we] commit no sin, however grievous, without first convincing ourselves that it is right and serves our better interest. . . the sins that are most apt to destroy the soul and undermine a nation and its civilization are not the obvious ones like murder, theft, and housebreaking, which everybody admits are wrong. The dangerous ones are the hidden sins—those which masquerade as goodness, which are often espoused as a matter of policy, and which are seldom recognized or condemned by the churches.[12]

The doctrine of sin, then, is said to recognize man's highest powers and capacities, but also to take account of the demonic depths to which humans can plunge in their own claims to virtue.

Here, then, is a significant watershed. Although both liberals and neo-orthodox understand the doctrines of man's goodness and man's sinfulness in different ways, their respective teachings have varied implications for the theme of victim and oppressor. These implications are much more fundamental perhaps than their common opposition to bigotry and ill-will, for the opposing doctrines lead to different claims on the part of both as to what types of action the doctrines evoke. The liberals are convinced that the doctrine of sin supports the bigot's hierarchical structure whereby the self-styled superiors dominate and oppress the alleged inferiors. The neo-orthodox claim for the same doctrine is that it undercuts all pretensions to ingroup superiority by placing faith not in man but in God's righteousness alone, thus imperatively directing the Christian to responsible awareness of the corrective action of God in human events. By understanding himself and all men as actual and potential oppressors, the neo-orthodox would destroy the oppressor within and uphold justice for others against the oppressors without. In contrast, the liberals believe that man's goodness is the only hope for the achievement of human rights, while the neo-orthodox

12. Ibid. (July 1955), p. 55.

contend that it makes for an unrealistic assessment of the human situation, does not understand and deal with the deep-rooted and demonic nature of prejudice, and plays into the hands of the oppressors.

In one important respect, the liberals and neo-orthodox are attempting to do the same thing in their approach to intergroup questions. Both are dealing with the fact of human alienation, man from man and man from God. But each states its understanding of the nature of this separateness in such a way as to rely ultimately on two different views of reality: the liberal on a unified nature, whose oneness lies beneath all human barriers in the natural experiences common to all men; the neo-orthodox on an objective divine action going on in human history, an action which is not simply man's and which is the ultimate hope for healing the nations. The two communicators therefore differ on the nature of the ultimate community they envision as well as on the manner in which it may be realized.

## The Relation of Ideology to Orientations to Other Religions

We have previously noted that the liberals present the non-Christian groups the most favorably in this study, with their scores for other Christians and Roman Catholics ranking third and fourth respectively on the scale. While the position they assign to Catholics is the usual Protestant one, the one they assign to non-Christians and other-Christians is atypical. The neo-orthodox, for example, reverse the order of the scores for the latter two groups, as may be seen in this table:

### General Intergroup Imbalances of Liberal and Neo-Orthodox Curricula

| | HIGHEST-SCORING COMMUNICATORS | | | |
| | LIBERAL | | NEO-ORTHODOX | |
| Intergroup Areas | Rank | Imbalances | Rank | Imbalances |
|---|---|---|---|---|
| Non-Christian | 1st | +80.0 | 3rd | +37.4 |
| Jewish | 2nd | +48.6 | 2nd | +44.3 |
| Other-Christian | 3rd | +45.9 | 1st | +79.3 |
| Catholic | 4th | +36.6 | 4th | +23.4 |

The reverse ranking of positive content about the non-Christian and other-Christian religions is interesting. When the broad contrast between the two curricula is scrutinized in the light of "identification" and "counter-identification," as these terms are understood by sociologists, its fuller significance appears.

The statements of the neo-orthodox curriculum place it within the central Christian tradition with which it constantly identifies itself. The "identification" position of the liberals is more ambiguous because of its left-wing theological stance. Liberal writers speak as Christians; even when a writer acknowledges that "religious liberals have rejected this traditional story of salvation at its most vital theological core—the supernatural nature of the world Saviour," the context shows that the writer does not intend to place herself outside of the Christian tradition. It is, however, also clear that the need of salvation, the conception that history is a definitive struggle between good and evil or that human destiny is in some manner tied up with this struggle—as well as other assumptions usually associated with the central core of Christianity—are explicitly rejected. The beliefs that replace them can be traced in large part to the influence of scientific humanist thought, of the general assumptions of American culture, as well as of the beliefs and claims of the non-Christian religions, in particular that form of Hinduism known as Vedanta. What one finds in the liberal curriculum might be called "a non-Christian particularism."

Christian tradition does, of course, bulk large in the materials. Considerable and sympathetic attention is given to the development of separate movements within Christendom. An entire course for the intermediate group is devoted to an eminently fair description of the life and influence of various Christian denominations and sects. Similarly, courses on the Old Testament and the life of Jesus are offered at almost every grade level; and even when the non-Christian religions are stressed in a course of study, both Judaism and Christianity are given prominent attention. In sum, one writer is constrained to say that the "way of complete rejection of this Christian tradition is the way which most of would like to avoid."

Nevertheless, certain traditional concepts in Christianity are explicitly ruled out of the liberal curriculum: creation by fiat, a God who is entirely other than man and nature, salvation from sin, and immortality as the perpetuation of the individual. Emphasis is given to truths which are said to have been supplied by science, such as the conviction that life is development, that man has the potentials for living the good life, that the cosmos is recreating itself, that man is a part of a unified cosmos, that the universal natural order resembles a democracy, and that life continues although individuals die.

Of the seven listed ways of dealing with the truths in the old story of salvation, one author prefers the realistic approach and "the way of searching for new insights." She cautions: "Those who advocate this realistic way would not belittle the emotional elements in the drama or fail to find value in [its] symbols. They intend merely to try to discriminate between an objective record of historical experience and any one interpretation of that experience." Such reading of the Christian message raises questions concerning its basic truth, so that "this realistic way of dealing with the story of salvation is fraught with real danger to the survival of Christianity, or at least so it would seem to many." If Christianity would save the life that is within it, the author suggests, it may better seek to lose its life in order that it might gain it. The same author adds that the perspective of the curriculum is a search for new truths and insights, for "those who no longer find the symbols and the myths and 'the lessons' embodied within this old story of salvation expressive of truth as they see it or inspiring to live by, are naturally left wishing for something else equally powerful in its emotional appeal to take its place."

According to the explicit beliefs of its own writers, the views expressed in the liberal curriculum do not coincide with the content of the central Christian tradition. This identification with the marginal in Christianity is reflected in the type of Christian thinkers recommended most highly as a Christian resource, such as Meister Eckhart and other Christian mystics, who expound a perspective which corresponds markedly with that of some oriental religions.[13] Ideologically, then, the liberal views occupy a marginal position in Christian thought, and their relatively lower ranking for other-Christian groups partly reflect this fact.

This analysis also explains the statistical findings for the kinship

13. For the affinity between the theology of Meister Eckhart and that of Zen Buddhism, see D. T. Suzuki, *Mysticism: Christian and Buddhist* (New York, Harper, 1957), chap. 1.

category,[14] in which the liberal lessons score highest in their kinship
with the non-Christian groups. A +57.3 imbalance links liberals
more intimately with the non-Christian faiths than it does to any
of the Jewish-Christian variations. In contrast, the neo-orthodox
lessons score highest in their kinship with other Christian denominations with an imbalance of +45.0, while the non-Christian category receives a score close to zero.

### The Liberal and Contemporary Christian Thought

The unique position of liberals among the four communicators
raises questions about the degree to which the liberals in this study
are conversing with contemporary Christian groups. In this respect
it is interesting to study liberal texts on the basic question of man's
nature, to which they give considerable attention. A typical interpretation of Christian doctrine on this question is as follows:

> Since according to this old story of salvation everyone is born
> with "a sinful nature," man's predicament is truly tragic. The
> demands of society and the demands of conscience, or (in the
> language of this story) God's commands, urge men to kind-
> ness, honesty, love, and self-sacrifice. On the other hand, man's
> sinful nature leads him toward selfishness, sexual excesses, and
> cruelty. As a result he is continually at war within himself,
> and his inadequacy makes him afraid of his own destruction.
> This is the doctrine of "original sin."        (UN376:131)

Much, of course, hinges on this doctrine and its interpretation;
as the author says: "Whether or not this doctrine truly represents
reality is a serious question, for if it is false, this whole story of
salvation loses its original meaning." The lesson recognizes that
there are variations in the ways Christians state the doctrine, but
the accompanying illustrative quotations do not explain what they
are. Definition of man's sinfulness as a conflict between inherited
*evil impulses* (sexual excess and cruelty) and the *good demands*
of society and conscience is nowhere defended in other Protestant
materials; it is nevertheless presented by liberals as the definitive
Christian doctrine of original sin.

The manner in which liberal materials discuss this crucial issue
underscores their marked tendency to converse with the highest

14. Analytical Cat. 10; see Figs. 13–14 and 17–18, Appendix VIII.

thought in the non-Christian religions but to neglect similar dialogue with the best present-day Christian thinkers. No heed is paid
to the profound ideological ferment going on within the churches;
nor do the faiths of the contemporary churches clearly emerge from
the lessons which purport to deal with them. This markedly contrasts with the meticulous exposition of Hinduism and Buddhism
that liberals draw from the most modern and learned students of
these religions.

In discussing beliefs which make for bigotry and prejudice,
liberal writers ignore the subtle and sophisticated Christian truths
that the contemporary radical theism finds in the traditional ideas
of "the chosen people" or of "special revelation." Since these doctrines are precisely those to which objections are made and which
presumably implicate Christianity (together with Judaism) in the
fostering of divisiveness, they are also by that very fact key issues
about which a significant conversation between the liberal and
other Christian points of view ought conceivably to take place.
This is true primarily because the methodology of the liberal curriculum is defined as the process of open-minded exploration of
alternatives; great emphasis is placed on the freedom of the child
to look at all of the varied answers to man's problems given by
the world religions. Yet this emphasis does not seem to inform the
liberal dialogue with other-Christian groups.

It would appear, then, that there are some limitations on the
exploration of alternatives in the liberal curriculum, just as there are
in the others studied here. The process of open-minded examination
is guided by an outlook that itself is not critically examined by the
pupil. The conversation takes place strictly between options circumscribed by the faith, and the alternatives offered the pupil are
preferential, not inclusive.

## Communication, Distortion, and Correction

An indication that one is communicating meaningfully with
others is accuracy, precision, in delineating their convictions. Similarly, distortions of the other point of view are presumed to be the
mark of the relatively uninformed. Both liberals and neo-orthodox
distort somewhat the life and teachings of Jews and Catholics.[15]
These distortions, however, are greatly offset by their practice of

15. Analytical Cat. 5; see Fig. 22, Appendix VIII.

often including corrective remarks and positive background information with the negative statement they make. This added material gives reality and sense to the actual, alleged, or misconceived negative actions, deficiencies, or attitudes of these groups.

At only one point in the distortion-correction category are the liberals and neo-orthodox unlike. The liberals have no negative distortions for non-Christians, and have a tremendously impressive corrective score of +54. In comparison, 13.1 per cent of liberal lessons mentioning other Christian groups are marked by distortion, whereas 42.6 per cent of the lessons contain corrective material. Liberal imbalances in the distortion-correction category for religious groups reach their lowest scores in the Catholic and other-Christian columns. The graph for the neo-orthodox shows the same phenomenon in reverse. There are no distortions for other-Christians. However, approximately 1 per cent of the lessons mentioning non-Christians contain distortions. This time, the lowest imbalance score among the four interreligious groups is found in the non-Christian column.

While both communicators are highly corrective in their approach to interreligious groups, the contrasts in this category highlight the stronger bond liberals have with non-Christian groups, and the stronger commitment the neo-orthodox have to the Judeo-Christian tradition.

### Liberal Inclusiveness—Opening the Door to the Non-Christian Religions

Since the Hebrew-Christian Scriptures have been central in Christian thought and since liberals are anxious to make their teachers and pupils think in more inclusive ways about truth and intergroup relations, they sometimes challenge the Judeo-Christian claim that the scriptural faith is unique. This claim, among others, seems to liberals to make for a lack of intergroup understanding; it appears to reject out of hand the insights of other world faiths.

"Archeologists, excavating in the Near East and elsewhere," says one writer, "have finally made intellectually untenable the idea that the Hebrews were the first monotheists of history or that they were a peculiarly religious people." The neo-orthodox, conservative, and fundamentalist writers believe that Israel was far superior morally and religiously to the polytheistic nations which surrounded her; the liberals take the opposite position, especially as this relates to Israel's earlier history. "Nor were the Canaanites as inferior religiously to the Israelites as the old Bible presents them." The Canaanites are said to have possessed a great civilization and to be the inventors of the alphabet. The Hebrews are portrayed as copying some of their Psalms from the Canaanites. Both Hebrews and Canaanites worshiped "with images, male and female. Both sacrificed animals and slaves and even children on their altars." To be sure, the prophets and "a small number of unknown and unusual persons" are credited with rising above these sexual and warlike excesses. But the Hebrew people as a whole are found to have been as degraded as were the other nations surrounding her. "Nor can the ethics of the Hebrew people be set off so peculiarly above these standards prevailing in other nations; the code of Hammurabi and the negative confession of the Egyptians both merit favorable comparison with the Ten Commandments, even though they are much more ancient." The exception to this generalization are the prophets; but the liberal writers point out that other religions have had their prophets. And, in general, all peoples have searched and found answers to the universal questions.

A text addressed to teachers and parents describes a Bible course taught to a sixth-grade class. The course apparently proved disappointing to the pupils because they had expected to find out about their own religion. The writer comments: "The children had been told (by others than ourselves) that the Bible was 'the book' about the Christian religion; that in it they would learn the truth about God; but they had found that it was about ancient beliefs which somehow were not very different from the beliefs of the primitive people they had already studied."

The teacher then explains that this version of the Bible story is the one now taught by those who "have studied it in a scientific spirit," i.e. as a man-made, primitive religion. When "the old story of salvation" is retold in the liberal curriculum, it is called the "old and unexpurgated" version of the Bible and its anthropomorphic aspects are highlighted. The questions reported as coming from children who studied this interpretation of the Scriptures indicates the elemental and primitive nature of its retelling: "God always seems to be angry in this story of salvation," says one child. "It seems that God is always picking out certain people to be his favorites," says another. The writer of the lesson guide explains:

> Naturally the teachers [who were teaching this course] dealt with the experiences of these biblical folk in the same manner in which they had dealt with the experiences of these other peoples the children had previously studied . . . but . . . [the pupils] soon sensed the fact that once more they were studying how primitive peoples of long ago had thought and felt and done, whereas the children had asked to study "our religion."                                    (UN395:90)

If the Hebrew religion is not unique, the question naturally arises: "Why not spend more time on other religions and less time on Judaism and Christianity?" By excluding the unique and universal validity of the Judeo-Christian faith the liberal permits a "wider" universality to be affirmed. This consists of mankind's "common human urge to understand the meaning of life and find a way of cooperation with the intangible powers about and within." The author reasons as follows:

> If [the Bible] is studied as a human book, as a source material available from which to gain a knowledge of the history of the Hebrew people and their great prophets, shall it continue to be used as our one major source of knowledge of man's ancient religious experience? If the Hebrew people is no longer correctly regarded as religiously unique above all other peoples of ancient times, should our children spend as much time as is customary on the history of this one people to the exclusion of that of other people? If Jesus is regarded as a very great religious genius or spiritual leader or ideal personality, rather than as "the only begotten Son of God" or as the one divine saviour, are there other great spiritual leaders of ancient times whose lives and teachings should also become familiar to our youth?                                    (UN395:87)

Given these teachings, the writer speculates, the pupils will then ask: "Why then should we not learn of other peoples also? Were the Hebrews the only religious people of ancient times? Why should we not learn of other great religious teachers as well as Moses and

Jesus?" The intergroup implication of this reasoning is then suggested as follows:

> Thus the door is wide open, leading into a study of the universal experiences of mankind in building religious faith and for more than both Bibles—the old Bible and the reinterpreted Bible. They will become curious about the world's other Bibles as well. As humanity seeks one common brotherhood, embracing all religious cultures, and differing religious beliefs are exchanged freely and sympathetically, we may discover the great ways in which we are all alike, and thus we may see our differences in true perspective.[16]

Liberal writers do not deny that there are universal and valid elements in the Christian tradition, but they stress that these must never be taught by fiat: "such teaching by simple affirmation and authority tends to develop authoritarian children, with hostile prejudices against those of a different point of view." Instead, the child should be taught to "feel spiritually related to all kinds of people," and therefore to come in contact with the varied religious heritages of the world. "Knowledge of our religious heritage is indeed important, but that heritage comes down to us from all quarters of the earth. No one can prophesy from which ancestral line some fresh insight may come."

### Ideological Identification with Outside Religions

The neo-orthodox curriculum, as indicated in the true-false category, finds the highest repository of truth in Judaism and the other-Christian religions.[17] This is also evidenced by the fact that its Roman Catholic and non-Christian scores are negatively imbalanced in this analytical category (that measures the extent to which the neo-orthodox assess the insights or ways of other religions as being valid or invalid).[18]

16. UN395:97. By "the old Bible" is meant the Bible interpreted as the authentic source book of Christian truth, for which the author would substitute "the new Bible," which is described as the "new Bible of human experience," covering all human insights including the Judeo-Christian.

17. See Analytical Cat. 7 (False-True), Figs. 10 and 14, Appendix VIII. For a description of Cat. 7 see Appendix II.

18. Not too much can be made of the differences in the liberal and neo-orthodox scores in the Catholic area, because while the latter speak specifically of variations within Christian thought, pinpointing precisely the groups which hold certain

The liberal false-true imbalance scores reveal a high imbalance of +30.2 for the non-Christian group category, which again strongly contrasts with the negative imbalance (−4.5) in the other-Christian group category. Judaism also takes a somewhat lower, although still positive, position on the scale for the liberals than it does for the neo-orthodox on questions of truth. These results are largely due to their de-emphasis of "traditional" and "conservative" elements of thought in the Judeo-Christian tradition and their emphasis on the affirmations of the non-Christian religions.

When liberals contrast their versions of characteristic Christian beliefs with those of non-Christian beliefs, the former are given a nonidentifying treatment. Even in national Shintoism, beliefs are found which are more acceptable than those said to belong to Christians:

> Since the Japanese feel that human beings are really good, they have never worried about being sinful. Men may make mistakes, which might be called "sins," but they are not *full* of sin. A Japanese worships more through giving thanks than through reciting his shortcomings and seeking forgiveness for them. No Shintoist is taught to think of himself as "a worm in the dust." (UN259:133)

The concepts of man as "being *full* of sin" and "a worm in the dust" (not, however, attributed to any specific group) are clearly directed to the interpretation of human sinfulness which most writers in the liberal curriculum presume to be characteristically Christian. What is thought to be the normative Christian view is further implied in this observation on the Jewish view of man:

---

views, liberals most generally lump all conservative, orthodox, or traditional Christians together indiscriminately. Many "Other-Christian" scores in liberal lessons may thus implicitly refer to Roman Catholics as well as to most Protestants. Liberal writers do not distinguish too frequently between Catholics and Protestants, because for them the definitive and contrasting categories are "liberal" and "conservative." Roman Catholic and Protestant thought appear to be less divergent than similar. Speaking of the Protestant Reformation, one author says that "most of the protests were against the (Roman Catholic) church system, not against the doctrine. For most Protestants, there are still no radical disagreements" (UN264:205). Another author writes a text in which Roman Catholicism and Protestantism are individually treated (UN229–UN244), but in a later volume few distinctions are made other than between the liberals and conservative-orthodox (UN364–UN385).

"Jews are not taught that mankind is basically sinful or that *normal needs and interests* are wrong." [19]

Another liberal type of nonidentifying comparison of Christian and non-Christian beliefs and practices springs from a monistic quarrel with the assumption that differences in social patterns stem from deeper, underlying differences.[20]

> Christians have made more attempts to "prove" things by appealing to their scriptures than many other people have. Such "proof" has not been of great concern to Buddhists and Hindus, for example. They believe that truth is timeless. It is as available to each person through his own experience as it is to important religious leaders.[21]

What is not explained in the context is that the "truth" which Christians on the one hand, and Buddhists and Hindus on the other, have in mind are of two different types, each of which arises from basic and radically different ideas about religion. The timeless "truth" affirmed in Hinduism is engendered by the subjective apprehension of identity with the divine; God is known in the inner experience of the solitary seeker.[22] For in Christianity, as we have indicated, God is revealed objectively in history where men actively relate to one another for better and worse in a community. The Christian's concern with the meaning of historical events thus fixes his attention on the here and now issues of personal and social history and on the Scriptures where he sees revealed the central meaning of this history. The Buddhist has no such concern for history as a part of his heritage. For the devout Hindu of whom the

19. UN261:160 (my italics). Although some Christians may be regarded as coming close to holding this view, the idea that "normal needs and interests are wrong" can hardly be said to be characteristic of most official Christian doctrines of the sinfulness of man.

20. Most of the quotations cited in this section are not scored in this study on the Other-Christian negative-positive sides, since the Unitarian-Universalist curriculum is measured as a Christian religion; e.g. distortions of Christian teaching are not scored unless a specific non-Unitarian-Universalist group is indicated.

21. UN262:170. The liberal writer here accepts the interpretation of Radhakrishnan, who often makes this point. Hinduism in fact does recognize a class of scriptures that are indisputably authoritative. Even Sankara, hero of the Vedantist, introduces proofs from scripture with great frequency.

22. Such apprehension must not be attributed to Buddhism as a whole, e.g. southern Buddhism, even though it is latent in all Mahayana and a central truth to several of its streams.

liberals speak, religion hinges upon a subjective uniting of Atman with Brahman rather than upon historical events. To explain adequately to liberal children why the Hindu does not need to appeal to his scriptures in the same way that the Christian does would require a clearer exposition of the different nature of the Christian and non-Christian religions—an exposition that the Christian finds wanting in this particular text.

In general, the question arises about the justice done to that vast Christian tradition by this teaching. For example, one author evaluates certain basic Christian motifs—such as the doctrine of the Incarnation. In the opening lesson on Christianity, the writer says that "to many Christians" Jesus "unintentionally *became* . . . God himself." In the next lesson, this idea is expanded:

> One of the greatest debates in Christian history was about whether Jesus was a god, like God, or the God. After a great deal of angry oratory, it was finally decided that Jesus was "very God of very God." This debate was only one of many theological wrangles . . . As it was, Jesus probably would not have been interested anyway . . . A man must live religion, not debate it.[23]

The author is probably describing the Athanasian-Arian debate at the Council of Nicaea, A.D. 325. Also, it is said that in Jesus Christ "many Christians have found the only god [sic] they know." One cannot expect this communicator, who rejects all Christologies, to give attention to the Christological problem. But one wonders why the actual views of trinitarians are not adequately made available to liberal pupils in this kind of exposition.[24]

23. UN263:186. Note the pejorative terminology—"angry oratory" and "theological wrangles" to describe debate—and the several downgrading devices. There is no discussion as to what issues were at stake in this controversy to those who participated in it; doctrinal discussion is compared with the necessity of living one's religion, as though the two activities were not necessary to each other, and the whole question is dismissed by saying that Jesus would not be interested in it anyway.

24. While trinitarian popular piety at times has led to what may be regarded as a disguised form of polytheism, nevertheless the official doctrines of the churches do not confuse the issue here. They are talking about one God; and when "the Son" is being discussed, it is always in relation to "the Father" as being two *persona* of one God and not about the relation of a "god to God." Popular piety oftentimes sacrifices the unity of the Godhead, equating "the Father" with God, addressing prayers not to God but to one segment of the

Christianity and Judaism are singled out by liberal writers from among all the world's religions and together with Islam are castigated for their intolerance and divisiveness. One source of divisiveness, they say, lodges in the proud claims these religions make for themselves; their insistence upon uniqueness, particularity, and the possession of revealed truth. On closer examination, the beliefs to which the liberals object are discovered to be precisely those incompatible with or irrelevant to a naturalistic-monistic world-view. The prime theological concerns of the traditional churches focus in those very areas in which the liberals disagree or else do not have strong convictions. The Judeo-Christian ideas of "revelation," "uniqueness," and "chosenness" are basically connected with (1) the locus of revealed religion in the particularity of human existence on the historical level, and (2) the transcendental element in human faith, specifically any idea of the supernatural or any clear-cut distinction between God and His creation. The liberal concepts of divisiveness thus point directly to the roots of the normative Jewish and Christian religions rather than to those of the nonbiblical religions.

## Authoritative Sources for Anti-Ethnocentrism

If liberals discover that the experiences, searchings, and dilemmas common to all humanity raise the fundamental religious questions, they often find their own answers to them in non-Christian sources. In fact, the bulk of liberal appeals to the "codes and authorities" category in interreligious relations comes from non-Christian sources, that is to say, the prestige figures, precedents, and concepts which authorize the crossing of group lines. In contrast, the neo-orthodox appeal is primarily to scripture and Protestant precedent.[25]

---

Trinity, and thinking of the Holy Spirit as a sort of impersonal force or power emanating from the Father. There is still enough truth in the unitarian characterization to give trinitarians pause to reflect. But the point is that, of course, these are variations and perversions and not essential ingredients in the trinitarian faith as held by the largest segment of American churches.

25. The liberal and neo-orthodox scores for Analytical Cat. 4 (see Figs. 5–6, 9–10, 13–14, 17–18) do not reveal the sources of the various teachings and precedents appealed to in furthering understanding of and positive images of other religious groups. However, in the General Group Category as well as in the interreligious categories approximately 82 per cent of the Unitarian-Universalist appeals come from non-Christian sources, while over 96 per cent of the Presbyterian appeals come from Christian teaching and biblical exposition.

In the liberal curriculum the answers to the world's common problems are, theoretically speaking, always universal ones. Based on human experiences, they are thereby self-authenticating; but the specific support to which they appeal is far from self-evident to those of another faith. One example is the doctrine that there are many saviours. In opposition to the Christian claim that Christ is the Saviour of the world and the world's only hope—a claim deemed divisive because it cannot be accepted by all humanity— an author says: "The liberal Christian group has been more tolerant than this . . . This group finds some salvation in Buddha and Mohammed as well as some in Jesus Christ." Support, however, for this article of faith is made not to universal experience or Christian precedent but to the teachings of Hinduism and Buddhism. Of course, neither this writer nor any other of the liberal curriculum specifically claims authority for such views. They are given as alternative and preferable answers to the questions of mankind; thus the view that there are many saviours is judged "more tolerant."

Distinctively Christian sources (such as the Scriptures) that are found to supply legitimate answers must be made consonant with Hindu-Buddhist affirmations. In answer to the central question "What am I?" Dr. S, a discussion leader, replied to his group, "We ourselves are part of God." He appeals to St. Paul's speech at Athens, "In him we live and move and have our being." Jesus' saying that "The Kingdom of God is within you," is interpreted as meaning that the Kingdom is inner and subjective. Another author suggests explicitly that Christians might find in their own religion what Hindus and Buddhists have found in theirs. "From Hinduism and Buddhism, for example, many Westerners can come (and have come) to a new understanding of the importance of the search for the real self." He adds that while such self-knowledge may come from a study of the "ignored aspects of Christianity," it is primarily through the study of other religions that many Westerners have come to "an extension of self-knowledge"—that is to say, an understanding of themselves as part of God.

## Conclusions

Our analysis indicates that more than one Protestant faith perspective provides an anti-ethnocentric basis for the amelioration of oppressed groups. Further, these anti-ethnocentric resources appear in faiths which are antithetical in their main doctrines.

It should be noted once more that the differences in liberal and neo-orthodox convictions make for distinctively different views of the nature of prejudice and its cure, as well as for quite different views of what relationships between groups ought to be. From this it is evident that an anti-ethnocentric orientation in itself tells us only one of the things we need to know about a faith, namely whether its approach to other groups is acceptive and positive, or rejective and negative. It does not tell us whether the intergroup understandings and program are socially relevant, adequate, or true. Nor can the truth of a faith be judged merely by its intergroup orientation, since opposite kinds of faiths can produce positive scores. Both intergroup programs envisioned in a curriculum, and the faiths themselves, are relatively independent of the achievements made on the ethnocentric-anti-ethnocentric scoreboard.

From this arises three points which need special attention. One is that the liberal and neo-orthodox faiths intrinsically sustain positive intergroup scores because of their unqualified universal perspectives. These faiths by their very nature must concern themselves with understanding other groups, with relating their adherents to all men, and with providing imperatives to cross group lines.

The second point is that these two communicators have thought through the meaning of their faith for intergroup relations. The converse of this statement also holds true. An intergroup sensitivity expressed in the way the faith is stated and a focus of the faith on contemporary intergroup problems are reciprocal phenomena; they have been noted in both anti-ethnocentric scorers, although in different ways and in varying degrees.

The third observation, however, is that the great divide of faith that separates the liberals and neo-orthodox from each other does affect the way in which interreligious relationships are regarded. Broadly speaking, *there is a strong tendency to picture outside groups more favorably when they share the same world-views, beliefs, and values,* and more unfavorably when they do not. For this reason, the neo-orthodox regard other-Christians more positively, while the liberals have similar regard for the non-Christian religions.

The world-views of the two high scorers also affect other differences noted in the intergroup content of their curricula. Liberal teachings are more *abstractly* relevant and the neo-orthodox more *concretely* relevant to the given social situations. The latter most frequently focuses upon the particular problems in American society and is more specific about the actual situations which Christians face in their daily decisions, particularly in their relations with other groups. The former tends to bypass the more immediate intergroup problems that the pupils confront in their particular American communities. These distinctions have some relation to the concepts of man, society, and God to which the respective communicators are committed. The liberal's predisposition toward abstraction, his search for "feelings of oneness," his veneration of shared fundamentals all move him to think of social situations, problems, and solutions less in specific, immediate, and historically conditioned terms and more in ultimate, global, and diffuse terms.[26] On the other hand, the neo-orthodox sense of the specificity of each intergroup situation—where God confronts the participant in the continuing present, where men respond to the actions of other men in obedience or disobedience to the requirements of God's actions—directly leads to preoccupation with the concrete social problems upon which American Protestants must act.

One notes, also, in the position of the liberals and neo-orthodox, a basic conflict of values which is reflected in their respective orientations toward other-Christian and non-Christian groups. Our analysis of the liberal position indicates that a highly positive orientation toward religious groups not normatively grounded in one's own historic tradition may lead to the loss of identification with this tradition and to a new grounding in the alien tradition. This development leads also to a tendency to reject, at least in part, one's historic roots.

In summary, each of the two faiths embodies a different kind of anti-ethnocentrism. The liberal's monistic view of reality leaves little place for the fundamental cleavages in society, for a recognition of basic conflicts which may perpetuate endless pluralisms, for the prime importance of the particular as against the universal

26. A more recent course in the liberal curriculum, however, does deal with more specific intergroup problems on the American scene: Dorothy T. Spoerl, ed., *Tensions Our Children Live With* (Boston, Beacon Press, 1959).

and the uniquely historical as against the natural. On the other hand, the neo-orthodox faith centers in a personal God who has acted in a specific history and in a specific person for man's salvation. This theistic and trinitarian view of reality, revealed to a particular people, makes a much larger place for deep and fundamental cleavages in society, for basic conflicts, for differences, concreteness, and specificity than does a monistic faith.

Each of these positions raises some questions of importance. Can good relationships between religious groups exist despite an insistence on their particularity and uniqueness? Does divisiveness consist in entertaining concepts which contradict the basic and central suppositions of monists, or radical theists, or whatever; or does it consist in the ways in which intergroup relations themselves are conceived? Is a faith universalistic by virtue of what it demands of the person who internalizes it, or because it is or is not sharable? Does tolerance consist of believing in many saviours and intolerance of believing in one only, or is tolerance an ability to affirm and uphold the person or group who disagrees with one on points considered fundamental by either party? Does anti-ethnocentrism make a place for all by affirming some common denominator, or does it do so by affirming the right of each group to its own particular existence, its uniqueness, or its right to be different and to contradict the assumptions of those who affirm a common core? The answers to these questions would seem to imply that there are a variety of ways of crossing group lines, and that there are different kinds of antidotes to ethnocentrism. What seems to be essential is that each faith affirms out of its own perspective the anti-ethnocentric ways that are indigenous to itself.

Ultimately, the positions and opposing contentions of the two high scorers also raise the question as to whether some form of exclusion and divisiveness is not inevitable in even the most positively oriented point of view. Are not all religious views to some extent particularistic, because when one has chosen one basic outlook, one has by this action excluded those presuppositions and values which directly contradict one's own? To declare a faith may be to a certain extent a divisive act, regardless of the faith's inherent good will and universal concerns, since its existence challenges the validity of conflicting presuppositions. This seems to be a characteristic feature of any belief or system of values, despite the eagerness of its proponents to be inclusive or to take an altruistic standpoint. This chapter has described a conflict of faiths as between the liberal and the neo-orthodox; must this conflict be interpreted as the consequence of intransigence and divisiveness on one side only? There are two other possible answers. One is that there are elements of divisiveness and even latent prejudice in both points of view despite their anti-ethnocentric orientation. The other is that conflict is indigenous to the existence of religious convictions, and although means may be found to mitigate this conflict and even to utilize it constructively, it will always be a component of the interreligious dialogue in society.

# 4. The Outside Groups as Victims

Our era has been marked by periodic outbreaks of violence ranging from lynchings and synagogue bombings to race riots and the near annihilation of European Jewry. Despite an increased public awareness of the dangers of prejudice, American society continues to discriminate against various religious and ethnic groups. Negro and certain ethnic communities, such as the Mexican and Puerto Rican, still suffer the effects of segregation, while various religious communities are subject to hate campaigns and to limitations on their religious freedom through legislation and practices which violate a free exercise of conscience. Hence the debate in American society over Sunday blue laws, religious observances in public schools, and the right of suppression by blacklisting and censorship.

An examination of intergroup teaching indicates that religious educators deal with the dilemmas of outside groups in a number of ways. A curriculum writer may avoid taking any position on the subject and remain silent. On the other hand, he may attempt to deny another group's predicament or its claim to certain rights. Or he may acknowledge a group's plight through one of two approaches which we will characterize as "identifying" and "non-identifying."

A writer who identifies with another's plight gives due consideration to the social problems and disabilities confronting the oppressed group in contemporary society. He may express his concern in a fairly general way by sympathizing with the group in question and by an outright disapproval of oppressive practices. However, he can take a stronger position by describing the plight of a particular group in sympathetic detail and urging his readers to take appropriate action to protect the freedom of the group or assure the achievement of justice.[1] On the other hand, a writer may ap-

---

1. The ability of lesson writers to make their concern for the questions of liberty and justice inclusive of outside communities is a significant indicator of anti-ethnocentrism. See definition of Analytical Cat. 1, Appendix II.

proach the identical issues in a non-identifying way and describe them in such a detached or negative way that neither he nor the reader can be said to pay real attention to the victim's dilemma. The following excerpts from the fundamentalist curriculum illustrate these two characteristic ways in which writers present the problems of outside groups:

*Identifying*

The policy introduced into Egypt by the new Pharaoh is now the old, sordid, tragic story of anti-Semitism. Again and again this ghastly phenomenon has reared its venomous head . . .

Pharaoh's fear was aroused by the manner in which the Israelites had multiplied. People today who claim that Jews control the press, the banks, commerce, etc., are modern counterparts of the Egyptian king. Some people are always looking for a scapegoat for their own failures and mistakes, and are glad to make such use of the Jews . . .

The same unpitying slaughter of Jews has been resorted to in nominally Christian cultures even today . . . What is *your* attitude toward Jews? . . . Do not allow yourself to develop a feeling of antagonism toward Jews. When you hear them criticized unfairly, or if hostility toward them is expressed in your presence, speak up in their behalf! Do it tactfully, but do it emphatically.[2]

*Non-Identifying*

God wanted to tell the whole world about Himself through the Jewish people. But for all the advantages God had given them . . . they were disobedient. They turned their backs on God, they refused His Son, and they worshipped pagan gods. And they have been sorely punished for centuries, as a result.

No other group in history has been persecuted like the Jews. They are not really wanted anywhere. Many nations have immigration laws to keep them out. Remember Hitler's purges? One wonders how many times in history, since Christ's time, Jews have been killed in masses. God said the Jews would be "a reproach and a taunt and an astonishment" wherever they went, and these predictions have been fulfilled.

In spite of the persecution, the Jews have prospered . . . Though they are despised and unwelcome in many instances, wherever they go they seem to rise to the top! Wall Street, railroad systems, newspapers, circuit courts, clothing firms—aggressive Jews have succeeded in all these ventures and in many others.[3]

2. The Scripture Press, *Studies in Exodus*, No. 1, pp. 138, 139, 140. The author is discussing Exod. I. Henceforth quotations from the Scripture Press are indicated by SP, followed by lesson number and page number.

3. SP839:47. The author is discussing the faithfulness of God in fulfilling His promises to the Jews in the light of Jer. 24:9; Ezek. 5:14, 15. It must be emphasized that this lesson also has identifying references to the Jewish plight in its other sections.

## ORIENTATION TO THE PLIGHT OF OTHERS

*The Scores*

On the whole, the Protestant communicators identify strongly with the rights and the predicaments of other groups.[4] Except for the conservatives, they devote considerable space in their curricula to a constructive discussion of these issues. Protestants pay proportionately greater attention to the more severe problems other racial, ethnic, and natural groups face today, despite their considerably greater preoccupation with religious than with nonreligious groups as a whole. In the neo-orthodox curriculum, for example, Jews are mentioned in over 60 per cent of the total sample of lessons and Negroes in only 4.3 per cent; yet only 8.2 per cent of the lessons which speak of Jews take account of anti-Semitism, whereas almost 54 per cent of those mentioning Negroes discuss racial hatred, segregation, and discrimination. More significantly, the disabilities from which both religious and nonreligious groups suffer are generally handled in Protestant lessons quite positively and with little ambiguity, despite the fact that the treatment given some of these problems is far from adequate.

Specifically, we note that while the fundamentalist lessons make some nonidentifying references, they also devote considerable positive attention to the sufferings and the claims of outsiders. The conservatives are the least disposed of the four to acknowledge the dilemmas of outsiders, and they are more ambiguous in their treatment of questions related to these dilemmas. Further, they disregard entirely prejudice toward Catholics and non-Christian groups. Later in this chapter we will examine the conservative approach to Jewish problems in its particulars; for now it is sufficient to note that the only negative imbalance the conservatives show in this category concerns Jews.[5]

The liberal and neo-orthodox approaches to other groups are those of complete identification with their aspirations, grievances, and predicaments. There is almost no negative spread in the scores for religious groups. Although the lowest imbalance scores are

4. For convenience, abstracts for Analytical Cat. 1 (Plights and Rights) are graphed in Figs. 23 and 24, Appendix VIII. For the full contexts of these abstracts consult the profiles in Figs. 5–20.

5. Analytical Cat. 1, Fig. 24, Appendix VIII.

produced by statements about Catholics and anti-Catholicism, there
are no negative references in the literature—the positive statements
merely appear less often. This means that in discussing Catholics,
the writers are less inclined to envision a Catholic plight than they
are a Jewish, non-Christian, or other-Christian plight when discussing these latter groups. The Protestant educators do not ignore the
possibility of anti-Catholicism. But their essentially positive approach to the question of religious liberty, coupled with a lesser
degree of preoccupation with Catholic problems, indicate that they
take Catholic freedoms for granted in the United States. On the
other hand, the higher other-Christian scores made by liberals and
neo-orthodox are largely due to an increasing concern for preserving the rights of smaller religious groups in this country, including
Jehovah's Witnesses, Seventh-Day Adventists, and other dissenters.

The only problem of any magnitude in this area concerns statements dealing with Jews. This becomes clear if we disregard the
relative scores for Analytical Category 1 (Figs. 23 and 24) and
determine instead the absolute distributions of scores within the
category for the Jewish religion. In 96 per cent of the references
pertinent to this category the liberals discuss the dispersion and the
suffering of the Jews in an identifying manner; in 4 per cent they
are balanced. The neo-orthodox treatment is identifying in 95 per
cent of the cases (2.5 per cent balanced), the fundamentalist in
57.5 per cent (27.5 per cent balanced), and the conservative in
only 22.2 per cent (with none balanced). As noted earlier, their
divergent theologies, their different uses of the biblical text, and
their hidden assumptions about the nature of society make it difficult
for some of the faiths under study to discuss themes related to an
outsider's problems in a clearly unambiguous way.

## The Neglected Areas

While is it impossible to set standards for the amount of attention
a communicator should give to the problems of other groups, it is
significant that some Protestants either completely overlook or give
niggardly attention to such problems. This is not always evident
from the graphs, because they merely indicate the general degree
and direction of statements made about the plight of outsiders
and say nothing about their specific nature. The lesson writers may
bypass serious problems confronting minorities in favor of more

remote ones. Almost all the liberal lessons dealing with white-Negro relations, for example, focus on the "brown baby" problem in Germany, where the offspring of American Negro soldiers and German white women currently face discrimination and dislike. Although this concern is commendable, it hardly does justice to the more intense issues of segregation and discrimination which face the Negro in this country and to which liberals pay little attention.

Far less adequate treatment of the American Negro's problems are to be found in the conservative and fundamentalist curricula— especially in the former. Each curriculum gives only slight attention to Negro problems, and this usually consist of generalizations and cautions. Certainly, all intergroup references cannot be specific or sufficiently detailed, and there is some value to be gained in stating even briefly the connections between the faith's ethical requirements and the issues involved in intergroup relations. But if these connections are only alluded to or are offered in the form of isolated generalizations, they are likely to be of little practical value in shaping a child's attitudes towards other groups.[6] There is a lack of response, or what we may call "silence," in this failure to treat questions of racial prejudice in sufficient depth.

These "silences" are noticeable also in the neo-orthodox publications which fail to analyze sufficiently the relations between Christians and non-Christians, other than Jews. Although there are many positive references to non-Christians, they are, with some notable exceptions, usually incidental or superficial. In this respect, the neo-orthodox contrast with the liberals in the way they express their concern for others; the latter are specific in dealing with interfaith relations in Asia, with ethnic-racial problems in Europe, and with the Arab-Israeli situation, but they tend to be more abstract in discussing the problems peculiar to American culture.

## "To Bigotry No Sanction"[7]

Although the textbooks of all the Protestant groups inveigh heavily against any form of bigotry, the neo-orthodox protest is

6. One of the earliest and most substantial bodies of evidence for this view is found in the Hartshorne-May analysis of character formation; pupils are seldom able to translate generalizations into specific action. Cf. Hugh Hartshorne and Mark A. May, *Studies in the Nature of Character* (3 vols. New York, Macmillan, 1928–30).

7. The phrase is George Washington's, who in a letter to the Jewish Con-

the most intense. The full weight of Christian teachings, precedent, and moral imperatives are brought to bear on the subject of prejudice, binding Christians to their oppressed neighbors and stressing that as Christians they take the responsibility for positive intergroup action. All forms of prejudice—exclusiveness, discrimination, hatred toward other groups, or failure to insist upon justice for others—are regarded as instances of the Christian's rejection of Christ and alienation from God.[8] Thus, the neo-orthodox maintain that "the termination of racial tension is not optional for the Christian." [9] In their view of history as the "scene of conflict" engendered by God's action, disregard of another's rights represents "a continual conflict between man's will and God's will." The Bible "proclaims the good news of God's zealous concern about the injustices of society, his radical intervention in the established order of men, and the dynamic working out of his redemptive purpose despite all human efforts to oppose it." Hence the Christian cannot have the right relation to God unless he relates justly to others. This is made particularly clear when one writer says, "We are told that Christ accepts our ministry to our fellow men as a ministry to him . . . those things we do to all men (and to any man) are done as to Christ himself." The Apostle Paul's description of men as being "slaves to sin" is also applied to intergroup attitudes: "He [Paul] is talking about those deep-rooted prejudices which hold us back from being friends with certain people and make it hard for us to accept changes in our life, such as the ending of racial segregation."

In the neo-orthodox view if the Christian is to be loyal to God, it is mandatory that he study and understand the society in which he lives and act so as to improve intergroup relations. Christ's sacrificing himself on the Cross binds us to others in such a way that the Christian is obliged to act responsibly in behalf of his neighbor in faithfulness to the universal nature of Christ's act. According to one writer, the crucifixion makes intergroup understanding an imperative:

gregation at Newport, R.I., described the "true spirit" of the newly founded American government as one which "gives to bigotry no sanction, to persecution no assistance . . ." David Philipson, *The Jew in America* (Cincinnati, U.A.H.C., n.d.), p. 20.

8. PR36,855:34; PR37,259:27; PR36,857:17.

9. More partial quotes are not being identified.

When I look across from myself to another person the most important fact is not his race or nationality, creed or color. The most important thing I know about any man is that he is a man for whom Christ died. Of course, I must deal with him as a particular person in a particular situation. If he is denied a fair chance to earn a living because of his color, I act either personally or through government to secure for him this right. But whoever he is and whatever his situation, I deal with him as one for whom Christ gave himself on the cross.

(PR37,491:26)

Note that this writer emphasizes that each person and each situation is particular, and that the issues confronting men must be handled concretely. A Christian is obliged, then, to learn about the specific conditions under which other people live in order to know how to act:

There is little value in trying to lead a class through a discussion on "One Human Race" unless the class is willing to use *facts*. The very word "race" is loaded. Some people begin to "bristle" as soon as they hear it. Others think the topic is too controversial to discuss in church school. In spite of such liabilities, we have no sanction from the Bible to avoid this subject; we have a *directive* to face up to it.          (PR37,096:77)

The neo-orthodox also insist that it is not enough for the Christian to acquire and face the facts of prejudice, but he is also directed to fight prejudice here and now:

God demands justice among us, not as some far-off goal, but now—this year, in this nation, and in this town. Even while he struggles with his own prejudices, the Christian will work in whatever way he can continually to overcome every kind of segregation and to secure equal justice for all men.

(PR37,493:32)

Although all three biblical communicators regard prejudice as sinful, only the neo-orthodox relate this understanding of prejudice to the whole range of specific Christian teachings. The neo-orthodox writer not only states his faith so as to make clear its relevance for intergroup problems but also involves both the student and the

teacher in these problems by beginning at any point in scripture—
using any doctrine or biblical incident—to clarify the meaning for
the Christian of prejudice, anti-Semitism, and racial segregation.
For example, the doctrine that "Jesus Christ is Lord" implies a condemnation of anti-Semitic practices. If Christ is Lord, his rule is
manifested in the way Christians treat others. As one neo-orthodox
writer puts it: "It is hard to imagine any greater offense to our
Lord than a sign, 'Gentiles Only'—a sign directed against him and
his people. The truth we must acknowledge is that anti-Semitism
and Christian faith stand in the sharpest kind of opposition. To be
an anti-Semite is to despise the Jews and their King; to be a Christian is to acknowledge their King as our King and to care for his
people."

## THE EXISTENCE AND PLIGHT OF THE JEWS

The fragments from both fundamentalist and conservative teaching which deal with the past and present suffering of the Jews
must be understood as reflections of Israel's self-image as found in
scripture. Historically, the oppression which Jews experienced took
two forms: the Exile, involving the destruction of the Jewish state
and the subsequent global dispersion of the Jews, and the rise of
anti-Semitism itself.

Why have the Jews been the victims of such terrifying abuses
at the hands of men? Why have so many attempts been made to
exterminate them, and why, despite these pogroms, do the Jews
continue to exist? What does the Jewish oppression signify for the
Christian? If the Church defines its role in the same way as did
Israel, it cannot escape facing these questions. They are pressed
home on the Christian by the fact that Synagogue and Church live
side by side and make for themselves many of the same biblical
claims. The liberals in this study find that they handle these problems in a different way than do other Protestants because, although
they acknowledge their Hebrew heritage, they do not define their
role in biblical terms. Concepts such as covenant relationship, gospel
and law, chosenness, divine election, and the messianic expectation
are irrelevant to the liberal communicator's understanding of his
own task; no question develops, then, as to how he shall interpret
the Jewish diaspora and world-anguish in these terms. The three
other commentators, however, since they lay claim to a "biblical

view" of both themselves and the Jews, cannot avoid using these concepts in their attempt to understand the nature and meaning of Jewish suffering.

The pitfall for some writers in discussing these problems comes at that point where the question of the Christian's responsibility for the suffering of the Jews is or should be raised. The remainder of this chapter therefore will examine the ways in which this complex problem—made more obvious and urgent to the Christian by the events that preceded and accompanied World War II—is handled by writers who hold to the four religious points of view represented in this study.

## The Conservatives

Unlike the fundamentalists, who view Jewish history by the two principles of divine judgment (dispersion) and providence (preservation), the conservatives regard Jews as part of a much larger group whom they designate as "unbelievers." The few references in conservative teaching which concern the Jewish plight occur in their discussions of judgment. Table 6,[10] for example, lists twelve negative indicators under the heading of "Jewish Disobedience: Judgment," with only one offsetting indicator. There are a number of reasons why conservatives cannot find a place for the Jews in either the present or the future divine economy. Central among these reasons is the conservative definition of the Church. For this group the Church is literally Israel itself—a remnant of the old Israel which preserved the faith by placing itself under the Saviour, thereby fulfilling Israel's obligations to mankind. According to them the Church was once composed of Jews; at present it is composed of both Jews and Gentiles according to a universal pattern. Nevertheless, it is the same Church, the same Israel; there is complete continuity between the two. This means that the Jews who did not accept Christ, because of their failure to believe, abandoned the Israel of God. They are thus unbelievers like any other non-Christian religious group.[11]

10. Appendix VII.

11. Jews are listed with "Mohammedans" (a pejorative term in the eyes of Islam), Mormons, Unitarians, Christian Scientists, Jehovah's Witnesses, Modernists, and "all anti-Christian cults and lodges" as being "outside the Christian Church." *Bible Student, 32,* No. 4 (1954), 21. This Church consists only of believers (the Church Militant on earth, the Church Triumphant in Heaven) and is essentially

Because the conservatives see an absolute continuity between Israel and the Church; they introduce Christians into Old Testament events and claim an identity with its teachings. A senior course on "the Church" begins not with Pentecost but with Adam and Eve, while a study of Genesis explains that it "has nothing to do with the Jewish race of today. What we have in the pages of Genesis is fundamentally church history." The following are further examples of this kind of teaching:

> Droughts and other disasters have also compelled Christians to seek new homes (e.g. Israel in Egypt).[12]

> The Jews [unbelievers] do not have the faith of the Patriarchs [which Christians do]. (MS39,004:60)

> The Gospel awakened faith in Adam and Eve and their believing descendants and kept them in the saving faith. They had only a meagre knowledge of redemption through Christ [but] clung to the divine promise [of the Savior] and eagerly looked forward to its fulfillment. (MS39,028:24–25)

Because the Church is Israel, the promises and blessings bestowed on the faithful believers of the Old Testament apply to the Christian, not to the Jew. The judgments and curses are warnings to Christians; as judgments however, they have already fallen upon Jews, while all the Old Testament prophecies as well as the future glories of Israel belong to the Church. Because they hold this definition of the Church, the conservative interpretation is that the Church (not the Jewish people) "will never perish." In Micah's and Isaiah's vision of the future, they say, Zion is the Church, and "the mountain of the house of the Lord" is "an expression used typically of the Church." Thus Jerusalem is exalted in a spiritual rather than a physical sense; the reign of Christ on the throne of David is a spiritual reign in the hearts of believers; and the everlasting kingdom is spiritual rather than earthly. The era of peace envisioned by the prophets applies only to the believers in all nations who willingly submit to the rule of God, who "no longer seek to fight one another

---

invisible, being known only to God; yet believers may know that the Church exists where the Gospel is preached. Ibid., p. 55.

12. The Missouri Synod—Lutheran (Concordia), "The Early Christian Church" (Acts), Teacher's Guide, p. 59 (my italics). Henceforth quotations from this press will be indicated by MS, followed by lesson number and page number.

for temporal gain." In short, the language used by the prophets is figurative. Consequently, in understanding the scriptural promises "Israel cannot be taken here in a physical sense . . . but it means the true, spiritual Israel."

Because they identify Zion with the Church, the conservatives believe that the existence of the Jews as a separate religious group claiming the name Israel is an anachronism. God, according to them, does not honor these claims, because the ceremonial laws of the Old Testament, together with the Old Testament sacraments (e.g. circumcision), were abolished by Christ. The Sacrament of the Altar has replaced the Passover, and the prophecies have been, or will be, fulfilled in the Church.

If the conservative interpretation of the Old Testament means that the Jews have no future role and that their understanding of the messianic age is mistaken, how do they explain the survival of the Jews through eras of persecution and attempts to exterminate them as a people? According to some conservative writers, the Jewish people exist today only as a warning to Christians about the danger of unbelief, and they list the Jews among their examples of "how severely God punishes sinners." It should be noted that this view does not accord with the conservative teaching about the preservation of the Jews in Old Testament times as the promise-bearers, the progenitors of the Messiah. Hence hatred of Jews in Old Testament times is interpreted as a hatred of believers, an attempt to extinguish the "Messianic line of Seth and Shem" which God was to preserve. However, the conservative view of Jews as believers applies only to the faithful in the period before Christ's birth. Following the Messiah's coming, all promises are understood as being fulfilled in Him, and there is no longer any reason for the Jews to exist apart. Inasmuch as the covenant whereby the Jews "were to be His people and enjoy His special favor" was contingent upon Jewish obedience to Christ, the Jews forfeited their privileges and ceased to be God's people.

When the conservative writer handles New Testament events, therefore, his tone toward the Jews and those who sought to exterminate them undergoes a change which is intelligible only in the light of his understanding of the Old Testament Jews. When the destruction of Jerusalem in A.D. 70 is described, the text does not condemn the oppressor. The event is described as a judgment upon and the end of "the old order"; and the accompanying description of blood, death, and misery is vividly nonidentifying. The text refers to the Jews who attempted to free themselves from the Roman conqueror as "disloyal subjects" and their leaders as persons who "continued to refuse the generous terms of surrender" offered by Titus. The account goes on to chide the Jews for preserving values which were praiseworthy in an Old Testament context, such as their love of the Temple.

The foregoing is sufficient to understand why the conservative point of view logically requires that rabbinic Judaism cease to exist as a religion. It also explains why the present sufferings of the Jews are considered in the context of disobedience and rejection. For example, an intermediate lesson dealing with the fall of Jerusalem asks the class member to "Give proof that the curse which the Jews called down upon their nation still rests on them and their children to this very day." This same text fails to explain what such a "curse" means in terms of today's realities. Hence the average American is left with only one possible interpretation: the anti-Semitic abuses which beset the Jew in the contemporary world. There are similar statements to be found in other lessons, and a number of them emphasize Jewish culpability. One text for teachers explains that, "Since that time [A.D. 70] the Jews have ceased to exist as a nation, and the Holy Land has been in the possession of Gentile nations. The Jews are scattered all over the world and have been frequently persecuted." There are references to Jesus' statement: "This generation shall not pass, till all these things be fulfilled," which the corresponding manual for students interprets as follows: "The Jews who live among us are constant reminders of Christ's words." Modern Jews live "under a curse they brought upon themselves."

What do these quotations tell us about the attitudes some conservatives have to the Jewish plight? Specifically, nothing is communicated in these statements about anti-Semitism. They are attempts to explain the collapse of the Jewish nation and to debate the theological issue as to whether the claims of the Church are true, or whether the claims of the Synagogue are to be acknowledged in any way by the Church as valid. For the conservatives, "the rejection of the Jews" means that they were no longer chosen to be the people of God; it is not intended to mean that God has abandoned the Jews to a tragic fate, that He no longer loves them, or that He sanctions their persecution. For conservatives this phrase implies that the Church now plays the role which Israel played in the old dispensation.[13]

In some of the lessons the phrase is also taken to mean that the Jewish task was completed with the coming of Christ, since all the promises to the Jews were fulfilled in Christ.[14] Still another understanding of "the rejection of the Jews" is that the Jewish nation existed temporarily in order to preserve the true faith during a preparatory period of the world's history and to produce the Messiah. And it is argued that inasmuch as its covenant was conditional, the dissolving of the Jewish nation was a part of God's plan.[15] Thus, in the conservative view, the continued existence of Israel is an anachronism, because God intended it to be part of the Church and not a community apart which might reject Christ and the Gospel. Consequently, in explaining the downfall of Judaism as a nation, the conservatives draw a sharp distinction between the Synagogue and the Church. This is their intention in the statements quoted above. They do not challenge the right of Jews to live in peace and to enjoy full freedom and opportunity.

But granting that the conservatives use the phrase "the rejection of the Jews" to make a spiritual point, what does the expression mean in relation to present-day Jewish suffering? In an interview the chief editor of the conservative lesson materials stated that he would "hesitate to indicate a precise relationship between rejection of the Jews and the persecutions they have endured." Although he finds a general relationship between sin and suffering, he feels that emphasizing this relationship in the curriculum might lead people to "try to justify the sufferings, often inhuman, that have been inflicted upon the Jews for no other reason than that they belong to the Jewish race. Persecution of any person or race is always a sin in the sight of God, and God is certainly displeased with those who persecute the Jews or any other race." [16]

13. MS39,386:45; MS39,327:45,47; MS39,134:141–42.
14. MS39,144:74–75; MS39,145:108–109; MS39,327:46–47; MS39,144:66–67.
15. MS39,470:29; MS39,461:76.
16. Interview with editor, Nov. 5, 1957. The use of the word "race" in this connection signifies "people," not a racial group, although in some of the lessons the connotation may be racial. It must be remembered that the Jews are thought of in the conservative curriculum primarily as descendants of Shem.

The references in Analytical Category I which offers so negative
an account of Jewish-Christian relations and the suffering of the
Jew (especially in the context of judgment and doom, Jewish
blame, the "blood curse," unbelief, and Christ-rejection) require
some clarification. First, although these references are occasioned
by certain passages from scripture, they are not always stated in
their full theological context. Writers generally fail to explain what
"rejection" means (e.g. the altered role of the Jews after the birth
of Christ), so that they risk being misunderstood. By omitting the
information which could make the term more exact for students,
they allow for the strong possibility that anti-Semitic currents in
our culture will supply the students with an interpretation which
conservative theology would not condone.[17]

Secondly, we note that with the exception of two brief sentences,
Christian moral judgments on anti-Semitism are absent from the
lesson material. Because of this omission, discussions of the negative
aspects of the plight could appear to the reader as an implied sanction of the Jewish plight or as an indirect way of expressing dislike
for Jews.

Finally, the references to Jewish disabilities do not reflect either
a love of Jews or a willingness for either the Church or an individual Christian to take the responsibility for Jewish oppression.
The treatment of the Jewish plight is nonidentifying, external, and
negative; whereas the conservatives' concern for "The Third Use
of the Law" logically should require them, as believers, to examine
their relations to the Jews in an anti-Semitic world.[18]

## Fundamentalism

The Jews occupy a vital position in the fundamentalist curriculum. Some of its writers hold that in the present age "only three
great groups of people" are recognized in God's program: (1)
Israel, (2) the Church, and (3) the Gentiles—the first two being
witnesses to the third. According to this view, "The Old Testament
is an account of God's dealing with the Gentiles through His chosen
nation, Israel. The New Testament introduces the Church, and

17. Even more urgently needed, because used more frequently, are explicit
interpretations of the concept of judgment. It appears to be used most often in
the materials in a wholly punitive sense, although this is not the usage of which
the denomination approves.

18. Article Six, *Formula of Concord*.

discloses God's plan for using Jews as His instruments in dealing with Gentiles." However, Israel and the Church are given different tasks. The Church is "God's spiritual people"; its purpose is to declare God's Word but not to exercise temporal power. Israel is "God's earthly people," whom God authorizes to exercise not only spiritual but also temporal rule. Israel is thus both a church and a nation—the only nation to whom God has pledged a land, a continued existence, and eventual "restoration."

These distinctions (although not shared by all fundamentalist writers) have various implications for the way in which the Jewish claim to human rights and the Jewish oppression are regarded. For fundamentalists the point in describing the Jewish plight is to emphasize that God's promises are dependable and that eventually the Jews will be restored. In fact, greater emphasis is placed on *restoration;* the plight as such is often incidental to the writer's primary interest in the eventual establishment of the Kingdom.

Another implication which this type of fundamentalist theory has for an understanding of the Jewish plight is that God has not abandoned His people nor deprived them of their blessings. Fundamentalist writers clash with conservatives on this point, the latter generally claiming, as we have seen, that the scriptural blessings and promises apply to Christians while the curses and judgments of scripture apply to Jews. But some fundamentalists take sharp issue with this interpretation, as in the following argument:

> Gentiles are willing to interpret literally the curses pronounced on the Jews in the Old Testament, but they deprive Jews of their blessings by "spiritualizing" the promises of the Bible's prophetic books. Some scholars believe that the kingdom-age blessings for Jews, mentioned in Old Testament passages, should be interpreted as belonging to the Church. "Zion" and "Jerusalem", according to these students, are "spiritual" references to the Church and the Gospel . . . It would be a more logical handling of Scripture to assume that the Bible means what it says and says what it means.[19]

19. SP944:177. This excerpt recalls a famous dispensationalist's denunciation of those who seek the Church as heir to the "glowing promises made to God's ancient people in the Old Testament" in the Psalms and prophecies. These Christians "appeal confidently to the fulfillment of curses against Israel . . . and triumphantly point the infidel to the punishment, captivity, and dispersion of

Fundamentalist writers, then, often believe that the Word of God will be validated by the final restoration and blessing of the Jews; the dispersion of Israel's people for disobedience testifies only to the faithfulness of the God who will restore them. The "judgment" upon the Jew does not mean to them that the Jews have been rejected by God—it signifies a temporary setting aside of His people from the role He has assigned to them. The Jews are still God's Chosen People; they have a reason for being as well as a future place in the divine economy. Hence their suffering is not to be understood as permanent, nor as justifiable. Christians have no license either to despise or to persecute Jews.[20]

Table 7 verifies the preponderance of statements dealing with the preservation of the Jews in fundamentalist discussions of Jewish oppression.[21] The view is that since God preserves His people, Jews rightfully exist today as a separate group. One text for senior students has a half-page drawing of an orthodox Jew with phylacteries and tallith standing in an attitude of prayer. It is entitled "What about the Jew?" and the legend reads: "Ungodly men say he is 'A byword, an outcast, hated, rejected, despised.' God's Word says he is 'beloved, chosen, precious, a king, a priest.' What Do *You* Say?" This suggests a high regard for the Jew as one expectantly

Abram's seed; and then coolly turn around, and appropriate to themselves every promise of forgiveness and restoration and happiness, given to the same scattered Israel. Let not a Gentile talk anymore after this of the meanness of a Jew." James H. Brookes, *Israel and the Church* (New York, Fleming H. Revell, n.d.), p. 4.

20. There is a potential negative orientation toward the Jewish plight in some forms of antidispensational fundamentalism which stand in contrast to that of Scripture Press. To Boettner, for example, the continued existence of the Jews is "sinful." It exists as a "bitter rival and enemy of the Christian Church." Only "divine disfavor" rests upon such a movement, "such as it has indeed suffered through the centuries." The revival of Judaism in our times makes "it extremely hard to reach individual Jews with the Gospel." The existence of the Jews has made "it possible to perpetuate through the centuries the distinction between Jews and Gentiles." "The continuance of this bitterly anti-Christian racial group has brought no good to themselves, and there has been strife and antagonism in practically every nation where they have gone . . . One need only think of the pogroms in Russia, the ghettos of eastern Europe . . . and in our own day the campaign of extermination waged against them in Germany by Hitler." The "great contribution" which the Jews might have made, but did not make to our American civilization, would have been to lose their identity, like the English, the Scotch, etc. Loraine Boettner, *The Millennium* (Philadelphia, Presbyterian and Reformed Publishing Co., 1958), pp. 313-15.

21. Appendix VII.

awaiting the Messiah and the kingdom. Indeed, unlike the conservatives, who tend to denounce the Jews for expecting an earthly messianic kingdom, fundamentalist writers are inclined to believe that there is considerable truth in that expectation. At times they refute the idea that "the only kingdom of God on earth is His spiritual rule in the hearts of men."

The question the foregoing discussion raises is how the fundamentalist concept of dispersion applies to present Jewish suffering. According to one lesson, there are four types of biblical prophecies that concern the entire range of Jewish existence in the Christian era.

1. The dispersion of the Jews (Deut. 4:27; 28:64)
2. The persecution of the Jews (Deut. 4:27; 28:64)
3. The preservation of the Jews (Jer. 30:11)
4. The restoration of the Jews (Isa. 60:10–22)

In fundamentalist thinking the diaspora itself is interpreted as a "judgment" or "punishment"—the result of Israel's rejecting its King, Jesus Christ. This view maintains that "judgment" began with the destruction of Jerusalem. There is scarcely any suggestion in the lessons that this first judgment upon Israel applies to anything beyond the scattering of the Jews from their homeland "as leaves before the wind to the ends of the earth." The phrase "scattered by the judgment of God" in this context clearly is not to be construed as Jewish "suffering in the purpose of God." [22]

Sometimes fundamentalist writers imply that the diaspora only *exposed* Jews to an already existent anti-Semitism, and cannot be made to account for it. According to the curriculum, the pagan Gentile world of ancient Egypt, Babylonia, and Rome was rife with anti-Semitism; Jews suffered unjustly at the hands of "evil men." In another place it is said that anti-Semitism is a "ghastly phenomenon" and that Jews have been subjected to "unpitying slaughter." However, fundamentalists believe that because God has complete foresight, he predicted in scripture the sufferings which the Jews would experience in the dispersion. In discussing this prophecy one writer says:

The Jewish persecutions are among the saddest facts of history. For the past 2000 years, the Jews have been driven from one

22. SP830:3 and SP963:53, among others.

country to another, and have been treated with the most horrible cruelties that Satan-possessed minds could devise.

(SP604:57)

However, the primary purpose of such a statement is not simply to sympathize with the Jews but even more to demonstrate the truth of God's Word in the hope of engendering belief in His future program, as fundamentalists understand it. Certain of the fundamentalist curriculum writers concentrate on a divine timetable of events and preoccupy themselves with textual and empirical proofs of the truth of God's Word; sometimes this preoccupation becomes so intense that these writers tend to bypass altogether the present ethical obligation of Christians to come to the defense of the Jews. Also, because of a writer's sole concern with making an exegetical point, Jewish persecution occasionally seems to be attributed not so much to the sinfulness of the persecutor as to the past and present ungodliness of the Jew who has rejected his own Messiah. Though these same references are generally accompanied by denunciations of anti-Semitism and by commands for Christians to love Jews, the distinction between the diaspora as judgment and anti-Semitism as sinful reactions to the dispersed Jews remains obscure.

In order for fundamentalist judgments on anti-Semitism to become practically meaningful, the curriculum writers would have to clarify in some detail the distinction between the "scattering" of the Jews and the "hatred" of them as a people. Their descriptions of anti-Semitism as "diabolical," a "murderous purpose instigated by Satan," "sadistic," "wicked" and so forth would then speak with greater force and relevance to the Christian's sense of obligation.

Such a treatment would logically require him to make a distinction between two types of Jewish suffering. The first type is the consequence of the Jews being expelled from Palestine. That is, many of the blessings intended for Jews are understood to be contingent upon their remaining in the Holy Land, where God will fulfill his purpose for them. According to this view it is the diaspora itself which is a judgment of God, and it entails one type of suffering. The second type—anti-Semitism—is quite different. For example, in what sense can anti-Semitism be considered a judgment? Some lesson writers say that Israel "is suffering a punishment commensurate with the seriousness of her sin in rejecting Christ as her Messiah." [23] Yet others point out that "Israel's survival is guaranteed by God, and God has promised to bless any person or people who will befriend the Jews, as well as to curse those who afflict His people. Setting himself up against God is the wildest mistake a man can possibly make." [24] These passages imply that there is a distinction in the background of fundamentalist thought between the "dispersion as judgment" and "anti-Semitism as sin," but the writers never quite make the distinction explicit. Some writers also add that hatred of the Jew is due to man's sinfulness and that the Jew has "God's seal of approval." Or again, Satan is said to have instigated anti-Semitism. Twenty-one lessons (with no negative instances) forbid and condemn anti-Semitism, holding that it is incompatible with God's will and with the imperatives of the Christian faith.[25]

The fundamentalist understanding of the concepts of judgment and rejection in the above context requires further clarification. First, judgment in their view has material consequences in that it deprives God's earthly people of their homeland. But it also has spiritual ones in that it deprives Israel of certain spiritual blessings, particularly in regard to salvation. The spiritual deprivation which follows from God's judgment upon the Jews in no way justifies anti-Semitism or limitations upon Jewish rights and status. According to fundamentalists, Jews can be saved, and "God always has His faithful remnant among Jews." Nonetheless, Israel has been "partially set aside" in regard to its spiritual status, because it demonstrated "a hardening in part" to faith in Christ, i.e. a "blindness in part" to saving truth. This does not mean that the Jew is any less kindly or worthy; lack of faith does not make a man inferior or dishonorable. In fundamentalist terms: "occupying the place of [spiritual] blessing is a matter of faith, rather than merit."

Further, fundamentalist belief in the partial rejection of the Jews does not imply that Jews are to blame for anti-Semitism. One of the lesson writers, in describing the spiritual blindness of Israel, takes into account the words of St. Paul and cautions against Gentile

23. SP, *Bible Knowledge* (Jan.–March 1955), p. 236.
24. SP, Ibid. (April–June 1955), p. 139.
25. See the comparatively favorable range of statements in Table 7, Appendix VII.

pride. He places the entire blame for anti-Semitism upon the
Gentiles and adds that "since the Christian's remaining in the place
of blessing depends purely on faith (faith being a gift), there is no
room for pride." He then points out that "Gentile feelings of superiority over Jews are a leading cause for anti-Semitism." To clarify
how these feelings operate, he continues:

> Pride comes easily to us, and humility is native to only a few
> choice souls! How proud Gentiles have been of their spiritual
> and cultural position! How they have "looked down their
> noses" at Jews, branding them with unprintable epithets and
> making all sorts of ridiculous accusations against them. It is as
> hard for proud Gentiles to come "down" to the place of spir-
> itual humility as it is for a high-altitude animal to come down
> to sea level!                                        (SP930:144)

Thus "the partial rejection of Israel" spoken of in the curriculum
is not intended as a justification for anti-Semitism. Anti-Semitism
is clearly man's guilt. The fundamentalist concept means that
"Israel" as a *nation* is partially rejected and not that God has abandoned His people, that He no longer cherishes them, or that He has
given Gentiles any warrant to abuse or hate Jews.

The fundamentalist writers also hold that Israel by definition
inevitably was to confront God's judgment in order to correct its
ways. Thus the curriculum states: "The humbling of the Jews has
been in accordance with the covenant God made with their forefathers." The Jews have been penalized for their "disobedience to
God's commands." However, the writers also emphasize that this
judgment gives no Christian the warrant to despise and condemn
the Jews. "They are God's peculiar treasure, and the day will come
when their renewed obedience will bring them into the place of
glorious blessing." "God's justice is not the 'mean' kind but is meant
for the good of the one who receives it." God chastizes the Jew as
he does the Christian—as a son. Further, the fundamentalists believe
that the Jews receive God's blessing along with His judgment, that
they are succeeding now through the grace of God. God, they say,
"preserves His people in love even though they miserably fail."
"It is because God loves us that He chastens us . . . and that love
will yet bring Israel—and us, if we are His—to the blessed port of
restoration."

The curriculum also emphasizes that all people are subject to God's judgment, especially those guilty of anti-Semitism. Some nations, such as Egypt and Germany, have already fallen because of the judgment passed on them for persecuting Jews, and the rest of the world will experience a similar fate for its participation. God's judgment is inevitable; those who escape judgment in this life will experience a catastrophic judgment at the end of the age, at which time it will no longer be remedial but punitive. Hence nations which have persecuted Jews will perish, and persons guilty of anti-Semitism, including the "wicked dead" will be thrown into everlasting hellfire.

In sum, fundamentalist writers regard historical judgment as a two-fold process by which both the people whom God has singled out for special responsibility as well as their oppressors are punished; for the former, judgment is intended as a corrective, while for the latter it is both corrective and distinctly punitive. The fundamentalist explanation for this is that since God's action is experienced through human action, he uses human instruments to realize them. Thus a group or nation which is disobedient to God undergoes punishment in the form of afflictions from others. Assyria and Babylon, for example, are understood as the agents of God's judgment upon Israel. But these nations were thereby guilty of carrying out their evil intentions against the Jews and were destroyed, while the Jews were preserved through divine mercy. The instruments of God are guilty and accountable because they act as free agents.

The foregoing indicates that although fundamentalist writers are outspoken against anti-Semitism, they nevertheless tend to regard Jewish suffering as a rightful judgment on the Jews even though the oppressors of Jews are guilty of a worse sin. Thus while condemning anti-Semitism, some of the writers still appear to hold the Jews at least partly responsible for their own sufferings. But, to emphasize an earlier point, were the curriculum writers consistently to make clear the distinction between the dispersion as judgment and anti-Semitism as sin, much of the confusion resulting from their presentations could be cleared up.

The fundamentalist position on the re-establishment of Israel is in harmony with their interpretation of the biblical text. There they find that the Jews were guaranteed external possession of the land of Israel; one writer notes that "many orthodox Jews and Bible-believing Christians have for years treasured the promises of God about Israel's coming restoration," and he urges his readers "to look into the faces of our Jewish neighbors, and to view the whole sweep of God's plan for this old world, with a keen consciousness that God has covenanted to restore Israel to a high place among the nations." Thus many fundamentalists view the return of Jews to the land of Israel as "the beginning of the fulfillment" of the prophecy of restoration. The fundamentalists do not believe in segregation, but they rejoice in the Jewish return to Israel because they believe the Jews will profit from re-establishing themselves in a homeland. "Jews who believe in the promises of God" will choose to go to Israel, asserts one educator who believes that the full economic, social, and spiritual advantages of the covenant are contingent upon the Jews being "in the land." Although fundamentalists regard Jews as among America's most valuable citizens, they feel that emigration to Israel is natural for those Jews who live in expectation of the Messianic hope. According to one writer, "God promised to bless Israel in the land He had chosen for her (Deut. 28:8). Have Jews, then, the right to claim these blessings when they dwell in other lands?" Another writer notes that "It is important to notice that God's covenant of blessing made a link between the people and the land. The relation of the Jews to Palestine became an index to the spiritual condition of Abraham's descendants."

From the above it is apparent that the fundamentalist's approval of the re-establishment of Israel is closely bound up with the idea that Jews will continue to suffer persecution as long as they are dispersed and remain a minority in a hostile world. Despite certain inadequacies which we have noted in their discussions of judgment and dispersion, it is evident that fundamentalists clearly condemn anti-Semitism.

## Neo-Orthodox Theology

Neo-orthodox writers do not teach that the Jews are rejected. On the contrary, they state that the Jews are still the chosen people; that they are prior in God's grace to the Christian; that the church is grafted onto Israel, which continues to perform a function in the divine plan. However, like the conservatives, the neo-orthodox think of the Church as the true Israel. This does not mean that God has cast off the Jews. Rather, the neo-orthodox understand that Christians are bound to the Jew in an intimate and significant way: the two communities share more than common roots; they share a common destiny.

This view closely relates concern for the plight of the Jew with the interests of the Christian. Neo-orthodox writers use anecdotes, illustrations, discussions, and other available material to call attention to anti-Semitism. These observations are likely to show up anywhere in the writers' expositions of the Bible. One writer even uses the "no room in the inn" phrase in the Christmas story to point out current anti-Semitic practices:

> Do the members of the class know of any clubs, hotels, or resorts that are for Gentiles only? Are they aware that the term "restricted clientele" generally means that Jews are excluded? Has it occurred to them that our Lord himself would be excluded from such places? It is likely that all of us have accepted privileges and services that would be denied Jesus.
>
> (PR37,534:39)

The neo-orthodox writer does not apply the concept of judgment to the Jew and to his suffering but, rather, to those who persecute Jews. This is consistent with his understanding of judgment as the expression of "divine action in history" which we examined in the previous chapter. Hence judgment, in his view, is invariably redemptive despite its severity. God's shattering of a social order inevitably entails that those who are relatively free of guilt will suffer along with the guilty. Americans, as much as others, need to realize that "the judgment of God falls on those who deny human rights of others." When Nazi Germany entered its "national security" crusade, it proposed to resolve internal problems in much the same way as did Egypt by killing off the Jews. "In both cases internal security was shattered." For the neo-orthodox, then, a denunciation of prejudice does not sufficiently reflect God's justice; God acts to destroy the institutions, structures, and agents of oppression; consequently, those who ignore the retributive justice of history contribute to their own destruction:

> We have again and again witnessed the fact that those who set about the persecution and elimination of other races or peoples

have succeeded ultimately in provoking wide-spread disruption of the social order, warfare, and the destruction of themselves. The chain of consequences flowing from Hitler's anti-Semitic policy needs no comment as an illustration of this principle in history. Even on the scale of the small community, we have many a time observed the utter disruption of community life where terrorism directed against Jews, Negroes, or Roman Catholics, has become rampant. The zeal to liquidate, or reduce to impotence, another race or people in the long run brings nothing but horror and destruction in its train.

(PR37,613:36)

In that the Church sees itself according to Israel's self-image, it must recognize that judgment begins in the house of God, i.e. visited upon Christians.

Because the neo-orthodox revulsion to anti-Semitism is so strong and because it so closely relates the Christian's role to the problem of achieving justice for the Jew, the curriculum is particularly forceful in its denunciation of anti-Semitism and in its directives to combat prejudice against Jews. Students and teachers are given instances of exemplary Christian behavior during the Nazi regime by those who forged passports for Jews, lied in their behalf, and even killed in order to save the Jews from extermination. The Christian is even urged to protect the Jew at the risk of his own life and security. Typical also of this communicator is the following story from a lesson which expresses the Jews' sufferings and vividly identifies with their world sorrow. An American church and its pastor, during the early stage of the Nazi terror, prayed at all church services on behalf of the persecuted Jews. This pastor was later visited by a rabbi, who produced several letters written in a foreign hand:

> They told of terrors, murders, starvations, hungers, deaths, and long-night vigils of prayer. They came from brothers and sisters of the rabbi, who lived in several cities of the Continent. "Why have you come to me with this?" the preacher asked the rabbi, finally, after his soul was almost frozen with the horror of it all. "Because I have to preach to my congregation tonight," the rabbi answered, "and practically every family among my people will be carrying letters exactly like these.

My heart is sick, and I have no word within me for them.
But I know you have been praying for my people, and I
thought that I could come to you and perhaps you could
give me some word of hope and courage that I might pass on
to Israel.                                    (PR37,144:38)

The neo-orthodox curriculum devotes relatively little space to
discussing the State of Israel; the position it takes on the re-establishment of Israel is always favorable, although discussion of Jewish
rights and sufferings do not figure in this context. Neo-orthodox
do not regard the re-establishment of Israel as the solution to Jewish
suffering. Anti-Semitism, for them, is a problem which God commands all men, and especially the Church, to solve as they confront
it—here in America, as well as in other parts of the world and at
the present time.

*Naturalistic Liberalism*

Liberal teaching univocally disapproves of anti-Semitism.[26] According to one text, "The Jews have suffered more severe treatment from their neighbors than any other single religious group.
Even today unscrupulous leaders can find a scapegoat in the Jews,
inciting hatred against them." The lesson books include photographs
of refugee Jewish children, and there is a reproduction of Arthur
Szyk's expressive painting which is dedicated to "the Hallowed
Memory of Europe's Martyred Jews." It shows a figure of a march-
ing Jew "defiant, unafraid" as he wears the yellow star and carries
the Torah. Some lessons have as their stated aim the improvement
of Jewish-Christian relations and understanding. The students are
given stories to read which describe the effects of Nazi persecution
on the Jews. Jews, it is stated, have been "lied about, cheated,
robbed, and made victims of the cruelest pogroms."

Liberal concern, however, for the Jews is directed primarily to
the Arab-Israeli conflict in Palestine. More than one-half of the
lessons concerned with Jews in Category 1 are devoted to this conflict. The preface to the student text in an Old Testament course
is entitled, "Why Tell This Ancient Drama?" According to the
text, "Palestine has taken on unusual importance and is often in
the news because some of the descendants of those people who

26. Table 9, Appendix VII.

first established the nation of Israel have gathered and organized a new Israel in that same land." One writer believes that the primitive origins of the issue are manifested in the current Arab-Israeli conflict. Another states that "The terrific emotional struggle between Jews and Arabs" over Israel's existence "goes way back to the conquest of Canaan," and it is impossible to understand these tensions or to be able to negotiate differences without a knowledge of their historical sources. As one manual for teachers phrases it: "Whatever position one takes today on the Palestine question, his judgment is colored by his understanding—or lack of it—of the past history of the country."

Although the liberals' position is never explicitly stated in this historical analysis of Arab-Israeli tensions, the logical drift of their discussion is opposed to the re-establishment of the State of Israel, not only because they cannot find any biblical sanction for it but also because they hint that it has little prospect for lasting success. They point out that past attempts at restoration have failed. But more central to their position is the contention that the Jews were never the chosen people and that God did not promise them Palestine as a possession. The Jews lived among the Arabs even during the period of conquest and occupation—hence Arabs also made Palestine their home. One chapter argues that historically Israel's rulers (e.g. Solomon) were military leaders who sought to glorify the nation and "largely by ambition to rival and surpass the other nations of their times," largely "at the expense of other peoples." This is the context in which the dispersion of the Jews and the modern attempt to re-establish Israel are presented. Although not actually stated, this account appears to assume that the Jews have no historical claim to Palestine.

However, liberal educators also point out that the present situation of the Jews—their suffering in the recent Nazi holocaust and the consequent problems which Jews face as refugees—contributes to the Zionist concern to re-establish Israel, and attempts are made in the curriculum to acquaint students and teachers with both the Jewish and the Arab versions of the conflict. Students are encouraged to take the part of Arab and Jewish refugees in the class activity known as "role playing." The class periods provide for discussions of the Palestine problem from both points of view, while the text gives the students further background through sympathetic, deeply moving accounts of the problems of Jewish and Arab displaced persons. Some of these detail the horror of the Nazi concentration camps or the anti-Semitism prevalent in Venezuela; others relate the experiences both of Jewish refugees in Israel and of Arab refugees on the other side of the barbed wire.

The lessons do not draw any conclusions from this historical analysis, but it is sometimes implied that the Jews share the greater part of the blame for the Arab-Israeli dilemma. For example, their analysis sets up parallels between the ancient Canaanite-Israelite struggle and the modern Arab-Israeli tensions: the inference is that in both cases the Jews "invaded" and created the Arab predicament. It is also intimated that the Jews violated the provisions of the Balfour Declaration in establishing Israel. However, another teacher's guide warns that "a study of the Arab-Jewish situation is likely to lead into a heated debate about which side is right and which is wrong." The "real problem is not to place the blame, but to understand the people, on both sides, who are caught in the teeth of the war, and to see their personal, human problems." The same teacher's guide provides only one attempt to evaluate the situation in Israel. This is written by an outside authority, a Christian observer with a definite point of view, who states that we cannot "now abandon our own creation," Israel, but must seek to draw up more equitable boundaries in Israel so that Jerusalem is internationalized and the Arab refugees resettled, for the most part, in Arab countries. His assessment of the part played by Israel's leaders in the dispute is as follows:

> We [Americans] are in an excellent position to exert a wholesome, moderating influence on Israel, whose very existence depends and must long depend on American support. Israel needs peace with the Arabs. Without access to raw materials, sources of power, or markets in the Near East, she cannot attain economic independence. Her leaders recognize this, yet they have done nothing beyond protestations and gestures toward a reconciliation with the Arabs.     (UN361:39 ff.)

Finally a lesson for seniors presents a lengthy history of the Arab-Israeli predicament in which Americans are not held accountable in any way for the events which culminated in the current impasse between the two nations. This lesson, it should be noted, also considers the Jewish plight in a nontheological context which implies that segregation of the Jews is self-imposed; it also leaves unexplained the terrible fact of Jewish persecution. In this respect this one isolated liberal account somewhat resembles certain non-identifying approaches we have cited in the conservative curriculum and stands in sharp contrast to the deeper and more committedly Christian attention paid to the Jewish plight by the fundamentalist and the neo-orthodox educators:

> For many centuries Arabs and Jews have been living in Pales-tine together, people of the same racial stock, but divided by religion. After the destruction of Jerusalem in the year 70 A.D. the Jewish people were scattered throughout Europe; later they migrated to America, and some went far into Asia. In most places they continued to live a separate existence, based primarily upon their unique religious convictions. In many countries they have been discriminated against and often bitterly persecuted. We all know the tragic story of their sufferings in Germany before and during the second World War.
>
> Out of this separateness, as well as the discrimination, grew the idea of a return to Palestine, the ancient home of the Jews, and later the idea of reestablishment of the Jewish nation. Palestine, however, was also the ancient home of the Arabs, and for centuries many more Arabs than Jews lived there.
>                                                    (UN410:39–40)

## CONCLUSIONS

It is important to note that religious convictions affect the ways in which educators interpret the plight and disabilities of outside groups. Even the liberal materials show this, although they are what may be called nondoctrinal in nature. The liberal's conviction that the Bible is a purely human document lacking divine authority not only allows them to declare that neither they nor the Jews are the chosen people but also influences their discussion of such empirical questions as the right of the Jews to establish Israel. The other three Christian groups struggle with such biblical doctrines as chosenness, rejection, divine judgment, and the question of continuity and discontinuity with the old Israel in discussions of the

Jewish plight. But these biblical communicators draw quite different conclusions about the meaning of these doctrines for Jewish suffering, and they exhibit different degrees of sensitivity to the responsibilities of the Christian for doing something concrete about it. Two extremes are noted in the biblical-oriented faiths: one shows an almost complete disregard for the questions Christians face in modern society with regard to anti-Semitism; the other, no less scriptural in its outlook, sees the scripture as a lens through which to view what is going on in the world, hence its intense fusion of Christian beliefs with its concern for Jews. Moreover, for the latter faith as well as for the fundamentalist one, certain of these beliefs make possible and even necessary a regard for Jewish suffering.

The great weakness of many lessons is that their writers preoccupy themselves so exclusively with the biblical text, and sometimes with historical data, that they overlook their contemporary responsibility as educators for inculcating intergroup attitudes and a sense of responsibility for intergroup relations in the minds of growing Christians. This problem has many aspects, but one of them is an unarticulated theory of society which enables writers to overlook the social implications of their remarks about other groups. The student is not addressed as a social being, who lives in a specific social order and who thus faces certain responsibilities; nor are the outside groups—such as the Jews—fully taken into account as an actual part of the society in which the Christian lives. There are other conclusions that can be drawn from our findings, such as the importance of describing the Jewish plight in its fullest historical context. However, the writer's main need in discussing prejudice in any form is to face the central leading question, "What is the Christian's responsibility in this area of concern?"

# 5. The Inside Groups as Victims

Most Protestant groups think of themselves as a beleagured minority
—whether actually or prospectively. This attitude has mixed implications for intergroup relations. Historically as well as psychologically, it has been associated both with ethnocentrism and its
opposite. The prejudiced person invariably pictures himself and
his community as victimized, and frequently shows paranoid delu-
sions along with repressed genocidal tendencies. Analyses of anti-
Semitic speeches reveal that the active ethnocentric has an indispensable need to create outside enemies; this need serves a socially
sinister purpose: The agitator, by implication, invites his audience
to ally themselves with the powerful of this world rather than
with the weak minorities, whom he assures the audience they will
be able eventually to persecute.[1]

However, Bainton, in an historical study, has called attention to
a powerful anti-ethnocentric tendency in the self-as-victim image.
According to his analysis of this conception, "Suffering is the lot
and mark of the Christian. He must be as the sheep and not as the
wolf." The history of some groups demonstrate a marked "incompatibility between the *cross* and the *stake*." [2] The experiences of the
heretic, the deviate, the man who protests against popular tyranny
are also part of the Church's history; these people, among them
some of the small Protestant groups in the left-wing of the Reformation, underwent severe persecution, yet held very firmly to the
conviction that men who "took up their cross" could not on their
part persecute others. It is entirely possible that groups which feel
victimized, whether with just cause or not, are restrained from
persecuting largely by the inhibiting influence of external social
checks; but Bainton's study reminds us of the vital importance of

1. Leo Lowenthal and Norbert Guterman, *Prophets of Deceit* (New York,
Harper, 1949), pp. 140–42.
2. Bainton, *The Reformation of the Sixteenth Century*, p. 227.

a controlling Christian self-image that also militates against the victimization of others.

The purpose of this chapter is to describe the different Protestant conceptions of their own groups as victim, to isolate the components of these images, and to discern their meaning for intergroup relations.

## Reactions to the Attitudes of Other Groups

The liberal writers are alone in depicting themselves in their official literature as the recipients of predominantly friendly deeds and kindly attitudes on the part of all contemporary outside groups.[3] The neo-orthodox appraisal of the present-day views that outside groups hold of them is somewhat ambiguous, as one can see from their imbalance scores which slither along the zero line, moving ever so slightly above or below. Although no negative attitudes are attributed to Jews, only .04 per cent of the total lessons mentioning Jews portray them as friendly. But among the religious groups, the Roman Catholics are the only ones whose amity the neo-orthodox writers seem to doubt.

The conservatives are unique among the four communicators in not having any positive references to the actions and attitudes of other religious groups toward them (i.e. the distributions are negative only).[4] The interreligious picture these findings present is that of an unrelieved hostility to and rejection of the Christian and the Church. Despite the fact that the fundamentalists say a number of favorable things about the behavior of outsiders toward them, they have an even greater preponderance of unfavorable references in this respect than do the conservatives. Of the four communicators, then, the conservatives are most significantly committed to an unqualified picture of themselves as victims, while the liberals draw exactly the opposite one.

The most intense negative imbalances occur mostly in the General Group Category for the three biblically centered communicators. This category measures statements about outside hostility without attributing it to specific groups, and is of particular importance, for it indicates how the various curricula express their

3. Analytical Cat. 12, Fig. 25, Appendix VIII.
4. Fig. 26.

rationale for the role as victim. We now turn to an examination of these statements.

## The Calling of the Christian

With the approach of Lent, lessons accentuate a typical theme—the Christian's call to suffer. The instruction of Christ that "whosoever doth not bear his cross and come after me cannot be my disciple" plays a dominant part in the Christian's understanding of his role, as do the varied directives of the gospels and epistles. St. Paul asks men to share in Christ's sufferings; Jesus promises persecution from city to city and proclaims a ringing beatitude upon all who suffer for the sake of righteousness. In "following Christ," or "taking the cross," the Christian accepts a hardship which the world imposes. Paul finds that men regard the cross as a "scandal" and a "stumbling-block"; Christ's followers must share this scandal and ignominy. The image is further sharpened by the historical memory of saints hated, scorned, fed to lions, and burned as tapers in the Roman carnivals. The apostles were peaceful and law-abiding, yet they were mobbed, stoned, flailed, imprisoned, and "fed as lambs to the slaughter."

But for an American Protestant to regard himself as such a victim must in the main appear ludicrous to outside observers. Even the faithful find it difficult to envision themselves in this role, for the leading currents of our contemporary culture run counter to this kind of self-image. The thoroughly acculturized American is committed not to self-sacrifice and hardship but to achieving comfort, acceptability, and success. Most people in our country are concerned with how to be proper, well-liked, and secure. In the eyes of our society, the victim is a failure; he is weak and not strong; he yields himself to something rather than gains power over it; he is used by God rather than using God for his own ends.

Not only the temper of our time but certain social realities as well undercut the concept of the group self as a victim. The biblical images were formed in a period when the Church was a tiny, powerless minority in a hostile world. This is hardly true today. Can a Christian justifiably maintain an identity with this victim when the Church itself can be held at least partly accountable for the forces of oppression, and when those who call themselves Christians are numerically a majority in America?

Nevertheless, to deny Christians any valid basis for such an image would seem to deprive them of an essential and admissible feature of their traditional faith. Such an image can be a legitimate one if it grows out of a more profound understanding than usual of the Church's mission and the way it is carried out in relation to modern culture. There is also the possibility in situations of real social conflict that a man who may be classified as belonging to majority groups on the basis of his color, nationality, and religious affiliation may belong to a minority in respect to his primary value-commitments. White Protestant "freedom riders," for example, have faced hostility, mob action, and arrest. Those of the majority groups caught in the conflict of social values can attract much the same hostility and rejection as do those who belong to racial and ethnic minorities. This dimension of the social problem is raised by the neo-orthodox writers in a basic way when they discuss the current trend toward conformity. To deal with these matters in terms meaningful to Christians we must therefore ask these fundamental questions: Why should anyone wish to persecute or defame Christians, or otherwise wish to afflict and oppress the Church? And what forms do these afflictions and oppressions, if any, take?

As can be seen in Table 10,[5] the liberals stand alone in giving no clue whatever (on either the positive or negative side) as to their general conception of their present intergroup status. This is not true of the conservatives, fundamentalists, and neo-orthodox, who in the General Group column of Analytical Category 12 make explicit the ways in which they conceive of themselves as victims.

The neo-orthodox see themselves as victims (with more minus than plus scores), yet this role is more qualified on the nonvictim side than are fundamentalist and conservative lessons. Since the statements of the two remaining communicators are qualitatively different from the others as well as from each other, let us first concentrate on their self-portraits.

## The Nature of the Fundamentalist-Conservative Images

Conservative and fundamentalist self-definitions of themselves as victim generally follow the forms designated in scripture. These

5. Below, Appendix VII.

forms, in fact, often appear to be the only ones with which the
writers are concerned—although this tendency is more characteristic of conservative lessons than of fundamentalist. Fundamentalist
literature is especially useful to examine on this point, because its
writers modify their exposition of biblical passages only when they
become aware of an incongruity between victimization in the past
and the actual social situation of those who use the lessons. When,
for example, an author says that Christians "in this world are naturally hated and oppressed" while the unsaved "naturally will pros-
per," he is not engaging in social analysis or stating a sociological
observation illuminated by scripture. He is expounding II Thess. 1:5
in the light of Eph. 2:2, II Cor. 4:4, and I John 5:19, on the basis
of his understanding that the Church is a distinct body of saints in
this age—a body to which the words of Jesus and the epistolary
writers on this subject apply in a literal sense. The lesson itself
plainly states this rationale:

> Christians invariably consider persecution as an unusual and
> disruptive thing which is contrary to God's plan. *They for-
> get that our Lord Jesus Christ said,* "In the world ye shall
> have tribulation" (John 15:19, 20). In reality, for a Christian
> in the will of God, *freedom from persecution is unusual*
> (cf. II Tim. 3:12).[6]

Noting that persecution is not limited to physical torture, the
section on "teaching hints" suggests that five or ten minutes be
devoted to "a panel discussion on forms of persecution that believers
must face in the community." The remainder of the lesson merely
assumes the reality of this image and does not examine it. Persecution is considered a normal experience for the Church on the
basis of Christ's promises.

All such fundamentalist portrayals of the Church as sufferer have
scriptural sources. They must be understood in part as a function
of the doctrine (held by some but not all writers in this curriculum)
that the Church Age represents a new and different dispensation—
one that is distinct from the dispensation under which Israel lives—
and that not only the prophets but also the New Testament writers,
and Christ in particular, predicted for the Christian a *distinctive role*
of suffering for the sake of righteousness. The lot of the genuine

6. SP967:276 (my italics).

Christian, then, in relation to the outsider, is often seen completely apart from contemporary social analysis.

In contrast to this tendency, when fundamentalist writers examine the present social realities in which the Church exists, they are likely to put scriptural interpretations in the future tense. The view of some writers is that the future fulfillment of yet unrealized scriptural promises applies primarily to the promises made to Israel "according to the flesh," i.e. to Jews: yet they also hold that other futuristic promises apply to the Church as well. These writers describe the Christian as only a potential victim now and suggest to their audience that they may have to face persecution shortly. "The day may soon arrive," says one, "when Christians, even here, will once more need to be unafraid before violent enemies." Or again: "Though methods of torture have changed in twenty centuries, it is entirely possible even yet that some of us in this room may some day be thrown to wild beasts, or burned at the stake, or stretched out of joint upon a rack—all because of our faith." [7]

Others add a conditional factor to both present and future prospects for suffering. "*If* you are [really] a Christian," says one writer, "you *may* have tribulation in this life (John 16:33). *If* you try to live a godly life, you *may* be persecuted (II Tim. 3:12)." "*Perhaps* some day some of you in this class *may* have to stand up for Christ before angry unbelievers." Any actual rejection the Christian may sense today becomes a foretaste of this grim possibility. High school classes are advised, "If some of the gang at your school are inclined to snicker at you for having 'religion,' or if some of your science teachers like to make sneering remarks about people who believe the Bible, don't take to feeling sorry for yourself. The worst, no doubt, is yet to come!" Continuing in this futuristic vein, the writer says:

> There is good reason to believe that bitter persecution of
> Christians will once more be common, in parts of the world
> where believers today take religious freedom for granted. God
> warns us in His Word that "all that will live godly in Christ
> Jesus shall suffer persecution."                    (SP889:35)

7. The reference is apparently to communistic countries, especially China and Russia. This, as well as preceding and following excerpts from the four curricula, will not be documented as to text and page (except for the larger, indented passages) because of their great number.

Thus certain incongruities between the fundamentalist self-image and current social realities are partially resolved by appeals to further hermeneutical principles that shift the context to that of a future time.

## The Absence of Overt Persecution

Other fundamentalist writers, however, explicitly give attention to the present-day situation of believers. They acknowledge that Christians in the United States enjoy actual freedoms and general acceptance, and make clear the distinctions between different levels of victimization. One may indeed be "criticized or laughed at," states one writer, because one is a Christian; but another observes that "most Christians today know absolutely nothing of what discipleship can cost. Only on the mission fields, as a rule, is there real persecution of believers." Christians should be mighty grateful, maintains another, "for . . . the privilege of living in a country where persecution and mass misery are practically unknown."

The relative absence on the American scene of a reality corresponding to the anticipated image of the Christian victim disturbs some fundamentalists. One author first notes that overt persecution is utterly foreign to Christians in their modern American setting: "Few Christians today have ever been beaten for the sake of Christ. All their lives long, American Christians do not suffer physically a single pang for Christ and His kingdom." The question for class discussion then proposes that, "Since we do not have to undergo very much severe trouble for Christ, can we be as faithful to Him as were those who suffered greatly?" A lack of persecution in the modern West thus calls into question the effectiveness and relevance of the Christian witness.

However, these fundamentalist denials of serious Christian persecution apply to the American scene, not to the global one. Comparisons are sometimes made between what American and non-American Christians must undergo; if it is conceded that "citizens of our nations know very little of any kind of bondage," their heritage being a glorious one of independence and freedom, then attention is called to "those who come from countries where another ideology has been forced upon them, and who have been enslaved politically." The writer concludes that our bondage is not political, but a bondage to sin. While overt persecution by non-

Christian nations is not charged, it is stated that Tibet, Nepal, Afghanistan, Mongolia, and other countries raise barriers "to exclude missionaries" or hinder the preaching of the gospel. A communist nation is specified in a graphic and inspirational story of a pastor who was seized in the presence of his congregation and led away to his persecutors.

## Distrust of the Martyr Role

Explicit disapproval of Christians who seek opposition and martyrdom is also characteristic of the fundamentalist interpretation of cross-bearing:

> Many early Christians, in days of persecution, were so eager to die as martyrs that they hurried to the magistrates and proclaimed their faith, demanding to be executed. Although on the surface such a practice may appear to be noble and commenable, it is not becoming in a Christian. (SP933:31)

The self-glorifying spirit of martyrdom is "shown by members of some present-day [Christian] sects who deliberately invite public disfavor and hatred." Such behavior is said to violate the command to live peaceably with all men, chiefly because it provokes extreme and uncharitable judgments on other groups. Persons of this kind are themselves said to be guilty of a hatred which they rationalize as antipathy of other groups toward them. An implicit danger to constructive intergroup relations in the "self as martyr" image is warned against in a lesson that quotes an extremist charge from a Jehovah's Witnesses publication: "The ecclesiastical systems, Catholic and Protestant, are under the supervision and control of the devil, and form a part of his visible organization, and therefore constitute the anti-Christ." Comments the lesson writer: "Such tactics, of course, have led to serious friction between Witnesses and people with saner views. As a result of the 'persecution' that has developed, the Witnesses have developed a 'martyr complex' that has convinced them of the righteousness of their cause."

More importantly, the same communicator readily acknowledges that many Christians believe that they are being "persecuted for the sake of Christ," when, in fact, they are merely guilty of a lack of sensitivity to other people or respect for others' feelings, or are merely "meddlers in other peoples' affairs." The writer cautions

the reader that the "chances are . . . that not all your suffering
comes to you because of your faith in Christ." Nearly one in every
three fundamentalist lessons on the theme of contemporary Christian suffering makes similar cautions. "God's people must be expected to be hated and persecuted, even when they have done no
wrong," one writer asserts, but then adds, "On the other hand, no
Christian should deliberately seek to make himself unpopular."

## The Christian as "Unrighteous Victim"

As the foregoing analysis makes clear, fundamentalist literature
distinguishes between genuine persecution for "the sake of Christ"
and other forms of opposition, criticism, and punishment due to
genuine evils committed by the Christian. Self-critical questions
for class discussion (e.g. "Are you suffering ridicule and shame for
Jesus' sake or because of the [evil] way you are living?") are based
on this distinction between the two types of suffering inflicted by
others. The same lesson states that God allows His people to suffer
only: (a) when they have done wrong and need to be corrected;
(b) when suffering will bring them some blessing they would
otherwise miss; (c) when their suffering will glorify their Lord
and, eventually, them. Only the second and third possibilities involve "suffering with Christ." It is presumed that the Christian
will be able to distinguish between the two types.

Correctives of the common Christian misunderstanding of the
teaching that Christians are to suffer are often quite specific. Paul's
"true meaning" of glorifying in persecutions does "not mean that
we are to glory in difficulties of our own making" as does the
Christian "who coldly disapproves of his unbelieving co-workers."
He "need not call it 'persecution' if they don't like him." If Christians are misunderstood by outsiders, this sometimes, "it must be
confessed . . . is their own fault . . . One earnest Christian, by
his constant haranguing of his fellow workers, was hated by everyone in his office." Christians are warned that they "often embarrass
and antagonize the very people they are trying to win for Christ"
by "crude methods" which are seldom successful and which antagonize unbelievers. Other lessons mention such offenses as a
"nosey" nature, selfishness, a holier-than-thou attitude on the part
of the Christian, boorishness and stupidity, tactlessness, careless-
ness, wickedness, unwise, untactful methods in personal witnessing,

and self-righteousness. In this manner the pupils' and teachers' attention is called to the dangers of self-righteousness inherent in a zeal for the gospel which has not properly been tempered by love of and respect for others.

Representing oneself as a victim, therefore, is not always defended in fundamentalist literature, and is often critically examined. However, such self-criticism is, first of all, directed largely to the attitudes and behavior of the individual Christian, rather than to the more generally approved behavior of the evangelical Christian community. Secondly, the weaknesses and failures that are exposed in criticizing the victim image are not consistently related to the doctrine of sin or to the Church's conception of itself.

## The Christian as Definitive Victim

Despite the relative absence of overt oppression of Christians in the United States, the fundamentalists believe that they do incur genuine disabilities which are no less real because they are subtle. The terminology their writers use to describe this actual form of victimization is notably less intense than that employed in the lessons produced by the more classically orthodox conservatives.

Taking the latter communicator first, references to the Christian's fate in the modern world are often put in the extreme. The world would "destroy the Christian" with persecution, temptation, and mockery. Scoffers and modernists try "to degrade the Christian religion in the eyes of the people." Modernists, unbelievers, and false teachers attack its doctrines and the Church undergoes the violence of the mob spirit by torture and burning. Malicious persons make fun of, attack, and slander the Christian religion and "infringe on our rights." The Christian is ridiculed and the Church branded as "narrow, old-fashioned, and bigoted." Teachers in high schools and colleges, popular writers, and speakers make "vicious attacks" on "our young people." Christians are despised and rejected as servants of Christ. Friends and relatives misjudge them. Spiritual enemies set out to destroy the Church. The wicked ridicule the godly. The Church's enemies in the world "fight to profane her" and "rejoice over her shame and sorrow." Vicious men would "tear Christ's followers to pieces."

The fundamentalist writers' most intense terms for the sufferings of Christians are "persecuted" and "hatred"; otherwise, they describe their disabilities more calmly than do the conservatives. They "are criticized and laughed at"; when promoting the Gospel they are "opposed"; they undergo "testing experiences"; and they may be "disliked" for their beliefs.

The reasons given by these two communicators for the injuries inflicted on the Christian mainly relate to their faith as preached and lived. Fundamentalist writers assert that one must be willing to be misunderstood and reviled for making a "separated witness." This separation does not mean exclusiveness; it means being set apart for God—obeying God rather than man. All disabilities endured for the gospel have an integral relation to this separation. Where the gospel is preached and lived, many will be offended. Similar reasons are given for hatred and ridicule of Christians and the Church in conserative lessons.

In summary, both the fundamentalist and conservative communicators characterize themselves as victimized for the sake of the cross mainly on the grounds of exegetical and hermeneutical considerations rather than those of an empirical examination of the contemporary churches and of the social realities in which they are placed and which confront the users of their materials with the necessity of making ethical decisions. Both these publishers see their victimization as not only an ancient but a present actuality and impending possibility in some parts of the world. Distinctions between what is past history, present fact, or future possibility, and between what is true on the domestic scene and what is true abroad, are more apt to be made in the fundamentalist literature than in the conservative. Of the two, the fundamentalists almost alone say that some hatred of Christians is a deserved punishment for their sins, suspect the martyr spirit, and acknowledge the real freedoms Christians enjoy. All these questions of the Christian life, however, are handled with minimum regard to their social dimension.

## THE LIBERAL IMAGE OF THE NONVICTIM

The above analysis raises questions about the relationship that exists between scripturally defined roles and those which modern American Christians actually play in the society that presumably scorns them. The two high-scoring communicators handle this problem in different ways. The liberal Universalists-Unitarians avoid it largely by picturing themselves independently of the scriptural prescriptions. For them, the Church is one among many human institutions and the Christian a believer in one of many religions. The modern church with its traditional doctrines is thought to be more apt to promote bigotry and transform its adherents into oppressors than to become martyrs for a cause. The liberal nurtures only an incipient image of himself as victim and one which is appropriate to any pioneer in new ideas and ways: the Jesus of history is praised as a glorious martyr and a victim of traditionalism. But every movement—including the non-Christian—is regarded as having produced its comparable prophet-heroes who have suffered for venturing beyond the accepted boundaries.

While the liberal pioneer may theoretically find himself such a martyr, there is another perspective in the curriculum that runs counter to it. Liberals see people today as looking for a religion that more satisfactorily fits the demands of our global, atomic era. The Hebraic-Christian dogmas are regarded as no longer satisfying: there is in the world a restless feeling for unity, a sense of oneness, and a rising universal consciousness that are frustrated by parochial perspectives. The assessment of our times fuses with the liberal view of human nature to discourage the construction of a victim image; by nature, people need and seek love, peace, and good will.

There is, therefore, an assumption that an inclusive, nonauthoritarian approach will break down barriers, ease tensions, and create harmony rather than conflict. The liberal believes that his tolerant, inclusive view of the problems with which humanity struggles encourages a friendly response. The outlook and method are expected to produce friends, not enemies. This nonvictim image is consistent with the overarching monistic faith. Yet in the background lurks an opposite assumption that is never explicitly stated in intergroup terms: the traditionalist opposes, the prophet suffers. This potential victim image springs from both scripture and history.

The liberals, then, see themselves as the object of benign rather than threatening behavior from outside their group. The correspondence between monism and these appraisals is striking, although a realistic appraisal of their status may also play a part. On the other hand, when the prophets, Jesus, and their own internal history are in view, the victim image appears, but not in an ingroup manner, nor does it contain intergroup content. The "suffering prophet" could as well be a Buddhist or atheist as a Christian or liberal.

## SOCIAL EXISTENCE AND THE SCRIPTURAL PARADOXES

The neo-orthodox self-image as victim must be treated separately because of the organic way it relates the biblical paradoxes to the concrete problems of existence which men face as American Christians. This paradoxical, existential, and relational way of thinking holds together seemingly contradictory biblical insights about life and focuses them upon the present concrete situations in which the pupils and teachers face the necessity of making specific ethical decisions.

The neo-orthodox writer does not assume that people are offended by the ordinary decency which many Christians associate with a Christian witness. On the contrary, the virtues of kindness, thoughtfulness, and graciousness arouse admiration. Our major contemporary problems, it is held, lie not here but in those areas of human life where God's righteousness judges man's injustice. This divine righteousness battles its way in the world and may be resisted as an evil by the ruling powers and respectable voices. In intergroup terms, this righteousness threatens the accepted social barriers which good and devoted men erect against their neighbors. When they resist oppression and injury inflicted on others, faithful men may have to suffer for the sake of Christ and the Gospel in heeding God's action upon them. So conceived, the neo-orthodox self-image as victim is defined by examining their cultural situation in the light of scriptural revelation. Suffering in this context concerns the response of the Christian to God's redemptive activity in the midst of a society of rebellious men.

### The "Real Threat" Defined

In the first place, neo-orthodox writers observe that the Christian lives in a changed situation, the reverse in many important respects to that which existed in the era of the great persecutions of the Church. Whereas Christianity was once a minority movement, outlawed by the Roman state and unpopular with the multitude, today in America precisely the opposite situation prevails:

"Christianity in the United States is more than tolerated; it is more than free; it is the *favored religion* of America. It is fashionable to join the Church. It is good for a man's business to be a Christian." [8]

This comment is intended as a rebuke to help the Church define its real problem. The early Church, in "passing over from persecution to privilege," suffered the tragedy of corruption by power and status. Our danger today comes precisely from this same state of affairs. In contemporary American society freedom is guaranteed by law and Christianity is legal, esteemed, and popular. The Church's basic problem is therefore one of "how to keep its own integrity amidst popular favor." This neo-orthodox fear of complacent conformity and respectability pervades its teaching materials.

Like the writers of the other curricula, the neo-orthodox recognize that there have been and are times and places in which genuine persecution of Christians occurs—but seldom in present-day America. This is a matter both for pride and regret: pride in our heritage of freedom and good will; regret, because this serene state of affairs denotes that the Church has defaulted in its prophetic duty to challenge the wrongs of our times and, instead, is acquiescing in them. Occasional allusions to situations of persecutions in other lands in the neo-orthodox curricula do not provide occasions for the writers to experience vicarious pride; primarily they wish to accentuate the contrast. The absence of real opposition to the Church in our culture, in view of the serious social evils which characterize it, demonstrates both the sheer irrelevancy of much contemporary Christianity and the judgment of God upon the churches for their concurrence in the pervasive sins of society.

In brief, the nominal, conformist Christian in America needs fear no actual cross. Vague calls to take it up may be compounded merely of hypocrisy and illusion. One lesson ironically observes "how little we understand the world or Christ by sitting so comfortably beneath our crosses." Another writer on this theme notes that the Church is reduced to inanity when "It doesn't really mean anything more to us than a congenial group of friends with whom to worship casually when the weather is not too bad."

8. PR37,656:41 (my italics).

*The Enemy Within*

Seeking as it does a religion of comfort, conformity, popularity, and success, nominal Christianity has become irrelevant to the crucial ethical issues of our time, and this development is more feared by the neo-orthodox than any outside threat to the existence of the Church. "The sharpness of decision for which a man is willing to die is a discomfort far removed from our comfortable church pews," observes the writer of a lesson on "Why Did the World Hate the Church?" His point is that "today's study of the [ancient] persecution of Christians under Roman rule faces us with a disturbing question: 'Is a Christianity that does not know persecution and misunderstanding a real and serious Christianity?'" The reply is no. The far greater threat to a real and serious Christianity is a Christianity that has so little connection with the deep, controversial problems of today that it arouses no opposition. Therefore, there is little need for pointing a finger at outside groups in order to identify the enemy, for the real enemy is within. As one editor puts it, "What frightens church leaders most is not the strength of the opposition outside the churches, but the weakness of the members within."

This weakness of the members within consists in giving their primary loyalties to the approved structures, institutions, and ways of a culture rather than to God. Such an accommodation to culture unilluminated by the biblical perspective is held to lead not merely to acquiescence in subtle and pervasive forms of evil in society, but also to the incorporation of those very evils into the life of the churches. Only a church that is made into the image of the world in which it lives could become fashionable and popular:

> The Church today often reflects within its own corporate life the standards of the nation. More often than not, churches perpetuate racial segregation and even discrimination. The Church cares too much about its own privileges and possessions and "good name" in the community and too little about the Kingdom of God. It seldom sees itself or the nation under the judgment of God, and it turns a deaf ear to those who would uncover the skeletons in its closets.          (PR37, 656:41)

Taking careful note of the ways in which the Christian minority directly challenged at its heart the pagan culture of the Roman world, thus arousing the opposition of both the righteous moralist and the sensualist, one neo-orthodox lesson measures this witness over against that of the Christian Church of today. The comparison is not favorable to the latter, which is seen to be so uncritically submerged in the cultural values that it has become insensitive to many obvious wrongs!

> We cannot study this struggle [between the Christian and pagan society in the Roman Empire] without asking ourselves where these sharp tensions between a church that obeys its Lord and the society in which it exists are to be seen in our own age. Does our society, not only in its sensuality but also in its idealism, feel that the Church is in some similar fashion an intolerable challenge to peace of mind?        (PR37,500:38)

The point is not that the Church should seek out some occasion to give offense, particularly to the non-Christian in our society. One author clarifies the neo-orthodox intent by saying:

> The lack of tension between the Church and our society should be a sign to us that our Lord, whom we and the world crucify, cannot be obeyed by a Church that fears to offend the world more than it fears to desert its Lord. Christians cannot be content to think no different thoughts about the issues of our common life than are found in every newspaper. And if, in the face of popular evils, they choose to remain silent rather than to suffer in protest, it will be only at the price of bringing down upon us suffering far greater than they avoid. When even the prophets fall silent, God must destroy. The history of Israel in the Bible and the history of the German Church in our own times have no plainer lesson than that.                                  (PR37,500:39)

The neo-orthodox materials are concerned, then, on the one hand, to free the Church from bondage to the popular prejudices, animosities, and twisted values of the society in which it is located; and, on the other hand, to enable it to witness, positively and prophetically, against social evils in obedience to God. These concerns lead the writers to scrutinize carefully the Church's self-image as victim: either the Church does not suffer at all, or, if it suffers in America, it probably does so in judgment. Its greatest threats are found to be not from groups without but from the perversion of the Christian response to the gospel inside the churches—in sinful conformity to popular prejudices and antipathies.

### The Witness of the Church

The Church, then, is seen to face an uncomfortable alternative in the present situation: either to challenge the culture in the name of Christ and risk the resulting misunderstanding and opposition, or to face "judgment," i.e. the suffering that accompanies the shattering of the social order (and of the Church) upon the rock of God's righteous demands when the consequences of our actions —or inactions—have at last come full circle. The churches— deeply compromised by racism, anti-Semitism, nationalism, and ecclesiastical pride—already stand under judgment; but this pre- vailing condition is deemed a denial of the Church's true mission:

> The gospel of love was not delivered in Jesus Christ in order that his followers might use it to foster self-righteousness, encourage animosities, and justify public opinion. What is more characteristic of the Church's mission is that it must as a rule *run counter to the currents of popular opinion*. Just as Jonah in his day was compelled to challenge the narrow nationalism of his countrymen, so the Church of God in every generation must invite misunderstanding and even persecution. But even persecution is wholesome and redemptive as long as God's grace has been manifested.          (PR36,854:33)

In short, the Church that becomes "a mere echo of the world's way of judging and the world's way of speaking" perverts its calling and is "a source of confusion, of false ideas of God, of distorted moral principles—sometimes even of hatred and blindness and fear." One aspect of the imperative mission of the Church is to surrender its reluctance to act in faithfulness to what God presently requires of it and, if need be, to suffer for its stand.

Examples of this position are found in profusion in neo-orthodox materials, and lend themselves to no simple analysis. The self-images as victim are expressed in various motifs derived from the doctrines of God and of man. These motifs include the concept of the idolatrous, obedience to the Christ who shatters the social order, or such concepts of the Christian role as that of reconciler, as making a covenant witness, or as a Christ suffering with and for the oppressed.

(1) The concept of the idolatrous is raised in a lesson that invokes the victim image in recalling the conflicting claims of the Roman Empire and the Church as to the proper center of man's ultimate loyalties. The Christian brought before the magistrate could escape punishment simply by affirming that Caesar is Lord; this "would testify that he was a patriot, an obedient citizen." But instead a countless number of the faithful chose to make the contradictory affirmation that Christ is Lord and to declare that in consequence the Roman Empire itself also stood under God's righteous requirements and judgment. For this decision they gave their lives. Says the writer:

> So today we have our moments offered to us, not so dramatically, of course, and with no such penalty visited upon us if we confess Christ. But the issue is there. When the vicious remark is made over the coffee cups . . . do we speak out or keep silent? . . . For whenever men are threatened [by such prejudice and slander], we face *in them* the Lord, who said, "Whosoever will confess me before men, I will confess before my Father." [9]

The point of the lesson is that "there is no community on the face of the earth where it is easy to live as that kind of disciple." Therefore, while the Nazi and Communist totalitarianism may be openly hostile to the full expression of the Christian faith, and while in America this hostility seems to be absent, yet here as everywhere is to be found a similar subtle enemy in the culture. It is specifically noted that this enemy is not simply an enemy of the churches, or of Christians as such. It is the enemy of God and consists of all the

---

9. PR37,500:39. Note that to "confess Christ, before men" is the actual response of the whole Christian man to the actions of others in a specific situation in the light of God's redemptive action—in this instance to the defamation of other groups. It is not simply a verbal affirmation of a theological formula, but a response to the hidden Christ in one's neighbor.

idolatrous forces of our society which subtly coerce us to conform pervasively to its demands:

> This same [brutally hostile] world is present also where we live, more courteous perhaps toward the Church, but at a thousand points exerting a pressure that discourages Christians from being definite and outspoken in their Christian witness. Jesus warned us that the Kingdom always meets resistance from men.                              (PR37,500:54)

(2) The motif of convenant witness enters into this self-portraiture in several ways. The biblical story is interpreted as that of a chosen people of the covenant who repeatedly tried to "be normal, that is, to be like other nations, to get out from under their peculiar providence." Like ourselves, they did not wish to pay the price of pain and opposition required of the living witness to the one God. Yet, "the Hebrew knew that God's history is never free from pain" and that the elect are called to live out its pages. Like those who would prefer to stay in Babylon, Christians are tempted to lose their identity and calling in the anonymity of the crowd. Asks the writer,

> Why hide from God? Because God is a terrible taskmaster. Psychologically, the Hebrew understands with most of us that survival depends upon being inconspicuous. He who hides in the mob, who never volunteers for committees, who leads no patrols, who, in brief, remains an ordinary sort of person, will live longest and receive least criticism. (We shall not forget, of course, that the safest refuge from God is always the pale gray of conventional religion.) [10]

The writer shows how "we also know something about this feeling of wanting to be left out of God's plan for the redemption of history." The early twentieth-century concerns for social justice, peace, the overcoming of poverty, unemployment, and prejudice have somewhat faded, because "under the threat of investigations and attacks from both the right and the left, men began, quietly and disconsolately, to forsake their common dream." Their courage collapsed; men tired of disappointments, of watching their hopes die.

10. PR, *Crossroads* (Jan.–Feb. 1959), p. 30.

And though a world "waits to be redeemed, children to be loved, the hungry to be fed, and the naked clothed," and mankind freed "from pride and prejudice," yet the Christian's reaction is apt to be, "Who wants to be a sucker? Better to till our ground, build our barns, and walk along the Euphrates. Better to join our country clubs . . . and buy our Jaguars."

But the neo-orthodox are convinced that the Bible shows us that God does not discard us or leave us alone. He pursues us and destroys "our laziness and shabby hopes. He remakes our spines and hearts. He sets us out on the front line. And perhaps, beneath our fawning about conspicuous comfort, we yearn most of all for this conspicuous renewal." This renewal "may mean, quite literally, hell":

> What if we should be required to sacrifice our middle-class lives, with all their easy securities? Renewal could mean that we would be shattered, lonely, and like Jeremiah, repudiated by every decent citizen. It could mean that we would share with our Lord his agony, his Godforsakenness. It might mean that we should, for Christ's sake, become homeless and help-less . . . [forgetting] purse and security.[11]

(3) The motif of Christ the disturber frequently appears as another constituent of the neo-orthodox analysis. In contrast to the idyllic picture of Jesus meek and mild, this curricula paints him as "the one who has raised our fundamental questions, the source of ferment and turmoil in the world." His teaching, "far from being a simple guide for our conventional moral behavior," instead "criticizes it and very nearly destroys it." This concept is not limited to Jesus' teachings but is extended to God's continuing activity in the world: Christ is "the Lord of history," the true God who bends history to His purposes, bringing down kingdoms and powers, and exalting those of low degree.

What has this concept to do with the image of the suffering Christian? According to the neo-orthodox view, it prevents him from sitting back in his easy chair. As a covenanted people, they believe that God throws the Church back into the stream of history whenever it seeks to hide from Him. "With Judaism, we too

11. Ibid., p. 30.

want God to be on our side, to do away with our enemies, and to baptize our every effort with success." But his call is "to *spend* ourselves for the sake of the world." Obedience to God, therefore, requires that the elect take upon themselves an intensified responsibility for the world in the light of a constant sensitivity to God's activity in it, a responsibility that may involve suffering as God's servants at the hands of sinful men.

Several propositions are involved in this analysis. (a) Although man seeks a comfortable place of safety, God calls him to take the risks of involvement in the world. (b) God continuously breaks up the pattern of the sinful social order, and this in itself precipitates conflict and suffering for the innocent and victim alike. (c) Those who acknowledge their covenant relationship but seek to escape responsibility will suffer; but if they are obedient, they also will suffer for the sake of God's righteousness.

(4) The prospective victim is also often conceived, in the words of Luther, as giving "myself as a sort of Christ to my neighbor as Christ gave himself for me." Being a Christ to one's neighbor means that one serves him in love, not saying "I love you" but expressing love by his actions. This service is uncalculating, given to anyone in need without thought of recompense and without any regard to its cost. The frequent analogy to the cross implies that this kind of service invites hostility. True service to the neighbor may threaten and rebuke the approved social codes of a community or nation, since it means crossing of the cherished social barriers it has erected against the despised, rejected, or down-trodden. Though the neo-Reformed see a danger in comparing our "little crosses" with Christ's cross and instruct that we must not equate them, nevertheless the command to take up the cross is plain.

Another way in which to view this same idea is to recall the neo-orthodox stress upon the unconditional identification with the neighbor. Differences in race, nationality, religion, ethnic origin, or class status are not to diminish but to increase one's concern for the neighbor's predicament. At this point the otherwise seemingly incompatible Christian roles of being a reconciler as well as a cross-bearer impinge directly on the plight of others.

Identification with the neighbor means that the Christian must share the burdens of other groups who experience discrimination, segregation, unequal opportunity, and abuse. He cannot bear these in exactly the same way as does the member of a minority group. If he happens to be a white man, he cannot escape the consequences of his whiteness. As a Caucasian, he is permitted to live where the Negro is excluded; but he can also try to meet his neighbor, to understand his condition, to labor for his fair opportunities to work, live, play, and worship. By fighting for the rights of the oppressed, by treating them as equals, by associating with them, and by resisting the subtle exclusions of his own groups, he becomes to some extent a target of the same resentment and hatred directed to the minority groups. He must be willing to suffer the onus inflicted on the minority, to become a victim on behalf of the victims. No Christian can, in this view, really bear his cross in twentieth-century America without taking upon himself the consequences of the sins which wreak havoc upon the Negro, the Jew, the outcaste, and the "stranger within our gates."

The Christian life, then, involves conflict with the world, and "those who are the world's" will be offended. Asks one writer, "Is the Church the conscience of the nation? If so, it must speak to the problems of our times, even if it treads on a few toes. If the Church is silent on social questions, then the painful victory has been lost." This witness is not a matter of belligerency, group pride, or self-assertion, since it is intended to speak from no ingroup standpoint but primarily about what God is doing in the events that befall the nations. Those who do so are not apt to be very popular, but the neo-orthodox are asked not to shrink from facing the reality that "no social progress is possible without controversy. No improvement is ever adopted without first facing trial by opposition . . . Conforming majorities do not ordinarily deal kindly with innovating minorities." [12]

## The Merging of the Self-Image of Victim and Victimizer

While in the neo-orthodox curriculum there is a clear assumption that Christians ought to be an oppressed minority, they are never unqualifiedly identified as such. For, although the Christian must resist the oppressor, he cannot do so as one who assumes that

12. This excerpt from the Presbyterian curriculum is a quotation from *The Church in Community Action* (New York, Abingdon-Cokesbury, 1952), p. 72.

he is entirely free from the evils he opposes. The neo-orthodox direct the learner to see the tensions between society and the Kingdom of God, but also to see that the Christian occupies a place in both. His danger is that he will not see this tension, but, in an uncritical and self-righteous manner think of himself as wholly standing within the Kingdom as though he were free from the world's evils. That is where it is said he ought to be standing according to the counsels of God; but since all men are disobedient, the Christian is judged along with society—therefore the neo-orthodox stress on the need for the Christian's continual self-criticism while, at the same time he witnesses to the reality of the Kingdom in the world:

> Considerations of the above questions [tensions between Church and State, e.g. nationalism, communism] might make for self-righteousness and pride unless we do some self-examination. This will be more difficult to discuss, and *it may be that the young people* [in the church school] *have been so reared that they see no tensions* between following Christ and being an American according to some present-day notions of Americanism.                                    (PR37,655:35)

This advice to the teacher envisions the Christian teacher and student as blinded by their culture and not as persons who, ipso facto because they are Christians or attend church school or belong to a church, are disliked for their assumed "witness" to the Kingdom in the perennial tension between the world and the Kingdom. The lesson addresses itself to those who to some degree have accommodated to the status quo, who have internalized idolatrous loyalties, yet whose will is to serve God in loving obedience.

A writer points out how the idolatrous pressures of the time and the Christian principles which contradict them find their lodging in the very same persons. As a result of a discussion on race relations, a church young peoples' group had unanimously agreed that "discrimination because of race, color, money or position was unchristian." Yet, adds the lesson writer, "in a school club that very same week several of these same young people voted against including a Jewish girl in their group." Their excuses in excluding the Jewish girl were that her admission might in some way demand of themselves some sacrifice of popularity and invite outside criticism or snubbing. The incident evokes this comment:

> Often it would be difficult for those of us who are the Christians in a community to be in any way distinguishable from the non-Christian population . . . most of us do not sacrifice very much because of our Christian faith . . . That following Christ might tend to isolate us from some friends, might antagonize some people in our communities, might give us a reputation of being a bit different—hence queer— would come as a surprise.[13]

Several incidents of such social isolation of Christians by others appear in neo-orthodox lessons. During a dinner party the host remarked that "the only good Asiatic is a dead one." One of the guests took issue with this opinion and, as a result, was dropped from the host's guest list. A civil rights' discussion in a church youth fellowship stirred up community controversy. Many of these young people were vilified for their stand, even by their own parents. An outstanding illustration, however, is one which could be provided by many a community:

> A young couple bought a house and moved into a suburban community of new, small, modern homes. Soon after they had moved in, a committee of these new home owners came around calling on them to sign a paper which was a neighbor-hood agreement never to sell their house to a Jewish family. The young couple refused to sign, much to the surprise of the committee. "Why not? Everyone else has done so!" The couple stated simply that they did not think it was the Christian thing to do. Thus in their new home in this area they were immediately ostracized and felt very much alone. Yet most of the people who had signed belonged to churches in that community.[14]

The victim image is here shaped to the requirements of prophetic self-criticism. *The total self-image is both that of a victim obedient to God and that of an oppressor disobedient to God. It is not a*

13. PR, *Counsel* (Feb. 13, 1955), p. 43.
14. Ibid.

portrait of an innocent and righteous Christian community beset by guilty and ungodly outside communities, but a group which is both obedient and disobedient to its Lord, and therefore both sufferer and afflicter.

These paradoxes prevent the neo-orthodox writer from picturing himself in such a manner that the non-Christian must bear the whole onus of prejudice. Not only is the Christian himself beset by the sins against which he witnesses, but the non-Christian also may give a witness within the Kingdom in this area of social concern:

> the fact that even though a Christian must take his stand and sometimes go against the crowd because of his Christian faith, he does not do so in a spirit of condemning the other person, but because he knows it is . . . in the end the only way to do God's will. *Then, too, many so-called pagans stand with them to support what is right.* In other words, in taking our stand as Christians, we should never do so in a superior and self-righteous way.[15]

The peril of self-righteous group pride and moralistic condemnation of outsiders is consequently mitigated both by the knowledge that Christians are sinners (and therefore tempted to prejudice and self-exalting pride) and by the awareness that if Christians do experience scorn for their stand on a crucial ethical issue, they are not alone in doing so. All who depend upon God are seen at the same time as both capable and not capable of righteousness: Because the Christian is capable and through no merit of his own included in the Kingdom, his "oughtness" is perfect obedience. Because he is not capable, and because he is also in the world, he must live in constant self-examination and continual repentance. This self-understanding involves a sense of the tension not only between God's objective Kingdom and the actualities of the world but also between the Kingdom and the world as they exist both within the Christian and the life of the Church. These polarized conceptions must always be seen together in order to understand how neo-orthodox materials are able to portray the Christian both as a victim (within the Kingdom over against the world) and as

15. Ibid., p. 44. Cf. *Crossroads* (April–June 1954), p. 31.

a victimizer (within the world that is in conflict with the Kingdom).

## CONCLUSIONS

The problem with which the four communicators struggle in these self-portraits is essentially the conflict between what H. Richard Niebuhr called Christ and Culture. From different points of view, although not always explicitly, they address one question: how to act and speak in obedience to God rather than to the norms of the society in which they live. They all give expression to the conviction that those who challenge and contradict the accepted ways may in some sense suffer; each group, therefore, regards itself as a victim in respect to its peculiar response to the problem of culture. The liberal feels rejected by those who resent pioneering in new ways and ideas; the conservative senses a hatred against him for preserving and preaching the gospel in its truth and purity; the fundamentalist expects hostility for his separated witness, and the neo-orthodox for challenging the cultural idols in obedience to the present action of God in history.

The fundamentalist and conservative protests, however, are primarily internal and individualistic rather than social. Their victim roles are described without relation to the intergroup issues which Christians face in contemporary society. Therefore the phenomena of discrimination and prejudice (judged as sinful by both communicators) are not explicitly discussed as aspects of the world against which they give witness, and consequently do not get into their picture of the Christian as victim.

The neo-orthodox curriculum is much given to social analysis, and the intergroup aspects of the Christian witness are constantly kept in mind. This is seen, for example, by the fashion in which the nonvictim as well as the victim roles for Christians are conceived. The fundamentalist nonvictim image is made up of acknowledgments that Christians in our society do not have to contend with persecution and that some Christians who are disliked are not necessarily suffering for Christ's sake; these observations are anti-ethnocentric in import but are not specifically directed toward intergroup questions. The neo-orthodox Christian, however, sees not only that as a nominal member of a favored religion he runs no risk of persecution but also that his main risk is accommodation to the prejudices of a culture in which segregation and discrimination bulk large. In this respect he is encouraged to assume responsibility for these wrongs and to acknowledge that God's judgment upon himself and his own groups for acquiescing to them is just. The positive intergroup implications of this position are noteworthy.

Even more importantly, the neo-orthodox teachings also clearly articulate a view of their own group as potential or actual victim in such a way as to provide it with a powerful anti-ethnocentric thrust. Their call involves the sharing by everyone, including the nominal majorities, of the plight of minority victims—the Christian being urged to bear the stigma of those whom the world rejects, discriminates against, and segregates, by defending the victims and giving them succour. Thus the ingroup member is led to sympathize with persecuted people everywhere and to allow himself to be persecuted on their behalf.

Perhaps at no point is a contrast more dramatically discernible in Protestant church school materials than in the basic assumptions of the liberal and neo-orthodox curricula as to what the responses of men will be to the intergroup aspects of their witness. Liberals most generally assume that the anti-ethnocentric approach they advocate will make for increasing social harmony and tranquility; therefore the prominence of a liberal nonvictim image—the liberal palm branch is most often envisaged as being grasped by a friendly hand across the barriers. The neo-orthodox, on the contrary, assume that their anti-ethnocentric approach must of necessity anticipate misunderstanding, resistance, and hatred; it will create fissures and tensions in the social structure at crucial points of struggle in human life. When these rifts are healed, new and unpredictable issues will arise, each of which will invite the antagonism of those who make idols of their own groups against those who obey God.

This contrast is not, of course, absolute. If the liberals stress the friendliness of other groups, they also see that the prophets of every age are being resisted by their contemporaries. However, the implications that the liberal must or will suffer because of this are very indirect. Unlike the neo-orthodox, the liberal materials do not call for martyrs in behalf of an intergroup ethic that must tragically fight its way into the life of the world against the opposition of those who live on the level of a generally accepted goodness; what is asked for are brave thinkers who dare to break new paths to larger and more universal concepts of truth. For this they may—and do—suffer some exclusion, if only from those Christian gatherings where cooperation proceeds on the basis of theological principles the liberals cannot accept.

It must be noted, also, that Protestant materials nowhere explicitly set forth the image of their own groups as victim as a pretext for hating or persecuting the enemy. Even the conservative materials say that the Christian's proper response to those who despise him is to turn away from them. The response of the victim to the oppressor recommended in fundamentalist materials is even more explicit. The fundamentalist is strictly forbidden to compound the evil of being hated by reciprocating hatred. God will judge the oppressor, and judgment is not the prerogative or the proper activity of the Christian. The scriptural imperatives not to resist evil and to humble oneself before persecution are taken seriously. The question of justice to the Christian must be left to God, and it is entirely "unnecessary for His children to waste their energies combating personal injustices." The Christian must defend the Jew, but he cannot defend himself. His only defense is in preaching the gospel, which in the fundamentalist view will correct the social evils, "such as oppression of the poor or discrimination against Christians," that grow out of "personal unbelief and rebellion against God." The fundamentalist's response to persecution is thus intended to be quietistic; to seek justice for himself is a denial of his commitment to a role of patient, unretaliatory suffering for the sake of calling men to Christ.

Many elements in the Protestant picture of itself as victim are thus seen to reflect the "incompatibility between the cross and the stake." Neo-orthodox writers reinforce this incompatibility by incorporating other clear anti-ethnocentric features which studies have shown are associated with a lack of prejudice: Unlike the ethnocentrics, the neo-orthodox ally themselves with the weak, i.e. those without power, rather than with the strong. They champion the victim rather than the oppressor. They entertain a conscious noninstitutional view of themselves—seeking not to save the life of the Church but to spend it unconditionally and without regard for consequences. Proclaiming an election faith rather than an institutional faith, they intend to risk the life of the Church by a nonconformist role and a maximum involvement in the life of society:

An obedient Church is a congregation of believers who live under the cross. It is a servant remembering at all times that Jesus Christ "came not to be ministered unto, but to "minister" (Matt. 20:28). It seeks out the hungry, the lonely, the miserable, the disinherited, and the sick. It is a Church that identifies itself with a godless, sinful and rebellious world, and yet refuses to conform to its methods and its commands . . . When the Church lives under the cross, it is a suffering Church. . . . the Church in America . . . is called upon to enter the struggle for racial equality, economic justice, political righteousness, and international understanding. Furthermore, a Church that lives under the cross is never static or secure in the world. It lives always on the boundary line of insecurity . . . It is ever alert to the call of God to strike its tents and move forward to unknown places. When the Church lives under the cross, one does not think of its churches as fortifications where Christians find comfort, security, and release from this world's trials. . . . The command of Christ is not to seek a safe place where we primarily indulge in beautiful worship services, celebrate the sacraments, evolve new liturgies, and edify ourselves with carefully prepared sermons. Let all these functions have their due place, keeping in mind always that the first command to the Church is to "go" to be "my witnesses," to "preach the gospel to the whole creation," to "take up the cross and follow me." Let the Church struggle against principalities and powers of darkness.        (PR37,146:32)

# 6. Images of Outside Groups as Oppressors

In the previous chapter we discussed the several ways in which Protestants do or do not see themselves presently as victims; it remains to examine how the various non-Protestant groups are depicted as either their actual or potential oppressors, both in the past and in the present. Oppressor images derive from the memories evoked by group histories and the interplay of current social roles. Almost all denominations have suffered persecution, and their own experiences in this regard, as well as of those of Christians generally during the first four centuries of the faith, still affect their teaching tradition. It is inevitable that the earlier struggles between religious groups should be discussed in Protestant literature because it is in the nature of a religious group to define and justify its reason for existence. Furthermore, many Protestants today live in hostile circumstances in nominally non-Christian countries, and nations under communist domination restrict and persecute Christians and Jews alike. Finally—as noted earlier—scriptural teachings contribute to the Protestant's image of himself as one who must bear hatred and misunderstanding, and this image, once evoked, is likely to encourage the writer to name specific enemies. Hence there are two leading questions that need to be answered in specific ways: Who are these enemies as Protestant curricula see them, and in what manner are the roles of these oppressors described?

Of all the contemporary non-Protestant groups, Roman Catholics and the Catholic Church emerge as the most hostile or threatening to three of the four communicators, the exception being the liberal (Unitarian), in 2 to 23 per cent of the lessons mentioning Catholics.[1] The least negative of these scores belong to the neo-orthodox (Presbyterians). The liberals do not see themselves victimized by

1. Analytical Cat. 12, Figs. 25 and 26, Appendix VIII. The liberals have no contemporary negative scores for Catholics in this category.

any religious groups, while the neo-orthodox show a similar attitude toward all contemporary non-Catholic religious groups. The fundamentalists (Scripture Press) and the conservatives (Missouri Synod) alone picture all four religious groups as being to some degree antagonistic; both regard non-Christians and other Protestant denominations and sects as potentially greater threats at present than Jews and Judaism.[2]

This picture changes radically in one respect when Protestants deal with the history of Christianity and that of their own specific religious tradition within Christianity. The unfavorable attitudes of Jews to Christians in the past now become the most prominent and also the most negative in the fundamentalist and conservative literature.[3] The neo-orthodox writers view the Roman Catholic and the Jews as equally hostile in the past, but their scores in this category are significantly less negative than those of the fundamentalist and conservative curricula. The liberals deviate from this pattern; they envision the Roman Catholics as the former oppressor. In describing these past and current conflicts Protestant educators both affirm and explain the symbols of their faith. Thus Jews and Catholics are referred to in church school lessons when the histories of the two religions figure as part of Protestant development. On the other hand, since Roman Catholics present a challenge to Protestants in contemporary American society—which is borne out by the many differences, conflicts, and misunderstandings between the two religions—Roman Catholics are more likely to assume the role of actual or potential oppressor in present-day Protestant thinking.

## ATTITUDES ATTRIBUTED TO THE ROMAN CATHOLIC CHURCH

The most bitter struggles within Christianity took place in the sixteenth and seventeenth centuries. The enmity between Protestants and Catholics that resulted from the split within the Church can still be detected in the way Protestants currently portray the

2. The fundamentalist and conservative scores for non-Christians are −3.8 and −8.5 respectively; for non-Catholic Christians they are −4.8 and −3.2 respectively; for Jews they are −1.2 and −0.7 respectively.

3. Analytical Cat. 11, Figs. 27 and 28, Appendix VIII. The General Group Category mentions no specific contemporary group but does include many references to the hardships Christians faced in the pagan Roman Empire.

schism and characterize the Catholic opposition. The scars left by the Reformation struggle are still evident in the treatment Protestants give Roman Catholic attitudes and behavior toward them not only in the past but in the present. This is least evident in liberal materials, where present-day Roman Catholics are pictured as friendly and where past attitudes of Catholics to Protestants are portrayed as only slightly negative. Neo-orthodox writers, however, highlight both past and present Catholic opposition to Protestants and Protestantism, and a negative picture of Catholic attitudes toward Protestants is even more prevalent in fundamentalist and conservative literature. Of the latter two, the conservatives are the most intensely negative; they fail to acknowledge either that Protestants persecuted Catholics or that some Catholics helped and protected Protestants during various periods of history.

Liberal, neo-orthodox, and conservative curricula discuss previous Catholic reactions to Protestants mostly in lessons dealing with the Reformation. This is especially true of the liberal curriculum which deals with Catholic-Protestant relations largely in terms of the rise of Protestantism. The neo-orthodox portray Catholic attitudes unfavorably for the period of the Reformation schism and for those periods immediately preceding and following it, but they create a more favorable image of Catholic relations to Protestants in the era immediately preceding the twentieth century. However, following the turn of the century, the increase in Catholic power in America encourages neo-orthodox writers to call attention once again to the Catholics' earlier anti-Protestant tendencies.

The different ways in which the liberals and the neo-orthodox characterize Catholic reaction to Protestantism must also be seen as a reflection of their diverse religious orientations. The liberals, for example, are not seriously involved with the issues at stake in the Reformation other than the question of religious liberty. Liberals discount the importance of the theological controversy, blurring distinctions between the beliefs held by the Catholic and Protestant communities. On the other hand, the neo-orthodox place themselves squarely within the traditions of Luther and Calvin and feel that certain vital issues were involved in the Reformation conflict—not so much questions of individual liberty and of the right to deviate, which they consider unintentional fruits of the schism—as other issues central to the schism itself. These are seen to be (a) the nature and source of authority, and (b) the nature of the Church. For the neo-orthodox, the conflict was rooted in the issue of whether the Scriptures should serve as the guide to the reformation of the Church, or whether the Church was to regard itself as the sole judge of scripture and thereby escape the severe biblical judgments and correctives. For the neo-orthodox, any view of the Church which does not intrinsically provide for the Church's continuous reform and radically limit its powers is seen to threaten the liberty of the Christian man and society. Neo-orthodox writers remain more deeply committed to the reformation views than do the liberals and consequently are somewhat more disposed to emphasize negative Catholic feelings toward Protestant concerns.

In dealing with contemporary Catholic-Protestant relations, liberals are either conciliatory or disinclined to analyze the issues which divide Catholics and Protestants today. The problems which Catholics face in Protestant countries or Protestants in Catholic countries do not particularly concern them. The opposite is true of the neo-orthodox writers, who deal directly with these and other points of conflict between Catholic and Protestant communities.

The neo-orthodox portray Catholic attitudes in the eighteenth and nineteenth centuries as favorable, because they find that the Catholic-Protestant picture altered rapidly at that time. As the Protestants gained power in England, Scotland, and various parts of the Continent they, like other groups in society, became corrupted by power and misused it in suppressing deviates, heretics, and dissenters. The neo-orthodox are, in fact, highly critical of the Protestant reaction to other Protestants as well as Catholics as they trace the precarious development of those traditions which formed the basis for American pluralism, religious freedom, and the right to dissent. They discuss this era of expansion and power differently than they do the Reformation when Protestantism was a minority movement and had to resist the formidable opposition which sought to destroy it.

Some important distinctions need to be made about the Protestant portrayal of the Catholic group.[4] First, whether Protestants picture Catholics as either friendly or hostile to them, they can

4. See Analytical Cats. 1–4, Figs. 5–8, Appendix VIII. Cf. Cats. 11 and 12.

and do affirm the rights of Catholics and deplore any signs of prejudice toward Catholics. The conservatives are the only group which is silent in respect to Catholic rights and problems, except by the implications of their general declarations which affirm religious liberty for all men. This general finding demonstrates that it is possible to picture another group as the oppressor (or even as the purveyor of false doctrine) and still defend the rights and the social status of that group. Moreover, when Catholics are given credit for their positive attitudes toward Protestants, or when Protestants admit that they, in turn, have negative attitudes toward Catholics, it is easier for the lesson writer to develop a more constructive concern for the problems which Catholics face in our society.

Secondly, as the neo-orthodox scores show, a communicator may express serious misgivings about Roman Catholic attitudes toward Protestants and yet not find it necessary to portray Roman Catholics unfavorably on every count. The total impact of neo-orthodox teaching about the Roman Catholics is quite positive, and this indicates that a religious group may feel compelled to describe an outside group unfavorably in one respect or another, but still present a generally diverse and even favorable image of that group.

## The Catholic Church as an Oppressor in the Past

In their approach to this problem, the liberal and the neo-orthodox curricula are sufficiently self-critical to show how Protestants have been guilty of persecuting Catholics in much the same way that Catholics have persecuted Protestants. Up to a point, the characterizations of the dispute between the Reformation leaders and Catholic authorities in each curricula follow the usual pattern. In liberal material, for example, we read that John Eck made a "sharp and vindictive speech" condemning Luther at the Diet of Worms in 1521. "France was a strong Roman Catholic country and the church had its observers everywhere who were spying upon all possible heretics." The Jesuit order, contrary to the intent of its founder, became "involved in political schemes and intrigues." There are the usual factual episodes, told with some restraint, concerning Socinus, Michael Servetus, Wycliffe, Luther, Tyndale, Cranmer, Calvin, and many others. However, both of these faiths are equally capable of highlighting the excesses of which Protestants were guilty. For example, on his way to Worms to challenge Luther, the papal representative, Alexander, is pictured by a liberal writer as a man who has also been forced to experience dislike and scorn: "Innkeepers refused to put him up, bystanders cursed as he passed. He saw caricatures representing himself hanging head downwards from a scaffold." [5]

When the Protestants gained power and the city's high council proclaimed Geneva to be Protestant, "The Roman Catholic Mass was no longer observed in the churches. The four monasteries and the one nunnery had been closed. A religion that endured for centuries could not be destroyed overnight. There were still many who preferred to remain Catholic." The list of misdemeanors the Council voted to punish included "having images or sacred relics of any kind in the home or church, or saying that the Pope was a good man." Other Catholics, including the Irish, "resented the attempts of the English crown to compel them to accept Protestantism and to require the use of the prayer book in the English language." "By order of the Crown, Roman Catholic landholders in Ireland were driven off their lands and Scottish Presbyterian settlers were brought in to occupy the country."

The liberal lessons, then, do not say that hostility and oppressive tactics, even in the early years of struggle, were true only of Catholics. Moreover, there is some recognition that Catholic actions could also be explained by the temper of the times and by the approved principle of territorialism in the West:

> the accepted practice of that day in almost every European country [required] the people to accept the religion of their rulers. Since King Ferdinand and Queen Isabella were loyal Catholics, they believed it to be their duty to force the Roman Catholic religion on all their subjects.          (UN234:53)

The ability to present a self-critical, judicious account of the Reformation—which we note in the above excerpts from the liberal curriculum—is even more obvious in the neo-orthodox material. For example, neo-orthodox writers state that Luther's student friends "rioted and pelted the priests with stones" in Wittenburg. In that portion of Switzerland where other territories overlapped Zurich, "Catholics and Protestants began to treat each

5. UN323:24.

other with killings and burnings." "Geneva would not permit Catholics any more than Naples would permit Protestants." Rather than rest content with a description of how Queen Mary tried to bring England back to Roman Catholicism by unrelenting measures, an author says, "Then the Protestants suffered as the Catholics had done under her father."

Some strange language is used in another set of lessons to describe the events of these periods. One neo-orthodox lesson writer, in discussing the Diet of Worms, gives some dramatic play to the unexpressed thoughts of the participants: "The emperor frowned, and Luther's enemies were displeased . . . His [Luther's] enemies were furious." Yet even this account goes on to say that Luther had set himself up as "an avowed enemy of Rome," that he "blasted out in anger at his foes," and that, at the close of the Forty Years' War, "The Protestant and Roman Catholic Churches became equal" in Germany.

If Protestants are depicted either as returning hatred in kind or as initiating the challenge to the Church of Rome, Catholics are sometimes portrayed by the neo-orthodox as anything but hostile to Protestants. Makemie, the Presbyterian, found that "Catholic Maryland offered freedom of faith and safety to those oppressed by their faith, and many who rejected the Established Church of England made their way to Maryland." Another tendency is to take both Roman Catholics and Protestants to task for a common guilt:

> There have been many times when the Church has felt justi-
> fied in using the powers of the State to persecute those who
> did not believe in orthodox Christianity . . . Lest we be
> overly proud, let us also remember that both the Roman
> Catholic and the Protestant branches of the Christian Church
> have been guilty of this excess.[6]

But in the conflict between the Roman Catholic Church and the deviates there are particularly sensitive issues at stake for both sides. The neo-orthodox often state the case for the Reformation eloquently and at considerable length, while recognizing that the Catholic was attempting in his way to preserve the unity of Christendom. Obviously men do not expose themselves to death and

6. PR37,143:23.

destruction unless there are serious values they are trying to preserve. The practice of stating the case for both the Protestant
Reformers who maintained a principle that aroused scorn from the
Catholic Church and for the Catholic defenders of their faith is
a characteristic one for the Presbyterian curriculum.

Both the liberal and neo-orthodox accounts are based on historical research, usually written by experts in church history who
have a fairly balanced historical perspective. The neo-orthodox
accounts are also conditioned by their belief in the universality of
human sinfulness so that they take full account of the Protestant's
own pitfall of pride and arrogance. On the other hand, fundamentalist literature contains only incidental references to this same
conflict. Rather than the careful conclusions of the neo-orthodox
scholars, who bring to bear both the canons of their faith and the
findings of their research on the problems of the Reformation, one
finds in fundamentalist materials only fragmentary, spontaneous
recalls of the martyred apostles, or analyses of scriptural predictions
concerning the tribulations of the faithful:

> According to secular history, all of the apostles except John
> suffered a martyr's death. In the early centuries, under pagan
> persecution, thousands of Christians were put to death, and a
> thousand years later, during the popish persecutions, millions
> perished.[7]

Such phrases as "popish persecutions" and "Bloody Mary," it
should be said, are not typical of fundamentalist lessons. But it
should also be pointed out that none of the instances which portray
Catholics as hating or persecuting Protestants indicate that Protestants also persecuted Catholics, or that Catholics also were sincere
in feeling that serious issues were involved in the conflict.

The references which conservatives make to the same period of
Catholic-Protestant conflict combine a church-centered view of
history, intense dyslogisms, and vague attempts at balance and self-
insight. Conservative literature abounds with references to "the
papists," "the Romanists" (both synonyms for the Roman Catholic
faction in the dispute), "Bloody Mary," "the wily Pope," and "the
enemies of the Gospel." Some of the issues between the disputing
parties are oversimplified, e.g. "The Waldenses were said to be

7. SP779:8.

models of Christian behavior, but they were hated by the pope at Rome, because they refused to obey him." The Catholic-Waldenses conflict is given a more adequate treatment later on. The chief omission in these lessons, perhaps, has to do with the shattering impact of the Reformation on the Catholic Church and the consequent sufferings of Catholics as well as Protestants. During the reign of Mary, it is said, Thomas Cranmer and "many other Protestant leaders were put to death." But in the descriptions of the English Reformation which precede and follow Mary's enthronement, there is not the slightest hint that Catholics suffered terrible persecutions at the hands of Protestants.

The conservative characterizations are not entirely negative. Conservatives acknowledge that Luther won friends and supporters among Catholics along with enemies. Staupitz, Luther's onetime abbot adviser, "continued his interest in Luther" after Luther quit the monastery. A "kindly old monk" comforted Luther in pre-Reformation times and prophesied his future impact for the good of Christendom. Peter Waldo and his heretical followers are favorably pictured in the words of "a Dominican monk." And Dr. Eck, who published the papal bull against Luther's teachings, is described as having been "hated and ridiculed" by German Protestants.

## The Catholic as an Oppressor in the Present

Protestants have many ways of expressing their anxiety about present-day Roman Catholic attitudes toward them. Even the liberals, who picture Catholics as predominantly friendly, indirectly express certain misgivings about the implications of the Church's teachings. The neo-orthodox are more explicit; though they usually picture the attitude of individual Catholics toward Protestants as a friendly one, they regard the position of the Catholic Church as somewhat hostile to Protestantism. However even in these contexts the neo-orthodox writers make critical references to Protestant action toward Catholics.

Mention of present-day Catholic attitudes toward Protestants occurs in the liberal curriculum mostly in connection with recommendations that liberals visit Catholics churches (along with other Protestant churches, Jewish synagogues, and "meeting places of Buddhists, Moslems, Hindus and others"). Students are told, for example, that Catholic priests, Protestant ministers, and Jewish rabbis "alike would welcome to their offices by appointment any group of interested young people who cared to ask them questions about the meaning of their rituals," and would also "welcome considerate visitors to any service of worship."

Several of the liberal references raise questions about possible prejudicial attitudes on the part of Catholics toward non-Catholics, but these are noncommittal. One lesson suggests that the class informally dramatize a situation that has been thought through by the class which has an element of conflict in it. After the situation and characters are decided upon, the actors are to talk briefly about how to present their spontaneous drama. Following the performance, the actors are told to describe how they felt in their roles, and the entire group is to join in a general discussion. One such example of a suitable situation is as follows:

> A Roman Catholic young person tries to persuade a friend of the value of becoming a Roman Catholic, expressing sincere concern about his not being a member of the only church instituted by Jesus Christ for the salvation of mankind. What will the friend reply? Can he disagree without offending the Roman Catholic? How does the Roman Catholic feel toward those who, he believes, cannot be assured of salvation?
>
> (UN289:12–13)

In explaining Catholic Canon Law, the Church's attitude toward mixed marriages and the education of children is described quite objectively. Only one sentence suggests that there is something besides mere difference of opinion in the relation between the two faiths. "The points at which the average Protestant is apt to come in conflict with this 'Code of Canon Law' are in its legislation regarding mixed marriages and the education of children" born of such marriages. This is the closest this curriculum gets to the subject of Catholic-Protestant tension. In a completely different context, which describes how a Protestant, the son of the pastor of an orphanage school in Naples, is "elected mayor by a large Catholic vote," we find one of the few references to the favorable political support Protestants get from Catholics.

An extreme contrast to the liberal view is that of the conservatives, which is completely negative in its portrayal of Roman Catholics.

They hold that in its teaching "the Roman Catholic Church has officially pronounced a curse upon everyone who says that a man is justified only by faith without good works." They also state that "the Papists are out to make America Catholic," and they stress that there is persecution of Protestants in Catholic countries: "Contrast the United States and Canada with Spain, where Protestants are still persecuted by the Romanists."

The majority of these references concern Catholic expansionist efforts and persecution of Protestants, and they usually come up in discussions of the rights, liberties, and civic duties of Christians. Here the issue involved is that of the separation of Church and State, and the discussions also criticize Reformed denominations and sects whose activities and attitudes they see as a threat to the liberties of the nation. Indeed, the names of the two groups are frequently linked together in conservative materials: "Point out that neither the Catholics nor some Reformed bodies wish to keep Church and State separate. Show what influence and power they have in politics. Catholics seek to get state support for their parochial schools . . ."[8]

It should be noted that in this category conservatives picture all religious groups in the same negative way. Non-Christians and Jews, however, are exempt from the charge of threatening civil liberties, because the conservative writers are concerned specifically with defining the proper role of the Christian Church in society and not that of the synagogue or the Buddhist temples. Therefore they address their own constituency with regard to what they consider to be proper and improper conduct for the Church as a divinely appointed institution. The only proper function of the Church, they feel, is to preach Law and Gospel, and this Law is not civil (which is within the ordained sphere of the state) but moral and ceremonial.

The conservatives also believe in the natural Law, and their objections to Catholic action can also be understood as following from this belief. Government, they say, should acknowledge and

8. MS39,548:27. The Missouri Synod prefers the phrases "Lutheran bodies" or "Lutheran" to describe the sphere of Christianity to which it belongs. Roman Catholics, Greek and Orthodox Catholics, and "Reformed bodies and sects" are their usual classifications for outside Christian groups. "Protestant" is sometimes used in place of "Reformed," and when used in this way the former term signifies non-Lutheran, non-Catholic groups.

respect, as does a democracy, "the rights which all men have by nature; it does not confer these rights, because God has given them." The Church is defined as a spiritual kingdom, and is forbidden to seek or exercise civil power. Luther's dictum that the Scriptures ordain that the State must rule by law and enforce it even "by the sword"—and not, in theocratic fashion, seek "to rule the world in accordance with the Gospel and Christian love"—is the source of the conservative's Church-State distinction: The State must not interfere with the spiritual activities and liberties of the Church; the Church, in its turn, must not interfere with the State. The Church has a right to instruct its members in civic duties and public issues, but it has not the authority to take direct action in influencing legislation. In assuming this authority it may be tempted to use the State to restrict the conscience and the freedom of non-Christians. Protestant—that is, non-Lutheran churches—are severely criticized on this score: "Some of the Reformed churches have been trying to force a theocratic form of government upon our country, e.g., by means of blue laws, Sunday legislation, prohibition amendment." Just as the state has no right to dictate what a person should believe in his heart or what a church may teach or to "pass laws which hinder or favor a particular church body," so too it is "wrong when churches meddle as busybodies in the affairs of the state, when they tell a government what laws should be passed, or demand that the state support their work and teachings." [9]

In the conservative view the violators of the civil liberties in America are usually the "Reformed" and Catholic churches, and "Roman Catholic countries" are held to be the principal violators of these freedoms outside the United States. A "church state" (controlled by a church or churches) is thought to be even worse than a "state church" (a church controlled by the state), and both Roman Catholic countries and Reformed sects are indicted for the

9. Ibid., pp. 25–28. Among violations of the principle of Church and State cited in conservative Lutheran literature are opening of legislatures with prayer, the reading of scripture in the public schools, teaching religion in public schools, Sunday "blue laws," prohibition of sale of liquor, Sunday closing laws, laws prohibiting parochial schools, forbidding use of a foreign language in church services, state financial aid to parochial schools, appointing an American representative to the Vatican, etc. Cf. MS39,546:14; MS39,548:24,25; *Concordia Bible Student, 41*, No. 4 (1952), 19-20.

former kind of tyranny. However, present-day persecution of Protestants and others by Catholics in Catholic countries is contrasted with the freedoms enjoyed by religious groups in certain Protestant countries, such as the British Commonwealth, Scandinavia, and Switzerland.

Thus the Missouri Synod regards the Catholic threat to their values and relationships as being qualitatively different from the threat posed by the Reformed groups because of their closer theological tie with the latter; still the former church is pictured as the most formidable competitor of the latter in gaining political power as well as popular favor.

> Protestants have become much alarmed in recent years because of the growing power, influence, and arrogance of the Roman Catholic Church. The Reformed churches have discovered in the Roman Catholic Church a strong competitor for gaining popular favor and political power. Rome has spared no effort in strengthening its hold on America. It has more parochial schools, high schools, colleges, and universities than any other church body, and it uses these means to win the youth of our country. Catholic books, newspapers, and other literature are conspicuous in public libraries and find their way into the homes of thousands of Protestants. The Roman Catholic Church gets plenty of publicity in the movies and the public press. Its voice is heard whenever it objects to matters of political, social, and moral significance. The special representatives of the Pope wield tremendous power in this and in almost all other countries in the world. Rome threatens to become the same strong controlling force that it was during the Middle Ages. Protestants [the word is used here inclusively] should therefore be on their guard if they wish to preserve their liberty.[10]

Although the various Catholic positions on social questions are never described or analyzed, the conservative writers feel that the social implications of Catholicism (not merely the Catholic understanding of the nature of salvation) warrants the concern of non-Catholics. Thus one curriculum writer would not vote for a Roman Catholic, Mormon, or atheist for public office; his objection to

10. MS, *Concordia Bible Teacher, 16,* No. 4 (1955), p. 75.

such persons is that their religion would contribute to forms of legislation inimical to the state. However, he would vote for non-Christians, other than those indicated, if he thought them capable:

> Luther said a heathen with the necessary wisdom and ability is to be preferred as a ruler to a godly man who lacks the qualifications. A good Christian may not make a good official. To elect a man merely because of his creed shows poor judgment. However, *a Christian should not vote for persons whose religion makes them dangerous to the welfare of the state. Roman Catholics* are pledged to further the interests of the Pope above all other interests. Mormons, atheists, certain religious fanatics, Communists, and other radical groups are apt to endanger the welfare of the state.[11]

The fundamentalist portrayal of contemporary Roman Catholic attitudes toward Protestants deals exclusively with the relations of the two faiths in countries other than the United States. The Catholics in question live in those nations (a) where evangelicals have missionary work, and (b) where the Roman Catholic Church is the religion of the State. The descriptions of Catholic actions are unqualifiedly hostile and are made particularly vivid and broad. A number of lessons, for example, adapt the current expressions to designate Communist forms of forced isolation—e.g. iron or bamboo curtain—in describing Catholic strongholds as "purple" curtains of the Roman Church, which are used to wall off people from "the glorious Gospel of Jesus Christ."

Unlike the conservatives, who feel that Catholic power is a threat to civil liberties at home, fundamentalists are mostly concerned with Catholic hindrances to their missionary work, and their portrayal of Catholic hostility focuses on the experiences of those who proclaim an evangelical message in a Roman Catholic land. These current difficulties are related in connection with discussions of the persecution of early Christians; for example, a lesson of the stoning of Stephen begins with this account:

11. Ibid., *13*, No. 4 (1952), 51–52 (my italics). Note that non-Christians (excepting atheists and political radicals) and Jews are not included in this prohibited list. The only religious groups mentioned, other than Catholics, are Mormons and "certain religious fanatics." The statement that Catholics are "pledged to further the interests of the Pope" above all other interests is unsupportable.

An hour before dusk, in a village not far from Cochabamba, Bolivia, a truck pulled up in the market square and Norman Dabbs and eight native Bolivians prepared to hold an open-air meeting. They had scarcely begun when a liquor-inflamed mob of natives, urged on by a Roman Catholic priest, converged on them . . . Before the men of the mob staggered drunkenly away, Dabbs and seven native Christians lay dead around the truck amid a pile of stones.                  (SP956:137)

There are numerous such examples with the identical theme. A senior's manual features a half-page drawing of a group of Latin-Americans stoning an "Iglesia Evangelica" church during services. The title of the lesson is "Suffering for Christ." The places named in this group of lessons are, Latin America or Central America (mentioned 6 times), Spain (6), those behind the "Purple Curtain" (5), Colombia (5), South America (4), Bolivia (2). The following countries are each named once: Mexico, Venezuela, Portugal, Italy, and "European countries predominantly Catholic."

As in the illustration quoted above, a Catholic priest plays a dominant role in three of the incidents described. "The whole world knows," according to one lesson, "that Protestant Christians are severely oppressed in Spain, but it is hard to believe that these priests even refuse to put their necessary signature on the ration applications for babies born into Protestant families unless permission is given to baptize those babies into the Roman Church!" This illustration is given as an example of "what God's People [the Jews] will be subjected to in the Great Tribulation, when Antichrist has full sway in this world" (SP834:28). Another story is told of a missionary who was distributing religious tracts in a Mexican village; a Roman Catholic priest "deliberately walked up to each person who had received a tract, took the leaflets from the people, tore them into small bits, and threw them at the feet of the missionary." In this case, however, there is the added detail that in response to the friendly and conciliatory reply by the missionary, the priest's attitude was altered.

It is instructive to note the difference between the above treatment of Catholic persecution of Protestants in other lands and that given in neo-orthodox literature. The neo-orthodox statements, as a rule, are much milder, generally qualified by details, and also less numerous in the curricula. One reference, for example, begins with a corrective statement: "Present-day Roman Catholicism does not make use of the Inquisition. As an instrument of papal policy, the Inquisition gradually died out, and such a method would clearly be inexpedient in a world where Roman Catholicism is not the dominant world religion from the standpoint of power." The writer then goes on to say:

> But the Roman Catholic Church has never formally disavowed the principle behind the Inquisition. And although all Protestants know good Catholics to whom the idea of the Inquisition is as abhorrent as it is to Protestants, it is necessary to remember that officially the Church has never claimed that in principle the Inquisition was wrong. Less extreme expressions can be found today in Spain and Latin America of attempts to get rid of Protestants by force if they try to remain in communities which are predominantly Roman Catholic.     (PR37,675:36)

Neo-orthodox lessons frequently present the Catholic side of the question: "Spanish leaders feel that Protestant views are wrong, perhaps dangerous, possibly even subversive. To them it seems quite natural and right that people who hold such views should be kept under control and scrutiny." Most statements concerning Catholic hostility toward Protestants clearly distinguish attitudes which some Catholics hold from those which all hold. Much more frequently than in the other curricula, a distinction is made between the Catholic Church and Catholics.

Sometimes the priest is thought to be responsible for inculcating in individual Catholics a dislike of Protestants, as in the following story concerning the problems of mixed marriages. Kathy, a baptized Catholic, is engaged to a Protestant. Her mother, who is also Protestant, explains to her daughter's fiancé: "Kathy's Church has taught her that everything I believe is wrong. And she's come to think that I'm a little feeble-minded because I don't see things the Roman Catholic way." Kathy protests that her mother and she have never "talked religion." Her mother replies: "If I talked to you about my beliefs, I would be committing a mortal sin, 'perversion of children' I believe it's called." Kathy is struck with this point and confesses, "I've always listened to what Father Patrick said about people who weren't Roman Catholics, but I never realized exactly that my mother was one of the people he was talking about and that she's been very understanding and good and loved me terribly all the time. I've hurt her often, I guess" (PR37,372:134–35).

However, the real difficulty in intermarriage which this story emphasized is that of reconciling the requirements of two faiths: the Roman Catholic Church requires that the Protestant sign a prenuptial agreement which contravenes his own scruples, and it forbids the Catholic, under penalty of falling from grace, to make accommodations. "Protestants and Roman Catholic young people are neighbors and fellow citizens," the writer explains.

> They often attend the same schools and belong to the same clubs. Despite some very basic differences in their beliefs, they may be very close friends, and it is only natural that Roman Catholic and Protestant young people should sometimes fall in love and want to marry. At this point they encounter a very difficult problem. It would be hard enough if they were free to work out the problem in their own way. But they really have no freedom in the matter, because the Roman Catholic Church demands the right to determine every condition of the marriage.                    (PR37,372:134)

Thus the neo-orthodox clearly distinguish between the Catholic Church and its members; the latter may be friendly to Protestants, but the Church erects barriers to certain relations between members of the two religions.

The neo-orthodox also take up the question of a possible union between the two churches. Many Protestant young people, a writer observes, cannot understand why Catholics and Protestants can't get together in one church. "They have Catholic friends who are very nice people, so they ask if the [division between the two churches] isn't rather silly." The text then asks class members to divide into two groups representing those who wish to argue for a possible union of the two communions, and those who think this is impossible because of existing barriers. The latter "should try to state the Catholic position and show why this makes it unlikely that the two Churches can unite." The neo-orthodox position on this question is clearly stated in another course. At the Council of Trent, the Roman Catholic Church is said to have so defined its own position as to make reconciliation with Protestantism impossible:

> Yet in becoming adamant on the points of difference between us, at Trent the Roman Catholic Church built firmly the wall of separation that stands betwen the two greatest families of Christendom today. It is hard to see how there can be much accord between us, since the issues are fundamental ones on which Protestantism cannot dare to make concessions. Personal relationships with clerical and lay Catholics can be cordial and co-operative, but ecclesiastical realtionships are almost impossible.                                      (PR36,849:21–22)

However, while the "intransigency" of the Catholic position may be viewed as an impediment to reconciling differences and overcoming hostility on both sides, neo-orthodox writers are not content to leave the matter there. They show that misunderstanding and hostile feelings are true of Protestants as well. Protestants, they write, are obligated to understand the Roman Catholic faith; most important, they must realize that Catholicism is not a monolithic entity and that improving the attitudes between the religions "calls for the exercise of that great virtue—charity." They point out that "there are Roman Catholics who are urging this attitude upon their own brethren (see, for example, Karl Adam's *One and Holy*), and we must remind ourselves of our own duty in this regard. Both groups must try to understand each other elsewhere than simply in the field of battle. We must not be satisfied with cheap anti-Roman polemics, and we must ask our Roman friends not to be influenced by the violent anti-Protestant attitudes to which they are often exposed." In sum, the portrait of Catholicism as evil and hostile to Protestantism must give way to a more realistic and charitable picture:

> To many Protestants, Roman Catholicism seems like a vast and menacing network of evil, bent on stifling democracy and freedom and making us all the unwilling slaves of the pope at Rome. Now there are elements within Roman Catholicism that give the Protestant this impression, and where such an attitude

is clearly present, he must of course resist it. But how meager this is as a total and adequate picture of Roman Catholicism! And furthermore, there are Roman Catholics who would resist such tendencies as militantly as any Protestant. We do a great disservice to the cause of Protestant-Roman Catholic relations when we think of Roman Catholicism simply as a political power. It is never enough to read only what angry Protestant writers say about Roman Catholics. We would hardly feel that our own religious faith had been adequately explained to a Roman Catholic friend if he had read only the interpretation of an angry Roman Catholic writer.          (PR37,686:7)

But while they teach that not all Roman Catholics are "knaves and inquisitors" and many have been "genuine men of God," the neo-orthodox urge that charity be combined with firmness in dealing with Roman Catholicism. This firmness is particularly necessary in handling issues which Protestants regard as a legitimate threat to Protestant values. However, here too they emphasize that one must first attempt realistically to understand the Catholic point of view by studying Catholic writings and conversing candidly with priests who "meet gladly with Protestant groups to answer questions." In general, the writer suggests that "We must try to see it as a Roman Catholic himself would see it, as far as possible . . . Otherwise we condemn ourselves to constant misunderstandings and difficulties." [12]

Through discussion, then, the crucial points of divergence between the faiths become clearer and can be dealt with more objectively, without loss of firmness. Protestants are deemed right in objecting to the doctrine that the pope does not err when speaking *ex cathedra;* this attributes to a fallible human being (and to an institution) a characteristic that belongs only to God. Such a claim "for any human being is a mark of spiritual pride." The neo-orthodox insist "that the office of the pope does not by definition

12. PR37,686:8,9. A book by a Protestant explaining Roman Catholicism to Protestants is Winthrop S. Hudson, *Understanding Roman Catholicism* (Philadelphia, Westminster Press, 1959). Even more useful books are Jaroslav Pelikan, *The Riddle of Roman Catholicism* (Nashville, Abingdon, 1959), and Wayne H. Cowan, ed., *Facing Protestant-Roman Catholic Tensions* (New York, Association Press, 1960).

exempt the one who fills it from human imperfection in understanding the divine will." For neo-orthodox writers, the Catholic doctrines of the Church imply institutional forms of idolatry which have negative social implications—that is, such doctrines do not provide any built-in curb on the Church's powers and its tendencies toward self-aggrandizement.

In brief, while there is no uniform analysis by various Protestant groups of the presumed Catholic attitude toward them, Protestants feel that a vital conflict of values still exists between the two communities and that this conflict has significant ramifications for the future of American society. There is evidence, too, that the Catholic Church and Catholicism are, for some communicators, recognized as a legitimate part of America and American religious life, but, for others, the rising Catholic status in the United States seems unduly threatening. Protestant teaching materials reflect considerable tension between the Catholic and Protestant communities which may continue for some time to come. It is evident, also, that while some Protestant portrayals of the Catholic attitude are partial, selectively negative, and even monolithic, others give fuller play to the varieties existing within Catholicism and are much more objective in their portrayals of these diverse attitudes.

## Jewish Attitudes toward Christians

The Jewish faith emerges as the persecutor in accounts of the very earliest period of the Church, beginning with the life of Christ and continuing up to the Roman persecutions. Although there are some references to this hostility in lessons on the Old Testament, they make reference to New Testament events and are mostly related to certain key themes:

    a. The conflict betwen Jesus and the Pharisees
    b. The crucifixion of Christ
    c. The themes of rejection and unbelief
    d. The question of gentile inclusion in the early Church
    e. The conflict between Church and Synagogue

The New Testament makes evident that there was a bitter struggle between followers of the early Church and the Synagogue. In a Jewish commentary on the Gospels, Montefiore notes that the same spirit that makes martyrs of men can also transform them into persecutors once the victim rises to a position of power, as in the case of the Maccabean heroes. He then adds:

> . . . the readers of the Synoptics must be prepared, both in the words ascribed to Jesus and outside them, to find a reflection of circumstances and moods which fall within those seventy years [of early church history]. And prominent among those circumstances will be this, that the young Christian community suffered persecution from the Synagogue. Even while the early Christians of the Jerusalem community observed the ceremonial enactments of the Law, there was still enough difference to make occasional persecution highly probable. It must, moreover, be remembered that the first Christians were Jews, and while they claimed or desired to stay within the Synagogue, they must have been a constant source of irritation [to the orthodox]. A family quarrel is often the bitterest of quarrels.[13]

It is natural enough, considering the early Jewish hostility to the Church which scripture describes, that Protestants refer less favorably to Jewish attitudes to Christians when discussing the history of the early church and more favorably when discussing current Jewish attitudes. It should be noted, however, that statements concerning the present-day orientation of Jews to Christians are relatively few among the types of statements in Protestant literature which mention the Jew.

In their treatment of contemporary Jewish attitudes toward Protestants, the liberals and neo-orthodox are again the unambiguous positive scorers, neither one attributing to modern Jews hostile views toward Christians. Directly opposed to this is the conservative practice of always describing the modern Jewish attitude as antagonistic. Although the fundamentalists feel there is some evidence of an amicable Jewish relationship to Christians, they more often picture the Jew as hostile.

The really difficult problems for Protestants concern their depictions of the attitudes of biblical Jews to Christianity. Evidence for this are the large negative distributions and the preponderance of minus imbalances (indicating unfavorable Jewish attitudes) which can be found in Analytical Category 11 (which deals with the

13. Montefiore, *The Synoptic Gospels* (London, Macmillan, 1927), *1*, civ.

past) rather than in Category 12 (which concerns the present).[14] In discussing biblical events however, conservatives also offer a negative picture of both ancient and modern Jewish behavior toward Christians.

In evaluating these observations, we must point out once again that the biblical texts present certain problems for the neo-orthodox, conservative, and fundamentalist writers which the liberal writer is free to disregard. The liberal theological position does not require that a curriculum writer consider charges such as "rejection and unbelief"; nor is the liberal treatment of the New Testament such that a writer must deal with any of the biblical themes other than the conflict between Jesus and the Pharisees. The liberal curriculum dispenses with the Gospel of John, the Book of Acts, the Epistles, and The Revelation, and confines its New Testament commentary to the Synoptic Gospels. On the other hand, the theological position of the other Protestant communicators necessitate that they treat fully the entire scope of the New Testament; hence all the biblical incidents and sayings associated with the ancient conflict between Church and Synagogue come up for discussion. Statistically, then, there are considerably larger distributions for the biblical communicators in the analytical categories dealing with hostility-friendliness of Jews in the past than there are for the liberals. Once again, though, the imbalances indicate that it is not simply a dependence upon biblical sources which accounts for negative findings. For example, the neo-orthodox score for Category 11 is −.02, while the fundamentalist score is −.18 and the conservative −.19. The liberals, who are not burdened with analyses of many of the biblical themes show a small positive imbalance of +.005. The slight difference between the neo-orthodox and liberal scores may also be accounted for in part by the liberal treatment of the biblical text which allows for a broad interpretation and gives the writers considerably more freedom to ignore a potentially negative or relatively difficult episode or passage in the Gospels.

Many of the references concerning Jewish unfriendliness to Christians occur in discussing the life of Jesus in relation to his time. In analyzing these discussions we note that among the factors contributing to the more positive approaches of the liberals and neo-

14. Cf. graphs for Analytical Cat. 11 (Figs. 27, 28) with those for Cat. 12 (Figs. 25, 26), Appendix VIII.

orthodox is a readiness on the part of these communicators to acknowledge that Jesus was both popular and unpopular among his own people. He is said to have had his friends and loyal supporters and to have been listened to eagerly, although the people misunderstood his intention when they wished to crown him king. However, sooner or later most people were "offended" by Christ, and in the end he was abandoned even by the faithful. In addition, both the liberals and the neo-orthodox distinguish between the various groups which opposed or criticized Jesus, and they are less inclined to make generalizations about "the Jews." Rather, these Protestants tend to deal with the opposition Jesus experienced as a human rather than a Jewish tendency. The over-all result of this approach may be judged by consulting the scores for Category 11: most of the scores for both groups are balanced—that is, negative references are offset by positive ones.

The fundamentalist and conservative treatments of these same themes is marked by an inclination to emphasize the inimical qualities of the Jews in the biblical drama; these groups offer a preponderant number of negative statements which are not sufficiently offset by contradictory material, correctives, or parallel self-criticism. Exactly 54 per cent of the fundamentalist lessons mentioning Jews and scored in Category 11 were unqualifiedly negative; the same holds true for about 79 per cent of conservative lessons in this category.

An attempt was made in this study to discover whether a text which gives prominence to the hostility of an outside group toward one's own groups will negatively influence the other facets of the outgroup profile. A conservative textbook was examined which strongly stressed the hostility of Jews and Pharisees to Jesus, the disciples, and Christians. Comparing the analytical-category profile of this text with the curriculum as a whole, it was found that the single text was considerably more adverse by 67 percentage points than the total curriculum.[15] The imbalances for the various facets of the Jewish portrait ranged from 3 to 53 per cent more negative in the textbook that emphasized outgroup antagonisms. Jews were presented as being considerably more immoral and ungodly in this text, and Judaism was represented as teaching only false doctrine and as awaiting divine punishment. While these results do not

15. The curriculum imbalance, Jewish category, was —15.4; the textbook was —82.5.

establish that statements scored in the "hostility-past" category determine other kinds of statements about Jews, there is clearly some relation between the two.

Inasmuch as later chapters will take up in greater detail the attitudes of Jews toward Christians, some attention should be given here to the lessons about contemporary Jewish attitudes toward Christians which will provide a background for the ensuing discussions. In fundamentalist and conservative literature, references to modern Jews generally take the form of extrapolations of biblical themes such as those discussed above which are used to make inferences about modern Jewish attitudes. For example, the words of Isaiah, "He is despised and rejected of men (53:2)," evokes an image of the Jew as the despiser. "This was true of Jesus in His life on earth; and ever since that time His name and person have been the object of contempt. *Especially among the Jews, His name is spit at and those who confess Him are cursed.*" [16]

A fundamentalist Christmas lesson intended to demonstrate that Jesus is Israel's promised Messiah includes (under the heading "True Story") the charge that "an orthodox Jew today, brought up on the Old Testament alone, believes that the Messiah is yet to come. *The New Testament is forbidden literature to him.* The Jew is told all kinds of false tales about the Nazarene Jew, Jesus Christ . . ." The theme of Christ-rejection in a lesson on prophecy (again from Isaiah) is the occasion for the statement, "to this very day, the name of Jesus incites contempt and abuse from some Jews and Gentiles alike."

These excerpts illustrate by what they both include and omit that New Testament events can be so interpreted as to make them a focal point for all references to the past and present Jewish attitudes to Jesus, the Gospel, the Church, and the Christian. To so interpret New Testament events is to produce lessons which may have severe negative intergroup implications. Thus, despite the repeated assertions in fundamentalist literature that (a) the Church consists of Jews and Gentiles, (b) the early Christian movement was Jewish, (c) a Jew who becomes a Christian can and must continue to be loyal to his own people, and (d) the national community of Israel is collective while the Church consists of *individuals* who are called out from among the nations, the charge remains that "the Jews

16. SP39:54 (my italics).

rejected Christ." It would be more consistent if the fundamentalists argued that there is always a Jewish element within the Church, but that most Gentiles together with Jews have rejected Christ. To say that the Jews have rejected Christ is to imply an obvious untruth—namely, that the Gentiles have accepted him.

Notice that the comments depicting the adverse attitude of Jews toward Christ and Christians are suggested by scripture rather than based on conclusions drawn from empirical or historical studies. However, it is obvious that these conclusions about Jewish attitudes do not derive only from hermeneutical and exegetical requirements; the tone of these remarks about Jews also indicates an attitude acquired from both culture and tradition, and is only occasioned, not determined, by scripture.

## CONCLUSIONS

This analysis indicates that (1) the various groups within Protestantism have different conceptions of the same outsiders' attitudes toward them and their concerns, (2) each of the groups maintains that each of the non-Protestant groups, e.g. Catholics and Jews, hold different views of Protestantism. Jews, for example, are pictured by some as disliking or even hating Christians; however, there is nothing in Jewish life and thought which is presented by any of the faiths as a threat to the freedom of Protestants or as a design to weaken or crush it. Moreover, we note that the alleged negative attitude of Jews is largely exegetical and expositional in nature. The Protestant portrayal of Catholics, on the other hand, is marked by anxiety about the increased status and acceptance which Roman Catholics and Roman Catholicism in general enjoy in American society. The improved status of Catholics appears (at this period in history, at least) to accentuate the Protestant-Catholic conflict rather than to mitigate it.

In discussing the Protestant-Catholic conflict of values, each Protestant group demonstrates a different approach. The conservatives fix on what they consider to be the major issue—namely, the respective roles which they regard as proper to church and state. In expressing their convictions on this point, they come into conflict also with most of the branches of Protestantism in respect to Protestant "political activity." The fundamentalists express their concerns about Catholics in a more oblique way by focusing attention on the fate of Protestants in Roman Catholic countries. The liberals are less specific about the nature of the tension between Catholics and Protestants; they simply point out that it exists and invite students to discuss certain aspects of the problem. The neo-orthodox approach shows an awareness of all these concerns, but it also stresses that a continuing debate is going on within the Roman Catholic Church on the issues that concern Protestants and that many Catholics are seeking a better understanding between the two religions. The neo-orthodox insist that Catholic attitudes toward Protestants are varied and complex and must be examined self-critically in all their complexity.

The communicators differ, too, in regard to the weight their lessons give to the historical background of the outsiders' attitudes toward Protestants and Protestant freedoms. Religious groups are born in the midst of conflict; and conflict too often seems to the insider largely a matter of victimization imposed from without. Fortunately, Protestants—and, hopefully, other groups as well— benefit from the correctives of this one-sided view that come from acquainting themselves with the inner histories of other groups. We learn from the neo-orthodox, for example, that "our groups" (Protestants, Americans, and so forth) do not always appear as innocent to outsiders as they do to us; that we, in turn, have victimized them, and—perhaps the most vital point of all—that all groups have been to an extent the creatures of their eras. Similarly, other Protestants present a more nearly realistic and historically balanced picture of those groups which Protestant traditions have often cast too exclusively in the role of persecutor.

It is, perhaps, because the Jews represent such a small minority in the world today that the Protestant devotes less space to Jewish attitudes in lesson materials than to Catholic-Protestant ones. Yet generalizations of past and present Jewish attitudes do enter into Protestant discussions of the biblical themes. These discussions of the Christian faith are colored by the age-old dialogue between the Christian and Jewish faiths. In the following chapters we will discuss two themes of prime importance for both Jews and Christians; these concern the way in which the Church defines its central task— the proclamation of the Gospel—and the interpretations it gives one of the most crucial events in Christian history—the death of Christ. Ironically, it is precisely at these two points of self-definition that the Church has impinged most decisively, and often tragically, on the life of the Jewish people. These two themes have been selected for detailed analysis in an attempt to determine how their presentation affects the images of the Jew's attitude toward Christians.[17]

17. For a discussion of another theme that also lends itself to depicting the Jew as the antagonist of the Church see Bernhard E. Olson, "Christian Education and the Image of the Pharisees," *Religious Education* (Nov.–Dec. 1960), pp. 410–17.

# 7. The Adversary and the Mission to the Jews

There are several topics in Protestant teaching materials which provide some lesson writers with an opportunity to impute to Jews a bitter hostility toward Christians and the Church. This chapter will discuss one of these subjects—the Christian's imperative to evangelize—and its importance for the Christian's understanding of the Jew. Particular attention will be paid to the ways Protestants state the Jewish reaction to this effort.

Two contrary opinions about any attempt to convert [1] a person who is a member of another group are found in Protestant literature. The liberals regard such efforts as divisive and bigoted. The majority of the denominations take precisely the opposite position: a failure to carry out the Church's mission is considered as a betrayal of the Christian faith, a fundamental indifference to truth, and a lack of love for people's souls. Further, fundamentalists and conservatives believe that to exclude the Jews from conversionist

1. The expression "to convert" is used here as a synonym for all the other terms used to describe the evangelical task. However, the reader must clearly understand that none of these terms—convert, mission, evangelize, or witness—have the same meaning for all the groups in this study. Most of the denominations attempt to convert the members of their own and other Protestant churches as well as persons outside the churches; for them the term "conversion" does not always signify that a person must shift his religious affiliation, if any. More often it means that he must "accept Christ as Lord and Savior" and consequently be changed fundamentally as a person through God's action (variously called "regeneration," "being born again," and so forth). While many lesson writers speak of this process as "becoming a Christian"—even when the convert is already a member of the Church—few, if any, refer to evangelistic activity as "converting people to Christianity." Christianity is a highly eclectic, diverse, and often corrupt medley of beliefs, practices, and rituals, and the attempt to convert people to it, or to the Church, would be, in their view, idolatrous. Nonetheless, the various Christian interpretations of the missionary task involve an acceptance of what, in this chapter, is called "the Christian claim," i.e. that Jesus Christ is Lord and that one must submit to him in saving faith; therefore, certain beliefs of this eclectic Christianity are inevitably present in the Christian mission.

efforts is to discriminate against them and to express profound ingratitude.[2]

Whether one agrees with the liberal position or with the traditional one, it is clear that proselyting is inevitable in a pluralistic culture where each religious group necessarily contends with others who adhere to different faith and value systems. If the convictions which each group proclaims are not simply minor issues, irrelevant theological points, or superficially held beliefs, they will have an effect on other groups. The rival ideologies of any group are therefore important as potential instruments of power; hence they cannot be ignored. Every person responds to these ideas in some way if only to reject them. In this ferment of competing faiths each person becomes a missionary for some ideology; he differs only in the ways he advances it.[3] Hence, whether the approach to others be crude or sophisticated, direct or indirect, exploitive of or sensitive to persons, each is characterized by certain elements:

1. A striving on the part of the person to make his viewpoint clear and significant to someone else

2. A desire to want the substance of this position and its implications to be understood by the other person in such a way as to influence him fundamentally (so that he will alter his view of himself, the social scene, reality, politics, salvation, etc.)

3. Often, but not always, a desire to press the conversation to the point of decision

2. Since for these groups all mankind is divided into two categories, the saved and the unsaved, the eternal fate of unsaved Jews depends upon the Christian's decision to take the Gospel to them. Because those who are presently "in Christ" are indebted to the Jews for taking the Gospel to the Gentiles, the Christian in turn must express his gratitude to the Jew for his own salvation by witnessing to the Jews.

3. The point of view of this study is that "religion" is not an option, even though one may exercise options between kinds of religious orientations— most of which exist in disguised forms (nationalism and communism are two excellent examples). From the standpoint of a sociology of religion, it is doubtful that any man is without any ultimate centers of loyalty, without meanings and purposes which fundamentally direct his life and constitute his gods. All ideology, then, which reveals man's basic commitments and grounds of meanings may be thought of as "religious ideology," even though those who hold it may shun

Thus the Unitarian liberals, who consider the missionary efforts of the churches improper, do not repudiate the right to express their own message. Since they believe neither in the traditional tenets of Christianity nor in Jesus Christ as Lord and Saviour, they do not wish Christianity to become the world's religion. They are not interested in proselytizing for a supernaturalistic religion, and consider the traditional attempts to do so divisive. Nevertheless, when they refute certain current ideas of God and man, they advocate other beliefs to take their place; they explicitly seek to clarify the issues as they see them so as to make them comprehensible and acceptable to the reader. While they address their texts primarily to their constituents, they offer suggestions to both the Christian and the Jewish communities which, if acted upon, would advance the causes for which the writers stand.[4]

The point of this analysis, however, is not to determine whether Protestants should or should not evangelize among Jews but to understand how this operation is conceived and carried out by the various Protestant communities.

Being apostles to the Jews is only one aspect of the churches' universal assignment to carry out the terms of the Great Commission. Consequently, although there is considerable missionary emphasis in all except the liberal curricula, there is very little stress as such on a special Jewish mission. Fundamentalist materials express great interest in the conversion of Jews, but the neo-orthodox and conservative literatures seldom mention it. Nevertheless, except for the liberal group, the other three denominations (and the independent churches who use fundamentalist materials) operate mission stations within the major centers of Jewish population in the United States.[5]

---

the term; it must also be clear that such ideology is not necessarily theology, "the science of God."

4. While some of the writers in the liberal curriculum describe their religion in essentially non-missionary terms, one of its writers credits Deutero-Isaiah as "giving the first great call to evangelism in the Judeo-Christian tradition" and as having planted at its center "the consciousness that any religion, which is worthy of the name, must be a missionary religion." It is notable that the Unitarian Laymen's League has for some years been conducting "experiments in Unitarian expansion," calling for a two-fold program of advertising and of training lay persons in skills for "initiating conversations with potential Unitarians." See the pamphlet *Five Steps Which You Can Use in Promoting Unitarianism* (Boston, Unitarian Laymen's League, 1957), pp. 2-4.

5. However, the Unitarian Church is widely regarded—along with Ethical

There is an increasing tendency in the world today to acknowledge that the freedom to persuade and to be persuaded, to convert and be converted, to evangelize and to change one's religious loyalties is an essential human right. The United Nations recognized this when they indicated that the freedom to change one's religion or belief, to engage in private or public teaching, and to receive and impart information and ideas through any media and regardless of frontiers are integral parts of one's right to freedom of thought, conscience, and religion.[6] "Religious liberty," says Miegge, "includes the right of every man to bear witness to his faith."[7] However, these just claims imply mutual obligations. Protestant denominations not only insist upon their own right to evangelize but also acknowledge that others have similarly legitimate rights— one of which is the implicit right to refuse to be persuaded without risking reprisal. In American culture, at least, the freedom to believe includes also the freedom to reject and to disbelieve.[8]

Nevertheless, religious groups seem to react negatively to the attempts of others to proselytize. The conservative writers, for example, at times rebuke one or another church within Christendom for its missionary efforts. One lesson specifically cites Seventh-Day Adventists, Mormons, and Pentecostals as "shameless proselyters," and one conservative book reviewer observes that the author "plays up the Baptists of the past as the real saints, but is careful not to mention the shameless proselyting which they practiced to seduce Lutherans away from their Church." This reviewer goes on to remark that "fanaticism and lovelessness are still to be found among people who bear the name Christian."[9] In a few instances, the recent upsurge of the missionary zeal of religious groups outside of Christendom is regarded as threatening; however, since most of these religions—excepting Islam—are not aggressively missionary, there are relatively few references to this

Culture and Christian Science—as a "transmission belt" between Judaism and non-Judaism.

6. Articles 18 and 19, Universal Declaration of Human Rights, adopted Dec. 10, 1949, by the United Nations General Assembly.

7. Giovanni Miegge, *Religious Liberty* (New York, Association Press, 1957), p. 80.

8. "The Christian has a right and a duty to express his faith and to seek to win everybody else for his Lord. Everybody else has a right to listen or not to listen to him, to believe or to disbelieve." Victor Buksbazen, "Niebuhr and the Gospel for the Jew," *Christianity Today* 3, No. 5 (Dec. 8, 1958), p. 12.

9. MS, *Concordia Bible Teacher* (July 1955), p. 76. Also MS39,441:79.

threat. Obviously, no Protestant communicator desires to have other Christian groups purvey their versions of the gospel among his constituents, nor is he particularly pleased by the prospect of non-Christian groups attempting missionary work among Christians.

All of these findings indicate certain common responses to conversionist efforts. The Catholic probably feels resentment for the Protestant missionary who approaches him in Colombia or Peru. But Jews have even more substantial historical reasons for distrusting missionary endeavors than do most faiths. Non-Christians also have always tended to look upon Christian missionaries in various degrees of friendliness, indifference, and resentment, depending upon their specific social milieu and the manner in which Christians approach them. The data in Analytical Categories 11 and 12, which portray the attitudes of other religious groups to the communicator's, indicate that Protestant writers sense this universal negative reaction on the part of outsiders to their conversionist activities. In conservative and fundamentalist curricula, for example, a number of the negative references that attribute outgroup hostility toward Christ, Christians, and the Church (or the Gospel) are found in accounts which refer to the resistance of others to the Church's evangelistic task. We will return to these portrayals later in this discussion.

## The Anxieties of the Jewish Community

Jews today are apparently more disturbed by the Christian's attempts to convert them than they are by their belief that Christians teach that the Jews killed Christ. The latter charge has caused them much suffering, but in their eyes the Church's attempts to convert them constitute a decided threat to their identity. Undoubtedly, the hostility of many Jews to other Jews who have become Christians is intimately bound up with their long struggle to maintain an existence and identity in a pagan and nominally Christian world.

Moreover, the Jew's response to the presentation of the Christian message has been necessarily conditioned by deeply imbedded memories of the seemingly endless wrongs inflicted upon his people by Christians in the last sixteen centuries. These persecutions were, in part, both attempts to coerce Jews into abandoning their religion and a punishment for refusing to do so. In seeking to carry out the terms of the Great Commission, the Church has shown the Jew a side of Christianity which an increasing number of Christians recognize as particularly shameful.

To be urged to embrace a religion which has become for him a symbol of oppression raises distinct personal problems for the Jew. The prospect of becoming a Christian arouses in him deep feelings of guilt which the zealous argument of the Christian missionary often helps to create. The Jew for whom the Christian message has an appeal experiences a conflict which arises from an identification with his own group and the implications of the charge that the Jews have rejected Christ; consequently, the problem he faces has more to do with whether he is to condemn and reject his own people for unbelief and "Christ-rejection" than with deciding any specific religious issue. For him, conversion often implies leaving the Jewish community, giving up the burdens of a suffering people, and joining the ranks of the persecuting majority. The issue the Jew cannot ignore is how he is to regard his own people if he becomes Christian.[10]

10. Some historical facts about conversionist attempts that are well known to Jews are apparently not too well known, or at least not often acknowledged, in the literature of the churches. Among the most prominent of these are the following: (a) Pogroms against Jews have usually followed or accompanied attempts to convert them. Failures successfully to carry through conversionist efforts usually resulted in renewed persecution. Cf. "Conversion," *Jewish Encyclopedia*, 4, 250. (b) The practice of the Jewish religion was considered an affront to Christianity and a stiff-necked defiance of the Church. Stern measures —including forced baptism, compulsory sermons, and restrictions on liberty— were often imposed in consequence. (c) Jews were proscribed by law from proselyting among Christians, yet they were also forbidden by law to place an obstacle in the way of a Jew's conversion to the Christian faith. One attempt on the part of the Jewish community to prevent some of their number from being proselyted led to a massacre at Frankfort in A.D. 1241. Solomon Grayzel, *The Church and the Jews in the XIIIth Century* (Philadelphia, Dropsie College, 1933), pp. 13–15, 226–27, and passim. (d) The pressure on Jews to become Christians resulted in a great number of forced conversions. These "converts" were called Marranos, or "secret Jews." This ironically brought them under the power of the Inquisition, which tried "relapsed Jews" and turned them over to the legal authorities for punishment. A. Hyatt Verrill, *The Inquisition* (New York, Appleton, 1931), pp. 33, 296. (e) As the dominant power group, Christians usually made conversion to Christianity the condition for exemption from the disabilities usually visited upon Jews. (f) Genuine, i.e. unforced, converts to Christianity took on the color of the anti-Judaism of the dominant culture and in many cases proved to be a source of great suffering for the Jew. Some Christians were only too willing to believe anything derogatory about Jews, and these converted persons often gained prominence by turning informer.

The social situation of Jewry has some bearing on this matter. When a converted Jew abandons a despised minority (and this is what the Church traditionally has required of him) to join a privileged majority, he is looked upon with distrust by both communities. His own group may suspect him of wishing to escape the persecution, ignominy, and social and economic disadvantages for the security and privilege which assimilation with the majority allows him. Gentiles may still regard him apprehensively, even disdainfully, because he is a Jew, and according to the popular anti-Semitic stereotype, must be "out to get something for himself." The Jews, in turn, may suspect the convert's motives while the Christians may withhold their full acceptance of him.

## The Protestant Response

Two contrasting Protestant responses may be noted to the Jewish anxieties and concerns aroused by conversionist efforts. Fundamentalist and conservative writers are most apt to focus on the Jews' hostile reaction without giving the necessary background information about Jewish-Christian relations which would make this hostility understandable. The liberals and the neo-orthodox, on the other hand, do not describe Jews as hating Christians; instead they direct their attention to those historical factors which Christians should understand in carrying out their mission.

For one thing, the liberals and the neo-orthodox take into account the past relation between Christian conversionist efforts and Jewish suffering, and they are responsive to the Jews' anxieties about missionary activity. One leading liberal writer says, "In spite of their Jewish Christ, Christians fostered hatred toward Jews who refused to accept Christianity." Some notable examples of the same emphasis also occur in the lessons produced by other Protestant denominations. A lesson on Christian and Jew in the Methodist curriculum, for example, strongly suggests that the religious origins of anti-Semitism are to be found in the "intolerance and hostility

---

Some of the Inquisitors were offsprings of converted Jews: "Apostasy and Apostates from Judaism," *Jewish Encyclopedia*, 2, 12–18. It must be remembered, of course, that this was not the whole story. Many Jews became Christians out of sincere conviction, and some of them were defenders of Jews. Today, of course, the situation is altered, and converted Jews are more and more attempting to stay within the Jewish community.

of early Christians toward those of another faith whom they were unable to convert." This lesson goes on to add that, in point of fact, the conversionist element "has continued to the *present* as a major factor in anti-Semitic feeling." Several pages later, the same author points out the connection between some Christians' aspiration to convert Jews and the hostility they still have toward them: "Even yet, consciously or otherwise, there are those who resent the fact that the Jews cling to their age-old faith and decline to admit the superiority of ours. 'I could forgive them,' said a friend of the writer, a genuinely pious Sunday School teacher, 'if they would only go on and accept Christianity.' " [11]

The most extensive treatment of this issue occurs in a neo-orthodox publication. Commenting upon the Apostle Paul's analysis of the relationship of the Jews to the Gospel in Romans 8–11, the writer takes pains to emphasize that significant changes have taken place in the world since Paul's time of which Christians ought to take specific notice in their relationships with Jews today. Acknowledging that "we do, however, have a particular duty to the Jew," this writer cautions students that

> We are in a different situation from that of Paul in our relation to Israel. Since Paul's time great changes have taken place that he could not possibly have foreseen. One of the more important changes is that the Jews and Gentiles have changed places. During Paul's life, among the people who believed in the living God, the Jews were in the majority, and the Gentile Christians in the minority. Today almost all the Western World is at least formally Christian. Today it is the Christians who rule the world, a world in which Judaism is only a slight, scattered, and fearful minority.
>
> *It is not hard, or pleasant, to understand why the Jews are fearful. Christianity has a long history of having tried to convert the Jew, not by the gospel of peace, but by the sword.* During the Middle Ages the Jews were sometimes given the alternative of believing in Christ or being burned at the stake . . . we need not cross the ocean to find examples of Jewish persecution. Large sectors of the American public are anti-Semitic. Jews are kept out of certain professions. Their num-

11. Eleazer, "Reason, Religion, and Race," an Adult Elective (Methodist), p. 49.

bers in colleges are frequently limited by a quota system. They
are refused admission to "Gentile" resorts and hotels. They
have never been given full citizenship in the American community. They have been mistreated by Christian civilizations
for centuries. Their dead is beyond number; their tragic
suffering beyond our comprehension.

The way we have treated the Jew creates a problem in our
relationship to him that Paul could not have known . . . This
will involve more penitence and self-criticism than we have
displayed . . . The Jew will not be able to forget until we
start remembering.[12]

Other curricula offer few such explanations for the Jews' anxiety
about the Christians' mission. There are many passages in fundamentalist lessons which insistently press upon the reader the task
of witnessing to the Jew. Although some of these passages take
note of the hostile Jewish response, none attempt to explain it or
to consider the special questions this hostility raises for Christians.

The conservative and fundamentalist images of present-day
Jews as haters and enemies of Christians are often evoked in
connection with discussions of the early history of the Church.
A comment on Matt. 10:24 ff., describing the reaction of the
Pharisees to Jesus, illustrates how a biblical episode can be made to
appear an implicit commentary on present-day relations between
Jew and Christian: "The Gospels illustrate how bitterly Jesus
was hated by the Jews. The Pharisees called Him Beelzebub (or
Beelzebul), a revolting title, which they applied to Satan. Cp.
12:24. Similarly *the Jews and other enemies of the Church have
called the Christians all kinds of bad names.*"

Here the writer uses the responses of a small group of Pharisees
to Jesus in a particular moment in history to project a series of
generalizations (1) from a few to all Pharisees, (2) from all Pharisees to all Jews in the time of Jesus, and (3) from all first-century
Jews to Jews of any time or place. Such a description conjures up
an image of the Jew who calls Christians bad names by its vague,
unqualified assertion, one which makes no distinctions between
a biblical incident and present-day realities.

Although the above illustration does not refer directly either
to Jesus' or to Christians' attempts to convert Jews, the conservative

understanding of Jesus' contacts with the people is that his ministry is to be regarded always as an offering of the gospel. Further, since Jesus' ministry is understood as intended for the Jews' salvation, the lesson writer tends to think of Jesus' conflict with the Pharisees as testimony to the Jews' unbelief—consequently, as a rejection of and hostility to Christ. This writer also couples this rejection of Christ by the Pharisees with Jewish responsibility for Christ's crucifixion, so that the continued existence of the Jews as a people separate from Christianity seems to imply Jewish hatred of Christians and of the Church. These connections are further reinforced by memories of the early persecution of Christians. One writer, commenting on the First Gospel, sums up all these ideological constituents in the following assertions taken from a single paragraph:

1. As a nation the Jews rejected Jesus.
2. They persecuted the Christians.
3. They were offended at Jesus' lowly birth, his dwelling in Nazareth, and his ministry in Galilee.
4. They regarded Christians as apostates from the Jewish faith.
5. They regarded Jesus as a deceiver.
6. They invented slanderous tales about his origin and life.                                    (MS38,996:7)

The conservative treatment of Jewish unbelief, e.g. the Jew's refusal to be converted or his reaction to missionary methods, is marked by a tendency to equate the Jews' refusal to accept the gospel with a hatred of Christianity. In one of a series of lessons on Palestine, the writer notes that Christians, Jews, and Arabs are interested in the Holy Land for different reasons—Christians because it was the homeland of their Saviour. He then adds: "Christians are tolerated neither by the Jews nor the Arabs, and it is difficult to gain converts from among either of these enemies of Christianity." The writer is referring to the situation in present-day Israel. It is not clear what he means by toleration, but taking the usual denotation of the word, it may more accurately be said that Christians and Christianity are tolerated in Israel.[13] Possibly

13. See Paul Rowden, "The Religious Situation in Israel," *Christianity Today*, 3, No. 6 (1958), 6–8, and Hans Kosmola, "State and Religion in the State of Israel," in Hedenquist, ed., *The Church and the Jewish People*, p. 99.

the lesson writer is referring instead to the widespread Jewish skepticism—sometimes hostility—to active attempts by Christian missionaries to convert Jews; or he may be equating intolerance with an outsider's inability to accept the Christian message.

While Jewish hatred for Christ is sometimes sharply pinpointed in fundamentalist materials, the emphasis usually is not so much on Jewish disdain for the Christian as on the Jewish hatred for other Jews who become Christians. Since of all the communicators, fundamentalists are the most interested in the conversion of the Jew, the lessons in the sample which discussed this issue were re-examined to see what additional statements they offered about the Jews. Most of these lessons stressed (a) love for the Jew, and/or (b) the evils of anti-Semitism. However, we also noted another pattern in these lessons:

Out of twelve lessons with conversionist statements:

(a) Nine raised the question of Jewish "unbelief"
(b) Eight dealt with the theme of the Jewish rejection of Christ
(c) Three raised the point that modern converts from Judaism are subject to attack by Jews.

The themes of unbelief and rejection of Christ almost always make themselves felt in the fundamentalist discussion of missions to Jews. A variation of these themes is resistance to truth. "The mission field," an author observes, "at home and abroad, is the same today—it is 'the Jews'—those who 'have religion'—who so often offer the most strenuous opposition to truth." The unwillingness of modern Jews to accept the Christian claims evokes images of the Jew's "blindness":

> As we examine some of the abundant proofs given in the Scriptures to convince man's mind, we marvel at the Jews' failing to see in Jesus the promised Messiah of Israel. The "stone of stumbling" to them was—*and still is*—their blindness to God's plans, and their failure to see in the "meek and lowly Nazarene" the King who shall sit on the throne of David.[14]

Passages such as these are fairly typical. One lesson contains the following statements: "In order to reveal the extent of [the Mes-

14. SP608:9 (italics mine).

siah's] exaltation, it was necessary to exhibit also the depth of His humiliation. *The Jews would not believe this latter truth, and will not to this day* . . . Paul referred to Isaiah's question (53:1) [Who hath believed our report?] in Romans 10:16, pointing out how difficult it is to get Jews to believe God's Word and accept the Messiah." The difficulty of conducting fundamentalist missionary work among the Jews is echoed by a number of passages in conservative literature, one of which calls attention to the Jewish mission in New York: "The great majority of the Jews are little interested in any religion, not even in the Jewish religion. Therefore mission work among them is very difficult." [15]

The fundamentalists never accuse the Jews of hating Christians as such, but they do say that they persecute the convert from Judaism. A question for discussion in the fundamentalist curriculum asks, "What does it mean for a Jew to be 'saved' (Rom. 10:1) and publicly confess Christ?" The answer given in the teacher's manual reads: "Ostracism by his relatives and Jewish friends, business loss, etc." Jewish persecution of the convert is also indicated by statements of this order: "Jews who receive Jesus Christ are considered dead by their families and funeral services are held for them." Sometimes accounts of Jewish persecution consist purely of quotes from converts to Christianity. One such convert, Moshe Emmanuel Ben-Maier, in describing his change of allegiance, climaxes his report by saying: "But ere long the door of my home was closed in my face. Though forlorn and forsaken by friends and relatives and loved ones, I was not forsaken by the Lord." [16] The lesson writer then adds his comment to Ben-Maier's: "Thus the follower of the Messiah-Saviour was despised and rejected as was His Lord."

It is, then, largely in connection with allusions to the ministry to the Jews that the contemporary hostility of Jews to Christians and the Church is mentioned. Interestingly enough, Jewish accounts of Christian missions make the Christian the hostile party. Hence, mission work tends to stimulate mutually negative attitudes for

15. MS39,169:559. The Missouri Synod bases the generalization that Jews are hard to convert on Romans 11:25–31. Israel is "blinded," but only in part; most of them (except the "spiritual Israel") are "hardened to the Gospel invitation." MS, *The Bible Student* (Senior Elective), "Epistle to the Romans," p. 39.

16. Two other fundamentalist accounts of conversions of Jews, told by the converts themselves, give no hint of persecution.

both of the religious groups involved. This, probably, is the explanation for Rabbi Leo Baeck's statement that "the usual, and inevitable, result of any talk [between Jew and Christian] was an increase in the feeling, on the Christian side, of being *uncompromisingly rejected by the Jew,* and on the Jewish side, of being *forcibly summoned and violently accused by the Christian . . .*" [17] The Christian's approach to the Jew has seemed to the latter to consist of more than just an attempt to have him share the gospel. The missioner has often created the impression that he is picking out the Jew for exclusive accusations of rejecting and crucifying Christ, of not embracing his own Messiah, of being blind and guilty of unbelief and of stubbornly clinging to his own faith. For his part, the Christian may feel that the Jewish resentment aroused by these imputations (which reflect the same quality of abuse he receives from the Gentile world) implies a clear-cut hatred and scorn for Christianity.

## Effect of Missionary Intent on the Jewish Portrait

Since accounts of the unfriendly reaction of Jews to mission activities seem to be accompanied by references to the conversion of Jews in the neutral and negative-scoring curricula, we should examine the impact on the total Jewish portrait produced by lessons which are concerned primarily with missions.

No activity of the churches has been more severely criticized for its negative intergroup implications than the missionary enterprise. Outsiders often feel that missionary efforts inevitably insult other faiths and reveal a certain amount of bigotry and intolerance. An attempt was made in this study to ascertain whether the claim holds true of those Protestant lessons which are intended to motivate the reader to convert others or simply to increase his interest in missions.

In order to determine whether lessons devoted to missions were more unfavorable than favorable to Jews and other religious groups than lessons with no missionary purpose, all the lessons were divided into three sections: (1) Those devoted primarily to missionary aims and content, (2) those with an intergroup theme or intent, and (3) those which contained neither. By "intent" we mean state-

17. Leo Baeck, "Some Questions to the Christian Church from the Jewish Point of View," in Hedenquist, *The Church and the Jewish People,* pp. 102–03.

ments of purpose such as "To inspire in the pupil a desire to take the gospel to the Jews" (missionary intent), or "To improve the relations of Christians to Jews" (intergroup intent).

For the purposes of the study two hypotheses were advanced. It was conjectured that lessons written specifically for the purpose of promoting good will and understanding between groups would yield more favorable portraits of outsiders than lessons with purely missionary purposes. It seemed reasonable to suppose that a writer consciously dealing with intergroup relations would be more concerned with factual accuracy and would be careful to present other groups charitably and objectively. On the other hand, with missionary themes one might expect that a writer would be more tempted to make derogatory references to other groups. We reasoned that if this were true, lessons which have neither missionary nor intergroup aims and content could be expected to score less favorably than the former and more favorably than the latter.

The second hypothesis was that if missionary interests adversely affected the portrayal of outsiders, communicators who demonstrated greater missionary concerns would produce a negative picture of the groups they were urging their audience to convert, while those who showed little or no missionary concern would offer a more positive picture of the same groups. Since the liberals were the only group which had no missionary lessons, the analysis applied only to the remaining three publishers.

Our findings for the most part failed to support the hypotheses —particularly insofar as the image of the Jew was concerned.[18] While the number of missionary and intergroup lessons are statistically small, the intergroup tendency of the lessons with Jewish content was on the whole considerably more favorable for missionary lessons than for the bulk of lessons in the curriculum. However, the scores for missionary lessons mentioning Jews were somewhat lower than those for intergroup lessons. But it should be emphasized that missionary lessons yield positive images of Jews in the fundamentalist and conservative materials, as well as in those of the neo-orthodox.

Two observations should be made about these findings. One is that the negative portrayals of Jews are mostly to be found in purely incidental references to the mission to the Jews in those

18. Tables 11 and 11a, Appendix VII.

lessons which do not have a primarily missionary purpose. The present Protestant trend is to write missionary lessons which demonstrate a high degree of intergroup awareness. This is particularly true of the neo-orthodox, who combine acutely sensitive intergroup interests with missionary concerns. Secondly, the negative Jewish portrayal, which occurs largely in fragmentary discussions of various aspects of the mission to the Jew, generally assumes two or three distinct patterns. In fundamentalist or conservative literature such statements often include expressions such as "unbelieving Jews." And when only biblical Jews are intended, the writer occasionally will use distinctly pejorative terms to underscore the Jew's resistance to conversion. For example, the fundamentalist writer who says that Jews offer "the most strenuous opposition to truth" uses such epithets as "the hard-hearted, stiff-necked Jews." In some of these same fundamentalist lessons, however, there are also directives to love the Jew, or statements which point out to the reader that the early Christians were Jews. The fact that these over-all references can be scored both positively and negatively on our quantitative scale accounts for their ambiguous intergroup coloring.

What has been said about the Jewish portrait is also true in general of the images of other non-Christians, of Roman Catholics, and of other Christian groups. It seems that a stress upon missionary themes as such does not in itself encourage negative statements about other groups. Yet some negative depictions of non-Jewish groups do appear in the fundamentalist and conservative literature, and these images are sometimes even more unfavorable than those in the general run of lessons. The decisive factor in creating favorable or unfavorable images of outsiders in missionary material seems to be the particular view a group takes of its mission and its manner of urging the Christian to see himself in relation to outside groups.

## Implications of the Jewish Image for the Christian Mission

It need not be denied that some Jews greatly dislike Christians and view all non-Jews alike, making no distinctions between hostile Gentiles and friendly Christians, or between the Christian who is kindly disposed to Jews and the Christian who is not. However, for Christians Jewish hostility has deeper implications. The

Christian writer who wishes to do more than refute the fact that Jews ostracize converts to Christianity or that they can be characterized flatly as refusing to believe the gospel must fully understand the Jewish response before he attempts to urge the Christian to witness to his faith among Jews.

Let us examine some of the implications for the Christian mission of viewing "the Jew as enemy." Although some valid empirical data can be found to support some of the statements about outgroup hostility, the question nevertheless arises whether the isolated, fragmentary, and negative statements we have described adequately prepare teachers and pupils to make a genuine Christian witness.

In part, the adequacy and effectiveness of the Christian mission depends upon whether or not the Christian understands and appreciates the people he is addressing. If Jews are seen realistically rather than through stereotyped images, it is likely that the Christian will experience a radically different response from them. We should ask, then, whether the image of the Jew consumed with hatred for the Christian is an accurate one.

To be sure, fundamentalists present several instances of positive Jewish reactions. One of the accounts describes a rabbi cordially welcoming an evangelical Sunday School teacher to discuss the respective Jewish and Christian views of the coming Messianic Age. The conservatives also take notice of and commend the friendly act of a Jewish hospital in Denver in volunteering to give medical treatment to an immigrant Lutheran family that otherwise would have been denied entrance to the United States. This type of material, however, is an exception. Most Protestant lessons are skimpy in acknowledging the friendliness shown by Jews today toward the Christian community, as well as the interest they take in matters that concern Christians. Many Christian missionaries to Jews are warmly received. Many rabbis support the Church's right to missionary work among the Jews. Jews also appear to be demonstrating an increased interest in the person of Jesus. Further, concern about Protestant-Jewish relations has led many Jews to make studies of Protestant thought; in Europe, especially, Jews and Christians frequently gather together at formal conferences to discuss their differences and to interpret their respective faiths to each other. Yet there is little Protestant disposition to express

in their curricula this positive side of the Jewish relationship to
Christians.

The neo-orthodox, nevertheless, take into account that Jews
differ among themselves as much as do other people; consequently,
they feel it would be just as mistaken to describe Jews as universally
or predominantly hostile as it would be to create an image of
them as uniformly friendly and receptive to missionary efforts.
Some Jews, of course, may greatly resent these efforts, but this
need not render them hostile to Christians in general or lessen
their ability to meet with other Christians on a friendly, non-
missionary basis.

A knowledge of the Jew which is based upon actual experience
and empirical data will radically qualify the context in which
statements about Jewish hostility occur. It is one thing to charge
that Jews (or even a few Jews) hate Christians. It is another to
note, as some evangelical writers in America have done, that many
Israeli Jews show animosity toward the attempt to missionize
Israel because "Jews have suffered during centuries of prejudice,
hatred and slaughter under the Roman Church and Protestants
and they have a pathological fear of the 'cross' . . . To the Jews,
these words [Christian, missionary] and these people [Baptists,
Nazarenes, Pentecostals, etc.] represent the hated instruments of
their oppression." [19]

If there is Jewish hatred of Christians in the Western world,
the lesson writer who fails to give an explanation for this hatred
does an injustice both to the gospel and to the Jews. The neo-
orthodox point out that the current animosity shown by Jew to
Christian and Christian to Jew are, as always, two qualitatively
different phenomena. Regrettable though it may be, a Jew's dislike
for the Christian is more easily accounted for than the corresponding hatred of the Jew by the Christian. The Christian may be
hated for having discriminated against and having ostracized the
Jews or for adhering to a religious group that has long been
identified in the Jewish mind with cruelty and vindictiveness.
He may be hated on the ground that as a member of a group with
greater status and power in society, he may have become utterly
or relatively indifferent to the recent destruction or the current
disabilities of the Jews.

19. "Freedom in Israel," *Christianity Today, 1,* No. 6, (Dec. 24, 1956), p. 20.

There are several dangers to the Christian mission in representing the Jew as an enemy. If Christian pupils and teachers are somehow led to believe that they are going out "in love" to witness to or convert a people who hate them, they are likely to become self-righteous and condescending in their approach and they, in turn, may further contribute to distorted views of Jewish attitudes. This is most likely if the image of the Jew is always presented in a negative context. Hence the greatest educational danger lies in the omission of material which could give the student a more balanced view. A Christian student cannot arrive at this historical understanding unless the lessons themselves provide him with it.

It is precisely at this point that conservative and fundamentalist communicators could demonstrate what Christian love means in concrete terms—a practice we are more apt to find in neo-orthodox writing. The child who is told to love the Jew as a manifestation of his Christian witness cannot do so unless love for the Jew is shown in the manner in which the Jew is described, and not merely in the command; the Jew must be made understandable and respected as a human being. This is not to say that prospective witnesses of the gospel should not be warned against disillusionment; on the contrary, they should approach their work realistically and not anticipate that every Jew will respond positively or that every effort will be successful. But it is also essential that Christians understand some of the reasons for the Jews' unfavorable response —what it is that makes the Jew a special case for Christians. For the Protestant to love the Jew for the sake of God is to know himself and all Christendom as standing under a shadow, cast not by the Jew but by the regrettable acts and attitudes of those in the Church.

Love for the Jew, therefore, requires an awareness on the part of Protestants that no treatment of the approach to the Jew is adequate unless the curriculum materials explicitly spell out certain acknowledgments at the appropriate places. As the neo-orthodox writers point out, these acknowledgments must include a confession that any negative attitude to Christians by Jews is a judgment upon the Christian Church for its historical involvement in the sordid tragedy of anti-Semitism.

Finally, the one-sided image of the Jew as hostile exposes the Christian to the danger of developing an aversion for the Jew or encouraging a highly qualified love for him. Some fundamentalist lessons, for example, persistently press upon the pupil the task of making an evangelistic witness. A number of these lessons urge the Christian to love the Jew by trying "to win him to Christ"; occasional contrasts are drawn between the attitudes of anti-Semites and those Christians who are interested in the Jews' conversion. But nowhere is there any indication that Christians who zealously set out to convert the Jew and fail can become hostile to him. Most fundamentalists assume that if a man accepts Jesus Christ as Saviour he will not harbor feelings of this kind toward those with whom he tries to share the Gospel. Similarly, the conservatives sometimes seem to urge love for one's fellow man as a *means* to convert him, rather than insisting, as the gospel does, on a love that is unconditionally required of the Christian simply because of God's unconditional and unmerited love for man. In short, a provisional kind of love and acceptance of others which is prompted by the desire to change them can easily develop into hatred if this desire is thwarted; thus, a love that expresses itself in this way may allow the Christian worker, who gives up a Jew or a non-Christian as hopeless, to feel free to abuse him.[20]

## The Conversation between Israel and the Church

Protestants have different presuppositions about their missionary approach to the Jews which are based upon differing theologies and experiences in carrying out their mission. But the focus is the same in each case—that is, the extent to which Christians can acknowledge a kinship with the Jew. Depending upon the extent to which they see themselves as either bound or not bound to the Jew, Protestants who would undertake an apostolate to the Jews may or may not distinguish between a mission to the Jew and that to other non-Christians. Similarly, those Protestants who see a close relation between Jews and Christians can address themselves

20. Martin Luther, seeing that the Jews had been horribly mistreated, took his stand with the Jews on the supposition that charity and kindness would convert them to Christianity. His failure to convert them in any significant numbers (together with their attempt to convert him) developed into a resentment against them which produced one of the two most unfortunate utterances of the Great Reformer. See The *Lutheran Cyclopedia* (Concordia), 1949 ed., "Luther's Attitude toward the Jews." The man who loves you in order to win you is tempted to love you only if he is able to win you.

directly to legitimate Jewish anxieties such as the concern about whether Jews will continue to exist as an independent people.

The neo-orthodox group both in its mission and non-mission references, expresses a kinship with Jews; this curriculum self-critically examines the Christian's share of anti-Semitism instead of giving free play to the hostility which Jews feel toward Christians. In the conservative curriculum, however, no distinction whatever is made between the missionary approach to the Jews and to others. This can be explained partly by the conservative doctrine of the Church as the true Israel. The Jews are looked upon simply as belonging to one of many false religions and not as God's elect; this cancels out the distinction between the Jew and other non-Christians. Because of the absolute discontinuity between the Synagogue and Church, the Jew stands apart from the Church with the rest of unbelieving mankind.

As noted in a previous chapter, some fundamentalists believe that the Jews are still God's earthly people and that they have been chosen for a high universal mission which they eventually will fulfill "in the land" at the second coming of the Messiah. According to this view, Israel is not rejected, but only temporarily and partially set aside until the chosen number of Gentiles shall be brought into the Church. Hence, the Christian of fundamentalist persuasion can converse with the orthodox Jew on the latter's own terms and interests, but he cannot do this with liberal Jews or with adherents of the non-Christian religions.

The Unitarian curriculum would like to break down altogether "the wall of separation" between Jew and Christian. One lesson points out that in "some places the two groups [Jews and Christians] are now beginning to work together toward ways of fusing the greatest common values in the two traditions, and hand-in-hand they are seeking to develop a richer common religious culture that will be adapted to a scientific age." [21] This culture would absorb the best features of Judaism and Christianity. Consequently, the liberals have no special approach to the Jew; they simply extend to Jews the same invitation they give to other groups—namely, to join them in their quest for universal truth.

The neo-orthodox believe that an adequate evangelistic approach must recognize the close kinship of Judaism and Christianity. For

21. UN244:250.

this reason they stress the radically different nature of the Christian's mission to the Jews. Apart from the historical and social considerations which should make the Christian repentant in his approach to the Jew, the neo-orthodox hold that the Church has been grafted into Israel and that through God's grace the Christian has been made one with the Jew. The neo-orthodox also point out that between Jew and Christian there is also a bond of common doctrine: "You will bring out such considerations as the fact that Christian tradition roots in the Jewish religion, so that there is established a basis of understanding that one does not have with a Hindu or a modern secularist."

It is an awareness of the Jewish element in Christianity, therefore, which prompts the neo-orthodox to define their approach to the Jew differently than to others. The Jew is regarded as prior to the Christian, not only historically but in other respects as well: The covenant and the promises are still with Israel; the Jews are still God's Chosen People; Jesus is understood as a Jew who never desired to sever either himself or his followers from their Hebrew heritage. In fact, it is said that Jesus "did not come to put an end to Judaism, or to start a new religion, but to build upon and complete the historic Hebrew faith." The Christian must take seriously the Law and message of the Old Testament; he must "be a Jew, as Jewish as he was, if we would follow him." This same writer continues:

> The church has not always understood the full import of this strand in the teaching of Jesus, and whenever and wherever it has not, the consequences have been dire. Misunderstanding at this point often has led not only to a crassly unchristian attitude toward the Jews, but also to a general impoverishment of the Christian faith.[22]

Under the heading "The Jewishness of Christians," the author discusses the significance for the Christian approach to the Jews of the precept that "although all Jews obviously are not Christians, yet in a quite literal sense all Christians are Jews." He quotes approvingly from David Noel Freedman: "A Jew who becomes a Christian is not converted in the ordinary sense of the term. He does not turn around, or change direction; he advances in faith

22. PR, Westminster Uniform Lessons, in *Crossroads* (Jan. 1957), p. 59.

from the Old Testament to the New Testament. To put it another way, a Jew remains a Jew when he becomes a Christian; or, to revise our statement, a Christian is partly a Jew." [23]

Hence, the neo-orthodox Christian cannot approach the Jew as though he had no valid faith but were simply another pagan. Although there are fundamental differences between the Jew and the Christian—particularly in respect to whether Jesus is understood as Christ—the Christian's Semitic heritage is to be regarded as normative and legitimate.

From the above analysis follows another theme that is characteristic of the neo-orthodox curriculum. It pays more attention to the offense which the Christian is apt to feel by the full realization of the essential Jewishness of Christianity, than he is by the realization that the Jew dislikes him for his missionary effort. This point is stressed in their curricula in some of the questions listed for discussion. For example, one class is asked, "Does such a phrase as 'the Jewishness of Christians' offend you? What does it mean?" The offense, apparently, comes from the realization that Jesus was a Jew; anti-Semites would make Jesus a non-Jew, offensive only to the Jews. But the neo-orthodox feel that such an image of Christ does not have the power to reveal to Christians and to all mankind the truth that everyone is offended by Christ. The corollary to this is that a non-Jewish Christ quiets the Christian conscience by masking and justifying the Gentile's hatred of the Jew:

> A church school teacher recently asked her high school class to repeat several times, "Jesus was a Jew." Several in the class said that they did not like to say it, because it made them feel queer. For them to say, "Jesus was a Jew," was to say something that did not seem quite right; it seemed a bit disrespectful to Jesus.[24]

In neo-orthodox writing, then, we note a reversal of the widespread Protestant tendency to begin with an account of Jesus and then to generalize about the Jewish rejection of him and the subsequent hatred by the Jews of Jesus' followers, the Christians. Although neo-orthodox writers begin at the same point, they

23. Ibid.
24. PR, *The Lord of Christian Faith and Life*, p. 62.

proceed to contemplate the possibility that Christians conceivably may reject Jesus' Jewishness (and with it an essential part of Christianity) because they are offended by the Jew. These writers point out that if both Jesus and Christians are essentially Jews, Christians cannot approach the Jews of today as if they had no relation to the Christian tradition.

The consequences of this view of Jewish-Christian relations are given in several lessons dealing with the rivalry between Jacob and Esau.[25] The writer pictures the Church as Jacob, who "receives the gift of grace through God's choice." Esau, his brother, is the "natural nation, Israel" who is "rejected" and whose birthright is claimed by Jacob. The points the author makes of this analogy bear directly on questions which are raised in a subsequent lesson on Romans 9–11, "What should be distinctive about our approach to the Jews?"

First of all, Jacob and Esau are said to be brothers in the same family of God. Secondly, Esau "despised his birthright and sold it for a mess of pottage," while Jacob "was not above taking advantage of his brother's hunger and worldliness to get the birthright away from him." Jacob "entered into the conspiracy with his mother" to steal the blessing. Both Jacob and Esau are described as perfidious. The point of it all is that God's choice has nothing to do with man's worthiness or moral superiority. Both Israel and the Church have failed; both depend wholly upon God's unmerited mercy.

Between the two communities there is a state of enmity. Esau resolves to slay his brother Jacob (Gen. 27:41). This "hatred" proceeds from a self-righteousness that "cannot abide those whose very existence is a testimony to the God who mercifully blesses sinners like Jacob." In other words, the neo-orthodox recognize the hostile attitude toward Christians and the Christian claim— at least during the very earliest period of the Church's existence.

One of these lessons raises three major questions about the Jacob-Esau (Church-Israel) conflict. The third question reads, "What must precede Jacob's reconciliation with Esau? How does this apply to our [the Christian's] reconciliation with the Jews?" This, they point out, is the core of the issue. God became Jacob's (the Church's) adversary in order to test his faith: Jacob met this

25. PR, *Crossroads* (Nov. 1955), p. 35; (Dec. 1952), p. 47.

test by declaring his own unworthiness and by throwing himself back upon the unmerited promises of God. Analogically, in this confession the Church becomes changed. The writer develops this point as follows:

> Then it is significant that as soon as the change was effected in Jacob, it became possible for him to be reconciled with Esau. Yet Jacob was astonished that Esau took the initiative in reconciliation. "Esau ran to meet him, and embraced him, and fell on his neck, and kissed him: and they wept." [26]

Only in a similar way, then, can the enmity between the Jews and Christians be made to cease: "Jacob . . . had to be reconciled with the brother he had wronged, once God had tested him and found his faith to be strong. So the Church, when it has endured its testing, must be reconciled with Israel before the Kingdom of God can finally come." Hence, it is clearly implied here that the Church must confess the wrong it has done to the Jews and give them its blessing before the union which the Christian mission seeks can be consummated. For "Jacob and Esau were reconciled after Jacob became the new man Israel, a penitent man . . . Jacob gave Esau his blessing." The decisive question, then, is, What is our attitude toward the Jews? How do we, Jacob, feel toward our brother, Esau?

An earlier lesson concludes with the suggestion that Israel's reconciliation with the Church is necessary because of God's plan for the Jews:

> here it is revealed that God elected Jacob and his people *ultimately* for the sake of the rejected Esau. Through the blessing with which God blessed Jacob with all things, Esau was also blessed. And without Esau, Jacob could not enter the Promised Land—a wonderful parable, surely, that without the Jews, without the reunion of the synagogue through the Jews' acceptance of the church's gifts of grace, we cannot inherit the Kingdom of God.[27]

26. Ibid.

27. "In so far as the Church believes itself to be a *people of God*, it will find a description of what it is meant to be within the destiny of Israel" (PR36,966:18). The Church must pattern itself after Israel, yet Judaism needs the Gospel to make it complete (PR37,031:15). "How can we explain the way in which the ancient

It is important also to note that this approach enables the neo-orthodox to clarify and put stress upon the reciprocal nature of the Christian's mission to the Jews. "Israel exists still," says one writer, "to remind men that God has chosen a distinctive people to be his own; it exists to bear witness to its faith in God, for our sakes (Rom. Chap. 11:11–15) . . ." Though God judges Israel, "he does not cast it out." For one thing, then, Israel keeps before the Church the truth of God's mercy by judging but not casting out the Church. In the Jew we see a divine witness.

Encounters between Jew and Christian have always led to conflict or to conversation, sometimes to both. However, past relations between the two have more often been marked by conflict and monologue. For the neo-orthodox writer, who looks forward to reconciliation—even though on the basis of a Christian understanding that both Israel and the Church will unite under a common recognition of one Lord—a dialogue with the Jew is indeed a possibility. There is every likelihood that speaking to Israel will also be followed by the silent listening, because Israel speaks to the Church simply by virtue of the fact that it exists. A significant conversation between Jacob (the Church) and Esau (Israel) means that the former repentantly acknowledges the grace God has shown it despite its rebellion against God; and in this way both the Church and Israel are enabled to renew their pristine faith. Thus the Church and the Synagogue are said to need each other in order to understand fully who they are and what their message and relationship to each other is. The Jew understood as adversary is not compatible with this approach. The words of Jocz, spoken from both a European and a Jewish-Christian standpoint, appropriately sum up the position the neo-orthodox curriculum has come to in its assessment of Israel:

> whenever believers from both [Christian and Jewish] sides have really met in faith, dialogue has been the result. Such an encounter creates an unusual situation, for both sides purport to speak on behalf of Israel. Herein lies the strange

---

history of Israel is somehow our own history, our tradition, the rock out of which we have been hewn?" (PR37,717:56). ". . . in this country Christians and Jews have other things in common besides our American citizenship, and . . . actually we as Christians owe a great debt to these people, for we are more closely identified with their religious heritage than with any other" (ibid., p. 60).

relationship between Church and Synagogue. In the Synagogue, the Church meets not another religion, but herself, yet in another edition, as it were. The same applies to the Synagogue. Church and Synagogue are like dissimilar twins, alike in some respects, different in others . . . The inner difference derives from the central fact: the Church draws her knowledge from Jesus Christ, the Synagogue by-passes him.[28]

Except for the conservatives, then, Protestants believe that in different ways and on different levels they can and do enter into conversation with the Jews by witnessing to them. Thus fundamentalists feel they can converse with orthodox Jews who, like themselves, are understood to be awaiting the fulfillment of the "scriptural promises" and looking forward to the kingdom. The liberal feels similarly free to converse with liberal Jews who can join in the quest for universal truths. And the neo-orthodox conversation with Judaism assumes that the two communities have a reciprocal relationship which God will eventually join into one.

In carrying out the mission, no Protestant communicator encourages the idea that Jews should deny their Jewishness by becoming Christians. For the fundamentalists as well as the neo-orthodox, Christians are "completed Jews." But even the conservative communicator indicates that the Jew who becomes a Christian has the right and obligation to identify with his own people and to continue to be a part of the Jewish community. While the neo-orthodox writers deplore the tendency within the Christian Church to segregate the Jewish Christian, they defend the right of the Jew (Christian or not) to be a Jew. The Jew, to be sure, finds this position basically incompatible; for him, the idea that one can be both a Christian and a Jew is a contradiction. However, the Christian, who emphasizes the importance of the Jewish element in Christianity and thinks of Jesus and the early Church as genuinely Jewish, also notices that a Jew can hold any view (even an atheistic one) and still be a Jew; such a Christian can easily reconcile the idea that a person can be both Christian and Jew. Thus, in the Protestant view of the mission, the Jew is not asked to abandon his own people. This point is made especially clear in the fundamen-

28. Jakób Jocz, *The Jewish People and Jesus Christ*, (London, S.P.C.K., 1949), p. 52.

talist and neo-orthodox curricula, where Israel is understood to be an integral part of God's plan for the ages.

It would seem, in the light of this discussion, that Protestants possess doctrinal resources that would allow them, in their explication of the mission to the Jews, to stress positive intergroup content rather than Jewish hostility to the Christian mission.

# 8. The Crucifixion, the Jew, and the Christian

One of the deep roots of tension between Protestants and Jews is frequently said to consist of teachings found "in Sunday School literature, especially in connection with the crucifixion story . . ." [1] Jewish apprehension on this score is well known. Ira Eisenstein deplores what he regards as Christian teaching "that Jews living today are guilty of killing Christ," [2] and another spokesman says:

> In most Christian churches even very little children are taught that the Jews killed Jesus . . . As a matter of fact, a large number of scholars today, including many Christians, have come to the conclusion that it was the Romans who killed Jesus, not the Jews. But many churches continue to teach the old story just the same. The result is that countless Christian children begin life with a prejudice: the "Jews" who killed Jesus, as they are told, are the same to them as the "Jews" who live on the next block. [3]

The crucifixion drama is also regarded, not without reason, as having played a prominent part in Jewish disabilities through the centuries as well as providing a major cause of negative attitudes toward Jews today. In the Middle Ages, when anti-Semitism was more socially acceptable than it is in contemporary society, recitals of the Passion of Christ were often followed by physical violence against Jews. Medieval Christians so frequently attacked Jews on Good Friday that in some countries the latter were forbidden by law to leave their houses on that day. [4]

1. Newton D. Baker et al., *The American Way* (New York, Willet, Clark, 1936), pp. 34–38.
2. *The Ethics of Tolerance*, p. 70.
3. Roland Gittelsohn, *Modern Jewish Problems* (New York, U.A.H.C., 1951), p. 152.
4. Jacob R. Marcus, *The Jew in the Medieval World* (Cincinnati, U.A.H.C., 1938), p. 35.

Three of the four Protestant publishers whose materials we have been analyzing agree that there is some relationship between antipathy toward the Jews and the charge that the Jews killed Jesus. Although some fundamentalist writers tend to make this accusation themselves, they attack many "so-called Christians" and Gentiles for having mistakenly hunted down and persecuted Jews on the assumption that they murdered Christ. The neo-orthodox curriculum notes that "in some localities Jewish people are dubbed 'Christ-killers,'" and poses for class discussion the question, "What is unfair about this kind of 'labeling'?" For neo-orthodox writers, any view of the Jews as definitive Christ-rejectors fosters Jew hatred. Liberal authors, in noting that "feelings of hate and . . . acts of violence (against the Jew) have a long history," explain that "Christians proclaimed a gospel that condemned the Jews as a people for the death of the Saviour of the world"; the result was that the "wall of separation between Christians and Jews in many countries became a wall of mutual hatred." On the question of the consequences for Jews of Christian teaching about the crucifixion, only the conservative texts are silent.

A neo-orthodox textbook examined in this study relates an incident which demonstrates the power of the crucifixion story to arouse hostile emotions. Twenty-seven Bilaans were listening to Bishop Dia tell the story of Jesus' death for the first time:

> He told finally how sinful man seized Jesus and nailed him to the cross to die there for the sins of the world, to die even for the Bilaans. . . . They looked at one another and muttered against the crucifiers. They murmured their sympathy for the Crucified.[5]

The immediate effect of this first hearing of the crucifixion story is described as a muttering against the crucifiers. When the story is stripped of its background, interpretive content, and self-illuminating impact, it has an obvious power to arouse feelings of outrage which may lead to an avenging attitude. Thus the question of who crucified Jesus and the Protestant answers are more than academic. They are contemporary issues with many significant implications for the Christian faith as well as for Jewish destiny.

5. PR, *Westminster Teacher* (Jan.–March 1955), p. 54. The quotation is from Samuel H. Moffett's *Where'er the Sun* (New York, Friendship Press), p. 41.

## The Teachings: "Who Crucified Jesus?"

To what extent do Protestant curricula teach that the Jews crucified Jesus? [6] Statistically, 43 per cent of the conservative lessons dealing with the crucifixion story contain variations of this generalization. Fundamentalists make this accusation in 36 per cent of the crucifixion lessons, and the neo-orthodox do so indirectly in about 2 per cent of the cases. The charge does not appear at all in liberal materials except for the purpose of refutation.

All of the curricula—except that of the conservatives—dispute or deplore the charge that the Jews killed Jesus. About 6 per cent of the fundamentalist, 10 per cent of the neo-orthodox, and 22 per cent of the liberal lessons describing the crucifixion criticize this notion. There are also other teachings that lay the blame for the crucifixion elsewhere than solely on the Jews. Thus Gentiles, the Romans, Pilate, Christians, all mankind, and "the multitudes" are likewise named as culpable. The neo-orthodox, for example, universalize the guilt to include Christians or all humanity in 40 per cent of the instances.[7]

Clearly, not all fundamentalist generalizations about "the Jews" are meant to denote all Jews, inasmuch as two lessons give a narrow definition of the term. Such distinctions, however, are omitted from most denominational writings, and the assertion "the Jews crucified Christ" does not usually make clear which grouping of Jews is intended, or if the term "crucified" is intended literally.

When such statements (or their equivalents) as "the Jews crucified Christ" are examined in their context, the actual participation of the Jews in the crucifixion seems, for the most part, to be viewed as indirect. Only one lesson in the entire four curricula explicitly ascribes to Jews the literal act of carrying out the death sentence; [8] all other lessons narrating the crucifixion make it plain

6. See Table 12, Appendix VII.

7. These percentages refer only to the lessons which specifically discuss the crucifixion in whole or in part, not to the total lessons in the sample. Out of a total of 2,304 lessons only 112, representing approximately 5-8 per cent of the lessons in the four curricula, expound the crucifixion. Note that more than one type of statement about direct responsibility for the crucifixion tends to appear in the units; also, that the conservatives name non-Jews in 37 per cent of the cases, and the fundamentalists in 45 per cent.

8. "Being restricted by Roman law from carrying out the death sentence, the

that the actual sentence was imposed and carried out by the Roman authorities, even where the main responsibility is attributed to either the Jews or their religious leaders. A great number of lessons, however, from the two theologically conservative publishers, merely characterize the Jews in a passing way as having crucified Christ, and no matter how the writers and editors might regard the meaning of this assertion, its plain meaning to the uninitiated (in the absence of any qualification or elaboration) is that the Jews not only instigated but executed the death sentence.

That it was the Roman authorities who condemned and crucified Christ is recognized by all four Protestant groups, but chiefly by the neo-orthodox and liberals. The fundamentalists and conservatives name "the Jews" as primarily involved, but their expositions also hold the Roman authorities guilty in 24 and 29 per cent of the lessons. "Jews and Gentiles" are also linked together as mutually guilty but in a very small proportion of crucifixion units. The absence of primary accusations against the Jews by the neo-orthodox and liberals makes more significant their more frequent naming of the Roman authorities. Given the above range and diversity of attitudes about the Jewish role, the question naturally arises as to what is signified by speaking of "the Jews" in connection with responsibility for the crucifixion.

The influence of the Gospel of John in the use of the term is notable. Writers often merely reproduce it from this text without elaboration or explanation. It is exceptional in the fundamentalist lessons to discover some attempt at defining the term. Commenting upon the statement in John 7:13 that "no man spake openly of Him for fear of the Jews," the writer interprets: "In this verse the word 'Jews' is used of the leaders of the nation, the chief priests and Pharisees who made up the Sanhedrin and who sought Jesus' life." [9]

In the same text it is explained that "the Jews" in John 12 are mostly Judeans divided into two parties, the Pharisees and Saddu-

---

Jews took the prisoner to the Roman governor Pontius Pilate, who *upon their demand turned Him over to them* [the Jews] *to be crucified*, even though Jesus was declared innocent. . . . The crucifixion and death of the Savior, while a crime on the part of the Jews, was a part of God's plan for the redemption of the world" (MS39,149:214-15, my italics).

9. SP947:70. In this lesson the "Jews" and the "people" are at loggerheads, the latter on Jesus' side.

cees. "The Pharisees were the real Jews, passionately devoted to the Torah and the Law." They were "the Jews" who engaged in debate with Jesus. But the Jews of the crucifixion story are the Sadducees.

> The Pharisees usually appear in connection with theological controversy, but it was the Sadducees, as "chief priests," who finally took over Jewish leadership, pursued a policy of violence, and eventually brought about Christ's crucifixion. Thus "the Jews," *originally the name of a nation, became* (in John's Gospel) *the name of a particular sect.*
>
> (SP949:116–17, my italics)

Both of these lessons use the word "Jews" to denote the Sanhedrin leadership and not the rank and file of Jewry. But other writers in this and other curricula are not this precise. The terminology of John carries over without specification in the following example from a conservative lesson based on the Gospel of Matthew:

> When Jesus was in the Temple for the last time, a few days before His Passion, He asked the Jews, "what think ye of Christ?" Their answer was a great disappointment to Him. But on Good Friday they showed what they thought of Him. Their hearts were so filled with hatred toward Him that they shouted themselves hoarse, crying, "Crucify Him!" That was the thanks He received for coming into this world to save and bless them. (MS39,194:46)

The Jews in this paragraph of whom Jesus asked the question were, in reality, a group of Pharisees or Sadducees. The writer proceeds as if he were talking of the same group of people when, on Good Friday, "they" showed Jesus what they thought of him. This cry was actually made by "the multitude," a group gathered by the chief priests or by the chief priests and officers—in any case, an entirely different group from "the Jews" indicated in the first instance. What the lesson writer has in mind is not easy to determine. One is left to assume that he regards each of these segments of the Jewish nation as symbolic of the whole.

The tendency to make one Jew, or several, represent all Jews —not only of ancient but also of modern times—is demonstrated by

another writer for the same curriculum. Whether he is speaking of
the Sanhedrin officials, the witnesses at the hearing before Caiaphas,
or the mob before Pilate's hall, he calls them "the Jews." "The
Jews had to brand Judas and themselves publicly with a cemetery
as a memorial." Matthew, he says, omits "the various accusations
of the Jews." Pilate should have "driven the Jews from his palace."
Pilate tried to appease them and thereby "played into the hands of
the Jews." Then, climatically, the clamoring mob which exchanged
taunts with Pilate emerges as all Jewry of all places and all times.
The Jews—through the mob's words—become fully accountable
for the death of Jesus, to this very day suffering under the curse
which they brought upon themselves.

Later we shall see that two ideological constructs lie behind
such a generalization. At present we can note that it is justifiable
to assume that the writers use the word "Jews" as signifying all
Jews, unless otherwise specified. On this account the generalization
can easily be seen as a distortion on several grounds:

1. It removes the crucifixion event from its proper context of
time and place. Since "the Jews" can mean any or all Jews anywhere, it is highly inaccurate and dangerous, giving leeway to
every pupil to interpret this in whatever illegitimate fashion he
desires.

2. It divorces Jesus from his own people and nation. "The Jews"
logically should include Jesus, the disciples, Mary, his mother,
"the people," and the many women who followed him from afar.
To refer only to Christ's enemies as Jews and not to his friends is
invidious.

3. The collective reference "the Jews" takes in too much ground.
It fails to distinguish between a mere handful of people who were
involved in the plot against Jesus and the vast populace who were
not. Even if limited to the Jews of this period, the generalization
is still factually inaccurate, for it implies "all the Jews" of Jesus'
time.

4. When an active verb is placed after the designation "the
Jews," it often becomes still more inaccurate. Actually, it was the
Romans who executed Jesus, whatever the reasons were and whatever Jews were involved. Any generalizations which omit the role
of the Roman authorities are inexact.

5. The generalization "the Jews" may originally (in the New

Testament) have been provoked as much by Jewish self-criticism and by the habit of thinking of themselves collectively, as by alleged Gentile emendations of the scriptural text. For non-Jews, however, to transform this Jewish prophetic terminology into an accusation is questionable to say the least.

## The Biblical Basis of the Collective Jewish Image

The tendency to think about Jews as a collective entity derives from biblical-historical as well as psychological sources. The biblical people thought of their leaders' deeds, or those of any member of the community, as ones for which the group was responsible. They were a covenanted people, and as such acknowledged their collective guilt and punishment. The Jews took seriously, in a way that many Christians do not, this idea of "representation"—that the few may stand for the many, and even that one righteous or evil man can personify the whole.

In the conflict between Jesus and the Pharisees and in the Jerusalem episodes, the New Testament writers represent Jesus as confronting not one segment of Judaism but, in effect, the authorities who stood for all of it. The early Church, Jewish to its core, spoke in corporate terms of what had happened, just as the Old Testament writers had. But they wrote this as Jews, about Jews, and to Jews who thought representatively and self-critically; they did not write as outsiders accusing another people.

There are two characteristics of the biblical concept of "representativeness": (1) The Jews interpreted other groups' actions in this way as well as their own. They did not merely think in general terms about others, but universalized the collective responsibility of whole peoples, including Israel. (2) Collective thinking within the covenant relationship enabled the prophets to call on Israel to judge itself the more severely, to regard itself as inviting the greater judgment, and to apply the universal principle to itself with the utmost stringency. Because God chose Israel, God demands more of it and punishes its trespass with pre-eminent severity.

These biblical modes of thought are not characteristic of the modern West. We judge the action of an individual—whether leader or follower of a group—as his own action, for which he is directly responsible. When the responsibilities of others are involved, care must be taken, in the interests of justice, to make distinctions between different degrees of involvement: accessory guilt, for example.

However, Protestant writers (especially in the low-scoring curricula) present generalized images of *Jews* where only a tiny group of them are actually in question. When the Sanhedrin arrested the apostles, "the Jews hounded and persecuted the Christians." In respect to *Christians,* however, responsibility for such evils as anti-Semitism tends to be placed in individual, not collective, terms. Qualifications are always clear: "Some Christians," "some so-called Christians," "a few people who call themselves 'Christians,'" "nominal Christian," or "this man who professes to be a Christian." [10]

In sum, partly because some writers have not made clear to themselves or explicitly acknowledged to the reader the sharp differences between the contemporary habits of judging our own groups as individuals and those collective ways in which the Bible judges Israel, the way of thinking about Israel (or Jews) is influenced by the textual sources, while statements about the guilt of our own groups are made according to the present-day habits of individualistic thought. A biblical notion of collective guilt is externally applied to the Jews, but not internally to Christians (or to all men) in a self-critical vein. This difference is partly a function of the loss of the Church's continuity with Judaism.

### Effects of the Crucifixion Story on the Jewish Portrait

This study throws some further light on the role which discussions of the crucifixion play in creating the over-all portrait of Jews and Judaism in teaching materials. If—as is widely thought —lessons on this subject are inevitably derogatory of Jews, past and present, this should show up statistically. First of all, the lessons which discuss the crucifixion would themselves score negatively. This would demonstrate the proneness of their writers to downgrade the Jews. Secondly these lessons should be more negative in imbalance than are the total body of lessons from which they are selected. This would show that crucifixion expositions not

10. Here, it must be acknowledged, the fundamentalist writers are affirming the essential incompatibility of anti-Semitism with Christianity, and not denying that these people were members of the churches.

only invite but intensify negative comment. Another possibility, among positive scorers, is that the crucifixion lessons might yield a less positive imbalance than the bulk of lessons from which they are taken—again indicating a tendency to omit favorable mention of Jews or explanatory and universalizing content to offset necessary negative comment.

Accordingly, all crucifixion lessons were abstracted from the total sample, and imbalance scores for the Jewish Group Category were obtained. These scores were then compared with the Jewish scores for the New Testament lessons as a whole. The results are shown in four parallel columns in Figure 29.[11]

Among the two high positive scorers, the Jewish imbalances for New Testament and crucifixion lessons are almost identical. (The liberals score slightly higher on the crucifixion units than on New Testament lessons; the neo-orthodox score one percentage point lower—neither deviation being very significant in view of the margin of error.) It is among the fundamentalist and conservative materials that one discovers two marked effects of their treatment of the crucifixion theme. Fundamentalist New Testament lessons have a slight positive imbalance, but on crucifixion units this imbalance becomes negative, reflecting a drop of 26 percentage points. The conservative curriculum, with an over-all minus imbalance for New Testament lessons of 49 per cent, dips to a minus 57 per cent when the crucifixion materials are isolated.

Some Protestants, then, actually do write about or refer to the crucifixion without being negative, and/or without becoming less positive, about the Jewish group. But it is also possible for a marginal positive scorer to alter his orientation with this material and become negatively disposed. Finally, lessons which are negative to begin with appear to be intensified in this respect in stating the powerful themes of the Passion.

Further, some correlatives of the crucifixion material may be noted in the general content of the two high and the lowest scoring curricula.

Liberal and neo-orthodox lesson writers are sharply aware that their teachings have implications of intergroup conduct. They take account of the plight of the Jews in discussing the crucifixion, and desist from including in their lessons the charges of blood

11. Below, Appendix VIII.

guilt or the implications that the Jews are rejected by God. Both welcome the corrective findings of sociological, historical, and biblical research, making them less apt to repeat uncritically some of the more traditional and stereotyped interpretations of the crucifixion episodes. There are significant differences between these two communicators in their approach to the crucifixion, and the above generalizations often involve opposite positions on central exegetical and historical questions. Nevertheless, both are capable of universalizing the meaning of the historical events—if in different ways. The capacity for self-criticism is undoubtedly the leading source of positive imbalances in neo-orthodox lessons on the crucifixion as well as in other types of lessons.

The intergroup orientation of conservative crucifixion material is considerably more negative than any of the others. The Passion story gives their writers what appears—to outside observers—to be a spiritual sanction for the continuing plight of the Jews. Their interpretation of the Jews' self-imposed blood-curse and Christ-rejection predominantly give their Plight Categories a negative orientation. Hatred of Jesus and of Christians by the Jews, as well as modern opposition to the Church and Christianity by unbelievers, is also a prominent constituent of these lessons.[12] Their teachings about the crucifixion are characterized by various kinds of downgrading, including a high proportion of distortions (consisting primarily of unwarranted generalizations) and pejorative phraseology. *If one were to subtract the crucifixion lessons from the total conservative scores for the Jewish Group Category, their negative imbalances in dealing with the Jewish plight would be transformed almost into neutral ones.*[13]

These two contrasting orientations to Jews and Judaism in the four communicators show that discussions of the crucifixion are not necessarily anti-Semitic and, in fact, can be and often are positive. However, these findings do demonstrate that—contrary to one communicator's declared desire—his comment on the crucifixion may produce a quite hostile picture of the Jews. There are,

12. See Analytical Cat. 11, Table 24, Appendix VII. For the ways that crucifixion discussions influence the Jewish portrait for liberals, neo-orthodox, and fundamentalists consult Tables 21–23. The general effect on the Jewish portrait is summed up in Table 14.

13. For the effects of the crucifixion story on the Protestant reaction to the plight of Jews see Table 13, Appendix VII.

then, patent dangers in the theme. Much depends upon how the historical facts (and contemporary implications) of the crucifixion are regarded and, perhaps more importantly, upon whether the cross is universalized in accordance with a specific world-view. For the liberals, Jesus is a prophetic martyr in an unpopular cause, put to death by traditional and entrenched powers which resist innovation in every age. For the neo-orthodox the Cross is a judgment upon all men, and a revelation of both man's sin and God's infinite mercy. When the cross is mentioned, the Christian is made to think of his own responsibility, not that of others; the Passion story becomes an occasion not for anti-Jewish polemic but for self-examination, humility, and repentance. One of the marks of the fundamentalist and especially of the conservative approach is to scant these latter theological universalizations, although they are a part of their essential position, and to describe the Passion in minute and conjectural detail, continually particularizing the events rather than elaborating upon their power to illuminate the human situation.

## THE QUESTION OF ACCOUNTABILITY AND INVOLVEMENT

In discussing teachings which assess guilt and assign responsibility for the crucifixion, it is important to note the several different, though overlapping, frames of reference that the writers use.

The query "Who crucified Christ?" may be understood historically, psychologically, or theologically. In actual fact, curriculum writers pass unannounced from one perspective to another. While it is true that the Gospel writers never distinguish between the narrative and theological aspects of their account, curriculum writers need to be conscious of the ways in which their readers do make such distinctions and to interpret to them the biblical events so as to convey more exact meanings.

When directed to the historical event, the question of responsibility may range from "Who actually sentenced Jesus to death and carried out the sentence?" to "Who are implicated, directly or indirectly, in the crucifixion?" The interest of the writer may be to discover who is mainly responsible for the actual death of Jesus. Or it may be to ask, "Who instigated the whole affair?"

These questions are historical. They deal with the facts of the case. But there is yet another kind of responsibility which the writer may have in view—the social-psychological one—although the answer to this is also partly historical and factual. Just as today we weigh the responsibility of the German people (or even the American people) as a whole for the crimes of Dachau and Buchenwald, so writers occasionally weigh the degree of responsibility of Jesus' contemporaries, who, by their permissiveness, indifferences, or indecision contributed to the agony of Golgotha. Whether to limit such social-psychological responsibility to the Jews of Jesus' day, whether to exclude it, or, if in affirming it, to include in such generalizations the Romans as well, are apparently questions to which writers give contradictory answers. We have already noted that the practice of projecting this responsibility of the Jews indiscriminately through time is common among certain writers. Thus the scene can suddenly shift from first-century Palestine to modern Jews living anywhere in the world, and the clause "the Jews crucified Christ" can easily suggest to modern readers "the Jews who live down the street."

But there is also a theological dimension to the question; the guilt for Golgotha is either particularized or universalized, i.e. the meaning of the event is applied either to particular groups or to all groups. Thus the simple historical accusation "the Jews crucified Christ" signifies, theologically, for many Christians that this accusation is itself a denial of the revelation of truth about man and God which came through the Cross. For some, the crucifixion stands as their call to martyrdom. For others, who particularize it, it signifies the rejection of the Jews and their abandonment to fate. To those who universalize it, it points both to the disobedience of all mankind (symbolized by Jew and Gentile together) and to the divine mercy conferred upon all humanity.

These varying frames of reference in which the questions of accountability for the crucifixion are raised will produce answers which, even if similar terminology is used, cannot safely be presumed to have the same meaning. Each separate term of the unwarranted charge "The Jews crucified Jesus" may differ in signification. Thus the word "crucified" does not always literally mean the torture and execution of Jesus upon the cross. It may be shorthand for expressing "the varying degrees in which persons were implicated in the events which led to his death," or simply be a synonym for any trespass against God. Also, as has been pointed out, the designation "the Jews" may be vague and undefined; or may denote only those Jews who actually participated (and no more); or the Jewish nation of that time; or all Jews in all places and ages since the beginning of the Christian era; or a very restricted group, e.g. the Sanhedrin. The conception of the figure crucified also alters the meaning of the phrase. If the victim is God incarnate, obviously the name "Jesus" signifies something different, theologically, than if he is thought of as a great Jewish prophet.

Any analysis of the crucifixion theme, therefore, must necessarily separate as distinctly as is possible the historical from the social-psychological and theological issues, and seek to understand what the various communicators mean by the phrases they use in their theological context. It is not always possible to identify exactly which of the possible meanings a writer may have in mind. In the absence of clear clues, explanations, interpretations, or denials, it must be assumed that the literal, historical crucifixion is signified.

However, in sorting out these intended meanings, it is helpful to bear in mind certain differences in orientation that distinguish the neo-orthodox from the liberals, fundamentalists, and conservatives. The latter three communicators stress, though for different reasons, the historical and narrative implications of the crucifixion. The liberal curriculum is interested primarily in the "Jesus of history" and not in the "Christ of faith." Believing that the Gospels obscure the "real Jesus" beneath an accumulation of theological interpretation, their writers try to pierce through the biblical texts in order to reconstruct "what really happened." To this end they use available archaeological and critical tools to reconstruct the event. It is not merely that they regard the theological significance of Golgotha as relatively unimportant but rather that they find a theological meaning read into the event which it is mandatory to read out again in order not to obscure the facts. Thus whenever the liberal writers speak of the crucifiers, they mean those who pronounced the death sentence and actually drove the nails.

The fundamentalists and conservatives both share this general interest in the pure event. They, too, try to describe what actually happened. Except for this similarity to the liberals, they greatly differ from them in their approach to scripture. They cannot conclude that the Gospel accounts are fallible, nor can they differentiate between the Jesus of history and the Christ of faith. To them, the Scriptures as written are verbally inspired and infallible, and Jesus is fully human and fully divine. What is contained in the Bible is to be understood as true history, so that the only valid critical problem is "What do the Scriptures say?"

These predominantly descriptive approaches of the liberal, conservative, and fundamentalist communicators are submerged in the neo-orthodox curriculum. Although free to use the methods of both the lower and higher criticisms of the conservative and liberal writers respectively, the neo-orthodox concentrate more upon the *meaning* of the events—the ability of scripture to illuminate man's life and to reveal to him the nature of God and of man. Writers in this curriculum are free to differ from one another about the historical facts, inasmuch as they are primarily concerned about the meaning of the crucifixion for man's contemporary plight.

These broad distinctions, however, while helpful as a guide to understanding what each communicator stresses in the crucifixion, must not be taken as absolute ones. There are, for example, in neo-orthodox literature full discussions of the what-happened aspect of the Passion, in order that the problems of what-is-happening in contemporary life can be more fully illuminated by it. Theological interests are also primary to the conservatives, but these are soteriological, and are not often expressed in ways which throw light on present-day problems, intergroup or otherwise. Consequently, while these levels of meaning—particularly the theological and the historical—provide convenient divisions for the following discussion, they will continually overlap one another.

### Historical Involvement of Jews and Gentiles: The Jewish Authorities

While Protestant communicators without exception recognize that the Roman government actually carried out the act of crucifixion, not all of Jesus' contemporaries and fellow countrymen are thereby regarded as innocent of any historical implication in the affair. All four communicators, moreover, agree that the arrest of Jesus involved some Jewish leaders who were responsible for turning him over to the Roman authorities. None assumes that there are any historical grounds for believing that the whole responsibility was Roman. This latter position, in all events, would be impossible for Christian groups to take: on the one hand it calls into question the veracity of the entire New Testament account, and on the other it milks the event of any significant universal meaning. A liberal writer begins by acknowledging that "although the Jewish leaders in Jerusalem surely shared the blame for Jesus' death, his crucifixion was the result of Pilate's decision. Crucifixion was a Roman form of capital punishment." [14]

The liberals, in fact, argue that "when the Gospel records are examined with a free and discerning mind . . . it becomes clear, at least to many scholars, that there was good reason for the Jewish leaders to wish to silence Jesus. He was criticizing both the Law and the Temple rituals of sacrifice. He also refused to play the role of Messiah that some of his enthusiastic followers were urging him to assume in order to lead their nation to victory against their Roman oppressors." [15]

Despite their tendency to generalize in this matter, the conservatives recognize that the chief priests and other more limited groups were involved in the plot to turn Jesus over to the Roman authorities. A lesson which ends with the statement "the Jews condemned Jesus as a criminal" begins by naming the chief priests as the "instigators of His trial and crucifixion; churchmen worse than any of the common people." Other more specific designations are "the Jewish leaders," "the Jewish High Council," "priests, elders, scribes, the high priest serving as presiding officer," the "Sanhedrin," "Sadducees," "the chief priests," or "the whole multitude."

When conservatives identify the religious leaders who plotted Jesus' death, it is most often the Jewish High Council, or Sanhedrin. But the real instigators within the Sanhedrin are also pinpointed as the chief priests or, sometimes, the High Priest:

> The leaders had long plotted Jesus' death. Two days before the Passover they met and finally resolved to act . . . "Chief priests, elders, scribes," three classes of men. They made up the Council or Sanhedrin, which consisted of 70 men and the high priest. The chief priests seem to have been the most influential members of the Council and, in this case, the ring-

14. UN150:52.
15. UN380:146.

leaders. Caiaphas had alerted all members who were in favor
of having Jesus put to death.                    (MS39,495:78)

The principals are here isolated as the chief priests, and, especially, Caiaphas, who is significantly regarded in this instance as
having alerted *only those members of the Sanhedrin who were
already in favor of sentencing Jesus.* In other words, even in the
conservative view not all members of the Sanhedrin were involved,
and those who were had apparently been selected by the High
Priest himself.[16] Some lessons mention the chief priests exclusively.
It is possible that where the designation "Jewish leaders" appears
by itself in a lesson, either the high priests or the group gathered
about the chief priest are intended. Jesus is said to have "told His
disciples that He would be arrested and tried by the chief priests,
then mocked and scourged and crucified by the Romans, Mark
10:33–34. . . . Meanwhile the high priests had been busy plotting
His death."

A similar account is provided by the fundamentalists, except
that the Pharisees are also included at times. Pharisees did in fact
belong to the Sanhedrin, but the high priestly clique was composed
of Sadducees. The significance needs to be noted. Up to this point
in the Gospels, the Pharisees are Jesus' main opponents. After Jesus
seized the temple, the Sadducees and high priests became the major
opposition. Quite often, lesson writers of most Protestant groups
assume that the earlier hostility of the Pharisees indicates that they
were responsible for accusing Jesus before Pilate. Actually, the
Pharisees were possibly not a decisive group in the Sanhedrin at
this time, the Temple and civil government being under the direction of the Sadducean-Boethusian priests. It has also been argued
that the scribes and elders named in connection with the Temple
were predominantly Sadducees.[17]

When various writers trace the principal source of Jewish in-

16. Conservative writers would specifically exempt Nicodemus and Joseph
of Arimathea, and the others as well. When a writer charges: "Without a dis-
senting vote, the Council passed the death sentence on the innocent Jesus," he
may be signifying that this action was taken only by the select number present.

17. The numerical strength of the Pharisees in the Sanhedrin cannot be determined, but the consensus of New Testament scholars is that the Council was
under strict control of the priestly and moneyed aristocracy, led by the high
priest and his followers. See Morton S. Enslin, "New Testament Times: II.
Palestine," *Interpreter's Bible*, 7, 106. Klausner believes that the Council was

volvement in the arrest and trial of Jesus to the Sadducean-Boethusian priests, their lessons indicate more visibly that other groups such as the Pharisees were possibly not involved, or, if at all, only marginally. This approach is also more likely to provide reasons why these "Jewish leaders" sought Jesus' death. Says a fundamentalist writer:

> The Sadducees were an organization of Jewish leaders, semi-religious and semi-political in nature. Their membership was composed of the most aristocratic, wealthy, powerful families among the Jews. On the whole, they were quite subservient to the Roman government. One contributing cause of their opposition to Christ may have been a genuine fear that He would bring Jews into conflict with Rome. Religiously, the Sadducees were rivals of the more conservative Pharisees. They were the "Modernists" of their day; the Pharisees were the "Fundamentalists." The Sadducees taught the doctrines of materialism, denied life hereafter, and the existence of the immortal soul. They did not believe in the resurrection. They were among the most violent enemies of Christ. (SP935:103)

This recognition of Sadducean subservience to the Roman government connects Rome more closely with the events that led up to the arrest and trial of Jesus than is commonly done in most lessons. The Jewish authorities involved acted more for Rome than for Israel in the opinion of one writer, who explains the economics of the crucifixion in this manner:

> In the days of Herod the Great . . . the Temple and its management had fallen into the hands of the Sadducees. They were *an insignificant group among the Jews*, there being no more than three thousand of them in Jesus' day . . .
>
> They were the monied aristocracy of the nation whose fortunes depended upon keeping the peace and an alliance with their Roman overlords. They were, actually, collaborationists, though they were thorough Jews. Annas, the father-in-law of the high priest, Caiaphas, had served in that office for a legal term, having bought his way into power by a huge bribe paid

---

made up primarily of Sadducees: *Jesus of Nazareth* (New York, Macmillan, 1945), pp. 334-35.

to the Romans. Coming into control of the Temple revenues
. . . he was in a position to pay further bribes to Caesar for
official endorsement of his sons, and, in Jesus' day, his son-in-
law, as high priests.

The arrangement was perfectly satisfactory to the Romans,
for whoever sat on the high priest's throne in Jerusalem was
the heaviest single taxpayer in the Empire . . . *No one could
be allowed on the throne without the approval of Rome,*
and that perpetuated Annas in power, *even though he and his
family were despised by the Jews themselves.*

It was a vicious arrangement. Annas supported the Romans,
and the Romans supported Annas. It was "a government of
the many by the few for the money."

When Jesus encouraged the people to believe they could
by-pass the Temple system in their approach to God, the
whole financial system was imperiled, and Jesus became the
object of the implacable hatred of the Temple hierarchy.

(PR37,190:33; italics mine)

Those authors who see the Jewish authorities as tools of Rome
succeed fairly well in avoiding the generalization "the Jews" in
connection with any part of the crucifixion story. This is not true
of those who interpret the respective roles of the Jews and the
Romans in the opposite fashion. Rather than regarding the Jewish
authorities as being used by Rome, these Christians describe the
Roman authorities (especially in bringing about the death of Jesus)
as having been the tools of the Jews.

The events leading directly to the actual trial before Pilate and
the condemnation of Jesus were the arrest of Jesus and the hearings
before the high priests and Sanhedrin. The treatment of the initial
events depends greatly upon certain conceptions: how writers
understand the relationship of the high priestly clique and the Sanhedrin to the Jewish nation and Rome respectively, whether they
regard the hearings before the High Priest and Sanhedrin as actual
trials, and whether they consider some of the charges brought
against Jesus as containing any element of truth or irony.

For conservative writers there appear to have been three trials.
There were (1) the night session before Caiaphas, (2) the morning meeting of the Sanhedrin, and (3) the trial before Pilate. Some

add a fourth—the trial before Herod. Since conservative writers assume that these can all be taken as trials, they tend to judge them all illegal.

For most neo-orthodox authors there were possibly two trials, the morning session of the Sanhedrin, and the trial before Pilate, with the night session regarded as a preliminary hearing. The liberals agree on this last point, but also look upon the morning session of the Sanhedrin as a meeting called for the purpose of confirming charges to be made to the Roman authorities, and not a formal trial according to Jewish law:

> As soon as it was day, Caiaphas, the High Priest, summoned certain members of his official council to meet in the palace to help in preparing the written charges to be brought before Pilate, the Roman governor. After some discussion, they agreed on three . . . When the group had agreed on the charges, Caiaphas ordered the prisoner brought before them for questioning. (UN172:150)

Since the conservatives regard the night session as a trial rather than a preliminary hearing, they assert that it was unlawful. "According to the law any session which the Council held during the night was illegal. This was a trial at which every rule of law . . . was trampled underfoot." The judgment is correct, of course, only if the Sanhedrin met at that time to conduct a formal trial. However, the high priests, who had the power to summon the aid of Roman cohorts at any time of the day or night, would not be restricted as to their convening of an investigative session. In this event, the rules that hold for trials for the entire Sanhedrin as a whole would not apply.

The illegality of the morning session is more widely asserted in the different curricula, except the liberal one. On the basis of rules laid down by the Pharisees in the Mishnah, a fundamentalist writer finds both the night and morning trials to be "illegal, by existing Jewish law, on at least five counts":

1. He was arrested, condemned, and crucified in less than 24 hours, though the law forbade execution until ten days after condemnation

2. He was tried at night, contrary to regulations for capital trials

3. False witnesses testified against Him

4. No one was permitted to speak in His behalf

5. Some of the Judges participated in gathering false witnesses

This indictment is partly vulnerable in that it ignores the fact that Jesus was condemned and crucified by Roman authorities who were obviously not controlled by Jewish law. Jewish law governed only the action of the Sanhedrin. The fact, then, that Jewish law prohibited execution so soon after condemnation could not make Rome's execution of Jesus illegal. Is, then, the writer assuming that Jesus was tried, condemned, and killed by Jewish authorities? [18] Likewise, the second point is valid only if the hearing before Caiaphas could be considered a trial.[19] Judgments would

18. There is much confusion in lessons which deal with these points, either because different writers come to different conclusions or because they are not aware of all the technical issues involved and therefore make contradictory assumptions. A careful analysis of crucifixion lessons dealing with the hearings before the Jewish authorities indicates that the writers need to study certain factual questions and also to make themselves aware that some of these cannot be answered dogmatically on the basis of any evidence we now possess: (1) Could the Sanhedrin try a capital case? (2) If it could, could it impose sentence? (3) If it could impose sentence, could it carry out the penalty? (4) Did the Sanhedrin have the power only to gather evidence and present a capital case to the Roman authorities? (5) Did it have the power to try a capital case and impose a sentence, but with the necessity of submitting it to Roman authorities for review and confirmation? (6) Did it have the power to try such cases and impose sentence in respect to offenses against the Jewish people only (with the necessity of Roman review), with all other cases to be tried before the Roman procurator? (7) Did it have the power to carry out the death sentence (when violation of Jewish law was alone involved and after Roman confirmation of the sentence), i.e. was the prisoner turned back to the Sanhedrin for execution? (8) Did the Roman power carry out all sentences of execution, regardless of whether they involved Jewish or Roman law? With the exception of question 3, writers seem to take for granted affirmative answers to all the questions.

19. "The simplest way to understand the story," says Sherman E. Johnson, "is to suppose that Caiaphas and some of his friends assembled at night in the hope of gathering evidence against Jesus. They were unable to find witnesses whose testimony agreed on any point that would make a conviction possible. It was a cardinal doctrine of the Pharisees that witnesses must be cross-examined separately and they would have taken every precaution to protect any man accused of a capital offense. Thus it would have been quite impossible to convict Jesus in a Jewish court. Accordingly the Sadducean priests tried to get Jesus

differ also on the morning session of the Sanhedrin, according to whether one believed this to have been a formal capital trial or an official confirmation of charges to be made to the Roman authorities.[20] If one is convinced that the real trial was conducted before the Sanhedrin, called into session for the purpose of condemning Jesus to death according to Jewish law and all that was needed to carry out the execution was Pilate's permission, then one's belief that the entire proceedings were illegal is probably warranted.[21] If one concludes, however, that the real trial was before Pilate and that the Sanhedrin session was for the purpose of indictment only, the charges of illegality would be more difficult to sustain.

One noncontroversial assertion of all writers is that Jesus died according to Roman and not Jewish law, and by Roman and not Jewish methods.[22] Nevertheless, the Jewish authorities are also

---

to say that he was the Messiah, in order to accuse him to Pilate as a pretender to the Jewish throne." "Matthew," *Interpreter's Bible*, 7, p. 486.

20. Kilpatrick examines the historical and Gospel evidences and notes a possible parallel between procedures permitted to local Egyptian authorities by the Roman government and procedures permitted to the Sanhedrin in capital offenses. In Egypt, "Local authorities dealt with minor cases and held a preliminary inquiry into graver ones. These last were reserved for the prefect to deal with at the nearest assizes. Thus in Egypt a prisoner in the position of Jesus would first of all be examined by the local authority and would then be reserved for the prefect's judgement when he was available. We must recognize that the trial of Jesus could, with but little modification, be fitted into this scheme. . . . the proceedings before the Sanhedrin contained an attempt to show Jewish opinion in the Sanhedrin that Jesus was guilty. For the rest the interrogation of Jesus by the High Priest would be the examination of a prisoner accused of a grave offence before he goes before the procurator for trial. And Jesus does go before the procurator for trial. Pilate tries him and passes sentence, and Jesus is crucified, a Roman form of the death penalty." G. D. Kilpatrick, *The Trial of Jesus* (London, Oxford University Press, 1953), pp. 19–20. For Jewish views cf. Klausner, *Jesus of Nazareth*, pp. 333–34; and Solomon Zeitlin, *Who Crucified Jesus?* (New York, Harper, 1942), esp. chap. 5, pp. 68 ff.

21. There is also a contradictory conclusion which may be drawn from the same set of facts, namely that the New Testament account is palpably false, inasmuch as all the rules whereby the Sanhedrin operated are contradicted by the events recited in scripture. For a representative view of this position see Roland B. Gittelsohn, *A Jewish View of Jesus* (pamphlet, Boston, Jan. 1954), pp. 4–5. Such a position assumes, however, that (1) the Sanhedrin sessions were actual trials, and (2) officials never violate official requirements.

22. Had Pilate merely approved a Sanhedrin sentence, he probably would have turned Jesus over to Jewish authorities to be stoned. Whether the local religious-civil authorities had the power at this time to carry out a Roman-approved death sentence is disputed by critics. The following fundamentalist sentences are juxtaposed: (1) ". . . the Jews could pass a death sentence, but had to get

presented as having various reasons for wishing to have Jesus condemned. At times, the Jewish reasons given by the writers are made the compelling ones. For the conservatives they are the sole reasons, the charges recited to the Roman governor being specious. Although agreeable in general to this interpretation, the fundamentalist and neo-orthodox would at times also include a genuine Roman anxiety over the messianic activities of Jesus, and also acknowledge that the high priests and Sadducees were responsible to Rome and were fearful of messianic pretenders as inviting the wrath of the Empire on the Jewish nation. Other reasons for opposing Jesus are given: interference with the Temple management, blasphemy, his teachings about the Law, his violation of established folkways and customs.

The liberals are the only ones who find the condemnation of Jesus to be legal, their assumption apparently being that the Jewish authorities had just reasons for getting rid of Jesus. Of all the charges brought against him, the teachers' manual takes seriously only the charge that "Jesus stirred up the people against the laws and customs the Jews regarded as divinely established." Or again, Jesus "had been found transgressing the covenant set forth by Moses and according to Jewish law he should be stoned to death." The writer quotes from another authority to support this point:

> It is surely appropriate to ask seriously why it is necessary for Christian writers to insist that Jesus was condemned illegally. He himself said that he did not come to destroy the law, and yet no true Christian believes that the teaching of Jesus was merely a continuation of Mosaic or rabbinical doctrine. He clearly modified prevalent teaching to such an extent that the Jews could truthfully say: "He stirreth up the people, teaching throughout all Judea, and beginning from Galilee even unto this place." It is hard to understand why the most devout Christian should hesitate to admit that Jesus broke the Jewish ecclesiastical law, and in consequence deserved an honest condemnation at the hands of the people whose whole criminal system had a theocratic basis. It is surely a grander thing to break the law gloriously in the interest of truth than

---

permission from the Roman governor to execute it," (2) crucifixion "was the Roman method of execution. He was not to be stoned, which was the Jewish method" (SP640:62). Are these statements contradictions?

to abide by a code now becoming obsolete, at a time when the world required a better code for its own true advancement. That is certainly a more inspiring thought than the assumption that the law was not broken, although the interest of civilization demanded that it should be broken.[23]

Though Jesus, then, deserved to die according to Jewish law, his defiance was justified according to this opinion, and his death, therefore, is to be regarded as a "martyrdom due to human misunderstandings and fears." Liberal writers, however, fail to draw the conclusion they imply—that but for the activity of the Jewish authorities, Jesus never would have been condemned to death.[24]

Unlike the liberals, the neo-orthodox writers believe that Jesus did make a messianic claim, and thereby left himself open to the Roman charge of sedition. The title of Messiah had no fixed denotation, but in the potentially explosive situation in Palestine it was generally associated with the nationalistic hopes of Israel—freedom from Roman bondage and the establishment of the Davidic kingdom:

> Since the term "Messiah" was an incendiary title, politically dangerous, there is every reason to see why Jesus should have wished to avoid its application to him and his work . . . if Jesus had allowed his followers to hail him as "Messiah," he would surely have aroused hopes of a sort that were out of line with his own intentions. That this would have been the case is evidenced by the fact that when "the messianic secret" was out, when the confession was no longer silenced . . . the immediate sequel was that Jesus was crucified as a political threat to Caesar's kingdom.[25]

Roman fears of a potential messianic uprising is perhaps the single most neglected feature of the crucifixion accounts. When Christians concede that the ruling Gentile conquerors of Palestine

23. UN150:53. The liberals are quoting from Richard W. Husband, *The Prosecution of Jesus* (Princeton, Princeton University Press, 1916), p. 13. Some Jewish scholars contend that "never did any generation of Jews seek to murder one of their prophets or reformers" (Gittlesohn, *A Jewish View of Jesus,* p. 3).

24. This illustrates that the liberal interpretation of the crucifixion also could, in its own way, reflect unfavorably on the Judaism of Jesus' day and imply that some Jews primarily were to blame for the death of Jesus.

25. PR, *Crossroads* (Dec. 5, 1954), p. 40.

—to whom the high priests and followers were answerable and utterly subservient—condemned Jesus to death as a pretender to the Jewish throne, the Gentile world is thereby implicated in the tragedy of Golgotha. "It must never be forgotten," says the author of a neo-orthodox lesson, "that . . . Jesus had been crucified as a seditionist. That was the meaning of the ascription fixed over his head. It was Rome's announcement of the reason for putting him to death, and a warning to any like-minded person.[26]

Historically, therefore, a case can be made out for the basic involvement of some Romans as well as some Jews. However, any view of the historical facts which ignores the complexity of the causes that led to the death of Christ and oversimplifies the case by isolating and exaggerating Jewish responsibility runs a double danger: first, of finding little or no significance for contemporary man in the events of the cross by overlooking certain theological considerations that will be analyzed in the next chapter; second, of falling into anti-Jewish attitudes that transform the cross into a weapon with which to castigate Jesus' own people.

### Historical Involvement of Jews and Gentiles: Pilate

The trial of Jesus before the Roman procurator is highly controversial. It is here that writers are directly confronted with the fact of Roman involvement. Complex and difficult exegetical questions are also posed by the scriptural account, not the least of which is the traditional interpretation that the Gospels present a Pilate who was relatively innocent.

Their understanding of the biblical sources leads conservatives and fundamentalists to stress the greater responsibility of "the Jews." Even while recognizing Pilate's guilt, they picture him as a more or less helpless victim in the hands of Jews. An instance of this emphasis is provided by one writer who directs the teacher as follows: "In treating the trial before the governor, present Pilate as an irresolute judge who let himself be driven by a bloody mob to condemn the innocent. *The Jews' sin was the greater.*" [27]

26. PR37,078:66. Cf. Matt. 27:37, Mark 15:26.
27. MS39,193:42. In these and other lessons Pilate usually represents himself, seldom "the Romans," while Caiaphas and the high priests are almost always identified as "the Jews."

The same lesson explains that Pilate "was, of course, guilty." But the reader is directed to John 19:11, where Jesus says, "he who delivered you to me has the greater sin." [28] The point is that while Pilate passed sentence, it was only the Jews who wanted him crucified. Another writer who believes that Pilate condemned Jesus but only on the Jews' insistence, drives home the guilt of the latter while never mentioning the guilt of Pilate. "A grievous sin indeed, for they [the Jews] have killed 'the Prince of Life.' Guilty of the death of God's Son!'"

In these lessons, Pilate is convinced of Jesus' utter innocence of all charges brought against him and makes one attempt after another to set him free.

These attempts are shown to have begun early in the trial:

> He was convinced of Christ's innocence and told the Jews so. They had no evidence to offer, but could only make a loud noise. Pilate wanted to be fair, but he lacked firmness. He should have set Christ free at once and driven the Jews from his palace. Cp. Acts 18:12–16. Unfortunately, Pilate showed that he was afraid of the Jews; he wanted to gain their good will. He wished that he could dispose of this case without offending the Jews, but also without condemning an innocent person to death.                    (MS39,193:42–43)

Finally, he is forced to bow down to the power of the Jews: "Pilate was not a willing tool of the Jews as later many kings and emperors obediently carried out the order of the papists to persecute and slaughter the true Christians."

These themes of Pilate's weakness—his futile attempts to free Jesus and his overwhelming fear of the Jews—are the earmarks of the conservative approach to the climax of the Passion story. Although Pilate believed him innocent, he proposed to scourge the prisoner and set him free, because a not-guilty verdict "did not satisfy the Jews." This only serves to demonstrate Pilate's vulnerability: "The Jews saw at once that Pilate was beginning to yield to them and that he would go farther to win their favor. There-

28. MS39,434:42. The "he" in John 19:11, however, is believed by many scholars to refer to Judas (not "the Jews" nor the Sanhedrin), although other commentators make a case for the chief priest.

fore they became more insistent with their demand that Jesus should be sentenced. From now on, Pilate's attempts to set Jesus free were futile efforts."

But Pilate "again and again attempted the impossible." He offered to release a prisoner, but "the choice of the Jews shows to what a low level of wickedness they had sunk." The climax of Pilate's increasingly frantic efforts comes when he attempts to appease the Jews by scourging him:

> Foiled by the unexpected choice of the Jews, Pilate tried to move them to leniency toward Jesus by appealing to their feelings of sympathy and humanity. He thought that when they saw Jesus suffering great bodily agony, they would feel sorry for Him . . . Severely bruised and with blood streaming from His body, Jesus was presented to the Jews by Pilate with the pitying appeal, "Behold the Man" (in Latin, *Ecce Homo*). . . . The hard-hearted, unbelieving Jews could not even thus be moved to pity.[29]

After this, "Pilate was baffled and helpless. He had yielded too much and could no longer stem the tide. The more he proclaimed Christ's innocence, the louder and more insistent grew the cries of the Jews that Jesus should be crucified." An interview with Jesus gave Pilate boldness again. "He was now determined to set Jesus free, but the Jews quickly drew their noose tightly about Pilate's neck . . . Fearing that the Jews might bring accusations against him before Caesar, Pilate finally yielded to their demands."

Few neo-orthodox lessons emphasize the more aggressive role of the Jewish authorities, but even these do not mitigate Pilate's guilt. "Pilate's part in the trial and crucifixion was pitiable, and the world can never forget that he lost a great opportunity to demonstrate Roman justice."[30] The stark picture of an utterly helpless Pilate caught in the toils of Jewish intrigue is greatly modified by other considerations. Pilate was indeed pressured, *and he did indeed seek to escape responsibility for his act; but so did everyone connected with the incident:*

---

29. MS39,193:49–50. The biblical incident in which Pilate washes his hands of responsibility is never interpreted, however, as actually releasing him from his guilt; in fact, the conservatives insist on Pilate's guilt when discussing that incident.
30. PR37,190:34.

Though Pilate himself had given the orders, he had tried to wash his hands of any responsibility, placing the blame on the Temple officials. The Temple officials had forced Pilate's hand by demanding that Jesus be crucified, but they had shifted the load to Pilate's shoulders by making it an issue of Caesar or Christ. No one seemed willing to accept the responsibility; somehow they all felt uneasy.

(PR37,627:34–35)

The neo-orthodox interpretation is also influenced by extra-biblical as well as biblical sources. Before taking up the trial of Jesus before Pilate, one lesson cautions the teacher to make certain that the pupils understand "that Pilate was generally a cruel and contemptuous procurator, and one who did not abide by the Roman policy of ruling subject peoples with some fairness and consideration." This manual then warns:

Help the class to see the turning point—when Pilate's own position was threatened. Be sure it is understood that Pilate had to be persuaded to condemn Jesus. *But do not be dogmatic about the reasons for this. For our Gospels do not make it clear exactly why he was reluctant.* Doubtless it was in part because of the impact Jesus made upon him. But remember that Pilate was very contemptuous of the Jews, and he may also have held back because he wanted to enjoy his feeling of power over them.                    (PR37,651:60)

The possibility that Pilate was pulled by several feelings—a desire to taunt and bait Jews, a superstitious awe of Jesus, and a contempt for messianic pretenders—is hinted at by several writers but is never fully developed in the neo-orthodox curriculum. Viewed in this way, Pilate's cry *Ecce homo* could as easily be derisive and mocking as an attempt to arouse support for Jesus' release. Were Pilate's protestations of Jesus' innocence partly a baiting of the high priest's mob, partly a vague fear that Jesus was a god, partly a conviction of Jesus' harmlessness, partly a pretension? It is hard to say.

The conclusion of neo-orthodox writers is that the trial before Pilate mainly implicates humanity itself and does not make any one group solely or chiefly responsible. Assaying the roles of the chief priests, the Council, Pilate, the people, Judas, the mob, and the Roman soldiers, one writer observes:

> Yes, every actor had an alibi, and every actor shared the guilt. Even the disciples who had fled in fear, and who had left Jesus alone in this hour of trial—even they were guilty along with Pilate, the high priest, and the mob. We have, then, a tangled human situation: as awful crime with no one present on whom the whole responsibility can be laid. What happens, then, to the guilt? It is shared by *all* those present. No one is exclusively guilty; *everyone is guilty with everyone else.*[31]

31. PR, *Westminster Teacher* (March 29, 1953), p. 82.

# 9. Intergroup Content of the Theology of the Crucifixion

Jesus is regarded by most Christians as the Messiah of the Jews and the divine Son of God. Thus statements about the crucifixion of Jesus naturally have broader and more significant implications than do statements about the death of other Jewish figures. For this reason, too, teachings about the crucifixion are bound to exert a profound influence upon Jewish-Christian relations.

The belief that Jesus is the Christ creates certain intergroup problems, the most important of which concerns the charge that the Jews were guilty of deicide. This accusation is sometimes made by conservatives and fundamentalists. For example, Stephen's defense before the Sanhedrin in the seventh chapter of Acts provokes the following commentary:

> Moreover, Stephen charged them with murder. Not just homicide (murder of a man), but deicide (murder of God). They had murdered the Just One (7:52), whose portrait was faithfully delineated by the prophets . . . Stephen did not imply that Christ was crucified by the Jews simply because they were Jews by race. It was their hard-heartedness, their blindness, their resolute stubbornness, that crucified the Lord . . . The nation was guilty of taking the life of the promised Messiah. Their guilt was doubly heavy.[1]

1. SP955:130. For conservative references cf. MS39,434:42 and MS39,495:79. It should be noted that such charges in Scripture Press and Missouri Synod materials are nontypical. Factually, and from our point in history, to limit this charge to the Jews is to ignore the involvement of the Roman authorities as well as the participation of a limited number of Jews. A recognition of this dual responsibility is basic to the conservative theological (and Pauline) dictum that God consigned the Jewish and Gentile worlds to disobedience in order that he might have mercy on all. Thus a conservative lesson says: "it was His [God's] will that the representatives of all mankind, Gentiles as well as Jews, should participate in afflicting Him [Christ] with the greatest shame and the worst kinds of torture" (MS39,193:41).

Such statements can follow—though not inevitably—from a belief in the divinity of Jesus, especially when they reflect unexamined teaching traditions the churches have inherited from earlier periods of their history. The question whether one can actually kill God is never raised by these writers, although one comment on the burial of Jesus implies that this is possible: "It exceeds all human imagination to think of the almighty Creator as lying lifeless in the earth, which He had made." [2]

In complete contrast to the fundamentalist-conservative position on Jesus is that of the liberals. The latter faces entirely different issues in portraying the Jews, and the theological points which are important to the conservatives are of no concern to the liberals. Jesus is interpreted as a great human prophet whose claim to divinity is said to be no different from that of all other men. His death, therefore, is considered a typical martyrdom, and the charge of deicide is no longer possible. Nor, from the point of view of liberal theology, can the Jews be denigrated because of their rejection of Christ or their presumed unbelief or apostasy. On the contrary, the liberal finds himself more or less in sympathy with the Jewish understanding of Christ.

The neo-orthodox, on the other hand, maintain some of the same theological presuppositions as the fundamentalists and conservatives. They, too, accept the full divinity of Jesus. But, like the liberals, they never make the accusation of deicide, and they treat the theme of Christ-rejection in a radically different manner than do either the fundamentalists or conservatives. The neo-orthodox handle the question of Jesus' death in such a way that the Christian, too, is implicated. In their interpretation the double guilt of the Christian is exposed rather than the guilt of the Jew alone.

There are at least three elements in the neo-orthodox approach to the crucifixion which should be noted. The neo-orthodox find positive intergroup significance in the crucifixion because they

2. MS39,199:76. How God can die is explained by a Lutheran theologian as follows: "There is such an ineffable union and communion between the divine and the human nature in the Person of Christ that it can truthfully be said that the Son of God suffered and died, although the divine nature can neither suffer nor die . . . For example, it may be said, 'God died,' because the Person who is God died in His human nature" (C. H. Little, *Lutheran Confessional Theology*, St. Louis, Concordia, 1943, p. 164).

view the function of scripture as that of illuminating man's condition. The doctrine of the full humanity as well as the full divinity of Jesus is central to their educational aims.

It has already been noted that the neo-orthodox believe the Scriptures reveal both man's true nature and God's self-disclosure. The cross, accordingly, is (among other things) a revelation, in that it shows man his true self—his rebellion against God even in what he assumes to be his noble acts. This revelation makes man capable of self-criticism, repentance, and faith. The illuminative function of scripture as it contributes to an image of the Jew is pointed out in the following passage:

> Readers [of scripture] are quick to identify their *foes* with the people who rejected Jesus and are equally quick to see themselves among those who followed Jesus. Their own face is reflected to them in a heroic light as the face of God's servant. Their enemy's face is reflected as a villain among the people whom Jesus condemned. When this happens, they have either failed to see their own face as it actually is, or else, as James writes, they have immediately forgotten what they look like. When we reverse this procedure, the truth begins to emerge.                                      (PR36,937:66)

This approach uses the negative portrait of humanity, as it appears in the Bible, to examine self-critically the Christian teacher and pupil as well as the groups mentioned in scripture. It includes the Christian with the rest of humanity as opposing Christ. In his portrayal of the crucifixion the neo-orthodox writer sees the human participants in the drama as so many images of himself. It is man's present failure which is discernible in the biblical drama, not simply the guilt of some ancient historical figures, either Jews or Gentiles.

The problem of establishing the guilt for Jesus' crucifixion is variously treated according to the use each of the communicators makes of the doctrine of the full humanity and full divinity of Jesus—a doctrine to which all but the liberals subscribe. The fundamentalists and conservatives explicitly affirm their belief in the twofold nature of Jesus, but the practical implications in both curricula, particularly as they describe the reactions to Jesus of his Jewish contemporaries, affirm the divinity of Jesus to the virtual exclusion of any consideration of him as a man. Jesus is pictured almost exclusively as the omniscient and omnipotent God; his knowledge of the world and of man, as well as his understanding of human events (including his own role and destiny), appears to be governed by few human limitations. The lesson writers sometimes regard his special nature as being apparent even to those Jews who did not accept him as the Messiah; hence the Jews are virulently denounced for their response to Jesus. In short, the divine nature of Jesus is overt rather than hidden, and "the Jews" of Jesus' time are often censured for failing to see in him what the Christian today perceives through his fully developed Christology.[3] But these writers never use the crucifixion to reveal to the reader how man responds when he confronts the divine in a concrete and practical situation.

One effect of subordinating Jesus' humanity to his divinity is that it colors the whole Jewish portrait in the negative-scoring curricula. The divine quality of Jesus is made so obvious in these expositions that the stubbornness of the unbelieving Jews becomes a recurrent theme. In crucifixion scenes, for example, the Jewish leaders almost always are described as more than blind in their hatred of Jesus; it is said that the Sanhedrin knew he was blameless, but that its members nonetheless invented charges which they clearly understood to be false, and that they manufactured evidence and deliberately sought witnesses who would not hesitate to perjure themselves. This same lesson urges the teacher to show the pupils "how the whole affair was manipulated to make the innocent Jesus appear guilty." [4] Jesus is sketched not merely as the victim whom God knew to be innocent, but as one whose innocence was quite apparent even to those who accused him.

If Jesus' divine righteousness was so evident, a reader—especially a child—cannot understand why the leaders should have hated him so intensely that they sought his death. In the absence of any understandable human motivation, their hatred appears purely arbitrary. For example, Jesus' opponents are presented at his trial as

3. The Missouri Synod doctrine is that Christ's two natures are so fused that one cannot separate them doctrinally, i.e. the human nature of Christ participates in all the divine properties. *Formula of Concord*, 4, 56; 8, 43, 84. One must, however, make a clear distinction between what Christ is in his Incarnation and how he was seen and responded to by man in his earthly ministry.

4. MS39,191:31.

"pretending" that the Saviour was guilty. The high priest is not represented as genuinely angered by Jesus' proclamation of himself "as the Son of God"; he is said merely to act "*as though* he were deeply offended.*" The Sanhedrin's "*professed* zeal for the law*" is described as "rankest hypocrisy"; its members only "*pretended* to be concerned for God's honor.*"[5] The fundamentalist writers are less apt than the conservatives to insist that the charges were trumped-up simply out of malice, but they make at least one similarly damaging statement. The Jews, according to one text, "pretended that they put him to death for a heinous sin of his own," and this pretense extends to all the charges.[6] There is little indication here that those who condemned Jesus for blasphemy sincerely believed that he was guilty of the charge.

By creating an image of the Jews as a people capable of unmixed evil, of committing acts which they themselves recognize as evil (here condemning a man who is clearly devoid of any wrong-doing), the writers present a Jewish hatred which is apparently unmotivated. Their portrait of the Jew thus makes him out to be diabolical.

In any act of injustice there is bound to be a mixture of motives, some of which appear to the ones who commit it to be worthy and seemingly to justify the act; in the negative-scoring literature, however, the Jews are assigned no motives, only arbitrary hatred. Certainly, a human being who took upon himself to put to death the divine Son of God would be convinced of the guilt of his victim; he would have to persuade himself that the prisoner is evil and ought to be done away with. According to these curricula, however, Jesus appeared before the crowd at Pilate's hall like "a harmless man whose innocence was evident to every fair-minded person. Pilate calculated that the Jews would be morally obligated to prefer Jesus to Barabbas . . . The choice of the Jews [of Barabbas] shows to what a low level of wickedness they had sunk."[7] The participants in this drama are described as if they knew their actions were equivalent to senseless murder.[8] While the Roman soldiers "did not know what it was all about," the

5. MS39,194:33 (my italics).
6. SP939:55.
7. MS39,193:42.
8. Ibid.

Jewish leaders "were seeking to destroy Him for no reasons with which they could justify themselves before man or God." [9]

Although some of these lessons imply that "the Jews" thought they were condemning not the incarnate deity but only an innocent man,[10] the Jew nevertheless appears almost subhuman for such an act. As such, the Jewish figures can serve only as foils for the Christian—and not as a mirror to show the Christian to himself—because the Christian understandably cannot identify with them. A pupil is more likely to respond to such teaching with hatred of the Jew rather than with the insight needed for conviction, repentance, and faith. It is thus clear that certain images of Jews hinder, rather than facilitate, the communication of the biblical message, and may implant unchristian attitudes as well.

Of course, Christians of all persuasions unequivocally defend the righteousness of Jesus. Although the liberals in this study think Jesus actually did violate the Jewish code and gave the Jewish leaders just cause for offense, they do not regard Jesus as unrighteous because of this. He is said to have overruled and violated an "outmoded code" in the interest of a higher righteousness. Thus he is guilty according to the laws of his own time and nation but righteous in that he was willing to break down an irrelevant and stultifying system of law. In this analysis the liberals acknowledge the sincerity and conviction of those who opposed Jesus, while at the same time defending Jesus' thought and action. This position differs from the conservative one which holds that Jesus was innocent even when judged by the law of his time. Their own conviction that Jesus was blameless is thus reflected back upon

9. *Concordia Bible Student*, *43*, No. 2 (Jan. 1954), p. 19.

10. Ibid., p. 51. A commentary suggests how the two assertions are reconciled: "Most of the Jews committed this great sin 'through ignorance' . . . They did not realize that they were crucifying the Son of God, although they did know that they had demanded the death of one who was innocent of the crimes with which they had charged Him" (F. Rupprecht, *Bible History References*, *2*, St. Louis, Concordia, 1935, p. 388). This distinction is probably made out of the necessity of harmonizing Matt. 26:59–61 with Acts 3:17 and I Cor. 2:8. However, the impact of the interpretations quoted from the conservative curriculum above is the same: instead of a revelatory account of how guilty men (who were certain of their own innocence) condemned an innocent man (whom they were convinced was guilty), the portrait is that of guilty men (who knew that they were guilty) condemning a man of whose innocence they were clearly aware. This places such action outside the pale of ordinary human action.

Jesus' contemporaries as though it were a conviction the latter shared.

Jesus' innocence and the culpability of his enemies is set in a very different theological context in the neo-orthodox writings, with startling implications for intergroup relations. As has been said, both the full humanity and the divinity of Jesus Christ are stressed in interpreting the crucifixion events. The neo-orthodox make clear that Christ's divinity did not obscure his human qualities. He walked, talked, and lived as a first-century rabbi whom his contemporaries regarded as no more than human.[11] Yet Christ was also fully divine—and this fact, as the neo-orthodox writers point out to their audience, has vital implications. Because man is universally a sinner—a creature who runs away from God—his response to the incarnate presence of the divine is negative. It is this phenomenon which the Christian is asked to observe in the mission and death of Jesus. Because Christians respond as human beings, they cannot divorce themselves from the picture of man portrayed in the Gospels; the Christian's natural rebelliousness against divine action is no different from that of first-century Jews. Hence, it all boils down to one point: in expounding New Testament events it is legitimate for Christians to identify with Jesus' humanity, but they ought not to identify in the same unqualified way with his divine nature. His righteousness is God's righteousness, and not man's. Although we are offended by this righteousness, it is just this which challenges, judges, and redeems us.

The neo-orthodox writers, then, do not denounce the Jews on the supposition that Christians are Christ's defenders. They understand that they, too, are among the offenders and must humble

11. This point is also made in a conservative family magazine not included in the statistical sample. Addressing himself to the oft-made criticism of the RSV (that, in addressing God, the translators used the pronoun "Thou" while, in his earthly ministry, they used "you" in passages representing address to Jesus, thus implying that Jesus was not divine), Dr. Arthur Katt, the Missouri Synod scholar, says: "it seems but logical that Jesus be addressed as 'you' in His human appearance among men, especially by His parents, brethren, intimate disciples, as well as by countless people, His enemies, for example, who did not regard Him as being divine. It was part of His human experience to be treated as 'man,' and His deity is by no means imperiled thereby" (MS, *This Day*, 5, No. 3, Nov. 1953, 38).

themselves before the Cross. Therefore, the reader is expected to identify himself not with the divine in Christ but rather with those Pharisees, publicans, Sadducees, sinners, and disciples who responded to this righteousness in their various but always human ways. And since it was the best people of Jesus' day—the most religious, dedicated, and sincere—who most strenuously misunderstood and opposed Jesus, they are made to seem no different from the religiously dedicated, sincere, and respectable present-day Christians in our American churches.

It is important to note how this neo-orthodox insight affects the image of the Jew. The neo-orthodox regard the plot against Jesus as arranged by men who ironically were convinced that they could justify their acts before both God and man. In the judgment of many of his contemporaries, Jesus was indeed a lawbreaker, a perverter of the nation, a blasphemer, and a seditionist. He was sincerely thought to epitomize evil.[12] But this tells us something significant about man; it is precisely in this negative way that man understands God's righteousness when it challenges him in those actual events where he meets his neighbor. The disturbing righteousness with which Christ challenged the distinctions, group lines, and exclusiveness of his age was considered sinful and unlawful, just as today segregation, discrimination, and Jew hatred are deemed by some "sincere and pious" Christians as God-ordained, God-sanctioned, and consonant with the American way of life.[13]

It is evident that the belief that "God was in Christ reconciling the world to himself" has positive intergroup significance for most

12. Jesus' opponents saw only Jesus the man, and they judged him from the point of view of their own conception of righteousness. The Presbyterian view is that existentially we are all in the same predicament and therefore our only safeguard is to understand that we must not confuse our ideas of right and wrong with the righteousness of God. Yet Christians are in a somewhat different position than Jesus' opponents, for the church sees the Christ of faith. How first-century Jews may have regarded Jesus' acts, therefore, must of necessity be distinguished from what is seen in him by Christians, who look back upon him with the eyes of faith.

13. In Presbyterian thought the irony of human action is that man opposes the righteousness of God on the supposition that it is man who is righteous. In any human situation he therefore tends to judge the righteousness that represents God's activity in the world as utter evil. Man's very goodness is thus often opposed to God, as when love of country or loyalty to group and institutions become ultimates and express themselves in chauvinism, isolationism, and various other forms of separatism seeking to maintain the supposed purity of the group.

neo-orthodox writers. The doctrine is universalized so that both Jews and Christians are understood on one and the same human level. Christians are not confused with the divine, nor Jews identified with the devil. Accordingly, Christians are not praised inordinately nor are Jews blackly depicted.

The neo-orthodox perspective on man's sinfulness is essential to this understanding. The curriculum takes with deadly seriousness the proposition that the crucifixion means that Christians, together with all peoples, are hostile to God. "To Paul," says one neo-orthodox writer, the power of Jesus' death stems from the fact that it shows God's 'love for us . . . while we were yet sinners.' Like Pilate and the priests, *we are really God's enemies*." [14] Therefore, through Christ's sacrifice upon the cross "we are enabled to know the truth [that our righteousness cannot justify us before God] and to pray, 'God, be merciful to me, a sinner—to me, the very kind of sinner who crucified Jesus Christ.'" [15] "The cross," adds another, "brings all of us—the proudest, the most virtuous, the most spiritual—under judgment and reveals to us the hidden possibility of our sin, that it crucifies the Son of God." [16]

Significantly, the charge of Jewish deicide and the one-sided accusation of the Jews as rejectors of Christ do not appear in neo-orthodox lessons. Instead, these writers equate their own contemporary hostility to God with that of the crucifiers (who, like ourselves, tended to think of themselves as God's champions). [17] What the neo-orthodox seem to be saying is that our human attitudes *imply* deicide; we would all destroy God if we could. Psychologically, we allow ourselves to do just this; we shut our eyes to the real God who manifests himself to us, and instead create

14. PR36,943:80; PR37,717:58.

15. PR37,570:30.

16. PR37,523:13.

17. "Ask the class, What can we learn from the fact that the people who demanded death for Jesus sincerely believed that they were following Scripture and obeying God's will? There was another Jew present who also believed that he was fulfilling the will of the Father . . . There is a striking contrast between *his* obedience and the behavior of the people who also thought they were obeying God. This suggests that when people think God has called them to launch a violent crusade against the enemies of God, they may be equally blind to what is really the will of God. It is important for people who feel that religion is always a good thing to realize that religion can also make people even more zealous in their cruelty and inhumanity" (PR37,547:23–24).

an idolatrous "god" shaped to our own desires, prejudices, and hatreds.[18] We strike out at man whom God has made in his own image.

It is, consequently, impossible for the neo-orthodox writer to discuss Christ-rejection without acknowledging that the redeemed Christian, like the rest of humanity, also opposes Christ. In fact, "the Jews were not alone in their rejection of Christ, for even we, as members of the Christian Church, still reject him."[19] Pupils and teachers are asked to discuss the various ways in which they see this happening.[20] The Christian's idolatrous denial of Christ for substitute gods is possible because a "suffering Christ is often just as much a stumbling block to us as it was to the Jews in the first century."

> We want no crucified Christ. When he confronts us, he exposes our kind of false righteousness. He shows us that the most dangerous sins in the world and in our hearts are not the obvious things which all agree are evil, but rather the very things that masquerade as goodness . . . We are prone not to like such a Christ, for he exposes us, even though he acts entirely out of love and a desire to save us. Because we do not like him and the demands he makes of us, we search for another who will give us what we want. In our own minds and hearts we permit the Christ of Christianity to be replaced by imaginary figures who are more in keeping with our desires because they have been created by our very wants . . . Thus Christ crucified becomes a stumbling-block to us all.
>
> (PR37,732:53)

18. Cohen recalls Nietzsche's creation of a madman who announces the death of God. "It is clear that Nietzsche construes the death of God as the work of man," he says, adding, "The course of the West since the sixteenth century has been to render God useless and without efficacy . . . It is not that man denies [that there is a] God, but rather that he seeks to interpose between himself and God the work of his own imagination. . . . the progressive withdrawal of areas of human life and understanding, previously conceived within God's provenance, has the effect of rendering God without role or significance. *In this sense is God slain*—or rather, the 'blood' of the divine life is drawn away by man's self-arrogation of the power and wisdom of God." Arthur A. Cohen, "Atheism," *A Handbook of Christian Theology* (New York, Meridian, 1958), p. 18.

19. PR37,463:54.

20. PR37,732:23.

Not only does this approach produce a genuinely human image of the Jew, as the neo-orthodox understand humanity, but also gives Christians an opportunity to see how they are guilty of rejecting the cross through their persistent anti-Semitism. One writer asserts that "in plain terms, the New Testament asks us to realize that we are the sort of people who crucified Christ," and that Christians "use even our religiousness to disguise from ourselves the fact that we acknowledge this Lord and yet remain our own masters." His conclusion is that "fixing on the Jews as those who were to blame for the cross spares us the sharpest offense of the cross. When we so righteously reject them, we are really rejecting ourselves [i.e. both the Jews and ourselves are on the same level of guilt]." [21]

It is a misuse of the Christian faith, according to the neo-orthodox, to point an accusing finger at the Jew. "No, the difference between Jew and Christian is not that the Jew is guilty and the Christian innocent of Christ's death. Both stand condemned there, at the cross which bears the lonely figure of this One who is Israel, God's Man. Christians have no ground to stand on here, from which to judge and condemn the Jews." Rather, the rejection of Jesus as Israel's king by Israel is but a mirror in which Christians recognize themselves, being bound, as they are, "in mysterious kinship with the ancient people of God." [22] A clear statement of this entire position is summed up in this neo-orthodox statement:

> Are we right, then, to understand the Jews as the particularly wicked people who murdered Christ? This has often been the attitude of the Church, and it has been used to justify the persecution of the Jews. Emphasize the point that the Christian faith centers on the cross, through which God triumphs over all man's rebellion and ungodliness. The difference between the Christian and Jew is not between the innocent and the guilty but between two who stand equally accused by the cross. This is what we naturally do to God . . . We dare not condemn them for rejecting Christ, when we ourselves so often reject him and sin against him. (PR37,717:160)

21. PR37,717:58.
22. Ibid., p. 58. In Israel's history Presbyterians see their own collective and personal history.

*The Oppressor and the Problem of the Christian's Inclusion
with Christ*

This self-critical analysis by the neo-orthodox places Christ
apart from ourselves and our own groups, and contrasts sharply
with the treatments to be found in the more traditional curricula.
The usual practice is to assume a close relationship or identity
between the modern Christian and the Saviour, because the Christian professes to be "in Christ." In the fundamentalist and conservative portrayal of the Jews, the writers tend to think of themselves as being with Christ in opposing his enemies. They feel
freer, therefore, to castigate these enemies. This I-with-Christ type
of identification is evidenced by the frequent denunciations of the
Jews as unbelievers and Christ-rejectors, as well as by the lack of
any substantial attempts at self-criticism. The I-with-Christ identification as opposed to an I-against-Christ kind of understanding
may be judged from the following excerpts from three of the
communicators:

   a. *Fundamentalist:* "We talk so freely about Christ's be-
      ing crucified by His enemies more than 1,900 years
      ago, that perhaps we fail to note the present signifi-
      cance of that fact . . . *Christ is in the world today
      through the presence of His spirit in the hearts of
      Christians. It follows, then, that Christians should ex-
      pect to be hated.*"         (SP831:12; italics added)

   b. *Conservative:* "In consenting to go this way of shame
      [the *via Dolorosa*], Jesus truly humbled Himself to the
      lowest depths, Phil. 2:8. *The same ungodly world
      loves to humiliate the Christians.*"
                        (MS39,195:55; italics added)
      "The Evangelists record six blasphemous utterances
      [at the foot of the cross], five by the Jews, one by the
      soldiers. *Show how Christ is blasphemed today when
      He, the Bible, and the Church are ridiculed. . .*"
                        (MS39,191:32; italics added)
      "For Caiaphas the silence of Jesus was more deadly
      than the breakdown of the false charges raised by his
      witnesses. He hoped that Jesus would say at least some-

thing to condemn Himself. *How eager the world still is to detect some fault in the Christians!"*

The mob before Pilate's hall reminds the writer that "Christians have often felt [the mob spirit's] violence, churches have been burned, believers tortured," but Christ's spirit of forgiveness also reminds us that "When we are obliged to suffer, we should follow His example."                          (ibid., p. 33)

c. *Neo-orthodox:* "But if we have really encountered Jesus Christ, we also know something with equal clarity: that the kind of love that was in him is not in us . . . Some people may think they are proving their loyalty to Jesus Christ by showing bitter hostility and contempt for people who reject our Lord. But in doing this they also reject him. What must determine our attitude toward another man is not his attitude toward Jesus Christ but the love our Lord has shown him."                          (PR37,556:59)

"[Peter] ended up . . . on the side of Jesus' enemies. And that is where we stand. Not literally, of course, but the human impulses that crucified or consented to the crucifixion of Jesus are the same impulses that find less dramatic expression in our lives in greed, cruelty, and indifference to the problems of human pain and suffering."                          (PR37,570:30)

Here we have two opposing reactions to the same event. On the one side, Jesus' death summons up for the fundamentalists and conservatives images of their own actual or potential victimization; for the neo-orthodox, it evokes the realization that they, too, are either actual or potential persecutors who are frequently indifferent to the plight of others. This is the crucial difference between the two perspectives. The I-with-Christ identification uses the Cross to demonstrate the culpability of others. The I-against-Christ identification points up our own guilt and our involvement in the deeper and more insidious acts of inhumanity which men everywhere are disposed to commit.

However, both the I-with-Christ and the I-against-Christ kinds of identification find support in the New Testament. Both are legitimate attitudes, and we have no desire to argue against either one. The question we must deal with in this study is how these identifications apply to intergroup relations. There are, of course, some lessons on the crucifixion in neo-orthodox materials which recognize the legitimacy of "suffering with Christ." But the writers' explanation of this role, as other chapters in this book amply show, produce trenchant insights for intergroup teaching, and in each case the accounts are also self-critical. One lesson, for example, which depicts the crowd demanding Jesus' crucifixion, inquires into the particular temptations Christians have to follow the crowd rather than to "stick up for their Christian convictions if led to take a stand different from others in their group!" The writer suggests that the teacher ask the students "what they would do if one of their friends were to date a girl (or boy) of another race and were dropped by the crowd for it. Whose side would they be on? Would they have the courage to stand up against the crowd for what they believed to be right?"[23] Thus inclusion with Christ may mean that the Christian "is bound, therefore, to be open to others, even at the risk of injury to ourselves, even as Christ exposed himself in reaching down to us"; he is committed to destroy the barriers between men. The implications of this position are explicitly made; the student is taught to identify Christ's reconciling activity with the sufferings of all oppressed people. The Christian's true response to the cross when "in Christ" cannot be that of Jew-hatred or condemnation of others, but rather involves attempts at reconciliation which may mean "suffering with Christ."[24]

The I-against-Christ kind of identification is also not entirely lacking in the other curricula. The statement that "we crucified Christ" appears to some extent in fundamentalist as well as in conservative lessons (although the expression "we reject Christ" never does). One Missouri Synod lesson sees "a little of 'Pilate' in each of us," and asks, "Do you always see clearly the role YOU played in Christ's Passion, or do you merely fault those who accused Him and drove the nails? (Is. 53:6; 2 Cor. 5:21)."[25]

Another conservative (and zero-imbalanced) lesson on the cru-

23. PR37,496:61.
24. *Crossroads* (April–June 1955), p. 53.
25. MS39,525:44–46.

cifixion warns against the prejudicial feelings a pupil might experience when learning about this event: "In the discussion correct
the child who is ready to condemn Pilate and the ungodly chief
priests. Help the children realize that it was their [own] sins that
drove those cruel nails through His hands and feet." [26]

Although these instances are exceptions, they demonstrate that
there is some capacity for self-criticism even in the more traditional
curricula which allows for anti-prejudicial teaching. But very
little is given by way of specific content to the conservative concept
of the Christian's role in Christ's Passion. When such references
are made explicit, they appear more relevant to the group itself
than to any intergroup understanding. Thus a prayer used as a
preface to an expository text confesses that "we have often been
guilty of the very sins committed by Thine accusers." The sins
which are then specified, however, are only those committed
against other-Christians: "we have brought false charges against
our brethren."

The nature of the Christian's sin is clearly spelled out in the
neo-orthodox curriculum. Their writers precisely describe those
sins which bind the Jewish leaders, Pilate, and the modern Christian in a common guilt. Among them are the sins of nationalism,
prejudice, institutional idolatry, ecclesiasticism, fear, hatred, and
jealousy—most of which have to do with the whole range of intergroup relations. By the same token, guilt for the crucifixion is
universalized, and it is made clear that man's *sin*—and not simply
"the Jews" or even "the Jews and Romans"—brought about the
death of Jesus.

It should be noted that the neo-orthodox group espouse some
of the same doctrines as the fundamentalists and the conservatives
and that these provide anti-ethnocentric force for the I-against-
Christ perspective. These doctrines include the sinfulness of man,
the role of God as the universal judge, and the definition of Christ's
righteousness so that it cannot be confused with the Christian's
human righteousness and religiosity. These conceptions are never
made explicitly relevant to the intergroup scene in fundamentalist
or conservative lessons, nor are they used self-critically.

Parallel treatments of certain biblical passages in the conservative and the neo-orthodox textbooks are instructive in illustrating

26. MS39,426:82.

the self-critical power of a universalizing perspective which implicates the reader as compared with the other-accusing tendencies of a perspective which does not. The Acts of the Apostles record several speeches in which the early Church sums up its understanding of biblical history in the light of the crucifixion. One such passage is Acts 7:2–53 (the speech of Stephen before the High Priest and Sanhedrin), which provokes these comments:

| *The Conservatives* | *The Neo-orthodox* |
|---|---|

His purpose in reviewing the long history of the Hebrew nation was twofold: he wanted to impress upon his enemies what great things the Lord had done for His chosen people Israel, but also how the Jews had always turned away from God and resisted His grace . . . His whole line of argument was meant to show that in the rejection of Christ by the Jews of his day history was repeating itself . . . The Jews in the days of Christ and the Apostles prided themselves that they were true disciples of Moses and were living faithfully according to his teaching. But they did not realize that they were just as ungodly and had ideas about Moses as wrong as their forefathers' who lived in the days of the Prophet. Stephen points out that the children of Israel did not want Moses for their leader . . . God had given them wonderful evidence of His love and grace . . . but these blessings meant little to these obstinate and faithless Israelites. How simple it should have been for Stephen's accusers to see that they were just as ungodly as their ancestors in rejecting Christ, who is greater than Moses.[27]

The Jews, therefore, are a sign of God, but a sign with two meanings. They are a sign that God has chosen to make himself known to men. But they are a sign also that men . . . have rejected God and tried to resist his real Lordship. Stephen sums up the whole of Biblical history and its meaning from this second point of view when he bursts out against the highest Jewish council, the Sanhedrin, saying: "You stiff-necked people, uncircumcised in heart and ears, you always resist the Holy Spirit. As your fathers did, so do you. Which of the prophets did not your fathers persecute?" Stephen pronounced his own death sentence when he fearlessly spoke those words, but he spoke true.

Too often, however, the Christian Church has been content to leave the matter there. And through the centuries the ancient people of God have many times been cruelly dealt with on the basis of such reasoning. This is entirely the wrong end of the stick. For it leaves the Jewish people as the particularly wicked people who murdered Christ. And it leaves us with the flattering thought that we, if we had been there, would never have done so. This is the exact self-congratulation

27. MS, *The Early Christian Church*, pp. 42–44.

### The Neo-orthodox

for which Christ himself denounced the Pharisees, who built monuments to the prophets, and congratulated themselves that if they had lived in the time of the prophets, they would have been on their side and guiltless of their blood: "Woe to you, scribes and Pharisees . . . Thus you witness against yourselves, that you are sons of those who murdered the prophets." Christ himself regards this righteous conviction that finds in its own heart no trace of enmity to God as proof positive that we are just the sort of folk who murdered the prophets.

This is a startling conclusion, but it is plainly the conclusion that is reached in the New Testament. In plain terms, the New Testament asks us to realize that we are the sort of people who crucified Christ.[28]

There is a vague similarity in these two accounts up to a point. Stephen proclaims the graciousness of God and the disobedience of man; God chose Israel and gave her every blessing, but Israel was unfaithful. However, the conservatives understand this recitation of biblical history to be a condemnation of the Jews as a people, who because of their disobedience can no longer be God's people. The neo-orthodox use the same passage to admonish Christians to apply the biblical truth to themselves.

There is a type of Christian thinking in which the phrase "we crucified Christ" has little more than a vague, analogical flavor. The neo-orthodox curriculum takes this statement with real moral earnestness and uses it to give the pupil a fuller and more responsible account of both ancient and modern Jews. The cross takes on contemporary meaning, and the Christian is forced to face up to his own rejection, unbelief, and rebellion, which, in the eyes of God, are just as serious as the acts of Pilate and the chief priests.[29]

28. PR37,717:57–58.
29. "The guilt that was shared by all the original actors was not limited to them. They merely illustrate a sin that is universally at work in men's hearts.

## The Impact of the Cross on the Jew

A final and important matter to consider are the ways in which various Protestant groups consider the objective effects of the crucifixion upon the life of the Jews. Since liberals regard the execution of Jesus as a case of human martyrdom, Jesus' death did not fundamentally alter human history—even though the Jew has tended to suffer from subsequent charges of deicide. All other Christian groups, however, believe that with the crucifixion mankind was reconciled to God; they differ, however, as to the way they understand such reconciliation to be manifested in history. Fundamentalists believe that the definitive split between Jew and Gentile no longer existed after the crucifixion. Prior to this time, the Gentiles had been excluded from the holy nation, and therefore from salvation; but with the death of Jesus, "a Jew," the "Gentiles who had been so far from the truth, from hope, and from salvation, were now brought right up to that truth in the shed blood of Christ (Eph. 2:13)." Thus:

> The partition, or wall, which had been dividing Jew and Gentile for centuries, came crashing down when the Lord of heaven and earth was nailed to the cross (Eph. 2:14). Jews and Gentiles had cooperated in putting him to death— the priests bringing the accusations, the Roman soldiers pounding the nails. And Jews and Gentiles, who shared the guilt of His murder, would share the grace of God that resulted from His death. He died at the hands of both groups, and His salvation includes both groups.                  (SP793:36)

However, this destruction of the barriers between Jew and Gentile concerns salvation alone; it does not specifically apply to the problems of intergroup relations. This is a salvation, moreover, which is considered possible only for those individuals who accept it by faith. The conservatives would add to this that the crucifixion also marked the end of God's purposes for Israel, which were fulfilled in the person of Christ; consequently, Israel's role now belongs to the Church. By itself this would amount to nothing

---

Had we been there, we would have been with Pilate, or the priests, or the mob, or the soldiers, or the robbers" (PR, *Westminster Teacher*, March 29, 1953, p. 82).

more than a description of the relation between Israel and the Church, but some writers ominously suggest that the Jews have been abandoned to God's judgment.[30]

One of the difficult scriptural passages which occasions such a punitive kind of interpretation concerns the statement "His blood be on us and our children." [31] This verse is invoked more than any other in scripture by the conservative and fundamentalist authors to connect the crucifixion with the subsequent plight of the Jews. The same statement is interpreted by liberals as a later addition to the original Gospel narrative, which they say "seems to represent an effort to throw the whole blame for the death of Jesus upon the Jewish people . . . It seems to justify the damnable but all too common charges of the Christian Church against the Jewish people of being the 'Christ-killers.' " [32]

A number of denominations do not discuss this charge. In the neo-orthodox sample no comment upon the meaning of the verse was found. On the other hand, the very conservative and fundamentalist denominations do not hesitate making interpretations of it. For the conservatives the saying is construed to be a self-imposed curse, which follows from the Jews' guilt for "their slaying of God's Son" and their refusal to accept Him as their Saviour. Thus Judaism fashioned its own tragic historical destiny: "When Pontius Pilate, a heathen judge, pleaded for the release of their own Messiah, they had taken the responsibility for His death by saying: 'His blood be on us and on our children.' The curse which they wished upon themselves was about to strike them as the judgment of a just and righteous God." [33]

Since the Jews "were willing to be held accountable for the death of Christ," the judgment upon them was severe.[34] "Terrible was their punishment for this blasphemous challenge to God. Since A.D. 70 they have been scattered all over the world, often persecuted and generally despised. To this day, the unbelieving Jews are

30. See above, Chap. 4.
31. Matt. 27:25.
32. UN150:52.
33. MS39,153:260.
34. A question many Christians would raise at this point is, "Were they willing to be held accountable, or is this a statement by the Church?" This question would have to be answered by the conservative communicators in the light of their own exegetical principles.

suffering under the curse which they brought upon themselves." [35]

The fundamentalists sometimes limit their account to quoting Pilate's statement ("I am innocent of the blood of this righteous man") and adding to this the above-mentioned verse without making clear its implications. At other times, a writer will add his views about how this pronouncement prophesies an historical judgment upon the Jews: "To this very day, the name of Jesus incites contempt and abuse from some Jews and some Gentiles alike. The Jews called down God's wrath on them when they chose to have Barabbas released instead of Jesus, and then accepted responsibility for his death by saying, 'His blood be on us and on our children.'" Says another writer, "Because they rejected their Messiah at His first coming, demanding that His blood be upon them and their children, the Jews have had an unhappy lot for centuries." [36]

There are several critical problems which this verse from Matthew presents. The liberals assume that the scriptural account is frequently distorted to conform to the variously developed theologies or church prejudices, and they dispose of it altogether in their curriculum because they feel it reflects the early Church's hostility toward Judaism in the period of "the great separation." But since fundamentalist and conservative editors accept scripture as verbally inspired and historically infallible, they would have to be convinced that the early biblical manuscripts did not contain this verse before they could reject the cry of the mob as unhistorical.[37]

The question then arises: How are Christians to understand this passage? If, as many scholars believe, the verse was in the original Gospel account, what did it signify to the writer?

It is possible to contend that this verse, along with many other sections of the gospels, is not anti-Jewish at all. Interpretations of

35. MS39,023:182; cf. MS39,194:51.

36. SP823:72 and SP944:116.

37. It is possible for evangelicals, who accept the verbal inspiration and infallibility of scripture, to recognize that some passages may have been modified by additions to and editing of the texts (e.g. by Marcion). The crux of the matter is whether they are convinced that the New Testament, as it has come down to us, has been divinely protected from error by editors and translators (the latter being under the necessity of choosing between textual variations among available Greek manuscripts as well as responsible for selecting the correct vernacular equivalents of the Greek words).

the passage depend upon (1) the author's understanding of Christianity's relationship to Judaism, (2) his reading of the phrase "his blood," and (3) the way in which he regards this event as throwing light upon the human scene today.

Most denominational writers believe that the author of Matthew was a Jew speaking to his own people. Matthew does not use the broad designation "the Jews," as do some Christians, to define the mob before Pilate's house. Also, the self-critical quality characteristic of the Jewish prophetic tradition can be detected in the narrative of Matthew. As a Jew he implicates his own people in the guilt for the crucifixion. This is understood by the neo-orthodox not as a denunciation from without of some or all Jews but as prophetic Jewish self-criticism.[38] It is the genius of prophecy that it always focuses most intently on one's own or one's nation's culpability. Understood in this way, the verse is not an anti-Semitic kind of accusation but an insight offered by one Jew to his fellow Jews to make them understand how they are implicated in the tragedy of the cross.

As Pilate washes his hands and cries out, "I am innocent of the blood of this just person, see ye to it," the people respond, "His blood be upon us and on our children." There are several possible interpretations of these statements. They can mean that Pilate has refused to accept his responsibility for the crucifixion but that the chief priests' followers have accepted theirs. But can this possibly mean, as some writers seem to imply, that from this moment in history the historical forces which God controls will work for the destruction and suffering of Israel, while the Gentile world goes free?

A contradictory interpretation is possible. Pilate protests his innocence. Yet it is Pilate who actually sentenced Jesus and delivered him up to his own Roman solders to be crucified. As the neo-orthodox point out, Pilate "passes the buck," but contrary to his own words, his act puts him at the very center of moral respon-

38. The attitude of the early Church (like that of the rabbis) was that the destruction of Jerusalem and the Temple was a divine judgment upon Israel, although the former held this conception in relation to the nation's failure to acknowledge their Messiah. This was a prophetic self-concept applied to Israel by Christian Jews who still identified themselves with the nation. The validity of applying this transtemporally to include persecutions of Jews today is questionable.

sibility. Had he not authorized it, Christ would not have been crucified. On the other hand, there were some in the mob whom the
chief priests had summoned for the occasion and who claimed that
they were willing to take upon themselves any consequences for
Jesus' death. The usual meaning of the key phrase "his blood" is
thus reversed in this interpretation. The blood that was spilled at
Calvary, which in the words of the crowd is "on us and on our
children" was the blood of redemption. Hence, Christ's blood becomes a symbol not of vengeance or retribution but of forgiveness
and grace. *The mob has one understanding of these words; God
has another.* The irony of Pilate's words and of those of the mob
is that the divine truth is exactly other than the way they see it.
Thus God's truth turns both the statements of Pilate and the mob
upside down, for they both stem from a universal human sin. In
the Cross God triumphs over man's sin, and His mercy prevails in
ways which baffle the ingenuity of a creative but sinful humanity.

If this interpretation has any validity, the words of the crowd
do not in any way justify or even explain the Jewish plight through
the ages. Rather, the cry of the mob illustrates the gospel theme
that this "Jewish Blood" [39] was poured out for all mankind.

Commentators have noted that the crowd before Pilate's hall
must of necessity have been small. There were so many Jews in
Jerusalem for Passover that not all of them could have been present
at the crucifixion or even have known of the event. To maintain
that a tiny, select group of people in the Jewish nation, more allied
with Rome than with Judaism, could have brought untold consequences to millions of Jews through a single utterance is to
combine a superstitious belief in the power of a curse with a belief
in a type of collective responsibility wherein a single group is
made responsible for all time for the action of a few members of
the group.[40] The concept of inherited guilt and the traditional use
of the blood-curse theme requires a fixed transtemporal perspective
that regards the modern Jews as essentially the same as the ancient
Jews and that thinks of them as inheriting a tragic fate. How, then,
is this cry to be understood—in the popular, secular, and super-

39. The phrase is taken from the neo-orthodox curriculum: PR37,092:54.
40. Corporate responsibility is an ancient Jewish concept; it has some validity
and has anti-ethnocentric uses; cf. the previous chapter. But this kind of
responsibility must not apply solely to Jews.

stitious sense or in the light of the entire gospel? [41] It is most significant that the words "Father, forgive them for they know not what they do" occur in the climactic part of the scriptural account of the crucifixion. Fundamentalists have tended to scrutinize themselves by asking which force controls history—a self-imposed curse by a few Jews, or a merciful God, who answers Christ's prayer for man's forgiveness—a prayer which asked for unqualified mercy. For example, one prominent dispensationalist devotes some comments to this question in the following passage:

> Ah, they say, the Jew forfeited every blessing, and annulled every covenant, and defeated every promise of future restoration by the frenzied cry, "Crucify Him! Crucify Him! His blood be upon us and on our children!" But what will they do with the prayer of Jesus, uttered on the cross, "Father, forgive them; for they know not what they do"? This is no mere expression of a kindly feeling for His murderers, but it was the earnest prayer of One who could say, "Father, I thank Thee, that thou hast heard me. And I know thou hearest me always (John xi, 41,42)." [42]

About this same prayer a conservative lesson writer asserts: "When Jesus spoke that prayer, He not only asked God to forgive the Jews and Roman soldiers, but he was also pleading with the Father to forgive us our sins, which likewise were the cause of His suffering." However, the writer also feels that this prayer could be fulfilled only for those Jews who became believers. "The people who had Christ crucified could have been forgiven. From Acts 2 we know that many of the Jews repented and were forgiven. The one sin that destroys men forever is unbelief. And unbelief is simply refusing to accept the remedy of the blood which God has provided for sinners." [43] Thus the unconditional request of Jesus upon the cross—a request made precisely because "they know not what they do" and not because they have seen and acknowledged what they have done—is understood conditionally by the conservatives to apply only to the believers. The passage is interesting for another

---

41. The "blood curse" interpretation is in large part consonant with the secular thought of the Middle Ages and has pagan sources.

42. Brookes, *Israel and the Church*, pp. 135–36.

43. MS39,197:65.

reason. The writer does not appear to distinguish between the Jews' persecution in this world and their individual fate after death. Because of their "unbelief" (if these blood-curse comments may be taken at their face value) the Jews seem to have forfeited their human rights. The hatred and deprivations visited upon them in this life seem to be of the same order as the future judgment made by a just and holy God upon individual souls. In contrast, though, it is not assumed that Gentile unbelievers live under any exclusive or unique historical judgment that implies or justifies their unending persecution.[44]

One of the neo-orthodox lessons already quoted holds that a man's faith or lack of it in no way alters the Christian's unqualified obligation to love his neighbor. The Jew's attitude to Jesus Christ ought not to affect the Christian's concern for his suffering. While the judgment of God, historically, is an essential ingredient of neo-orthodox theology, a distinction is always made between man's action and God's. The Christian cannot think of himself as an instrument of judgment but must accept the judgment of God upon his own action. The belief that Israel was to be a holy community does not change this responsibility, for the Church is also summoned to this role and, like Israel, it too continually fails God. Thus the neo-orthodox again develop a self-critical analysis. According to them, the Church should discern a judgment against itself. The malicious persecution of other groups therefore cannot be viewed complacently as "the judgment of God" upon them.

## Some Observations on Commentaries of the Crucifixion

Self-portrayal is at best painful and difficult and, like all other insights, the truth about ourselves that emerges through Israel's history may be bitterly resisted. It is simpler to sketch and caricature outside groups than to assess our own relationships to them. The neo-orthodox curriculum is a valuable contribution to all Protestant communicators who accept the Bible as the inspired record of God's revelatory acts. In effect, these neo-orthodox writers say that the crucifixion story inevitably is distorted unless Christians honestly

44. Another distinction which high-scoring writers make is between the forgiveness of the sins of individuals and the mercy of God that does not hold the sins of a whole people, or of their representative few, against them for unlimited generations.

place themselves with the Jews. Only by sympathetically understanding them in and through the activity of God in Israel's history,
can we observe ourselves realistically.

In fact, were all the editorial groups to be consistent, they would
make much the same emphasis in their curricula, inasmuch as all
of them readily admit—when the question is put to them—that it
was the sins of all mankind, the Christian's included, which allowed
both Jews and Gentiles to put Jesus to death. The purpose of narrating the crucifixion is admirably set forth in the conservative
curriculum through quotations from Luther which point out that:

1. Recitations of the bare historical facts of Christ's life
   and death do not "suffice for the conduct of life."

2. To relate the crucifixion episode in order to breed
   "sympathy with Christ" or "anger against the Jews"
   is a misuse of the Gospel story.

3. The purpose of meditating upon the sufferings of
   Christ is to produce true contrition and repentance on
   our part.[45]

These can become useful directives for curriculum writers. The
many lessons which offer nothing more than a dramatic recital of
the crucifixion need to be restructured with a view toward the
larger intent of a Christian curriculum. Indeed the crucifixion story
is sometimes described heatedly, and considerable invective is
leveled at the Jew. Both "sympathy for Christ" and "anger against
the Jews" are expressed in some lessons which encourage similar
feelings in pupils.

It is the third point mentioned in the conservative curriculum
which needs most to be elaborated upon by editors in their specific
curriculum policies. Too frequently writers simply urge pupils

45. The quotations come from two different lessons and contain the following
lines: "And now there are not a few who preach Christ and read about Him that
they may move men's affections to sympathy with Christ, to anger against the Jews,
and such like childish and womanish nonsense. Rather ought Christ to be preached
to the end that faith in Him may be established . . ." (Bible Discussion Guide,
Senior Teacher's Manual, Course I, "What Is My Life Worth?", 1955, p. 13).
"We ought, first of all, to look into the wounds of Christ, and see in them His
love toward us and our ingratitude toward Him, and thus, with heartfelt affec-
tion to Christ and detestation of self, to meditate upon our sin. That is true
contrition and a fruitful repentance" (ibid., p. 58).

to develop "true contrition" and "fruitful repentance" without providing the kind of detailed self-scrutiny needed for repentance. Writers tend rather to state the purpose of the lesson by means of a parenthetical statement such as "Christ died for us"; or they may add some material which exhorts the pupil to manifest gratitude for the love of God who suffered in our stead. But the deeper meanings of contrition for man's relationship to others are seldom enlarged upon. And when a fuller treatment of the Crucifixion is given, the critical orientation is lost. The writers do not recall the Christians' actual or possible hatred for the Jews but rather the Jewish hatred of Christians or the hatred evoked by the name of Christ. The contemporary plight of the Jews does not make the Christian feel penitent about the Church's traditional attitude toward Jews; instead Christians are absolved from responsibility by placing it on the Jews instead.

A specific, self-critical type of intergroup orientation, however, is not the only major shortcoming of the negatively disposed lessons. A reader can hardly avoid the impression that, despite the communicator's theological convictions regarding the universal significance of the crucifixion, he has not made these theological points sufficiently relevant to man's actual social situation. The theology of the conservative communicator logically should require that the Christian recognize how his own sin placed Jesus upon the cross. Instead, it is generally only the sins of the Jews (or of others) which are elaborated, while the Christian is placed along with Christ as the object of enmity and hatred. The sins of the Jews are stated concretely, but no connection is made between these sins and our own. In short, the conservative insight that "we crucified Christ" needs to be given a specific and unmistakable intergroup relevance through a concrete, self-critical, and insightful use of scripture— a use which is so notable in Luther's sermons.[46]

Again, self-scrutiny needs a more accurate Hebraic context. One question which lesson writers should decide is whether the New Testament narrative is to be read as a document foreign to Judaism or whether it is to be understood as a book written from within the Jewish community. Are the theological interpretations of events described by the Evangelists to be divorced from their Jewish

46. Luther's own self-critical approach is a model; he directs these dicta to the main issues of his age.

context, or interpreted in the light of presuppositions alien to those which the Gospel writers themselves entertained?

Finally, we feel some editorial boards should adopt the policy of reminding commentators on the Passion story that the teaching of this story has had terrible consequences for the Jews, and that centuries of Jewish oppression, deprivation, and torture should encourage them to treat more humbly and with repentant awe a theme that lends itself to the designs of Satan as well as to those of God.

# 10. The Protestant as the Oppressor

Despite the deficiencies we have noted in some of the curricula, Protestants are generally highly self-critical; they are willing to admit their own prejudices and call attention to their share of the responsibility for anti-Catholicism, anti-Semitism, and racial hatred. For some curricula, this ingroup self-scrutiny runs through the preceding chapters like an unbroken thread. Facing up to one's past and present record of prejudice toward other groups is a highly anti-ethnocentric practice. The prejudiced blame others, whereas the unprejudiced hold themselves responsible.[1]

In this study, those communicators who candidly face up to their past record and freely admit their prejudices show the least prejudice and the greatest anti-ethnocentrism on the objective scales. Conversely, the group which is the least inclined to do this manifests more prejudice and less anti-ethnocentrism.[2]

All Protestants, however, are self-critical to a certain degree and are willing to deal with the objectionable features of their relationships with others. The neo-orthodox have by far the most favorable scores in this regard, the conservatives the least. In some respects, the fundamentalists are even more prone than the liberals to admit their prejudices toward other religious groups.

Protestants are more ready to admit their full share of responsibility for current relations between race, national, and ethnic groups than they are when dealing with tensions between religious communities. Moreover, the tendency to make outsiders partly responsible for intergroup conflict and, at times, outgroup suffering is more characteristic of the discussions concerning interreligious relations. Liberals and neo-orthodox, for example, make Roman Catholics somewhat accountable for the tensions in our society.

1. Adorno et al., *Authoritarian Personality*, pp. 149, 391, 394 f., 430. See also Allport, *The Nature of Prejudice*, pp. 170, 237, 383 ff., 437 ff., 496, 508, and chap. 20.

2. See Analytical Cat. 3, Appendix VIII, Figs. 30 and 31, which chart the degree to which explicit intergroup self-criticism is engaged.

Because Americans interested in intergroup relations are more concerned with the Catholic-Protestant and Jewish-Christian conflict, the following discussion will deal with these problems.

## PROTESTANT RESPONSIBILITY FOR ANTI-CATHOLICISM

Fundamentalists and conservatives in one respect confess their anti-Catholic tendencies more unambiguously than do the liberals and neo-orthodox: they condemn Protestant anti-Catholicism (however they may understand it) without offering any qualifying statements about the Catholic responsibility for Protestant-Catholic tension. This may seem strange in view of the tendency these same communicators show to suspect that Roman Catholicism represents a threat to true doctrine or to social freedom.[3] If, in one set of lessons, conservatives and fundamentalists depict Catholics as the enemy and persecutor, in an entirely different set—none of which mentions Catholic responsibility—they criticize their own groups for anti-Catholicism. In other words, there is a clear separation in these materials between criticism of the outsider and self-criticism.

Of the two communicators, the fundamentalists are the more clearly self-critical. For example, they sometimes give their students a check list, on which the students are asked to indicate whether they have ever been "guilty of feeling superior to anyone because he or she is . . . a Roman Catholic." Jews, Negroes, foreigners, and non-Christians are also included in the list. At other times fundamentalists reprove Protestants for trying "to set Roman Catholics straight in all their false doctrines." The latter type of reference is made with a view to witnessing to the Catholic, and the audience is told that "the Catholic will resent being told about [these doctrinal matters] by someone outside. Do not feel that Catholics must necessarily be set straight on all these points before they can be saved. You will learn that it will only widen the gap between them and you to center your discussion on such matters."[4] Or, again, an illustration shows how interest in intergroup relations can be combined with the effort to win souls for Christ:

A prominent New York pastor tells of a young woman who called on him one day to confess that she was unhappy.

3. See the discussion above, Chap. 6.
4. SP954:119.

The source of her misery, he discovered, was a sustained hatred of Jews, *Catholics*, and Negroes. "As a Christian clergyman," says the pastor, "I advised her to get down on her knees and ask God to help her get rid of her hates."

The advice was good. If, as a Christian, you find your service for the Lord paralyzed by prejudice, dislikes, and suspicions, get on your knees and ask Him to unshackle you. Then open your eyes to a possible mission field in the hearts of the very ones you despise. Take them the Gospel of Christ. Teach them the Word of God. Lead them into a saving knowledge of Christ—and you will see how your unshackling has led to this.                                                        (SP959:37)

In contrast, conservative self-scrutiny is general and implied. One lesson confesses that earlier Lutherans (under the instigation of Carlstadt) were guilty of breaking into a church "where the priests were reading Mass" and driving the worshipers out "in a brutal manner"—an act which Luther would not have condoned. But the following is more typical: In an intermediate workbook the student is asked, "Do you treat other children so as to show you love them for Jesus' sake? Test yourself by putting a check mark in front of the things you do as a rule." One of the statements is, "I make fun of Jews and Catholics." As in other types of conservative references, a critical social and theological analysis is not applied to either the direct or indirect acknowledgments of guilt for the disabilities which others suffer.

The liberal and neo-orthodox are self-critical about their relationships to Catholicism, but their accounts usually distinguish between *anti-Catholicism* (or the plight of Catholics in our society) and any intergroup *tension* that may exist between Catholics and Protestants. The liberals do not explicitly admit that currently there is any anti-Catholicism among Protestants, yet they do provide a number of examples of Protestant persecution or dislike of Catholics in previous eras. On the other hand, the current conflicts between Catholics and Protestants are attributed not to any Protestant misconceptions and prejudices but to canon law legislation regarding mixed marriages as well as to the Catholic system of education.

The neo-orthodox make an even more explicit differentiation

between outgroup plight and intergroup tension. Insofar as Protestants exhibit any dislike for Catholics, disseminate anti-Catholic propaganda, or deprive Catholics of any of their rights, they are held guilty. As for tension between Catholics and Protestants, the neo-orthodox feel that the Roman Church not only shares the responsibility for this but in many cases is said to have initiated it. Pointing out that the animosities, and the "sense of separation that make it practically impossible for us and for them to find a common ground for understanding," are deeply rooted in history, one writer claims that the Roman Catholic Church is responsible for the barrier between Protestantism and Rome:

> Who is responsible for this isolation of one part of Christendom from another? The Roman Catholic, of course, answers that this is the evil work of the Reformation. Many Protestants accept that answer too readily. It is startling to them to discover that the steps which made the break permanent were taken by the Roman Church. As this lesson will show, a deliberate policy fostered by Rome, when relationships were still more flexible than they have ever been since, committed the Roman Church to a kind of an "iron curtain", making it exceedingly difficult for Protestants to have fellowship with Catholics.[5]

The present wall between the two communities, then, is judged to have been erected by the Catholic hierarchy; the moderate elements at the Council of Trent who wanted some basis for reconciliation between Protestants and Catholics were defeated.

> The representatives of the pope seem to have set themselves the task of making the Roman position as rigid and ironclad as possible. In other words, they were guided by the purpose not of holding the door open to Protestants but of shutting the door once and for all to any possibility of compromise or reconciliation. To this end, they defined Roman Catholic dogmas in a way far more inflexibly than had ever been done before. For the first time, the Roman Church emerged with a cut-and-dried system of belief which allowed no dissent or even further discussion. (PR36,830:61)

5. PR830:60.

The problem of intermarriage seems to be one cause of contemporary tension according to neo-orthodox references; but differences in Catholic and Protestant views regarding censorship, birth-control legislation, and other matters are also dealt with. However, Catholic-Protestant feelings are not regarded in any categorical way. Some non-Catholics, for example, are severely criticized for surrendering their own religious freedom by adopting a policy of not voting for a Roman Catholic for public office. In the main, then, anti-Catholicism unequivocally is seen as a Protestant problem; but the roots of the conflict between Catholics and Protestants today are largely regarded as proceeding originally from Roman Catholic action.

## CHRISTIAN RESPONSIBILITY FOR ANTI-SEMITISM

Anti-Semitism is by no means a distinctive phenomenon of the Christian era, nor can it be said to exist primarily among Christians —since most Gentiles in the world are not Christians. But the fact that anti-Semitism has existed within Christendom and that Christians have inspired and maintained anti-Semitic practices is something fundamentalists, liberals, and neo-orthodox all acknowledge with regret. Among fundamentalists and conservatives, however, there is also a tendency to state the Jewish plight in a theological context which implies that Jews are responsible for the suffering visited upon them.

The distinction the liberals and neo-orthodox make between plight and tension does not hold true for their descriptions of Jewish-Christian conflict except for one point. The neo-orthodox, in one atypical instance, say that if minorities have rights which the majority must respect, "it is also true that majorities have rights that minorities ought to respect. This matter of 'respect' is a two-way street." The account continues:

> The record of Christians in their treatment of Jews leaves much to be desired. It has been Christians who have created the ghettos, instituted pogroms and carried on inquisitions. . . . For all such unchristian conduct and attitude the Christians should be in full repentance, of course, but the full obligation does not fall upon Christians alone. Jews also have their responsibilities and stewardships.                    (PR37,096:75)

There are no similar assertions about the responsibilities of Jews, nor of any racial minority elsewhere in neo-orthodox literature. This lesson, however, is concerned with an issue about which there is growing conflict in American society today—namely, the singing of Christmas carols in the public schools. The writer's assumption seems to be that Jews ought to tolerate this practice as a token of good will to Christians.

Neo-orthodox self-criticism functions to soften the picture of the persecution of the young Christian community in the New Testament era:

> Although the greatest threat [to the Church] came from the pagan forces, Judaism was the first to attempt to exterminate the Christian community. Whenever Judaism had the strength to attack Christians and whenever Judaism was not held in check by its wise men, it did all that it could do to eradicate the Christian Church. (Acts 8:13 describes one such attempt.) It was not until a much later period that Christianity itself became anti-Semitic. When it did, it was of course a thousand times more sinful than Judaism had ever been.
>
> (PR36,974:40)

Thus in dealing with the status of the Christian community in its early period, nothing is omitted concerning the hostility of the Jewish authorities. But the matter is given a sound perspective by including also some account of Christian hostility—for example, *the greater sin of anti-Semitism in the later Church.*

Neo-orthodox lessons offer a host of statements describing certain objectionable features of the modern church. Class members are asked to note, e.g., "Jewish-Christian Churches" that are segregated by the main-line churches, and "walls of separation which we are constantly building" in order to keep some racial, ethnic, or Christian-Jewish group out of church membership. Christians are said to have often accepted the privileges and services of places that are denied Jews and "would be denied Jesus." Christians have been guilty of anti-Semitism. Tyrants and "the Christian Church" have persecuted the Jews. Primarily it is these statements and others like them which (a) serve as correctives to the supposition that only others persecute, (b) point to the conditions that Christians must examine if they are to exercise faithful obedience to their calling, or (c) become the basis for insight into the meaning of prejudice and anti-Semitism.

The liberals also freely admit that Christians are responsible for anti-Semitism. How, for example, did Hitler get the kind of mass consent he needed to massacre the Jews? Certain "conditioning factors already in the cultural life of Europe" and Germany are thought to explain this:

> This terrific human destruction must be seen as a climax of centuries of persecution of the Jewish people. Isolated in ghettos, deprived of citizenship in many countries, lied about, cheated, robbed, and made victims of the cruelest pogroms— the Jews have lived with tragedy from generation to generation.
>
> It was in nominally Christian lands, for the most part, that this long tale of sorrow became history. The Christian peoples of Europe must plead guilty before the nations for the major responsibility for this accumulation of crimes. Nor can Christian America wash her hands of the guilt. Here, too, have been Jew-baiting, anti-Semitic riots and even murder of Jews simply because they were Jews.[6]

Most of the liberal references are shorter variations of this theme, e.g. the Christian Church has charged the Jews with being Christ-killers. Christians, in particular, have persecuted Jews. Only a few excerpts also involve the reader: The leader of a group is told that he and the pupils will probably have some bias about the "Palestine political situation," and therefore ought to (a) recognize it, and (b) "put it in the background in order to receive with an open mind all the material you can find from both Israel and the Arab countries."

## The Problem of Sin in the Church

However, in relation to anti-Semitism, the liberal curriculum omits certain identifying phraseology such as "we," "our," "lib-erals," or "Unitarians" which would specifically locate the guilt. The reason for this may be that the context for the kind of self-criticism indicated also contains indictments of certain beliefs which, it is contended, have grown out of the "Old Story of Salvation"

6. UN244:255.

—a story the liberals no longer deal with. Only to the degree that liberals consider themselves Christians can admissions of the Christian guilt for anti-Semitism involve them—except, perhaps, in a most marginal way. That liberal Christians in the tradition to which these writers say they belong have hated, disliked, or rejected Jews is never actually stated, although it may be implied.

Self-indictment is characteristic of the neo-orthodox curricula in a way that is not true of the liberal. The context for the former's remarks, as we shall see, requires them to admit that their own people (pupils and teachers, as well as the writers and publishers of the denomination using the materials) are guilty of some form of prejudice.

In addition to the neo-orthodox doctrine of sinfulness, their doctrine of the Church also contributes to self-inquiry. For the liberals, the Church is an institution, but for the neo-orthodox it is more than that; it is a *people*, the "body of Christ." This is a concept of the Church which transcends denominational lines and institutional Christianity and encourages the neo-orthodox to employ sincerely a collective "we" or "us." No member can be thought to divorce himself from a body like the Church; one cannot say, "I am no part of thee." The liberal curriculum, on the other hand, assumes that each person is responsible for his own religion; religion is not a communal heritage; nor is there any concept of Church but only of sectarian churches. The neo-orthodox, when speaking of the Christian's sinfulness, makes plain that no Christian can wash his hands free of the guilt for a fellow Christian's sins.

The conservative communicator finds it considerably more difficult than the neo-orthodox to face up to the presence of sin in the Church. While the fundamentalists are freer to admit the Church's guilt, they do so cautiously; the word "Christian" is usually modified. Thus fundamentalists assert that "If any group has suffered at the hands of so-called Christians . . . it is the Jewish people. Down through the years since the Christian era began, these people have been tormented and persecuted and put to death." Here the term "so-called" sharply modifies the word "Christian"; bigots may only pretend to be Christian, which is to say that they are not really Christians. The qualifying phrase, however, can be understood to serve another purpose—to indicate that anti-Semitism is not Christian and is therefore forbidden, that an anti-Semite cannot belong to the Church.

This fundamentalist qualification of the word "Christian" comes up repeatedly. "In mistaken zeal, so-called Christians have hunted them down, tortured them, and killed them . . . many Gentiles (not real Christians) accuse the Jews of killing Christ." Another lesson says that "some saved Gentiles" during Paul's day "were antagonistic toward converted Jews." In the last instance, there is no hint that these were not "real Christians"; yet, when the fundamentalist writer gets close to home he admits, "And many who call themselves 'fundamentalists' are distinguished for virulent anti-Semitism." [7]

Here, again, the writer is approaching other fundamentalists with a problem he feels applies to them. The same author says, "In America, Jews face a rising tide of anti-Semitism which at times is spearheaded by professedly evangelical groups." [8] Quite obviously, many of the flagrantly anti-Semitic movements in America are led by men who call themselves "fundamentalists," "evangelicals," and "Christians," but with whose literature and point of view other fundamentalists and evangelicals such as Scripture Press would not wish to be identified. The following story clearly distinguishes between Gentile and Christian—an extremely important distinction for the fundamentalists:

> A Jewish shopkeeper said to a Christian worker who called on him, "Why do Christians hate us Jews so?" What Christians?" asked the worker. He then pointed out the distinction between the terms "Gentile" and "Christian"—for all Gentiles are not Christians. The worker proved to his Jewish friend that true Christians love the Jews. Do you?     (SP940:71)

Regardless of whether such statements are really adequate, they reflect a certain amount of self-criticism. Fundamentalists admit that anti-Semitism is a problem for which evangelicals have a direct

7. SP783:55; SP784:57; SP793:35; SP928:110.

8. SP930:125. Fundamentalists rebuke that segment of Christendom which uses their materials yet fails to apply the teachings to their attitudes toward Jews. Says one, "If God has not cast away His people Israel, have I, as a Christian, any right to give them an 'outcaste' rating in my own thinking or speaking?" (SP987:Pt.II).

responsibility. Yet the distinction "not real," "who claim to be," etc. tend to soft-pedal their criticisms.

An example of the rather infrequent conservative attempts at self-criticism appears in connection with a lesson on Jonah. Just as Jonah became angry at the mercy God showed to Nineveh, so "There are still many members of Christian churches who would become furious if they saw Negroes, Jews, Asiatics, or other foreigners, or social outcasts worshipping in their sanctuaries. The spirit of Jonah has not died down in the church . . . Have we ever committed this sin of Jonah?" [9] This is an in-the-church situation rather than a broader description of the social scene. As has already been implied, the bulk of the references in the category are negative, and they mostly concern issues which were raised in previous chapters.

The ways in which the four communicators relate to the dilemmas of both Catholics and Jews reveal their respective attitudes toward the problem of sin in the Church. For liberals, of course, sin is not regarded as a problem, because it is not believed to be a useful category of thought.

Of the other communicators, the neo-orthodox have accepted most fully the Church's involvement in sin—especially as this effects the welfare of other groups. While the fundamentalists recognize that some Protestants are guilty of anti-Semitism, they are also anxious to dissociate the true Christian from any possible involvement in the vile anti-Semitic references to be found in the professional Jew-baiters' journals. Yet such a position has its dangers, because by limiting their analysis of sin in the churches in this way, these writers fail to observe how even the best and most sincere Christians are involved in the sins of anti-Semitism or prejudice.

There are really two problems here. The first is the way in which a writer conceives of the social order and the individual's place in it—that is, the extent to which he believes sinfulness is part of the very structure of the prevailing cultural mores, institutions, and social patterns. The second issue has to do with the nature of the Church itself.

The fundamentalist and conservative faiths think of the Church

9. MS39,217:32–33.

as a community that is invisible to man and known only to God, so that the individual Christian who is a member of *a* church may or may not be a member of *the* church. This view often encourages these writers to view the Church uncritically, as if the problems of a sinful social order or the moral ambiguities of the lives of church members did not touch the life of the Church itself. Moreover, the fundamentalists in particular regard the response of the Christian to the Gospel in his everyday relations as individualistic—that is, in harmony with their view of society, which appears to be a nominalistic one. Society is seen as an aggregate of individuals; therefore, the only way to alter society is to alter the people who live in it.

There is considerable truth in this last contention, of course, and all the evangelical movements of the past which have operated according to such assumptions have greatly benefited society, directly as well as indirectly.[10] Moreover, some fundamentalists say that the basic task of the Church is to witness to the world, not to change it. But given this as a starting point, the question of *the Christian's responsibility for the society in which he lives* has yet to be answered. The question here is not one of salvation; it has to do with the Christian's awareness of an unavoidable involvement in society, of the obligations he has to act and to challenge society—not to win or be assured of salvation, but to express his Christian responsibility (obedience to God).

Neither fundamentalist nor conservative views of society and social structures take full account of the Christian's role in society. They do not examine how both the Christian and the churches as they exist in reality are molded by and imbedded in society, nor the way in which society, in its turn, depends on and reacts to the activities of Christians and their churches. The Christian is viewed as somehow distinct from society—either by transcending it or simply by being dissociated from it. Conservative materials for example are silent about many social issues; it is as though these had only a personal (i.e. individual) dimension. Yet these problems also have a broader, social, intergroup dimension. The fundamentalists discuss social questions to the extent that they believe that all problems of social justice will ultimately be solved in God's

10. Cf. the thesis of Timothy L. Smith, *Revivalism and Social Reform* (New York, Abingdon, 1957).

plan in the future Kingdom age. This view, however, need not overlook the question of the Christian's responsibility *now* (nor the responsibility of the editors and writers of the curriculum to speak to other Christians about these issues) so that proximate solutions can be found and the Christian accept the responsibility for his society (whether or not his actions will have any profound effect on society).

The fundamentalist and conservative concern that the main task of the Church ought not to be obscured by preoccupations with marginal affairs understandably is bound up with certain precautions concerning the social gospel. Social-gospel proponents have tended to confuse salvation with social reform; they believed that a man must deserve salvation, and that by being indifferent to social issues a man forfeited his right to salvation. But to "earn" or "deserve" one's salvation is now regarded by all of the communicators except the liberals as a form of self-righteous striving. These communicators argue that in view of man's universal disobedience, who could possibly be righteous enough to "deserve" salvation? The fundamentalist and conservative response to the social-gospel movement was to make a thrust in the opposite direction. Salvation history and salvation doctrine are the definitive focus of all evangelical writing. But these central soteriological requirements of the fundamentalist and conservative faiths should not be threatened by an awareness that the Christian must deal with ethical questions which have social dimensions; hence love and justice can be made specific and relevant to the areas of social concern raised in a study such as this.

The further distinction between the Church as invisible to men (known only to God) and the existing individual churches as visible congregations also allows conservatives to resolve the problem of sin in the Church by locating the blame for unhealthy intergroup attitudes and relationships primarily upon the unbelievers in the churches. The conservative believes that existing congregations consist of both believers and unbelievers, and that only God can know the sheep from the goats. This distinction is made in order to support the validity of the sacraments even when administered by evil men. Such a view in part accounts for the way in which conservatives bypass the believer's involvement in and responsibility for intergroup relations and assume that it is the unbeliever in the churches who is prejudiced, anti-Semitic, and bigoted.

Although such a distinction has dangers, certainly, it could be of some use. Perhaps there *is* a dimension to anti-Semitism which should be acknowledged more explicitly—namely that the Christian who does not really believe (i.e. who stands in rebellion against God but is afraid to admit this to himself or to others) may actually be the anti-Semite who practices his idolatries under the guise of Christian, biblical, and theological doctrine. Perhaps anti-Semitism is possible only for the Christian who unconsciously rejects his faith, who projects *his* own lack of belief onto the Jews and accuses *them* of unbelief. This may be the real purpose in the fundamentalists' search for some qualification here, e.g. it is the so-called Christians not real Christians who are anti-Semitic. On the other hand, this way of putting the matter may assume that both writer and reader are "real Christians," and not morally involved in the sins of society despite their inevitable participation in society's evil institutions and mores.

The neo-orthodox, on the other hand, see both the Church and society in a way that implicates the Church and the Christian in the social sin. Their thinking about the Church involves certain paradoxes, e.g. the Church transcends social boundaries, yet is involved in the life of the culture; it is both a holy unity and a group of individual and sinful congregations; it is both within the Kingdom and outside of it; it is the body of Christ and the communion of saints and at one and the same time a fallible human institution. But these paradoxes tend to broaden the neo-orthodox thinking about the Christian; e.g. he is the doubting believer, the sinning saint, the one who challenges a society judged by God, yet is himself judged by God as a responsible member of that society. This complex understanding of Church and Christian is analogous to the neo-orthodox view of the Kingdom of God—it is both present and future, heavenly and earthly, social and individual.

On the other hand, the biblical concepts of collective responsibility are applied by the neo-orthodox to the Church and to society as well. These canons of thought are partly biblical, partly sociological. Israel thought of itself as a people; each member of the community was responsible for the other and for the whole.

In our day the nation is, of course, distinguished from the Church; yet the legitimacy of collective responsibility in respect to the life of the nation (or culture) as a whole is acknowledged. As the neo-orthodox references to the nature of the self or society amply demonstrate, the idea of collective responsibility has important ramifications for an improved intergroup scene.

For one thing, the biblical view is held to require that Christians recognize that they are morally accountable for society's ills. Christians are involved in each other's sins and in the sins of the nation, Church, or culture. For this reason, the neo-orthodox challenge the right to point an accusing finger at others. Scripture directs us to recognize our collective guilt and responsibility. In the Bible this recognition is primarily directed toward Israel; that is, it is an insight Israel applied to her own life. But if Israel is taken as a model for the Church, this principle should apply also to Christians. Moreover, the biblical injunction is considered universally valid, i.e. for all people. For Christians it means primarily recognizing their own involvement and culpability.

The neo-orthodox view, then, accomplishes two things. (a) It presents the Christian with the inescapable fact of moral responsibility for his and other groups, an obligation which has even more serious consequences if he chooses not to become personally involved. (b) This view makes the Christian more critically aware of his own group than of other groups.[11]

Consequently, the neo-orthodox make every effort to educate Christians in such a way that they know they are socially implicated. The curriculum writers point out that as social beings Christians in one way or another are bound to participate in social structures

---

11. This does not mean that other groups should never be criticized, nor that self-criticism does not have its risks. The danger of the latter is that the enemy may use the prophet's evaluation as support for his polemic. Any American, reading another American's legitimate stringent analysis of what is going on in America, understands that this is a self-evaluative way of facing fellow Americans with their responsibility. However, as soon as this self-criticism is utilized by an outside group to accuse America to other outsiders, or in order to establish a rationale for a negative image of the United States, it is demonically perverted. We recognize this difference in the use of the same data when we distinguish between Americans who examine and criticize the American scene and Russian communists who propagandize against the United States in order to justify Russian national policy. Anti-Semites traditionally use characteristic Jewish self-criticism as justification for their rejective and negative portrait of the Jew!

which institutionalize segregation and discrimination. The curriculum examines this involvement and the responsibility it places
upon the Christian. The following, for example, is one illustration
of this practice:

> A Negro family moved into an all-white community. Only
> one family in the community called on them to make them
> welcome. Other neighbors tried to force the Negro family
> to move, but without success. The good neighbor was made
> the victim of a whispering campaign of slander.
>
> What should be the attitude of the white family toward
> their neighbors? Should they sell and move? How can they
> demonstrate their forgiveness of those who have wronged
> them? What should they do about the slander? What should
> the churches of the community do about the situation? How
> can the neighbors be led to see that they are wronging both
> the Negro and white family? Does the white family need
> to feel any involvement in the social sin that has created this
> problem? Does it need to seek the forgiveness of the Negro
> family for this? How might this be done?
>
> This example may serve to illustrate that we are all involved
> in the sins of society. Social sins are complicated matters.
> Everyone needs forgiveness.[12]

The Christian's responsibility for society is examined repeatedly.
The following is typical of the neo-orthodox emphasis:

> Who is it that treats these people as objects rather than as
> persons? Who is responsible for the conditions in which they
> live? How can these people have any dignity, any sense of
> being someone, when a hostile society tries to keep them "in
> their places" and will not allow them to better their condi-
> tions?
>
> What do we owe these people? Do they want pity and
> charity? You will want to help the group to see that this is

12. PR, *Westminster Teacher* (March 10, 1957), p. 77. The very man who
supports and benefits from the social arrangements and institutions which result
in synagogue bombings or race riots may insist on his lack of connection with
these events. But if the biblical notion of collective guilt has any validity (and
where is it more valid than in our interdependent and closely knit society?), his
lack of *direct* participation in the event does not excuse him from the fact that he
does participate in and helps shape the life of the nation, that he and all Americans everywhere share the guilt.

not the answer. We have robbed them of their precious rights to be persons. As Christians, we believe that man was created in God's image, to be a free and responsible person. As Americans, we assert that there are certain basic inalienable rights that belong to all men, and yet, in many areas of our land, we have deprived people of the right to be persons, to have dignity.[13]

## THE PREJUDICED CHRISTIAN AND THE NATURE OF PREJUDICE

The neo-orthodox consider that prejudice is an inescapable and insidious form of human sinfulness, and that the most harmful kinds of prejudice occur precisely because people convince themselves that they are free of prejudice. This point is related to the stress on collective responsibility. Even good Christians may be somewhat indifferent to problems of justice or assume a neutral attitude toward them; but this means that a Christian implicitly acquiesces to sin and thereby surrenders his Christian responsibility. For example, if he ignores the critical state of racial relations in America today, the Christian, in effect, sides with those who resist changes (by law or otherwise) in the social patterns of racial segregration—patterns which have been shaped by the law, custom, folkways, and mores of the community. The Christian's silence is considered tantamount to actively supporting those institutions and customs which enforce and perpetuate segregation and discrimination. Therefore, for the Christian, social action is not a matter of choice. Nor is social action desirable as a means of earning individual salvation; rather it is an expression of obedience to God's action in the world and a sign of gratitude for this guidance.

### The Concept of the Idolatrous

"The idolatrous" is a basic idea that appears repeatedly in connection with neo-orthodox self-analysis. It describes the sin man commits when he places something between himself and God.

13. PR37,365:74. The ideology discussed in the remaining portion of the chapter is largely taken from Analytical Cat. 2, where discussions of the nature of prejudice and its manifestations in the Church and society are classified. See Figs. 32 and 33, Appendix VIII. Any consideration of the nature of prejudice against others is an indirect form of self-criticism, because it assumes that the Christian audience needs to understand the etiology and structure of prejudice in order to become free from it, i.e., prejudice is implicitly assumed to exist within the Church.

In intergroup relations, such idolatries take institutionalized forms (such as substituting the nation or the Church for God), ethnic forms (the race or ethnic group), and creedal forms (a creed or even the Bible itself). In each case it is the group, the formulation, or the institution that takes the place that only God should occupy in the life of man.

What constitutes an act of prejudice? One neo-orthodox answer is that in the act of discriminating against another because of his creed or color a man affirms that his center of value is his own group. The god of the nationalist is his nation; and even though he may invoke the name of God, deity is useful merely to assure victory for national policy. The idolator, then, does not believe that God judges this policy or forces him to rethink his program; instead, God is purely instrumental to the idolator's purpose. The racist is always affirming both in word and in action that his own race is supreme and should determine the destinies of other races. So, in the neo-orthodox view, the Church that regards itself as absolute fails to recognize that it is being judged; it loses its capacity for self-criticism and sits in judgment on others.

This way of looking at man's relationship to God illuminates the age-old hatred of the Jews. The neo-orthodox feel that anti-Semitism is more complex and more resistant to correction than other forms of active prejudice because the Jew is a symbol of man's fundamental difficulty: *he arouses in other men the knowledge that they are obstinately prone to idolatry.*

> But there is more than a psychological and sociological explanation of anti-Semitism. There is a theological reason. Haman put it in Esther *Ch. 3:8.* The Jew's worship of God stands in the way of his allegiance to any nationalism. For this he is persecuted. (PR36,857:17)

The neo-orthodox argument goes on to say that the Jew, then, in the covenant relationship, understands that he has only *one* loyalty, i.e. God. This loyalty colors the Jew's relation to everything else in life:

> But when modern nationalism demands the loyalty of the whole man, making the State of supreme authority and the final security for its citizens and therefore the equivalent of

their god, this clashes with the loyalty of the Jew. It senses in the God of the Jew an enemy. And there are a great number of people for whom nationalism is their only religion. The nation symbolizes their self-interest. It is the answer to the problems of their existence. All their needs, their life, their destiny are tied up with it. And they hate the Jew because they hate the God of the Jew.[14]

The anti-Semite therefore not only seizes upon the Jew as a symbol of his rebellion against the true God of the Jews (and of his substituting the false god of nation or race) but projects upon the Jew his own rejection of God, charging the Jews with that rejection. Hence this communicator holds that anti-Semitism is, in the deepest sense, a profound indication of man's rejection of God. Such an approach to anti-Semitism helps to explain why American nationalism should be so closely tied up with anti-Semitism, and why some typical anti-Jewish charges hold that the Jew lacks loyalty to his country, that he is homeless throughout the world, that he is distinguished only by his rejection of Christ.

There is, then, a profound religious dimension to prejudice and, in particular, to anti-Semitism as the neo-orthodox understand it. Whenever a man—Christian or other—becomes anti-Semitic, it is a sign that he has become unfaithful to God. On this score, the neo-orthodox severely criticize anti-Semitism and identify strongly with the Jew:

> But the God of the Jew is the God of the Bible, the God who sent Jesus Christ into the world. And this explains why *any nation that persecutes the Jew will eventually persecute the Christian Church.* The Christian faith through the New Testament is so rooted in its Jewish past, so deeply grounded in the Old Testament that it can never in the end escape the hatred directed against the Jew—unless, of course, it compromises with the nationalism around it. But this eventually means that it denies that Jesus is the Christ and proceeds to make of him a harmless, insignificant man.
>
> For we must not forget that the name "Christ" is a title. It is a title that has meaning on only one condition—that the covenant and promises are true. If these are not true, if

14. This part of the lesson is a quotation from J. Stanley Glenn.

God did not really make them, if they are only certain ideas the Jews themselves acquired, then the title is an empty title. It has no significance. Therefore, when anti-Semitism denies the covenant and promises made to the Jewish people, it denies the one thing that the title "Christ" is meant to fulfill. It, therefore, denies Christ. And so the real conflict in anti-Semitism as it gradually works itself out from one stage to another is not with the Jew but with Jesus Christ. When we persecute the Jew, we do it because of his religion; and his religion is fulfilled in Christ. Therefore, in the end persecution is a war of the evil power of this world with Christ and his Church. In the end the offense is not the offense of the Jew, but the offense of Christ and his cross.[15]

## A Remedial Curriculum

If this ideology (of the anti-Semite as the idolatrous Christ-rejector) is at all effective in neo-orthodox theology, the Jew cannot very well be made the scapegoat for the world's ills. But neo-orthodox theology goes further than recognizing that the Christian's Christ-rejection makes anti-Semitism possible as a form of idolatry. It offers an alternative to the anti-Semite's habits of anxiety projection. It provides for both pupils and teachers a community of faith which confesses its common guilt for prejudice and Christ rejection, and it offers a release from anxiety through the doctrine of unmerited forgiveness. The Christian's knowledge that he participates in universal sin is balanced by his knowledge that he can enjoy God's acceptance and forgiveness. The community which continually examines itself and confesses its wrongs is also a community which constantly seeks repentance and forgiveness.

Thus the perspective of the neo-orthodox curriculum makes the classroom a place where pupils and teachers can confess their prejudice openly without fear of being condemned or rejected by their own group. One of the greatest difficulties in the attempts to change the attitudes of prejudiced persons has been the lack of adequate methodology. Recommended classroom procedures were thought to have too stringent requirements for Sunday School teaching, and the problems connected with this appeared too com-

15. PR, Crossroads, 2, No. 4 (1952), 35-36.

plex. As this study indicates, the typical treatment of prejudice in the class is too often moralistic, condemnatory, and seldom related to both the essentials of the Christian faith and the child's experience. In the neo-orthodox curricula, however, a new pattern seems to have been developed—or is developing—along the following lines:

1. A group situation is provided in which it is possible freely and without condemnation to bring one's prejudice out in the open without risking isolation (where prejudice is condemned) or loss of status (as is the case when the group assumes that some or most are free of prejudice).

2. The security to admit and examine one's prejudices in a group is provided for by the following:
   a. All members, including the teacher, are placed on the same level. That all men are prejudiced is the basic assumption on which the group proceeds; all men are sinners, all men are involved in the sins of society; all men need to confess, to know forgiveness. None of the neo-orthodox lessons assume that the teacher is less prejudiced than the pupils, or that the pupils can be divided into two groups: the prejudiced and the unprejudiced.
   b. The element of permissiveness is also present to a strong degree. No one is condemned for facing up to the fact of prejudice in himself, the church, or society; admitting to, and showing the ways in which one is prejudiced, has group support.

3. At the same time, prejudice itself is seriously condemned. There is no support for prejudice; but every encouragement is given to cross group lines and to take action, as well as to "talk out" one's prejudice in a group that provides each member with status and security to proceed and face up to prejudice.

4. Finally, the nonmoralistic context in which such discussions take place is with the knowledge that God's

free and unmerited forgiveness applies to all men, and
that God does not condemn us for our sins, but saves us
from them.

This approach to intergroup problems, then, is both self-critical
and remedial; the classroom procedures are so arranged as to allow
for discussion and clarification of the Christian doctrines of sin,
confession, grace, repentance, forgiveness, and obedience to the
divine command.[16] Hence Protestant theological analysis—when
sociologically informed and consciously applied to intergroup problems—has something vital and fresh to contribute to our understanding of intergroup phenomena and the meaning of prejudice.
It is quite possible, for example, that both prejudice and the lack
of it are religious phenomena which are rooted in the nature of
man's ultimate commitments. There are objects, groups, and forces
—both real and imaginary—which can be endowed with ultimate
value so that they tend to elicit the kind of behavior appropriate to
the object of worship. The neo-orthodox analysis, then, is particularly valuable, because it clarifies the nature of prejudice and makes
us aware that, theologically, prejudice is but another aspect of the
old problem of idolatry. Inasmuch as the churches take as their
central mission the tasks of serving and declaring the one, true God
and of calling men to repentance, the intergroup issues raised in
this study—particularly in relation to the problem of idolatry—are
much closer to the root concerns of Christian faith than some might
at first suspect.

16. Note that these procedures conform to what the doctrines *require*—e.g. they
ensure that the sin of prejudice is faced up to and confessed, they lead the
students to seek forgiveness and reconciliation and to be obedient to God's call.

# 11. Conclusion: A Critique

No one clear conclusion can be drawn that will embrace the complexity and range of intergroup images which we have found in Protestant textbooks. Yet the various analyses of the four communicators on the basis of the leading issues of their intergroup content do lead to two summary observations. While some Protestant teachings can conceivably implant or nurture certain types of anti-Judaism and anti-Catholicism, they also disseminate valuable remedies for prejudice as well. Some denominations (such as the positive scorers in this study) use their anti-ethnocentric resources very nearly to the full. Even more significantly, these antidotes to prejudice are plainly more indigenous to the essential, declared faith of Protestants than are the instances of bias. These central findings must not be overlooked in the inevitable tendency of our study to focus much of the time upon the negative content of teachings that involve this or that delicate issue.

Thus it remains to explore more generally the ethnocentric and anti-ethnocentric potentials of Protestant teaching and the forces which produced them. In so doing we can clarify certain basic problems which writers, teachers, and preachers need to be aware of when they deal with outside group in the course of expounding their religion.

## The Areas and Degrees of Ethnocentrism

Protestants clearly have many more problems in depicting outside religious communities positively than they do nonreligious ones; but even those who present their readers with predominantly dim views of other religions and denominations, do not reject all of them. Even in this area, there is no full ethnocentrism. Fundamentalists demonstrate a considerable sensitivity to some intergroup problems and manage a low positive orientation toward Jews. Analyses in this work of certain historical and biblical themes which encourage and complicate the mention of outsiders indicate that the conservative denomination, which gravitates toward negative scores for religious groups, could indeed have been quite positive in its teachings without endangering either its theological position or its principal concerns as Christian educators.

In any case, when we look at the negative references to Jews and Catholics, it is clear that we are dealing with ideological patterns that are radically different at many points from contemporary anti-Semitism or from the earlier anti-Catholicism of the Know-Nothings or the Ku Klux Klan. To be sure, some themes associated with religious anti-Semitism are found in the conservative curriculum (Christ-rejection, divine judgment, deicide, the curse); but most references to Jews that derive from these themes signify, in their theological context, different realities to the conservative Protestant mind than they do to the professional anti-Semite. It is precisely at this point, of course, that the danger arises of planting in young minds the seeds of anti-Semitism, despite the intent of the writers to the contrary. These writers handle biblical and historical themes according to unreconstructed traditions (formed by both secular culture and inherited ways of depicting Jews), and divorce them from the deeper layers of theological insight proclaimed elsewhere by the same communicator. Still, our major distinction between conservative Protestantism and contemporary religious bigotry holds true.

Among the contrasts to be drawn, one notes that anti-Semites display no solicitude for the rights of other ethnic, racial, or religious groups, except possibly those of Arabs and Gentiles. This is not true of the conservatives, even though the scriptural passages which provoke mention of the Jewish plight often betray them into placing these tragedies in a context of Jewish culpability without the critical benefit of other facets of their own theology. Again, racist attitudes are prominent in anti-Semitic statements. While the conservatives occasionally refer to Jews as a "race" (meaning "people"), or lump prejudice to Jews and Negroes together as "racial," no overt racism appears in the materials, nor is any intended. Racial attributes are not assigned to Jews, nor are racial differences used to justify discrimination or segregation of any kind. Of even greater importance is the fact that nationalism, the real and virulent religion of the anti-Semite, is absent in evangelical teaching.

The Protestant image of the Jew as oppressor occurs largely in reference to the biblical record and early Church history, where there is some limited justification for it. In contrast, the anti-Semite is preoccupied with present Jewish hatred of Christians. Here again, the conservative communicator is often so unaware of the real issues that exist between Jews and Christians that he refers to Jewish hostility from a noncritical and improper historical perspective. Nonetheless, the antagonisms of Jews toward Christians is largely set forth by conservatives in a framework of actual past events (the conflict of Church and Synagogue, etc.), while the anti-Semites treat Jewish hostility, whether past or present, in terms of a world-wide plot to destroy Gentiles, Christianity, and the United States—all of which are loosely identified with each other, the "nation," and the white race. Even in its punitive statements, the communicator's focus is upon divine judgment and does not hint at any pogrom against the Jew, nor does he incite or approve of such action, as does the anti-Semite. Judgment is regarded as a divine, not a human, prerogative.

The anti-Semite's general score for Jews (and the resultant profile imbalance) is more intensively negative ($-97.4$) than is the conservative's score ($-15.4$). This significant difference is due partly to the theological orientation of the conservative writers in which concepts such as "judgment," "chosenness," "rejection," and others mean very different things than they do to the anti-Semite. The contrast is seen in the way the self-other group roles are envisioned. Conservatives, fundamentalists, and the neo-orthodox never confuse the Gentile with Christian, as does the anti-Semite. The churches require a clear-cut distinction between "Christian" and "Gentile," and the Christian is defined so as to include the possibility that Jews as well as Gentiles will be found within the faith. This self-definition affects the portrait of the victims and oppressors. Anti-Semites, for example, charge that the Jews earn the opposition of Gentiles on the grounds that those who set themselves up against God deserve and invite the contempt of others—a proposition that is abhorrent to the conservative communicator as to all the others. All men, Gentiles as well as Jews, sin and have set themselves against God. Since men are disposed to hate God, it is those who are faithful to Him who earn and invite the contempt of others. Thus the Christian's vocation, in the conservative view, is to suffer and not to inflict suffering.

On this and other grounds, the conservative communicator does not hesitate to condemn prejudice and anti-Semitism as sinful—something the anti-Semite does not do.

Both the fundamentalist and conservative scores for Roman Catholics are intensely negative and frequently may be classed as anti-Catholic. Again, however, it must be noted that the fundamentalists explicitly uphold the rights of Catholics and condemn prejudice against them. They do not charge contemporary Catholics with actual oppression of Protestants except in some Catholic countries abroad. While they take a monolithic historical view of Catholic action against Protestants, they also criticize Protestants for their anti-Catholic prejudice. The conservatives do see a threat in the Catholic viewpoint, not only to the "true faith" but to American freedoms. Yet when we come to the real value-conflicts posed today by Catholic-Protestant relations, the two remaining communicators (liberal and neo-orthodox) demonstrate that it is possible to take account of them and still give a positive view of the Catholic group.

On the basis of the criteria adopted for this study, we can conclude that not even the most negative-scoring communicator is ethnocentric. While the Missouri Synod feels threatened by some groups, it does not feel threatened by all, nor is its dogma inherently rejective. The equivocal over-all scores of the Scripture Press communicator reflect a capacity for self-criticism, even when it views others in a predominantly negative way. It is not rejective of all groups, nor of all segments of a single group. Fundamentalists, for example, admire the orthodox, Bible-believing, observing Jew much more than they do the liberal secular Jew or the "modernist" Protestant. This phenomenon is noted even in positive-scoring curricula. The liberal Christian admires the liberal Jew but not necessarily the orthodox Jew or the fundamentalist Christian.

*The Effect of Faith Perspectives on the Portrayal of Other Groups*

The basic faiths of the communicators are not threatened by our findings in any way. But the study does address some questions to the faiths. Ironically, it is in lessons that set forth the faith—whether in the form of doctrinal, biblical, or historical exposition—that the problems of intergroup writing become crucial. Lessons written with an intergroup intent—i.e. specifically to discuss relations between groups—have a positive impact which begins to break down the moment one gets into *religious* teaching. Here, other groups are brought associatively, incidentally, and cursorily into the discussion, but these generally fragmentary images comprise the bulk of the outgroup portraits. Thus they are the most important type of reference as well as the most problematic. Consequently, some final attention should be paid to the influence and resources of the faith perspectives in portraying outsiders, particularly Jews.

Faith perspectives do not affect the ways in which other groups are envisioned in a univocal or determinative way. But this study does shed some light on the various relationships that exist between the faiths—or how they are stated—and the negative and positive portraits of other groups in our society. These points may be summarized as follows:

(1) A negative intergroup portrait in some respects is a matter of a partial rather than a full-fledged exposition of a given theological position. It is often associated with what each communicator himself can recognize as an inadequate or fragmentary statement of his own faith, i.e. as bad theology.

The adverse picture painted in some conservative lessons of the Jewish plight as being a consequence of Jewish sinfulness and divine judgment reflects certain isolated facets of biblical thought. But this construct does not at the same time do justice to the same communicator's views of man's sinfulness in hating and persecuting Jews, nor to the concept of God's mercy in the preservation of Israel. Nor does it bring to bear the conservative's self-critical perspective on this question; where the divine judgment is invoked only against Israel, the communicator's doctrine that all men and all groups stand under God's judgment and mercy is lost to the reader's view. This illustration, then, involves an important principle: many of the images which contain bias are contradictory to the tenets of the declared faith. The use of theology in a more complete and searching way can help to resolve these questions, and to improve the portraits of outside groups.

(2) When Protestants have not explored their faith fully in regard to a given theme—such as the crucifixion—certain other factors tend to determine the images of the outsiders involved. One

of these is the complex tradition of Christian teachings about other groups which have been formed in other periods of history and which Protestants have inherited as part of an uncriticized body of church culture. These teachings have been handed down in many ways, not the least important being in the form of commentaries used by some lesson writers as well as the beliefs that have been part of their background. This instruction, while not constituting the core of the faith, has been circulated widely by both clergy and laity and has found its way into treatises and the learned works of scholars. The origins of these teachings are exceedingly complex, reflecting many social and historical forces and faith conflicts. An earlier chapter in this book, for example, describes certain textbooks which claim that Protestants laid the foundation for religious freedom and that Roman Catholics have always persecuted Protestants. Nothing is said about the converse truth—that when Protestants were in power, they restricted the rights of Catholics and sometimes put them to death, as they also did to other Protestant deviates. Roland Bainton's *The Travail of Religious Liberty* shows how terribly unfair this kind of one-sided teaching is; yet it is the way Protestant churches were one disposed to handle the problems of religious persecution and the rise of religious freedom. Fortunately, not only individual lessons of all denominations, but the entire curricula of many, demonstrate that this tradition is being radically reconstructed.

Similarly, the unrelieved past hostility of Jews to Christians is a traditional teaching whose negative implications can be corrected only by putting the facts in their proper biblical and historical context. Teachings about Jews comprise a unique problem because of the way pre-Christian anti-Semitism crept into the Church with the influx of those Gentiles who had no appreciation of the Hebraic heritage of Christianity and who produced various non-Hebraic heresies, such as Gnosticism, Marcionism and the like. Portions of Christian teachings began to take on a strong anti-Jewish tone. The doctrine of the impartial and universal judgment of God was transformed into a particular and irrevocable curse on Jews; the inclusion of the Gentiles into the chosen people became an inclusion of Gentiles to the exclusion of the Jews; what had once been an internal conflict within Judaism was externalized as a conflict between Jews and Gentiles. Despite evidence that a great deal of these sentiments have been re-evaluated in the light of scriptural teachings, the traditions still influence innumerable lesson writers to make invidious comparisons, negative selections, and adverse interpretations to the detriment of the learners' images of Jews. This points up the crucial need to re-evaluate Christian teachings about other groups in the light of Christian faith and biblical teaching as well as historical research. Without this effort writers often continue unconsciously to pass on the prejudices of their culture and the stereotypes inherited from their past.

(3) Behind the negative intergroup image there often lies not only an inadequate explication of the faith but also a lack of sensitivity to the meaning of that faith for the Christian's relations to other groups. The positive-scorers see the relations of their theology to the issues in the world about them, and they show more concern about the specific import of any given theological point. Those writers whose lessons score negatively do not usually pay enough attention to the intergroup significance of the biblical insights.

The way a faith is stated is important in a more specific way. It can make the involvement of the learner in intergroup concerns either inevitable and important or optional and auxiliary. A faith may be so stated as to inspire or not to inspire an awareness of the existence and problems of other groups in our culture. It may or may not compel the readers to ask searching questions about the society in which they live. What is needed is to tie intergroup concerns to as many central doctrines of the faith as possible so that they cease to be peripheral.

When intergroup problems are taken seriously as a faith requirement, they are not necessarily expressed in the same way by any two equally anti-ethnocentric communicators. This was pointed up in Chapter 3. Liberal naturalistic monism makes a concern for all outsiders mandatory through its search for a oneness which can overcome barriers that divide human communities. Intergroup relations come thus to stand at the center of the liberal's perspective of the world. The neo-orthodox writers must also come to grips with intergroup questions because these are crucial to the situations in which Christians are asked to act obediently to God's action upon them and their neighbor. The man of faith who accepts the gospel is directed to make an assessment of his relation to all men, for whom Christ died. Intergroup relations, as embodied in these two perspectives, cannot be an optional interest for the Christian. They are linked with so many vital components of the faith that the learners cannot ignore their social responsibilities without repudiating the faith. This is an important distinction: the fundamentalist and conservative communicators have yet to make explicit in their materials the real connections between their central concern to preach the gospel and their task to educate those who accept the gospel about their relations to outside groups with whom they live in society.

The unused and potential anti-ethnocentric resources inherent in the fundamentalist-conservative views have been previously pointed out. We have also repeatedly noted that such anti-ethnocentric attitudes must and can be consonant with their conception of their primary task as communicators of the gospel. An interest in ethnic, racial, and interreligious relations cannot and need not supplant the Gospel in the course of deriving from it.

The fundamentalist writer divides men into two classes, those saved or lost; he tends to see other Christians, non-Christians, Jews, Negroes, and alien ethnic groups primarily in this way, rather than as communities whose existence God calls him to understand and toward which he must establish attitudes. Men are in need of a saviour, to be "born again" in Christ. These are their primary needs. Thus one can see why writers of the fundamentalist and conservative materials tend to think of Negroes, Jews, and others almost solely in terms of declaring the gospel to them and why so often the urge to love and respect them is expressed exclusively by the act of bringing them to a saving faith. If fundamentalist and conservative lesson writers are to work out an intergroup policy, they must do so within this soteriological perspective, but include in this policy other neglected resources of their faith.

Deep intergroup concerns are often instanced in informal conversations with the editors and writers of the conservative curricula. But these interests have not yet been expressed in the materials, or else have not been stated so as to have binding relevance to their declared faith. In order to understand this reticence, outsiders must realize that intergroup concerns historically have been associated in part with such movements as the "social gospel," which have been felt to subordinate or sacrifice the Gospel. Social gospelers were intent upon "building the Kingdom of God" or "bringing in the Kingdom" by their action. Conservatives and fundamentalists as well as neo-Reformation Protestants believe that only God can "build" or "bring in" the Kingdom, since it is God's kingdom, not man's. Nor can men earn salvation by their good works—according to the doctrine of salvation by faith—since it is God's free gift and due to His prior action.

It is easy to see that one can deal with intergroup problems in such a way as to obscure and pervert the core concerns of an evangelical faith. Yet the problem of man's response to the Gospel in his ethical life still remains a burning one for the evangelical. To recognize that the prime task of the Church is to preach the Gospel does not justify neglecting the question of how the Christian should respond to the Gospel as it affects the neighbor whom God calls him to love. To reflect upon these responses and to emphasize their importance in teaching materials (specifically, in the field of intergroup relations) is in no way to subordinate the primary task of the Church as fundamentalists, conservatives, and neo-evangelicals conceive it. If a den of vice were operating in the vicinity of an evangelical church, its members would not hesitate to work to eliminate it without thinking that they were bringing in God's Kingdom or earning salvation thereby. Similarly, Christians may seriously attempt to eliminate prejudice, and take account of the problems which other groups face in our society, without compromising the Gospel one iota. One simply thinks, acts, or raises questions with respect to the welfare of other groups as a trustworthy response to God's saving grace. Careful theological statement can guard against the traditional perversions of the Gospel that have at times accompanied social concern. But not to state this concern at all, as this report shows, ironically results in the very kind of accommodation to a sinful culture that the communicator wishes to avoid.

Of course, the Christian lives in this culture and cannot escape the consequences of some accommodation to it. But this does not mean—and fundamentalists, conservatives, and evangelicals would agree—that the Christian must remain mute in the face of intergroup problems. All these faiths have begun to work toward improving their ethnic and racial images and relations. It remains for them to develop and extend this social awareness to the interreligious area.

For the conservatives, intergroup concerns have an additional dimension in their preaching of "Law" rather than Gospel. The "third use of the Law" has to do entirely with the nature of the believer's moral duty to the neighbor. In this communicator's view, Law and Gospel must never be confused, nor must either one be neglected. The Gospel tells of God's action in justifying, regenerating, and sanctifying man. Law tells of man's ethical duty and speaks of human relations as a legitimate area of concern where careful thought and action are needed. An obedient response of Christians to the gospel requires the conservative communicator not only to disseminate the Gospel but also clearly to speak to Christians about those intergroup issues which they face and to which they can find proximate solutions.

The two positive scorers are notably successful in bringing the concrete issues of intergroup relations into the exposition of their respective faiths. The neo-orthodox see the actual daily situations that confront Christian pupils and teachers as those in which they are divinely called to love their neighbor and seek justice for him. One function of scripture is to illuminate these situations, but the specific social problems they present must be looked at and understood in order to determine how a loving, just, and relevant response can be made. Neo-orthodox writers are convinced that the biblical viewpoint requires a Christian curricula to involve the readers in these problems by questioning them as to their real attitudes and feelings and by directing them to scrutinize their own actual relations.

Thus pupils and teachers are instructed to involve themselves actively with specific issues in the concrete situation. We cannot talk, for example, about the political responsibility of the Christian in our society without engaging in some way in politics, in joining a party, working for a candidate, studying political positions, voting, and running for office. This does not mean that the Church must enter politics; for the conservative communicator in this study, such a demand would violate his doctrine that the task of the Church is spiritual and that it must not impose its will upon the state. But this restriction does not absolve the Church from its responsibility to direct Christians to involve themselves in the actual conflicts where serious questions of Christian duty arise.

The same principle is true of intergroup relations. The Church can call the reader's attention to the crucial areas that are pertinent to the Christian faith. The Church can raise the issues, discuss them, call the Christian's attention to his situation in the community, and provide for responsible reflection and action upon them—not as a substitute for or a supplement to the Gospel but as a response to the Gospel. An excellent illustration of this function is found in the electives from extant Missouri Synod literature such as the Lutheran Round Table Series, where biblical perspectives and empirical data are utilized to enlighten the Christian reader about the problems, issues, and solutions to racial prejudice, segregation, and discrimination. The low-scorer in this study produced a study unit (first published in 1955 and not included in the statistical analysis) which declares that the "church always faces the problem of the social order":

> Wherever church members live and congregations exist, they face the responsibilities created by a society of sinful men. To evade its obligations in this area is to belittle the church's task. . . . As soon as [church members] exclude from their lives the problem of responsibility for social order and limit themselves to the question of personal relationships, they may indeed become partners in conditions that cause grave injustice.[1]

The saving purpose of the Church—embodied in the soteriological aims of the curriculum—is not lost in this approach. Rather, it makes a place for imperative intergroup concerns within the larger framework. It is not surprising, then, that the lowest-scoring communicator has shown the most openness to this study and has made the most positive responses to it. It is currently in the process of mustering its own resources of faith in behalf of an anti-ethnocentric approach.

(4) Some forms of doctrine illuminate, while others obscure, the nature of intergroup problems and the self-other portraits.

The theological concept of prejudice as idolatry, for example,

1. *The Christian and Race*, p. 22.

serves as a focal point for organizing and making meaningful empirical data on the nature of prejudice. Projection—the psychological term for blaming others for one's own inadequacies, frustrations, and shortcomings—takes on a new meaning when it is seen as a function of the worship of one's own group or groups as a substitute for God. The relationship of Judaism to Christianity and the vocation of suffering take on a crucial significance the moment anti-Semitism is discerned as a basic form of idolatry. This insight is one of the few that is capable of being expounded from within different perspectives of faith, whether liberal or fundamentalists, or those that stand between them.

An example of how the exposition of a vital doctrine can obscure intergroup issues appears in that devoted to love of neighbor. In one curriculum love is never discussed with regard to the inequities experienced by other groups in our society. Love of neighbor is urged; but seeking justice is never specifically mentioned as a necessary condition of this love. There are many illustrations in the literature of how love of the outsider is expended in seeking his conversion or showing him friendliness, and not in seeking to right the wrongs he suffers. In another curriculum, on the other hand, considerations of justice are seldom omitted in any discussion of the Christian doctrine of love or of the neighbor's plight.

Again, certain writers pose general solutions to the question of intergroup justice in terms of acceptance of Christ. Here both the anti-ethnocentric strength and weakness of religious conservatism in America becomes evident. The weakness probably derives from an omission: once the writer has stated that the only ultimate solution to human conflicts and injustice is to be found in God's final action in history, he may be content to let the matter rest.[2] The proper *human* response of the believer in a situation where he can seek relative justice for oppressed groups is thereby ignored and

2. In addition to being silent, some writers seem to imply that the rights of Jews are in some way dependent upon their acceptance of Christ. The biblical view, however, is presumably that accepting Christ is a question of the ultimate salvation of the person and not an issue which can be used to justify a Christian's lack of active concern for an unbeliever's rights and freedom from persecution. A Christian's attitude toward another man is to be determined not by whether he accepts Christ but solely by what God has done for all men regardless of their merit.

the options of decision and action which are open to the believer are never seriously explored.

The potential anti-ethnocentric strength of the conservatives lies in the very pessimism for which they have been criticized by secularists and some liberals—that is, the conviction that ultimate solutions to intergroup problems are impossible apart from Christ and the universal acceptance of salvation. The valuable insight in this position—which varies from communicator to communicator—lies in its rejection of an "illusion," i.e. that final solutions for these problems can be found in history. Moreover, no envisioned final solution is without its ethnocentric dangers. For the neo-orthodox writers, this insight is no justification for inaction. Man must be obedient to God even if only relative justice can be achieved. Faith in God involves the knowledge that God uses and overshadows man's own action in establishing that justice which is truly divine. The conservatives need to elaborate their theology precisely at this point; otherwise they leave the impression that the believer need do nothing.[3]

Beliefs, then, may be stated so as to set or remove limits to the kinds and degrees of social concern in which a Christian might be engaged. The doctrine of the Kingdom of God is another case in point. The Kingdom may at times be defined as so internal that the Christian loses contact with the objective world where the issues of intergroup relations come to light. Or the Kingdom may be seen as so spiritual and so much in the future as to turn the illumination of doctrine away from the contemporary scene. The kingdom may be so closely identified with the Church—if not the churches—that the religious body receives a certain glorification at the expense of neglecting the world as it relates to Christian faith. But the kingdom of God may also be envisioned as both earthly and heavenly, both material and spiritual, both inner and outer, both present and future, both within and without the churches, so that no part of life and no ethical question is without importance or relevance.

The views which lesson writers convey of scripture and its uses

3. Christians must not "play God" or try to bring in God's Kingdom; yet, in the evangelical view, this does not excuse the faithful from the duty to fight evil and to do good in the situation, culture, and time in which God has placed them.

have grave intergroup consequences in this regard. (These convictions have nothing to do with the acceptance or rejection of the views of inspiration or infallibility.) When scripture is looked at as almost wholly predictive or as having a value entirely apart from the contemporary situation in which the believer finds himself, the reader is not forced to look at the realities of history, at the contemporary conditions in which he lives, or at himself. The focus is not upon man's real, present situation as a requisite for understanding and appropriating the Word of God. The Scriptures become a source of true doctrine, but the importance of the doctrine for the conduct and self-understanding of man is not discerned and its positive intergroup aspects are scanted.

On the other hand, the anti-ethnocentric use of scripture appears to be tied up with a curriculum theory that gives to it a contemporary meaning, which regards it as addressed to "us." Such a curriculum requires some degree of realistic examination of the contemporary scene in which men must act in obedience to God, and encourages unrelenting and continual self-examination. A Presbyterian U.S. publication warns the teacher:

> This lesson will be effective as Philip's experience takes on meaning for us. A discussion of prejudice among the first century Jew has little value unless we can see ourselves in them and find the common denominator of a Christian solution which fits twentieth century America as well.[4]

This quotation questions the value of scriptural expositions which portray the Jews in a negative way without involving the student in its implications. Unless this is done, a discussion of Jewish prejudice in the first century becomes primarily an occasion for denouncing Jews, for using them as bad examples, for tempting the writer to "apply the lesson" by moralizing about how Christians should try not to be like these people, or for making invidious comparisons based on the supposed moral superiority of Christians over their spiritual predecessors. The Word of God is in this way robbed of its power to speak the unwelcome word to ourselves and our accepted group. It makes of the Word of God an unattractive snapshot of some other group rather than a mirror reflecting the

4. Presbyterian U.S. Graded Series, *Pioneer Teacher's Guide* (July–Sept. 1956), p. 14. Not to be confused with the United Presbyterian curriculum.

image of one's own and all groups as given in the divine revelation.

The characteristically anti-ethnocentric evangelical writers say that scripture is meant to stimulate self-insight, self-examination, confession, repentance, and faith. What scripture says is related to the actual situation in which the pupils and teachers live. This approach encourages open and rigorous examination of both the Christian and the social scene:

> It is natural for Pioneers [the name for Presbyterian U.S. intermediates], preoccupied as they often are with their own group, to be indifferent or even hostile toward people who are different. Indeed, there is little in our contemporary American society to discourage such an attitude and much to encourage it. The Church must make a conscious effort to help its people recognize their prejudices for what they are and learn to look out on the local neighborhood and the world neighborhood through the eyes of Christ . . . Think of your group, your church, your community. What prejudices exist in school and community . . . Who are the "Samaritans" of your community? [5]

(5) When the world is looked at *solely* through one's faith commitments, the social images tend to be unreal. It is only when these commitments are brought into some meaningful relation to the actual events in the world today that the images bear some relation to reality. The kind of mythical Judaism and monolithic Catholicism that crop up in many lessons would be eliminated if writers took full account of relevant historical and empirical data.

The need to be accurate and specific has been noted throughout this study. Even positive scorers may so view intergroup problems through their faith perspectives as to misconstrue the real situation of the outside communities they seek to portray sympathetically. The liberal's monistic view often leads him to ask the Jewish and Christian communities to merge their religious festivals on the basis of their primitive meanings, as though two people whose celebrations take on significance mainly from their respective histories can find a solution to their differences by reverting (as Jew and Christian would interpret the request) to their pagan residuals. The other communicators also tend to give at times an uncritical and

5. Ibid.

distorted view of themselves and others. Drawn from primarily exegetical sources, the images of the outsider are too exclusively those of the persecutor, and the images of the ingroups too often those of the persecuted. The Jew is often no more than a theological-exegetical abstraction. When correctives to these images appear, it is usually from the consideration of empirical evidence.[6]

This study has considerable import for the current disputes in sociological and theological circles concerning the influence of certain Christian doctrines on the intergroup orientation of the communicator. Beliefs in a supernatural God and of man as sinner have been too easily mistrusted by outsiders because of their supposed prejudice-producing potential. Belief in an objective God is also suspected by students of intergroup relations of promoting authoritarian submission. The argument is that the individual who subscribes to the idea of God as supernatural is more apt to be submissive to outside powers and persons. An item in the scale for measuring the relation of religious ideology to prejudice in *The Authoritarian Personality* reads, "Every person should have faith in some supernatural force higher than himself to which he gives total allegiance and whose decisions he does not question." The authors express the opinion that "agreement with this statement, which expresses very firm belief in the supernatural and an attitude of submission toward it, would be associated with prejudice." [7] This item correlated significantly with the rest of the scale for measuring ethnocentrism.

However, no communicator in this study requires unquestioning obedience to an institution (such as the Church) which is thought of as embodying or dictating the will of God. Even if they assert that His will is not knowable apart from the existence of the community that interprets scripture, each of the biblical perspectives has a center that looks beyond the churches to support its values. Submission to the dictates of churchmen, authoritative spokesmen, or any other institution is not for them the equivalent of submission

6. These empirical considerations can also appear in the exegesis itself. Cf. Bernard Ramm's discussion of the interpretation of biblical words and passages in his *Protestant Biblical Interpretation* (Boston, Wilde, 1956), pp. 131–32, 136. To this must be added all that we know about ancient and present-day Judaism from archaeological, historical, and sociological sources.

7. Adorno et al., *The Authoritarian Personality*, p. 218.

to God. On the other hand disobedience to human tyranny is always to obedience to God.

The neo-orthodox curricula in particular recognizes that just as the idea of God can be idolatrously utilized as a power in the service of the real gods of national, racial, economic, and social caste, so can the idea of deity be pressed into the idolatrous service of the Church. Self-exaltation, self-centeredness, hatred of outside groups, provincial loyalties and concern with maintenance of ingroup power rather than with the kingdom of God, idealization of ingroup leaders, withdrawal from the responsibilities of the social order—all can and do appear in the churches, even as much as they mark those nationalists and racists whose ultimate commitment is to the nation or to their race.[8]

God is conceptualized far more objectively and noninstitutionally by neo-orthodox writers than by other biblically centered communicators. Their awareness of God's action requires not only that the Scriptures must be heeded (although open to constant and varied scrutiny), but that God's present action must be discerned in the human events that involve us all. Scripture provides the proper understanding of and perspective toward those events. This shifts the center of human commitment significantly to a divine action that transcends group action. The submission demanded is one that makes a place for the human voices, the human authorities, the social institutions, but absolutizes none of them. This submissive attitude frees men from bondage to all relativisms, all authoritarianisms, all despotic leaders, and all institutional idolatries.

In brief, the neo-orthodox curriculum points to a corrective action going on in the world, one which is not its own action or the action of others—an action to which the Christian must give heed and which scripture gives him power to observe. It is to this divine action (judgmental and redemptive) that the individual is committed to respond. His ideas and goals are constantly being remade in the light of the scriptural illumination of what is going on in contemporary life. Primary attention must be given to the grace and judgment contained in the actions taking place outside the group as well as within it. Ethnocentrism, or the glorification of

8. Some writers of lesson materials fall into this trap. Cf. my introductory essay in Jules Isaac, *Has Anti-Semitism Roots in Christianity?* (New York, N.C.C.J., 1961), pp. 21–24.

the group, is impossible where commitment to the divine is made in these terms. Submission to God in this sense is to ensure against authoritarian submission—indeed, it is the opposite of and the antidote to both authoritarianism and individualistic subjectivism.

It is also true that the liberal monistic view of God results in a highly positive intergroup outlook. Here again, the implications of the idea of God are universalized—all men are affirmed and included in its purview. Men are called to be responsible, for they depend on nothing but their own powers, which are part of reality itself. A sense of dependency on outside powers is discouraged. This may deter conformity, just as does the positive outlook of the neo-orthodox. The sense of dependency in both faiths is not to authoritative creeds, churches, leaders, or groups; but only for the neo-orthodox is man dependent upon an objective, divine action judging and redeeming him and all men.

Similarly, the doctrine of man as sinner—examined in Chapter 3 —can and does have positive intergroup implications. It becomes anti-ethnocentric once it is not restricted to a given cultural context but instead is universalized. The doctrine of man as sinner does not denigrate man when it is meant to denote the difference between deity and humanity and is not confused with the passing cultural judgments of what is right or wrong. This, too, is the neo-orthodox view: what is sinful is not always determined in advance but is discerned in the continuing (and present) conversation of action and response between God and man, a conversation that can be grasped and illuminated only in the light of the scriptural revelation. The believer must point not to himself and his own group, but to God.

In short, the doctrine of the supernatural as easily lends itself to a position that short-cuts authoritarian submission as do nonsupernatural ideas of God, such as that held by the liberals. In this connection it is worth repeating that the two communicators who have ambiguous or negative interreligious scores are not prevented by their religious beliefs from scoring positively in their teachings about other racial, ethnic, and national groups.

(6) Scripture, the scriptural themes (such as the crucifixion), and the exegetical data derived from them do not necessarily affect the portraits of outside groups in a negative or positive way. The

themes may be handled in an ethnocentric or anti-ethnocentric fashion according to how the more basic issues or motifs are understood: God, man, scripture, revelation, sin, and many others. It has already been demonstrated that the intergroup scores in the various curricula have a certain independence of scripture and of scriptural themes, including that of the crucifixion. The same differences are also found in discourses based on history rather than scripture.

There is, then, an intergroup attitude that is expressed as a function of the larger perspectives that are brought to the scriptural passages being expounded. These perspectives are informed partly by scripture and partly by traditions and social forces. They affect the ways the biblical themes are universalized and made relevant to the pupil and teacher by illuminating the areas of present controversy, encouraging self-criticism, and making intergroup concerns and actions imperative. The crucifixion may be handled so as to accuse the Jews of Christ rejection and deicide, or it may serve to show the reader what he himself is like in his response to deity, what his great need is, and what God has done about it.

In a fashion, the whole problem may be approached by way of the basic purposes of Christian education. When scripture talks about the conflict between Jesus and the Pharisees, to take but one example, the writers may ignore the good points about the Pharisees (even the friendliness of some to Jesus), paint them entirely negatively, criticize and denounce them and generalize about "Jews" and Jewish hostility. But does this serve the ends of Christian education? Is not one function of the Jesus-Pharisee conflict to enable the Christian (as well as the non-Christian) to get some insight about himself and his spiritual condition? Can the biblical portrait of the Pharisee provide the Christian with self-insight unless the writer is willing to see the positive human qualities of goodness residing in the Pharisees, what it was they thought they were defending, their commendable motives and piety as well as their hostility to Jesus, their inability to keep the whole counsel of God, and the like? When the Pharisees are understood as truly human—which they were—then their portrait in scripture can become a source of spiritual illumination for the pupils and teachers. The most conservative communicators can thus show men their need for a saviour, and the Christian his need for continual repentance. Thus the illuminating uses of scripture necessitate that both the negative and positive aspects of the scriptural portrayal of the Pharisees be kept steadily in view.

Scripture need not be the less inerrant or less the literal Word of God because it is used to illuminate the concrete problems of man's existence. The Christian's need to know himself and the specifics of the situation in which he seeks to act in obedience to God's action does not detract from the prior necessity of knowing what the scripture says or what it is that God has done in and through Christ's life, death, and resurrection. Concern for justice does not conflict with, but properly springs from, a genuine Christian love for other persons. In brief, there is no threat to any of the faiths in bringing scripture into intimate relation with the inter-group facts of life. But each communicator must work out his own way of stating it. The antidotes to prejudice are there, but not all lesson writers make use of them.

## Effect of Empirical Factors on the Portraits of Other Groups

Not all the data in the analytical categories can be understood in doctrinal terms. The negative imbalances in the categories which measure the extent to which outgroup hostility is felt by a communicator reflect past and present clashes over issues which at times have bred considerable animosity. The group's image of itself as victim is a response not merely to the memory of martyrdom in its own history, of the struggles to win the conditions for its existence, but is also formed by various influences in present-day culture.

(1) Part of this self-image comes from the bitter dialogue in which religious groups are sometimes engaged in present-day America. The kinds of negative statements made by some of the conservative writers can be partially understood as a response to the scorn heaped upon them by larger and more popularly respectable groups. The establishment by this denomination of parochial schools in many American communities, for example, invites accusations of divisiveness and intolerance from outsiders. In addition, the motivation, intellectual respectability, modernity, wisdom, etc. of the conservatives have been questioned. The actions range from bitter verbal attack to quiet airs of superiority, much of this coming from presumably liberal sources. For example, the desire of the con-

servatives on religious grounds to remain aloof from the ecumenical movement has been construed as a form of prejudice.

On the other hand, liberals as well as others have felt the sting of the larger denominations in their attempt to find a place in American religious life. The refusal of the trinitarian churches to include the Unitarian liberals in the varied Councils of Churches is one of the reasons for the phenomenon of counteridentification with Christianity analyzed in Chapter 3. To be sure, this reaction reveals itself in lower positive scores, rather than in negative scores for other Christian groups.

(2) A second and closely related ingredient of the Protestant self-image as victim (and the corresponding outside images of the oppressor) is derived from the problem of the relation of the churches to American culture. The low and ambiguous scorers take many positions that are at odds with the norms, values, and ideas generally accepted in our society.

To illustrate, there are competing insights, doctrines, and values at stake between the Missouri Synod position and the majority positions in America. This holds true whether one is evaluating the Lutheran position from the standpoint of general culture or of the culture of the churches. The attitude toward religion as an elective, that religions are alike (or of the same value, or achieve the same goals), that what people believe in common is more important than their differences, that it is more important to pursue social goals than to take account of the salvation of the soul—these and many other contentions place this communion in opposition to groups which define their position in one or more of these ways.

The churches in their trend toward union and ecumenicity at times slur over doctrinal differences in the interest of intergroup harmony. They encourage a consensus theology making for co-operation, unity, or merger. In America itself there is pressure to achieve conformity, accompanied by suspicion and criticism of those who maintain minority or unique positions. The common acceptance of evolution, certain presuppositions of liberal "higher criticism" of the Bible, and the manifold ways in which the distinction between Law and Gospel are seen as blunted in the teachings of the churches all confront the conservative communicator with certain problems.

The conservatives have many allies and opponents within the churches. Many of their positions and doctrines are affirmed by the Christian majority. But the Missouri Synod theology is uniquely constituted and is dependent upon certain specific historical formulations of that faith (among others, the Formula of Concord and the Smalcald Articles). These have certain implications for intergroup relations, such as in their views of the Church and State question or of the Kingdom of God.

In response to the positions of other groups, and in order to protect its principal soteriological concerns, the educational literature of this Church is inclined to define its position over against that of other denominations and sects. In this way its members are educated to avoid the numerous pitfalls which they will encounter in the ordinary everyday relations between Missouri Synod Lutherans and non-Lutherans. The trends of the times are seen as opposed to their own goals and convictions. As a guide to the unwary, conservative teaching in respect to truth is weighted to warn the readers against the false teachings of other churches and groups.

This defensiveness may be related to denominational maneuvering and maintenance of power positions in American society, but it is also tied up with the question of the right to dissent from the norm in behalf of doctrines and practices deemed to be inherently true. Dissent requires a well-knit community in which faith can be nurtured and given common support. The positive-scoring communicators may not feel this need to the same extent. The liberals find strong support for their position in certain trends in American culture (toward unity and a common consensus on religion, toward the secularization of American education as well as the acceptance of evolutionary theory, to name but a few). The neo-orthodox find considerable support for their fundamental position in the ecumenical movement, if not in society in general. Therefore these latter two faiths feel less threatened and permit more fredom in dialogue and communion with those who differ with them.

But such minority communities as the fundamentalists and conservatives do not find it easy to advocate the same degree of dialogue and interaction with competing groups. The problem is dramatically that of how a religious community can best maintain and express its faith. It is partially a problem of survival—of the faith, and of the group that holds it—in order that the faith may be witnessed to. Such a group needs to be well integrated and united.

The problem of many minority Christian groups is then to create a community with deep commitments, self-discipline, and close mutual ties. To witness to and transmit a heritage against the weight of cultural opinion is possible only when those who have been nurtured within the community of faith shore up its structure by the collective strength of their commitment. This of necessity can involve a marked degree of ingroup loyalty and outgroup rejection.

(3) Because the portraits of other groups are at least partially forged in the heat of value-conflict and not merely by historical prejudice, negative imbalances in some of the analytical categories in this study are not necessarily invidious. It is not only true but appropriate that Protestants speak of outside groups from concerns that differ in kind and degree.[9] A different image is reflected in its lessons of Roman Catholicism from that of Judaism or of other Protestant groups. These variations are due to social as well as religious factors. In the first place, Catholics, unlike Jews, now constitute in America an established near-majority—if not in the country as a whole, at least in the major centers of population. American Catholicism shares not only actual power with Protestantism but also its responsibilities. The liberal and neo-Reformed writers regard Catholics particularly as sharing some responsibility for Catholic-Protestant tension, whereas they do not blame Jews on similar grounds.

Secondly, where Protestants are a minority in America and where Catholics exercise powers commensurate with their numbers, Catholic doctrine—especially as it relates to traditional concepts of American freedom—arouses some misgivings among Protestants. The Roman Catholic doctrine of the Church, for example, raises questions central not only to the faith of Protestants in regard to the issues of truth and human destiny but also about the nature of group freedoms in a pluralistic culture.

Where the issues of conflict involve the rights and freedoms of all groups, this study raises the possibility that one religion may

9. The Protestant profiles for religious groups vary according to the group. Consult graphs for the Analytical Cats. in Figs. 5–20, Appendix VIII.

oppose another, not because it is prejudiced but precisely because it is not. A religious communicator may be compelled to oppose any threat to the freedoms—as he sees them—by opposing the activities and beliefs of some groups that threaten them. Realism demands the recognition that other groups as well as our own are capable of despotic action. Yet whether such a concept of another group is justifiable is always a question to be decided on the basis of evidence.

Interestingly, no religious group other than Roman Catholicism is opposed by Protestants on grounds that may be interpreted as anti-ethnocentric convictions. Jews in some cases may be portrayed as not proclaiming the true faith, but nothing in Judaism or Jewish life is ever presented as a threat to the freedom of other groups. The conservatives, on the other hand, have at times painted some of the Protestant groups and sects as embodying such a threat, especially in employing pressure upon government to legislate their distinctively sectarian morals into law.

There are real conflicts over values in our society, and they are found at different levels. The world-views of any religion may have implications for action that others decry. It is inadequate, therefore, even to speak of interreligious relations as a single phenomenon. One must specify the group and the kinds of relations. It is hardly sufficient, for example, to say that some Protestant groups consider Jews, Catholics, and non-Christians different or similar. The question must be, What kind of differences and similarities? This differentiation must take account of both the Protestant communicator and the group that he names. The liberal assessment of Roman Catholics is not the fundamentalist view, nor are their respective images of Catholicism applicable to Judaism.

(4) But it is important to note that some Protestant groups, despite their controversy with Roman Catholicism, Judaism, and other religions, manage nevertheless to be positive in their general images of these groups. It is obvious that the liberals and the neo-orthodox deal with this area of value conflict in a different manner from that of the negative scorers. The liberals partly achieve this by ignoring most conflicts betwen Catholicism and Protestantism— passing over the differences between them and taking an irenic view

of the tensions as a whole. The neo-orthodox, however, explicitly meet these conflicts head-on.

The issues posed by the existence and claims of the Roman Catholic Church, Judaism, and other religions may be raised in many ways, e.g. in the narrow context of Jew versus Christian, or Catholic versus Protestant. But such a context makes self-defensiveness and polemic against others inevitable. It encourages writers to attack groups instead of issues. The self-critical stance of the neo-Reformed curriculum is made possible partly because it analyzes intergroup conflict in the broad and more inclusive context of "Christ versus culture." The main questions are put as Christ in opposition to the churches, Christ in opposition to man, government, and society. The conflict is defined in a broad theistic fashion, rather than in terms of one group versus another.

This is a very important point, and it may prove to be the most fruitful for intergroup writing. While all Protestant communicators are actually struggling with the larger problem of a minority witnessing in and against a culture in which they participate, very few writers raise the issues in this way. The neo-orthodox group does so, as do other conservative groups not included in this report. The centers of conflict are found respectively in "Christ" and "culture," rather than in "our group" versus "their group." The Christian writer and reader, then, come to understand themselves as standing (with the Roman Catholic, the Jew, or whoever) in both camps, and not exclusively in one camp with outside groups clustered in the opposing camps. By visualizing value conflicts as essentially one between God and human institutions and groupings, the issues are elevated above ethnocentric partisanship. Thus the neo-orthodox are enabled to universalize the issues. Catholics, Jews, or non-Christians are never looked at monolithically, because they are seen as participating in the divine-human dialogue—at times by our side, at times against us.[10]

## Solving the Problem of Conflict

The differences between the positions of the four communicators in this study and between them and outside groups may never be

10. For different ways in which Christians view the conflict of Christ and culture see H. Richard Niebuhr, *Christ and Culture* (New York, Harper, 1951).

fully overcome. As long as a pluralistic society and religious freedom are accepted, conflict is inevitable. There are a variety of
Protestant answers to life's ultimate and immediate questions, and
their proponents take them seriously. The question, however, which
each of these Protestant groups must face in their own way is how
to raise the conflict from the level of mere ingroup partisanship
to genuine dialogue.

Each group in this study tends to see itself in one fashion or
another as a minority against culture, as contending for the faith in
the midst of conflicting forces. The chasm that separates one group
from the others bothers some more than it does the rest. But all
Protestants in their own ways are seeking an ultimate human unity,
though none can quite envision the nature of that unity. For liberals
it is an emergent; for the more biblical communicators it is God
who will bring unity, and He will do it in a way that man cannot
foresee.

The real differences between religious groups come at this high
level of faith, whatever else they have in common as human beings,
as groups, and as sharers in the rights and privileges of society. This
type of tension—rooted in deep personal commitment—cannot be
solved by appealing to whatever else is held in common. To attempt
to solve this problem on the ultimate level of faith is to make real
community impossible, because it cannot be achieved without converting everybody to a single point of view. Stated in secular terms,
the problem of a pluralistic society is to achieve sufficient unity
within our diversities to prevent the disintegration of the social
order, and to maintain such diversities within our unities as will
restrain tyranny and correct our excesses. The stress on human
rights made by the denominations, the recognition of what different groups have in common as human aggregates, are important.
But the vital value differences between the faiths point to the need
for a genuine conversation between them where differences are
anticipated, frankly looked at, accepted, and even valued. Out of
this dialogue a better understanding of each of the communities
emerges. The hope of achieving justice for some groups, and for a
fairer and more objective presentation of others in Protestant lessons, depends to some degree upon the extent to which editors,
writers, ministers, and laymen are willing to engage in the dialectic
of coming to understand the outsiders. All of this must, of course,

be subordinate yet integral to the larger aims of declaring the faith and strengthening the believer in it.

In this dialogue, our differences may become more clear; at least, we will come to know what our genuine differences are. Real divisions, when discerned and honestly discussed, can lead to better understanding. Bogus issues cannot be discussed dispassionately and create unjustified fear and misunderstanding. Lesson writers—often reproducing an uncritical tradition of Protestant teachings about Jews, Catholics, and other Protestant groups—may fix before the eyes of the student spurious issues that becloud the real ones. False images of the Jews, for example, tend to obscure rather than facilitate the communication of the biblical message.[11] Each faith has its own problems in this respect; each must work them out from within its own declared faith.

Since there are ambiguities in each denomination in regard to the way it portrays its own groups and others, one must question whether it is possible altogether to shun a certain partisanship and particularism in setting forth one's faith. Judgments of other groups will inevitably be colored by it. By far the greatest danger is that Protestants will relax their vigilance in their fight against their own prejudice in the delusion that they are free from it. But while there are real issues between groups in American society, a realistic handling of these issues need not, and ought not, to eventuate in images of outside groups that are wholly negative and rejective.

A promising omen is the fact that the Protestants involved in this study have been open to receiving these findings without defensiveness and with an eagerness to make needed changes in their curricula. In this lies a great hope for the future of freedom in America, where faiths may be stated without prejudice against others, yet where each group is genuinely free to be itself and to declare its faith with candor and zeal.

11. An understanding of the development of anti-Semitism in the Church and its pre-Christian sources sheds much light on the manner in which the biblical message is fractured and even annulled in stereotypes of the Jew once common in Christian teaching. See Isaac, pp. 14–16.

# APPENDIXES

# Appendix I. Some Basic Concepts

This section seeks to answer several technical questions raised by Protestant editors who attended the Yale Conference on Intergroup Writing in Curriculum Materials, Jan. 2–4, 1958.

The basic concepts of ethnocentrism and anti-ethnocentrism, the general criteria for determining each, the descriptive nature of the statistical analysis, and the necessity for negative distributions have been described briefly in Chap. 1. Since the inevitability of negative distributions is acknowledged in this study as not being in itself invidious, however, a fuller explanation and illustration of the important concept of imbalance seems required in view of the questions raised at the conference.

In addition to the significance of imbalances, another issue of importance was raised. We were asked how, in view of the fact that scores are not weighted, the intensity of intergroup statements is handled here. In a descriptive study such as this, weighting is impossible; the graphs and tables simply give information as to the number of lessons in which statements occurred of a given kind, their direction, and the preponderance, if any, of plus over minus occurrences.

## The Concept of "Imbalance" as a Directional Indicator

If the scores in the Analytical Categories are descriptive only, how do they get translated into normative scores, i.e. into over-all indices of "direction" upon which judgments of various kinds can be made? The reply, on the statistical side, is "in the scores of imbalance."

The meaning of "imbalance" for this study is best seen in relation to the distribution scores, or in the negative and positive spreads in each Analytical Category above or below the zero line. The distributions tell us what percentage of all lessons with content in a certain (e.g. Catholic) intergroup area fall within a given Analytical Category. This information has two parts—(1) a figure representing the proportion of the total units conforming to positive indicators (and therefore graphed on the upper side of the zero line, and (2) the proportion conforming to negative indicators (and therefore graphed on the under side of the zero line).

One of three possibilities now occur:

1.  The plus distribution may be greater than the minus distribution.  This signifies a positive imbalance.

2.  The plus and minus distributions may be equal, canceling each other out.  This indicates ambivalence, neutrality, or an ability to offset necessary negative scores by positive scores in the same category.  This is called a zero imbalance.

3.  The minus distribution may exceed the plus, yielding a negative imbalance.

Upon examination, materials with positive imbalances have a greater tendency than materials with negative imbalances to omit all but relevant negative statements about other groups, to offset negative references with positive ones, to have less distortions and more correctives, and to make observations conforming to indicators in a variety of descriptive categories.  Materials with negative imbalances make other than relevant negative statements; the mention of one negative instance occasions other negatives.  There is a tendency to greater distortion, a lesser capacity to offset negative with positive content, and a temptation to proliferate the negative all along the analytical profile.

The imbalance scores, then, are descriptive, but also indicators of the total impact of a curriculum.  Seen in conjunction with each other, they are signs of the direction of the references as a whole, as to whether they conform more in some or several respects to the negative than to the positive indicators or vice versa.  These scores are significant, because they may easily be compared with the imbalances obtained by other communicators as to both direction (plus, zero, minus) and intensity of direction (as represented by the sizes of the percentages).

In brief, the imbalance scores have the power to reveal intergroup orientation.  Since these scores are available for each segment of the profile as well as for the total picture, it is possible to evaluate the communicators' materials in respect to the findings in each Analytical Category by applying the E-A criteria and other relevant sources for judging the significance of the findings.

For example, it is important to evaluate any imbalance score by the nature of its content.  If a communicator makes a very

high plus imbalance score by simply ignoring the whole question of social conflict, historically and in contemporary society,
this is itself a fact of tremendous importance.

### The Problem of Intensity—The Multiple Relevance of Intergroup Statements to the Analytical Profile

Since the imbalance scores .serve as indices of intergroup
orientation and therefore have a qualitative import, a further
question arises as to the adequacy of the imbalance scores to
represent the intensity of intergroup content.

The question is a difficult one, for this study eschews the
task of weighting scores in order to indicate intensity. By intensity is meant the degree of seriousness of an intergroup
statement, determined mostly by its potential effect on the audience, or by the degree of its potential recoil on the victim.
An example of the latter type of scale is found in Allport, who
suggests three levels of intensity of ethnocentric attitudes:

1.  Antilocution (verbal rejection)
2.  Discrimination (including segregation)
3.  Physical attack (of all degrees, including extermina-
    tion)[1]

The first degree of intensity (antilocution) is limited to verbal
portraiture, such as is measured in Analytical Categories 6 to
9 inclusive in this study. Within this lowest level, however,
Allport finds it necessary to rescale antilocution from "mild
animosity" (e.g. relating ethnic jokes) to "intense hostility"
(epithets, like "nigger"). These factors are further complicated
by such considerations as the "spontaneity" and "irrelevance"
(i.e. irrationality) of the utterance. For the purposes of our
study, the remaining two degrees of intensity, which refer to
action, would have to be translated into verbal statements about
action. To denounce, advocate, or defend discrimination would
be an example of references on the intensity level of two.

However, since our categories and scoring procedures are
purely descriptive, to attempt to introduce a weighting factor
would render every percentage figure meaningless. The numerical scores are not value scores.[2] Does this study, then,

---

1.  Allport, The Nature of Prejudice, p. 45.

2.  Even though a statement may appear two, three, or four
times in a lesson, or be thought "mild" or "potent," it is scored

in its statistical design, bypass or ignore these crucial differences between the seriousness of one kind of statement and another?

In one sense, the measurement of intensity is ignored yet, paradoxically, is provided for in an almost automatic way. The degrees of both ethnocentric and anti-ethnocentric concern manifest themselves in the materials in at least three ways:

1. A very anti-ethnocentric or ethnocentric writer will disclose the intensity of his orientation by the multiple relevance of his remarks to the analytical categories. (In other words, a prejudiced writer will say more negative things about an outgroup which can be scored in many, rather than in one, analytical category; an unprejudiced writer likewise, will touch several indicators in a number of Analytical Categories.)

2. Since outgroup acceptance and rejection tends to be generalized, the prejudiced writer will mention more than one outgroup when making negative statements, thus scoring in more than one intergroup category. (If he makes an intensely derogatory statement [with relevance to four analytical categories] about Jews, Catholics, and Negroes, the statement scores twelve times, four in each intergroup area.)

3. Since ingroup appeals to codes as well as tendencies to distortion are characteristic of ethnocentrics, intensity of intergroup statements are likely to be marked by relevance to these additional categories. The opposite is, of course, true of anti-ethnocentrics. (Thus, to a condemnation of anti-Semitism will be added the weight of the church's teachings, making for two positive scores. Or to a negative moral portrait of Jews may be added an additional score for a factual distortion, making for two negative scores.)

That the descriptive approach is itself an index of intensity the available data amply proves. These confirm the hypothesis, for example, that "potent" statements have verbal accompaniments which fall into a multiplicity of categories. Intensely negative remarks occur in lessons with as many as 7 to 8 more minus than plus scores, while potent positive statements are associated with an 8 to 9 preponderance of plus over minus

---

only once. There is no attempt to indicate the number of times such a statement appears in each lesson, but only the number of lessons in which such statements appear.

scores. [3] Similarly, the analytical profiles show that the making of negative statements in one category is accompanied by negative statements in other categories, and vice versa. The inclination also to make references to more than one group in the same lesson is evidenced by all scorers, as shown in Table 15. [4]

The degrees of <u>intensity</u> of intergroup statements are therefore manifested in the aggregate imbalance for a given intergroup area. Let us take the following hypothetical statements as an example:

  1. "Peruvian Catholics . . . mobbed a Protestant church at . . ."
  2. "Roman Catholic official policy operates with impunity in South America. It issues, for example, into riots against Protestant churches and the persecution of missionaries."
  3. "The sinister designs of the Roman Catholic hierarchy are only temporarily frustrated in the United States by a militant Protestantism. Not only does this false Church infect the South American people with its diabolical dogmas, but it keeps its victims economically impoverished, ignorant, and slavishly submissive to its dictates. When the Church wishes to destroy the teachers of the true gospel, the Catholic mobs burn and wreck churches and boycott the business places of converts to the faith."

These three hypothetical statements are all relevant to the Catholic intergroup area, Data-Gathering Category 12 (Hostility-Friendliness). The statements are all negative.

Example 1 is a simple statement that Peruvian Catholics mobbed a Protestant church at such a place and time. Let us assume for the moment that this statement is verifiable as factually correct. There would be only one score (negative for Category 12) for this sentence as it stands.

Example 2, however, is more complex and intense. It describes Catholics as hostile to Protestants ("riots against" and "persecution of"), but attributes this to "Roman Catholic official policy." Here a factual distortion is introduced into the

---

3. Cf. Fig. 21, Appendix VIII.

4. Below, Appendix VII.

picture, and a minus score is given to it in the factual Distor-tion-Correction Data-Gathering Category (No. 5 as well as No. 12).

Example 3 repeats the two negative scores of the previous reference. The "designs" of the Roman Catholic "hierarchy" are called "sinister," it "infects" the South American people, its dogmas are "diabolical," and it keeps its people in various forms of submission. These statements call for a minus score in the Moral-Godly Category 6. The church is called a "false church" which seeks "to destroy the teachers of the true gospel." This is scored negatively in the False-True Category 7. Cer-tain "other characteristics" are also mentioned: the South American people (Catholics, largely) are "economically im-poverished," "ignorant," and "slavishly submissive" to the "dic-tates" of the Church. Another minus is consequently checked in Category 9. Finally, since the Christian faith is set opposite the faith of Roman Catholicism, a negative is also given in the Kinship Category 10. This paragraph, in short, rates seven negative scores in all.

The above illustrates how the intensity of statements show up in the scores simply by becoming increasingly relevant to more categories on their negative side. At the same time, these percentages do not themselves become meaningless. They always represent something specific. This would not have been the case had a different, and normative, scheme for scoring been adopted.

# Appendix II. Synopsis of Analytical Categories

## Outgroup Plight and Intergroup Tension

The following four categories are concerned almost exclusively with the outgroup plight and the response of the ingroup toward it. The "plight" is the actual or presumed deprivation of rights, and the discrimination, segregation, and persecution of those who have minority status in our country. "Intergroup tension" means the conflict between outgroups and ingroups which is a component of the plight.

|                    Negative                    |                    Positive                    |

1. Rights–Status. Assertions concerning the status of other groups; their inherent rights; their deprivation of rights; their experience of hatred, discrimination, segregation, persecution; and programs and solutions in the area of intergroup tension.

| Negative | Positive |
|---|---|
| Supports discriminatory and segregative practices; defends denial of basic rights. Denies existence of plight; or admits it, but justifies its being. Warrants ignoring plight. Opposed to organized efforts to alleviate plight through agencies, legislation, social reform, good will efforts. Solutions to tensions unacceptable except on hierarchical, dominant-submissive terms; denies possibility or desirability of solutions. Gives directives to social action designed to maintain present status of outgroups or to | Aware of and concerned with plight and tensions, and joins variously in attempts to gain rights and status for others. Asserts rights for other groups; rejects discriminatory and segregative practices against others, and deplores prejudice. Instances of plight given; plight described; suggests activities that call attention to plight. States aims that include bettering relations, and supports programs and organized efforts to this end. Delineates friction areas and describes their history. Seeks solutions to plight and |

prevent sharing of ingroup rights and privileges. Rejects content of books, etc. concerned with bettering intergroup relations. Opposes special observances dedicated to improvement of intergroup relations. Key: Counter-identifies with out-group plight.

destructive tension free from hierarchical, dominant-submissive patterns. Gives directives to social action, recommends resources (books, persons, agencies, audio-visual aids, etc.), approves special observances, institutions, and efforts directed toward alleviation of tension and achievement of rights and status for "theygroups." Key: identifies with theygroup attempts to achieve rights, status.

2. Prejudice. This category is distinguished from the first by the fact that the subject matter is here the prejudiced person. The focus is upon prejudice itself, upon understanding it, and analyzing its mechanisms, functions, and etiology. Statements scored here constitute an indirect form of self-criticism in the intergroup area.

The characteristic response is silence, i.e. disregard of this area, not measured except by lack of scores on the positive side; the significance of absence of scores to be determined by presence or absence of other kinds of content.

Defines prejudice; analyzes prejudicial attitudes and behavior; describes the psychological and/or sociological origins, functions, mechanisms of prejudice in individuals or groups, e.g. answers such questions as: How do we know we are prejudiced? How does prejudice express itself? What function does this have in our lives? etc. Key: attempts to understand prejudice in fundamental manifestations.

3. Self-criticism (responsibility). This category measures the degree to which the communicator is disposed to involve or separate his own group from responsibility for the plight of

outgroups or for existing tensions.   This is measured by the presence or absence of self-criticism in the intergroup area as well as by direct statements of responsibility.   Self-criticism not relevant to intergroup relations is not scored.

Holds outgroups responsible for their own plight or for existence of problems, e. g. they brought it upon themselves, deserved it, due to their acts or inherent nature, etc.  Pictures own groups as free from guilt; its involvement in prejudice denied, defended, idealized, or explained away.  Asserts ingroup too tolerant of and complacent toward threats of outgroup.  Categorically rejects criticism of ingroups by outgroups in intergroup area.  Belittles warnings against possibility of ingroup intolerance.

Holds own groups responsible for "theygroup" plight and accompanying tension.  Denies primary responsibility of outgroups. Engages in self-criticism in intergroup area; existence of ingroup prejudice, persecution of or hatred toward other groups in past or present admitted or described ("wegroup" involvement); provides self-critical class activities; accepts, weighs criticism by nongroup members; warns against possible ingroup intolerance, etc.

4.   Codes—prestige—precedent.  This concerns the fashion in which the codes, creed, ingroup authorities, and precedents are brought to bear on the problem of intergroup relations, including, in this case, interaction (cf. Category 13), although the fundamental focus is on the outgroup plight.  The bearing of the Christian and American creeds, as reflected in the faith of the communicator, in the prestige persons and official statements appealed to, etc., are in view here.

The creeds and authorities appealed to in the intergroup area are ingrouped, i. e. against concern for the problems of tension and outgroup plight, against the sharing of rights and status.

The creeds and authorities appealed to are theygrouped, i. e. oriented to the breaking down of barriers, toward interaction, toward alleviation of theygroup predicaments, toward sharing of rights and status.

## Outgroup Portrait

The next five categories are designed to gather information
on how the communicator views other groups as such, quite
apart from the question of intergroup relations.  Taken together
they constitute a portrait of a given group, but not a complete
one (cf. also next section).

Negative                                Positive

5.  <u>Factual:  Distortion—correction</u>.  This is a device and not a
    content category.  It is the only device category of the
    fourteen.  It seeks to measure the amount of distortion or
    correction of the outgroup portrait, in factual material.  It
    ignores wholly evaluative and conjectural material.  Any
    statement or description which pictures outgroup beliefs,
    practices, customs, and history, and which is also subject
    to factual check, is scored here, regardless of its rele-
    vance to other categories.

|  |  |
|---|---|
| Factually distorted ma-terial that is unfavorable (i.e. which conforms to the negative indicators in cate-gories 7 through 14 and/or contributes to a negative por-trait of an outgroup) is clas-sified according to a number of devices, among them: Significant omission of facts which would alter the direc-tion of the statement; his-torical inaccuracy; mis-statement of belief and practice; invidious and mis-leading comparisons; un-warranted conjecture; un-warranted generalizations. The content of these devices is scored in the relevant portrait categories. | Corrects factual distor-tions of outgroup life, be-lief, or practices.  Pre-sents informational ma-terial for its own sake—describes theygroup festi-vals, holy days, observ-ances, practices, organiza-tions, etc.  Cites factual achievements of theygroups and theygroup members. Gives background informa-tion on events and beliefs which, if omitted, would alter the direction of the content negatively.  Ex-plains theygroup disvalued beliefs in context.  Gives bibliographical material of theygroup leaders and pres-tige persons.  Fairly states theygroups' views.  Directs teacher or pupil to sources of dependable factual infor-mation (resource persons, |

books, organizations). Employs such devices in citing factually unfavorable beliefs and practices of theygroups as, e.g., objective-explanatory: It was the Pharisees' view that. . . because they believed that. . . or were concerned that. . .

6. Moral: Good—evil, Godly—ungodly. Assertions imputing goodness or evil to another group or members of that group in any form or degree are scored in this category. Also, denials and qualifications of such assertions or descriptions. For the purposes of this category, godly or ungodly qualities are considered as good or evil.

Outgroup person or persons are portrayed in immoral roles, assigned negative moral qualities. Outgroups and outgroup action are evaluated or designated as evil. The acts, intentions, motives of the outgroup member or members are corrupt, ungodly, exploitive, hateful, obnoxious, deceptive, selfish, materialistic, etc. (They hate goodness, are covetous, cheat, blaspheme, disobey God, abuse divine things, exploit others, rob widows, etc.) The groups themselves are said to be immoral, lax, killers, idolators, children of the devil, tools of Satan, and other generalizations tacked to the outgroup name. (If an outgroup is said to hate, persecute, etc. another outgroup, the

"Othergroup" person or persons are pictured in positive moral roles or assigned positive qualities. Evaluates and designates theygroup and theygroup action, intentions, customs, etc., as good: they are honest, godly, kindly, considerate, helpful, morally attractive, etc. (e.g. they are noble in deeds, use fair methods, are faithful to God, appreciative of His blessings, value human life, respect people, their motives are good, they are children of light, enemies of evil, devout, etc.). Refutes stereotype of evil in theygroups; universalizes disvalued acts as common to all mankind. Self-criticism is present, i.e. balancing assertion that wegroup performs same disvalued moral acts as theygroup. (If theygroup is said statement is scored here; but if the ingroup is the victim, it is scored in categories 11 or 12)

(to love wegroup, the statement is scored in categories 11 or 12.)

7. <u>True-false characteristics</u>. This evaluative category embraces any characterization or assertion that other groups or their representatives are teaching, believing in, possessing, or practicing (1) that which is not in accord with reality, i.e. anything erroneous, distorted, false, rejected by God, or (2) that which is actual, conformable to fact, correct, the true teaching, the "pure doctrine," or approved of God. Further, included are any assertions representing other groups as deceivers or false teachers or conveyors of falsehood, or their representatives as distorting, twisting, or destroying the truth, or, conversely, defending, purifying, and perpetuating the truth.

Rejects particular teachings and practices as false, untrue. Makes unconditional claims to truth, excluding others from its possession. Rejects teachings, beliefs, practices of others as invalid, unscriptural, worthless, and unauthorized. The outgroup and its members are ignorant of real truth; are apostates, unbelievers; caricature the truth, falsify, are mistaken, credulous, prejudiced against the truth, proceed on erroneous assumptions, censor the Bible, pervert the Gospel, etc.

Accepts particular teachings and practices as true and valid. Pictures others as having claims to truth, and own group as also possessing error. Others are said to seek, value, and defend truth, to give their lives for it. They are pictured as sincere in their search for truth, or open-minded in seeking it and as having given truths to the world.

8. <u>Superior-inferior characteristics</u>. This category is primarily racial in emphasis, i.e. refers to inherent traits. Religious superiority is usually put in terms of moral or truth characteristics, and is scored above.

Assigns trait of inherent inferiority to outgroup or

Affirms equality of endowment. Denies that

outgroup members, or implies this by statements containing racist presuppositions, e. g. "The Negro is descended from Ham," "the Jews are a mongrel race." Affirms or assigns innate traits, e. g. "Jews are by nature endowed with acquisitiveness." Denies equality of endowment. Affirms inherent endowment or superiority for ingroup.

nate traits characterize theygroups. Contradicts racist claims and stereotypes; affirms that there is no superior or inferior race.

9. <u>Other characteristics</u>. A general category embracing all content in the basic outgroup portrait not scored in the moral, false—true, or superior—inferior categories. Also excludes elements of portrait found in the relational categories to follow.

Attributes specific characteristics to outgroup person or persons, or to group as a whole, or assigns roles to them, all of which may be classified under the headings: manner, appearance, disposition, intellectual qualities, education, attitude, quality of responses, personal adjustment, and others (e. g. "their religion is gloomy," they are discourteous, fierce, they "chatter," are cowardly, etc.).

Assigns positive roles or traits to individuals or group, under the same headings as in negative column. Examples: they are polite, pleasing, clean, humorous, joyful, valiant, learned, etc.

<u>Outgroup Portrait: Relationship of Outgroup to Ingroup</u>

The following three categories continue the outgroup portrait but in a different context: Every communicator sees an outside group as related to his own in some way, as responding to ingroup action or as taking attitudes or initiating actions toward the communicator's own groups. While other categories have focused upon the way in which the communicator regards the plight of other groups, or regards the groups themselves in their essential aspects, these categories concern themselves with the way these groups are seen as impinging upon the life of the ingroup.

|            Negative            |            Positive            |
| ------------------------------ | ------------------------------ |

10. <u>Kinship: Differences–Similarities</u>. This category seeks to determine whether the communicator views other groups as related or similar to his own, or as unrelated and different. While it is closely associated with the true-false category, it is milder on the negative side and more factual on the positive. For example, whether a religion is false or true is a matter of faith and evaluation; but whether a religion is related to one's own may be a matter of historical and observable fact.

Asserts differences between outgroups and ingroups in belief and practice; denies common elements. Disavows contributions of outgroups, dependency upon, or indebtedness to them. Denies historical roots in other groups. Rejects leadership of outgroup members. Asserts need for, or gives examples of, conversion of outgroups to ingroup faith. Deplores differences, and stresses need for believing or practicing the same thing.

Asserts that theygroups have elements in community with wegroups: common origin or heritage, shared elements of faith, practice, and value. Recognizes likenesses and similarities, and includes them in a common fellowship. Avows contributions of other groups to one's own. Acknowledges and may follow outgroup leadership (e. g. accepts teachings of Maimonides on charity, uses outgroup resources in worship). Deplores or rejects attempts to convert other groups. Includes deviating groups with one's own, e. g. calls Catholics "Christian." Stresses unity, interdependence, and indebtedness. But values, or is permissive of, differences.

11. **Hostility—Friendliness (past)**. What sort of attitude and action have outside groups taken toward the communicator's own groups? This category seeks to answer this question—as far as the past is concerned; e.g. this category gathers data on the mutual persecution of Catholics and Protestants during the Reformation, but not for the contemporary scene.

Claims outgroup is ingroup enemy; denies outgroup has friendly intention. Asserts outgroup is hostile to ingroup, that it rejects and opposes it; criticizes, slanders, assaults, has contempt for, despises, hates, fears, plots against, persecutes, kills, destroys, punishes, harms, wars against, is prejudiced against ingroup, deprives it of rights, withdraws from fellowship; or threatens ingroup freedoms. Gives instances of above. (Includes statements using past tense.)

Asserts theygroup is wegroup friend, denies unfriendly intention. Asserts that theygroup supports, helps, encourages, likes, cooperates with, befriends, has fellowship with, defends rights of wegroup. Explains or defends theygroup criticism or opposition. Makes mitigating observations ("This was an intolerant age, and we must not hold this against the . . .") or balancing wegroup criticisms ("Christians were also opposed to Jews").

12. **Hostility—Friendliness (present)**. This category is the same as the previous one, except that it is limited to the twentieth century, or such context as indicates that the positive or negative attitudes are still existing ones.

## Relationship of Ingroup to Outgroup (Other than Outgroup Plight)

There are two categories in this division. They seek to measure (1) the extent to which barriers against interaction are erected or broken down by the communicator, and (2) the basic attitude of the communicator toward other groups as indicated by punitive and sympathetic statements.

Negative                    Positive

13. **Interaction**. The kind of interaction here visualized does not involve segregation-desegregation, etc., but is limited to intergroup contacts. The areas of interaction between

groups which are praised and recommended or feared and opposed are taken into account.

Opposes intergroup contacts and joining organizations not under strict control of ingroup. Opposes associating with outgroup members in various contacts. Opposes outgroup dating and intermarriage. Not willing to cooperate with other groups or to engage in fellowship across racial, doctrinal, national, or church lines.

Approves or recommends intergroup contacts, cites instances, describes how to arrange for interaction. Willing to engage in fellowship across group lines, to cooperate with other groups for common ends, to join "mixed" groups. Is permissive of intermarriage, may advocate it. Depicts possible interrelations.

14. Punitive–Sympathetic. This category compiles various expressions of a punishing or sympathetic nature directed toward another group.

Asserts that the outgroup should be punished, or that succor and blessings should be withheld from them, or that such a punitive state of affairs exists, that God has or is punishing, or that a judgment or impersonal doom has overtaken them (e. g. God withdraws His blessings, doom and punishment will come upon them, they are rejected of God, they condemn themselves out of their own mouths, God "strikes out" at them in fury, their fate is certain, etc.). Similar assertions are made involving ingroup action against outgroup. Opposes aid or help to needy outgroups, or organizations that give succor.

Asserts that theygroups should be blessed or prayed for, or that they have been blessed and rewarded, that God loves them and provides for them His mercies, and protects them and pours out His grace upon them. Urges service projects, programs of giving, sharing with other groups. Supports or commends the work of service (aid) agencies, such as UN relief agencies. Asserts that wegroup members should love, serve, etc. theygroup members, and extend the hand of friendliness.

# Appendix III. Statistical Design and Procedure

The key to the statistical design is the set of Analytical Categories. The verbal and pictorial content of a given unit is scored in these categories, which provide the raw data upon which generalizations about content are made.

The basic unit for counting is the complete "unit," or item, rather than the reference. An item is a complete segment of material unified by theme, authorship, or function, such as (1) an entire article, (2) a complete lesson, or (3) any other material which shows continuity (an editorial, a page of poems, a devotional plan for a single day).

A unit of material is analyzed for its intergroup content, using the indicators of the Analytical Categories as a guide. If an assertion conforms to any indicator, it is scored in that category, plus or minus as the case may require. If it conforms to both the positive and negative indicators in the same category, it is scored in the "both" column.

A unit containing intergroup content may be relevant to more than one of the Variable Categories, of which there are seven.[1]

The most likely multiple relevance to the Variable Categories will occur in the intergroup areas (Group Category), e. g. Catholics, Jews, and Negroes may be mentioned.

## Scheme for Scoring

A data-gathering instrument is used to record data and to facilitate their transcription to IBM cards.[2]

The name of the publication; its date of publication (if elective) or date of intended use; the author, if any; and the title of the unit (article, lesson, etc.) are recorded on the top two lines. On the top of the right margin are five spaces in which to record the serial number of the unit. This serial number remains

---

1. Publisher, Age Group, Series, Group, Period, Form, and Content Categories.

2. See p. 318. This explanation of procedure refers to the form and cannot be understood without studying it.

Publication_____ Date_____

Author_____ Title_____   / / / / /

| PUBLISHER | | AGE GR. | MANUAL | SERIES |
|---|---|---|---|---|
| _01 Am Bapt | _11 Nazarene | _1 All | _1 T | _1 Vac |
| _02 Nat Bapt A | _12 Presby | _2 Int | _2 P | _2 WkD |
| _03 Nat Bapt US | _13 Prot Epis | _3 Sen | _3 TP | _3 Uni |
| _04 South Bapt | _14 Unitarian | _4 I-S | _4 Of | _4 GG |
| _05 Cong-Chris | _15 Quaker | _5 YP | _5 OT | _5 CG |
| _06 Disc of Chr | _16 Dav C Cook | _6 Ad | _6 Fam | _6 Elec |
| _07 Luth (M Sy) | _17 Scrip Pr | _7 YP-A | | _7 Oth |
| _08 United Luth | | _8 Jr-I | | _8 4, 5 |
| _09 Meth | | | | _9 3, 4   / / / / / |

| GROUP CATEGORY | PERIOD CATEGORY | FORM (Unit) | CONTENT CATEGORY |
|---|---|---|---|
| _1 Jewish | _1 Bibl-OT | _1 Article | _1 Mission |
| _2 Negro | _2 Bibl-NT | _2 Lesson | _2 Inter-Gr |
| _3 Catholic | _3 Bibl-Both | _3 Story | _3 Other |
| _4 Other Chr | _4 Early Church | _4 Poetry | |
| _5 Non-Chr | _5 Middle Ages | _5 Devot'l | |
| _6 Other Eth | _6 Reformation | _6 Feature | |
| _7 Internat'l | _7 Pre-20th C | _7 Picture | |
| _8 Gen-Racial | _8 Contemporary | _8 Editor'l | |
| | | _9 Other | / / / / / |

INFORMATION-GATHERING CATEGORIES

|   | 1 | 2 | 3 |
|---|---|---|---|
|   | + | − | + |
|   |   |   | − |

Outgroup Plight-Human Rights
1.  Rights-Status. . . . . . . . . . . .
2.  Prejudice (Examination of). . . . . . . .
3.  Self-criticism (Responsibility) . . . . . .
4.  Codes-Prestige-Precedent . . . . . .

/ / / / /
1 2 3 4

Outgroup Portrayal
5.  Factual: Distortion-Correction . . . . .
6.  Characteristics: Moral (Evil-Good) . . .
7.  Characteristics: False-True . . . . . .
8.  Characteristics: Superior-Inferior. . . .
9.  Characteristics: Other . . . . . . . . .

/ / / / /
5 6 7 8 9

Outgroup Portrayal: Relationship to Ingroup
10.  Kinship (Differences-Similarities) . . . .
11.  Hostility-Friendliness (to Ingroup) Past. .
12.  Hostility, etc. Present-Future. . . . . .

/ / / /
10 11 12

Ingroup Relationship to Outgroup
13.  Interaction . . . . . . . . . . . . . .
14.  Punitive-Sympathetic . . . . . . . . . .

/ / /
13 14

the same for the one unit, regardless of how many instruments it is necessary to fill out for that unit in order to record certain variables.

The most simple example of scoring occurs where all factors are constant except for the relevance of the Analytical Categories. Assume that a David C. Cook publication for senior pupils in the Uniform Series is being examined. This information is recorded in the "Publisher," "Age Group," "Manual," and "Series" columns, and the number 16323 transposed to the appropriate spaces in the right-hand column. The unit being analyzed is a New Testament Bible lesson mentioning Negroes only. These data are recorded in the "Group," "Period," "Form," and "Content" columns, the numbers 2223 being transposed to the margin.

The lesson is then carefully read, and all assertions about Negroes or Negro-White relations are classified in the Analytical Categories according to direction and kind of statement made. Let us assume that the author (1) deplores segregation, (2) says that discrimination against Negroes is a denial of essential Christian principles, and (3) accuses the church itself of practicing segregation. These conform to the indicators on the plus side, and relate respectively to the subject matters in categories 1 (Rights–Status), 4 (Codes–Prestige), and 3 (Self-criticism). These categories are then checked in col. 2, and the figures again transposed to the corresponding blanks in the margin.

These references are clipped, or copied, in context, and fastened to separate yellow sheets. Certain information is then added: page of reference, identification numbers, and the theme and occasion for the reference. Three sheets, each with a separate reference, would be required in the above example.

The analyst is now ready to proceed with the next unit. The serial number is moved ahead by one numeral. Let us suppose that this unit has no intergroup content. The instrument is filled out as before, with the exception that there is no check in the "Group Category" (with a corresponding zero placed in the first blank in the margin), and consequently no checks in the analytical categories.

Another possibility is that reference to some group may be found in the unit, but no relevance to the analytical categories is discernible. Suppose, for example, in a lesson on the Old Testament, that the only reference to Jews is one which says, "The ancient Jews had to dig wells in order to get water, because running streams were very scarce." This would be a statement about physiography without direction and without relevance to any of the indicators. In this event, the "Group Category" would be scored "Jewish" and the number 1 transposed to the margin, but with the analytical categories left blank.

When one or more of the nonanalytical variables occur in the same unit a more elaborate procedure is dictated. The rule, in general, is that when more than one nonanalytic variable occurs in the same unit, a corresponding number of instruments bearing the same serial number should be filled out. (In some cases this is not necessary—as, for example, when the content is the same for certain variables and applicable combinations of these variables are provided for in the instrument, i. e. some units are for both teacher and pupil, for teacher and officers, or may be intended for two age-groups. These frequent combinations are anticipated in the "Manual" column, and are checked on one instrument.

## Group Category Variables

When, however, a unit contains content pertaining to several intergroup areas, a separate instrument must be made out for each area. In cases of multiple group references, the relevant analytical categories and direction of content are apt to vary somewhat as the intergroup area varies. A unit on the Reformation says:

It is true that Catholic churchmen and rulers have subjected Protestants to persecution, but persecution was not renounced by the Reformers. Catholics as well as Protestants were put to death in England. Even Protestant heretics like the Anabaptists were hounded by the Reformed rulers; Servetus was burned at the stake by Calvin; and Christians of all persuasions have through many centuries persecuted Jews.

Such a reference is multiple in the "Group Category" as follows requiring three instruments with the same serial number:

No. 1.  Jewish:  Cat. 3, plus.
No. 3.  Catholic:  Cat. 11, plus and minus; Cat. 3, plus.
No. 4.  Other-Christians:  Cat. 3, plus.

The rule is that the serial number identifies the particular unit regardless of the number of variations with it. To complete the

record, the quotation likewise is clipped or copied in quadrupli-
cate, each sheet representing one Analytical Category for each
intergroup area.

## Form (Unit) Category Variables

Pictures, worship services, poems, and prayers are considered separate units when found alone. For example, a full-
page picture of Jesus and the little children of the world may
not illustrate an article, poem, or other feature, so it is considered a unit in itself, and given a separate serial number.

However, often these same types of material appear as
integral parts of lessons or articles. Articles and lessons are
frequently illustrated. Poems, prayers, and worship materials are often included within a lesson. In this event, these
various features would not be considered separate units but
parts of one unit. However, there are several distinctions:

1. If a poem or prayer appears in the body of the article
   or lesson, and is integral to it, no separate instrument
   would be made out.
2. If a worship service is appended to the lesson, as it frequently is, it was considered part of the same unit, but a
   separate instrument was filled out for it:

| Unit No. | Unit Title | Form Category |
|---|---|---|
| 5004 | "Being a Christian at Home" | x 2 Lesson |
| 5004 | "Being a Christian at Home" | x 5 Devotional |

3. If a picture or pictures illustrate the text, they would be
   treated as part of the same unit, and a separate instrument would be filled out for them.

This procedure assures that (a) the same content relating to
many variables would not be counted more than once in the over-
all materials, and (b) no content pertinent to a variable would
be omitted when abstracted from the whole.

## Units Not Scored

Not all the units in a periodical are necessarily scored. For
example, a publication frequently includes a wider age range
than this project embraces. Lessons and features designed for
Primary teachers are, quite often, found in the same periodical issued for older age-groups. These nonrelevant items are
skipped.

Other types of printed material that are not considered ana-lyzable units are advertisements, title pages, tables of contents, indexes, puzzles, cooking recipes, Bible-reading lists with-out comment, charts of forthcoming lessons, abstract filler de-signs, music without words, and other noncontent features.

## Summary

The above-described method of recording information pro-vides data in various combinations; e.g. all IBM cards pertain-ing to variables may be sorted out and statistics for that selec-tion compiled.  Pictures which also occur in the lessons would comprise part of that data, so that where pictorial content over-laps verbal, it will not be counted twice.  But if the data for pic-tures are sorted out of the verbal material, a complete picture of the verbal material is given.  Likewise, if any other variable is sorted out, a complete picture of that variable is available.

It was necessary, consequently, to lay out a step-by-step procedure for sorting the IBM cards and tabulating the data in accordance with the requirements of the design as a whole.

Attention is now turned to the formulas with which to repre-sent some of the more important findings.

## Coefficient of Preoccupation (Predominance Score)

The visibility score shows to what degree a given commu-nicator is preoccupied with a specified group.  It indicates how "visible" othergroups and intergroup relations are in the ma-terials examined.

The extent to which a communicator is aware of and con-cerned with the existence of outside groups may be expressed numerically by figuring the ratio of units containing intergroup content to the total number of units analyzed.  The result is ex-pressed in percentages of lessons in the total curriculum which contain references to the outside groups in question.

The formula:  $\underline{Cpre.} = \dfrac{r}{t}$

Where $\underline{r}$ equals relevant content (1. Total intergroup units)  (2. Total units for a single intergroup area)
Where $\underline{t}$ equals total content (the total of all units in the sample)

Scores of preoccupation are useful, experimentally, in

seeing whether any relation exists between preoccupation and direction, and, also, in evaluating various types of materials. For example, if, in New Testament lessons, Catholics and Catholicism are highly visible, this may indicate overpreoccupation with, or excessive consciousness of, the existence of Catholics, and it is presumed may possibly correlate with negative scores of imbalance.

## Coefficient of Imbalance

The coefficient of imbalance, devised by Janis,[3] expresses numerically a complex relation between the positive, negative, and neutral units in the sample. Neutral units are those with intergroup content conforming to none of the directional indicators in the analytical categories. When the number of units scored positively increases, the positive imbalance increases. When the frequency of units scored negative increases, the negative imbalance increases. The imbalance always decreases in absolute value, i. e. tends toward neutral, when the total of neutral units becomes greater.

The formula is to be applied specifically in this study to the separate analytical categories as indices of direction.

The formula, adapted from Janis, substitutes "positive" for "favorable," and "negative" for "unfavorable."

1. For <u>Positive</u> imbalance, where $p$ is greater than $n$:

$$C_{pi} = \frac{p^2 - pn}{rt}$$

2. For <u>Negative</u> imbalance, where $n$ is greater than $p$:

$$C_{ni} = \frac{n^2 - np}{rt}$$

Where $r$ equals <u>relevant content</u>

Where $t$ equals <u>total content</u>

All the units scored in one Analytical Category regardless of direction is "relevant content." "Total content" always means the total number of units containing references to a given intergroup area.

---

3. Irving L. Janis and Raymond H. Fadner, "The Coefficient of Imbalance," in Lasswell and Leites, eds., <u>Language of Politics</u> (New York, Stewart, 1949), pp. 153–89.

A General Score of Imbalance

General imbalance scores are used in this study to summarize statistical findings for the combined analytical categories.
There are two kinds of general scores.

The first consists of the total analytical plus-minus scores
for all 14 directional categories, providing a convenient indicator of the general orientation of a communicator for a single
intergroup area. A +.25 general score for the Negro Group
Category in curriculum B means that 25 per cent of the analytical scores in units with Negro content are positive, after the
minus are subtracted from the plus scores.

The second and broader general imbalances would apply to
similar scores for combined intergroup areas; e.g. for all religious groups, or for racial-ethnic-national groups, or even
for all eight of the intergroup areas.

The value of general scores lies in their ability to provide
statistical indicators of the general intergroup impact of a curriculum. Because the scores are reduced to percentages, they
may usefully be compared with the scores for the same intergroup areas in other curricula. They lend themselves also to
comparative uses within a single curriculum. For example, in
this study they provide a simple means whereby the effect of the
crucifixion story on intergroup content may be determined by
comparing the general imbalance scores for crucifixion lessons
with the imbalance for all New Testament lessons from which
the former were taken. The degree and direction of the difference indicate whether crucifixion lessons tend to be more positive or more negative toward Jews than noncrucifixion lessons.

It may be objected that a General Imbalance Score for all the
intergroup areas is unwarranted because of the impossibility of
comparing, let us say, Jewish-Christian and Catholic-Protestant relations on the one hand, and interreligious and interracial
relations on the other. Yet such a combination does indeed provide a fair picture of the total intergroup direction of the total
curricula, inasmuch as it does justice to the multiple intergroup relevance of lesson materials. Some lessons mention
one, some two or three, and some as many as all eight intergroup areas.[4] In Scripture Press lessons, for example, out of
the 433 units analyzed, 288 made intergroup references. If
these 288 lessons had referred only to one outside group, the
total of intergroup units would have been 288. Instead, they

_____
4.   Table 15, Appendix VII.

total 803, an average of over 2.8 different groups for each lesson. Since another religious group is often used negatively in
order to make a positive interracial point (e.g. "Jewish prejudice" against Gentiles as an illustration of the sin of race prejudice against Negroes, or the dislike of Muslims for Jews to
illustrate the need for a greater American concern over what
is going on in the Near East), the combined scores give a true
picture of what the lessons look like as a whole in respect to
the other group portraits.

The general score is not composed of an average of other
imbalance scores, but compiles the negative and positive scores
for the intergroup area in question, subtracts the lesser frequency from the greater, and divides by the number of analytical categories scored. The general formula is:

$$C_{gs} = \frac{n - p}{r}, \text{ where } n \text{ is greater than } p, \text{ or}$$

$$\frac{p - n}{r}, \text{ where } p \text{ is greater than } n, \text{ where}$$

        $n$ equals number of negative scores in the
           analytical categories
        $p$ equals the number of positive scores
        $r$ is the relevant content, i.e. the total of
           $p$ and $n$ scores.

## Positive and Negative Distributions

A distribution merely shows what percentage of units are
represented in the positive or/and negative scores in the Analytical Categories.

Distribution of scores in the Analytical Categories. A simple way to portray the direction and classification of content in
the Analytical Categories (for a given intergroup area) is to
graph the data for each category according to the formula:

$$C_n = \frac{n}{t}, \quad C_p = \frac{p}{t}$$

Where $n$ equals negative content; $p$
equals positive content; and $t$ equals
the total number of units with content
pertaining to the intergroup area being
measured.

Distribution scores, when graphed, are boxed above (+) or
below (−) the zero line, while imbalance scores (with some exceptions) are generally represented lineally.

# Appendix IV. Definition of the Nonanalytical Categories

A definition of most Nonanalytical Categories is unnecessary, but the Group Category requires explanation.

The Group Category assumes that the writer of any unit[1] can be considered within the groups predominantly represented by the communicator. Many denominations, for example, have white churches, biracial churches, and Negro churches—but the church at large is predominantly white. Assertions about Negroes or Negro-White relations in the publications of these denominations are judged as made by non-Negroes.

The analyst consequently must shift his perspective when he shifts from one kind of intergroup statement to another. When a writer talks about non-Christian religions or Judaism, his standpoint is taken to be the broad area of Christianity. If interdenominational relations are dealt with, the position of the writer is assumed to be that of the particular denomination issuing the publication. The fixed point shifts again when the writer mentions Roman Catholics, inasmuch as such statements must be judged in the light of the fact that the writer is to be considered Protestant. If international issues are discussed, the writer is assumed to be American, and all statements concerning other countries and peoples are to be judged by the indicators in the Analytical Categories in this light.

Now the question arises, "What is a 'Jewish' reference?" Many statements do not always use the words "Jews," "Jewish" or "Judaism," but other equivalents and near-equivalents. Equivalents are such designations as "Hebrews," "Israelites," "Israel," etc., and near-equivalents consist either of subgroups within the Jewish category or identifying symbols. The "scribes," "Pharisees," "Essenes," "Zealots," "rabbis," would constitute some biblical Jewish subgroups. Such words as "synagogue," "Sanhedrin," and "Torah," and mention of such exclusively Jewish holidays as the Passover, are sufficient to

---

1. The "unit" for counting, e. g. an entire lesson, article, poem, standing alone as a separate, self-contained entity. See Form (Unit) variable on data-gathering instrument, p. 318.

classify a reference within the unit as belonging to the Jewish Group Category.

On the other hand, even though the context is potentially Jewish to the analyst, if none of these symbols appear in the unit, the unit is not scored "Jewish." Thus, mention of "the people," "some persons," "the leaders of the country," "a man" or "a woman," "a paralytic," "his hearers," and "the common folk," if not specifically identified as Jewish are not scored in the Group Category.

A third possibility now arises. Jewish symbols may occur in the unit, but so may nonscoring terminology. The unit is then scored Jewish, and the individual references judged in the light of the above distinctions; e. g. a writer says, "The Pharisees hardened their hearts against the plain evidences . . . But the people realized that Jesus had displayed divine power." The people are not identified as Jews. Therefore, this part of the statement is not pertinent to the indicators in the analytical categories. But the statement about Pharisees is pertinent because it specifies a Jewish subgroup. It is characteristic of some writers to make generalizations of a negative kind about Jews or near-equivalents, and to assign favorable acts and traits merely to unspecified persons. Similarly, for the purpose of scoring, a particular individual is not to be considered Jewish unless he is identified as such.

Other difficulties encountered in the Jewish Group Category are illustrated by complications stemming from the historical roots which Christianity has in Judaism. For the purposes of this study, roles and qualities attributed to Jesus and the disciples as such are not considered Jewish unless so identified. Unless it is otherwise stated, Jesus and/or the disciples and apostles are "wegrouped" as Christians. Several examples may suffice to illustrate how the above principles operate:

> Jesus went to Jerusalem for the Passover in order that He might declare his Messiahship. But upon entering the outer Temple courts, he saw moneychangers and merchants selling animals for the sacrifice. He upset the boxes of the moneychangers and set the animals free, saying, "God said, 'My house is to be a house of prayer for all people,' but you have made it a den of thieves."

The above quotation is scored "Jewish" in the group category, because of the presence of the symbols "Passover" and "Temple courts," indicating a Jewish context. But the assertion is neutral and nonrelevant to the Analytical Categories because none of the people who figure in the event described is identified (either in the reference or its context) as Jews or equivalents. In other words, a Jewish reference is not always relevant to the Analytical Categories, either when (1) it is not directional, or (2) when the principals (actors, customs, factors) are unidentified. The utility of such a distinction is evident when the previous quotation is compared with the following:

> When Jesus entered the Temple, he saw Jews who had journeyed from afar, poor and rich alike, buying doves and lambs for the Temple sacrifices. The men who sold them charged exorbitant prices which the poor could not pay. Their very own leaders, however, cared little for the commands of God. They had their eyes set upon the accumulation of mammon. (Italics added).

The victims are named as "Jews" and the victimizers also as "their very own leaders." Here Jews are pictured as cheating their own people, caring little for the commands of God, etc. The presence of a group designation makes the quotation directional.

There is consequently a distinction between the relevance of an assertion to the Group Category and to the Analytical Categories.

The assumption that Christ and his followers stand within the Christian circle makes it possible to measure the number of times writers tend to cross over this line into the Jewish camp. If Jesus is said to be a Jew discussing contemporary controversial issues with other Jews (Pharisees), the line is crossed. But this is not the case in the following example:

> Jesus knew that the Jews had false ideas about the Messiah. Therefore He decided not to do anything that might encourage them to think of Him as their earthly King. By leaving them, He severely rebuked them for their blindness.

This quotation serves to demonstrate how Jesus is often set in opposition to the Jews, as someone standing outside of the Jewish community, in a universal or Christian context. Jesus, in this instance, must be rated an ingroup member.

A similar problem arises in respect to the Catholic-Protestant intergroup area. The church throughout the Middle Ages is considered by some writers to be Roman Catholic, while others assume it to be simply Christian, with the distinction between

Protestant and Catholic not considered valid until the Reformation Period. For the purposes of scoring, however, any unit that deals with the Middle Ages, if distinctively modern Roman Catholic symbols are there, is considered Roman Catholic. Any discussion of the acts of "the Pope," or "Cardinals," or even just "the Church" of this period, if the setting is the Western church prior to the Reformation, meets this rule. The Kinship Category should indicate whether or not the communicator identifies or counteridentifies with the church of this period.

Other kinds of problems in respect to the scoring of Group Categories arise. The Negro group, for example, is simple to handle on the American scene. But in dealing with Africa, a question arises. An African may be a white African or a Negro. Sometimes the primitive religions of Africans are mentioned. Such references are considered relevant to the Non-Christian Religions Category. The subject of the suppression of Negro Africans by the white man belongs in the Negro Category. If speaking only specifically about an African nation, the unit is scored International. Everything depends upon the context, however, and in some cases more than one Group Category must be checked for the same set of statements.

The Other-Christian Group Category shall be defined to include all non-Roman Catholic churches or sects, e.g. all churches which claim to be Christian, whether regarded as so by a specific communicator or not—all Protestant denominations, the Greek Orthodox and Russian Orthodox Churches, the Copts, the sect denominations, and many fringe groups (e. g. Christian Science, Jehovah's Witnesses, Seventh-Day Adventists, Mormons). In all cases the denomination represented by the communicator shall be excepted (content relating specifically and only to it is not considered Other-Christian).

# Appendix V. The Materials

This project involves a qualitative analysis of all the texts and periodicals published over a period of three full years. The full number of texts and periodicals amounts to 9,528 for the three years (of which a one-third sample is 3,176). These figures, however, include story papers. The total of 9,528 texts and periodicals includes 3,771 story papers with slightly over an average of 7 units per issue.

In length, these texts and periodicals range from lesson sheets of two pages to books of over 500 pages. Much of the material is in book form, either soft or hard cover, and ranging from 120 to 520 pages in length. Some communicators publish only in book form (e.g. Unitarians, Episcopalians) or publish certain curriculum series in this manner. The vast majority of the texts are manuals, ranging in length from 48 to 168 pages.

Since the basic counting unit of this study is a large body of content (e.g. a single lesson, a chapter in a book, an article, a page of poems, an editorial, a full-page picture), the frame of materials was selected upon the basis of the number of units rather than upon the number of pages involved. It was determined that there are 127,599 units (articles, lessons, etc.) in the total range of material for the three-year period (42,589 units for a single year).

## Limitations Imposed on the Quantitative Study

With a total of 127,599 units to be investigated in texts published within a three-year period, it was clearly impossible to subject all of them to precise structural analysis. Accordingly, the quantitative study was delimited in the following ways:

1. Limitation by communicators. Three denominational publishing houses and one independent publisher were chosen for intensive quantitative analysis. These were chosen because of their differing theological views and potentially contrasting positions on the E-A scale. The publications of these four communicators pose the basic problems and issues in intergroup relations. [1]

---

1. Several denominations will be added in a later stage of the survey.

2.  Limitation by curriculum series.  Only the major curriculum offerings of the denominations were chosen.  These are
the Group Graded, Closely Graded, Uniform, and Elective series.  Because they are not really integral to any particular series, the story papers, devotional manuals to be used by individuals in their private devotions, family magazines (but not
home study manuals), and technical materials were excluded
from quantitative analysis.  Under the "elective" series are
included also Sunday evening youth kits and parochial school
texts on religion.  The teacher and pupil manuals in these four
series represent a sort of "core curriculum" which adequately
represents the viewpoint of the communicator.
3.  Limitation by age groups.  Since a number of editors
have suggested that adult materials were the ones most in need
of analysis, and since previously published content studies have
reported only on primary and junior materials, [2] the quantitative study was confined to materials prepared for the intermediate, senior (high school), and adult age groups. [3]

The Problem of Sampling

One further possible delimitation on the statistical side involved sampling.  The first problem of sampling is that of adequate size.  Assuming that a particular curriculum series is to
be sampled, within reasonable limits what proportion is likely
to indicate the content of the whole?  No sampling experiments
have been conducted with curriculum materials produced by
churches.  However, the value of small samples has been adequately demonstrated on newspapers and magazines. [4]
While 10 per cent samples of some newspapers have been
found efficient (3-day samples for the month), the themes and
content of curriculum publications vary so greatly and range
from the present day so far back in time that small samples
are to be considered suspect.  A 33 1/3 per cent selection was
adopted for the following reasons:

---

2.  Eakin and Eakin, Sunday School Fights Prejudice.

3.  All of the above delimitations refer to quantitative analysis
only, and do not exclude from consideration in this report qualitative data derived from the curricula of other communicators
and texts of the four publishers not listed in this appendix.

4.  Cf. Berelson, Content Analysis, p. 176.

1. The variables should be adequately represented in the sample. In order to do this most adequately, a large sample seems called for.

2. In the quarterlies, a smaller (e.g. 25 per cent) sample for the three-year period would exclude the materials for óne of the quarters.

A curriculum composed of a small number of units, such as the Unitarian, presents a different kind of problem. The limited number of units in each variable sampled would result in too great a margin of error. Therefore, the entire curriculum was analyzed.[5] The general rule adopted was: the greater the number of publications, the smaller percentage allowable in the sample; the fewer the publications in a curriculum, the larger the sample.

Sampling poses other questions of method. It is possible to sample texts by selecting every third or fourth unit. However, there is a distinct advantage in sampling according to texts. The exact proportion of articles, lessons, stories, poetry, devotional materials, editorials, pictures, and other features will be obtained by the simple expedient of analyzing the entire publication. The automatic proportion of kinds of units, therefore, can be achieved by analyzing a periodical or text as a whole, provided that all the series are sampled in the same proportion.

The method employed in this study is that of sampling by texts. Several variable factors were taken into consideration in laying out sampling patterns. The first is that variations of lesson themes are used for the four quarterly periods of the year. The trial and crucifixion of Jesus, for example, is customarily dealt with in the March through May issues, depending upon the date for Easter. Much intergroup material seems reserved in some series for the summer or fall months. Catholicism is most likely to be mentioned in material directed to discussions of the Middle Ages, the Reformation, and modern interreligious tensions rather than in Old Testament exposition. Jews and Judaism, naturally, are more likely to figure largely in biblical materials, and, perhaps, more intensively in lessons on the New Testament. Similarly, other cultures, especially more primitive cultures, are more in focus in courses on mission work than those on other broad themes, and Negroes

---

5. Except ror one adult text prepared for parents and teachers of preschool children.

appear more than any other single group in material directed toward the problem of intergroup relations in general.

Experiments were made with these variables in random samplings of texts, resulting in the design of eleven sample patterns. Each pattern included one text from each quarter over the three-year period, but not less than one text per year nor more than two. This ensures that each year of the three years' materials is covered, as well as all the quarters.

A comparison was then made between the estimated degree of appearance of the "content" and "period" categories in a given series, and their appearance in the sample. This process was repeated for several series. It became evident that each series of lessons would have to be sampled separately and a pattern found which would fit the variables in that series most perfectly.

Once a fairly acceptable pattern for a given curriculum is worked out, however, it becomes necessary to select a number of units from other manuals in order to obtain a proportion of variables large enough to be able to make valid generalizations as to the content of those variables. This increased the sample percentage for half the communicators.

The sample pattern for Counsel, teacher's publication for the Presbyterian Group Graded intermediate curriculum, indicates how the sample technique worked in practice (see Table 16). [6] Table 17[7] shows how certain contemporary, mission, and intergroup lessons were oversampled in order to obtain reliable statistics on certain variables. Table 18[8] indicates the degree of sampling (from 33.3 to 95.6 per cent) to which the materials which form the base for this report were subjected.

---

6. Below, Appendix VII.

7. Ibid.

8. Ibid.

Missouri Synod Lutheran Materials Analyzed

| Unit Number | Publication | Date of Use |
|---|---|---|
| 38995–39024 | Studies in St. Matthew<br>Senior Teacher | Undated |
| 39025–39097 | The Beginnings according to<br>the Book of Genesis<br>Senior Teacher | Undated |
| 39098–39111 | Our Creed<br>Adult Pupil | Undated |
| 39112–39137 | The History of Israel<br>Senior Pupil | Undated |
| 39138–39170 | The Church through the Ages<br>Intermediate Pupil | Undated |
| 39171–39184 | Concordia Bible Teacher*[9]<br>Senior Teacher | Oct.–Dec. 1953 |
| 39185–39199 | Concordia Bible Teacher<br>Senior Teacher | Jan.–Mar. 1954 |
| 39200–39212 | Concordia Bible Teacher<br>Senior Teacher | April–June 1954 |
| 39213–39225 | Concordia Bible Teacher<br>Senior Teacher | April–June 1955 |
| 39226–39238 | Concordia Bible Student<br>Senior Pupil | Jan.–Mar. 1953 |
| 39239–39250 | Concordia Bible Student<br>Senior Pupil | July–Sept. 1953 |
| 39251–39252 | Concordia Bible Student<br>Senior Pupil | Jan.–Mar. 1954 |
| 39253–39265 | Concordia Bible Student<br>Senior Pupil | Oct.–Dec. 1954 |
| 39266 | Concordia Bible Student<br>Senior Pupil | Jan.–Mar. 1955 |
| 39267–39278 | Concordia Bible Student<br>Senior Pupil | July–Sept. 1955 |

---

9.* The "Concordia" series is intended for grades 10 through 12; however, the materials denoted "Intermediate" in the Missouri Synod scheme embrace grades 5 and 6, while the "Senior Bible Lessons" are for grades 7 and 8. This classification differs from the scheme used by the other Protestant communicators. Age-grade variable scores for this denomination are, therefore, not comparable with those of the other communicators.

Missouri Synod Materials (Continued)

| Unit Number | Publication | Date of Use |
|---|---|---|
| 39279–39280 | Senior Bible Lessons Senior Pupil | Oct.–Dec. 1955 |
| 39281 | Senior Bible Lessons Senior Pupil | Oct.–Dec. 1954 |
| 39282–39298 | Senior Bible Lessons Senior Pupil | July–Sept. 1955 |
| 39299–39315 | Senior Bible Lessons Senior Pupil | July–Sept. 1954 |
| 39316–39332 | Senior Bible Lessons Senior Pupil | April–June 1954 |
| 39333–39350 | Senior Bible Lessons Senior Pupil | Jan.–Mar. 1954 |
| 39351–39356 | Concordia Bible Student— Pictures | Undated |
| 39357–39373 | Intermediate Bible Lessons Intermediate Pupil | Oct.–Dec. 1954 |
| 39374–39390 | Intermediate Bible Lessons Intermediate Pupil | Jan.–Mar. 1955 |
| 39391–39408 | Intermediate Bible Lessons Intermediate Pupil | April–June 1955 |
| 39409–39425 | Intermediate Bible Lessons Intermediate Pupil | Oct.–Dec. 1955 |
| 39426 | The Concordia Sunday School Teacher Int.–Senior Teacher | Jan.–Mar. 1953 |
| 39427–39441 | The Concordia Sunday School Teacher Int.–Senior Teacher | April–June 1953 |
| 39442–39460 | The Concordia Sunday School Teacher Int.–Senior Teacher | July–Sept. 1953 |
| 39461 | The Concordia Sunday School Teacher Int.–Senior Teacher | Jan.–Mar. 1954 |
| 39462 | The Concordia Sunday School Teacher Int.–Senior Teacher | April–June 1953 |
| 39463–39479 | The Concordia Sunday School Teacher Int.–Senior Teacher | Oct.–Dec. 1954 |

Missouri Synod Materials (Continued)

| Unit Number | Publication | Date of Use |
|---|---|---|
| 39480–39496 | The Concordia Sunday School Teacher<br>Int.–Senior Teacher | Jan.–Mar. 1955 |
| 39497–39509 | Love One Another: The Letters of John<br>Adult Pupil | 1955 |
| 39510–39527 | The Ministering Christ Who Gave Himself<br>Adult Teacher–Pupil | Undated |
| 39528–39545 | Practical Christianity<br>Adult Teacher–Pupil | Undated |

Presbyterian Materials Analyzed

| Unit Number | Publication | Date of Use |
|---|---|---|
| 36803–36831 | This Generation | Jan.–Mar. 1954 |
| 36832–36836 | Crossroads | April–June 1953 |
| 36837–36850 | Westminster Teacher | Jan.–Mar. 1954 |
| 36851–36853 | Crossroads | Oct.–Dec. 1954 |
| 36854–36856 | Crossroads | July–Sept. 1954 |
| 36857–36864 | Westminster Teacher | July–Sept. 1954 |
| 36865 | Crossroads | July–Sept. 1953 |
| 36866 | Crossroads | Jan.–Mar. 1954 |
| 36867–36907 | Crossroads | April–June 1953 |
| 36908–36957 | Crossroads | Jan.–Mar. 1953 |
| 36958–37004 | Crossroads | Oct.–Dec. 1953 |
| 37005–37025 | Crossroads | Jan.–Mar. 1955 |
| 37026–37043 | Westminster Advanced Quarterly | Jan.–Mar. 1955 |
| 37044–37067 | Church of Our Fathers | Oct. 1953–Sept. 1954 |
| 37068–37080 | Westminster Teacher | Jan.–Mar. 1955 |
| 37081–37095 | Westminster Advanced Quarterly | Oct.–Dec. 1953 |
| 37096 | Westminster Teacher | Dec. 13, 1953 |
| 37097–37112 | Westminster Home Department | Oct.–Dec. 1953 |
| 37113–37126 | Westminster Advanced Quarterly | July–Sept. 1953 |
| 37127–37142 | Westminster Advanced Quarterly | April–June 1955 |
| 37143–37145 | Westminster Teacher | July–Sept. 1953 |
| 37146–37147 | Crossroads | July–Sept. 1953 |
| 37148–37172 | Westminster Teacher | April–June 1955 |
| 37173–37183 | Crossroads | Jan.–Mar. 1954 |
| 37184–37205 | Westminster Teacher | April–June 1954 |

Presbyterian Materials (Continued)

| Unit Number | Publication | Date of Use |
|---|---|---|
| 37206–37240 | Westminster Teacher | Oct.–Dec. 1952 |
| 37241–37255 | Westminster Home Quarterly | Oct.–Dec. 1954 |
| 37256–37265 | Westminster Teacher | Oct.–Dec. 1954 |
| 37266–37272 | Crossroads | Oct.–Dec. 1954 |
| 37273–37300 | Westminster Teacher | July–Sept. 1955 |
| 37301–37361 | Youth Fellowship Kit | 1953–54, Vol. 11 |
| 37362–37364 | Youth Fellowship Kit | 1955–56, Vol. 13 |
| 37365–37376 | Youth Fellowship Kit | 1954–55, Vol. 12 |
| 37377–37421 | Junior Hi Kit | 1954–55, Vol. 11 |
| 37422–37426 | Westminster Home Quarterly | Jan.–Mar. 1953 |
| 37427 | Westminster Home Quarterly | Oct.–Dec. 1954 |
| 37428–37441 | Westminster Home Quarterly | Jan.–Mar. 1953 |
| 37442–37459 | Westminster Home Quarterly | July–Sept. 1954 |
| 37460–37464 | This Generation | Oct.–Dec. 1952 |
| 37465–37469 | This Generation | Jan.–Mar. 1953 |
| 37470–37488 | This Generation | April–June 1953 |
| 37489–37497 | This Generation | July–Sept. 1953 |
| 37498–37503 | This Generation | Oct.–Dec. 1953 |
| 37504–37509 | This Generation | April–June 1954 |
| 37510–37513 | This Generation | July–Sept. 1954 |
| 37514 | This Generation | April–June 1953 |
| 37515–37543 | This Generation | Oct.–Dec. 1954 |
| 37544–37547 | This Generation | Jan.–Mar. 1955 |
| 37548–37556 | This Generation | April–June 1955 |
| 37557–37582 | This Generation | July–Sept. 1955 |
| 37583 | Westminster Home Quarterly | April–June 1953 |
| 37584 | Westminster Home Quarterly | April–June 1954 |
| 37585–37589 | Westminster Home Quarterly | April–June 1955 |
| 37590–37594 | Westminster Advanced Quarterly | Jan.–Mar. 1953 |
| 37595–37621 | Counsel | Oct.–Dec. 1952 |
| 37622–37626 | Counsel | Jan.–Mar. 1953 |
| 37627 | Counsel | April–June 1953 |
| 37628–37653 | Counsel | July–Sept. 1953 |
| 37654–37658 | Counsel | Oct.–Dec. 1953 |
| 37659–37684 | Counsel | Jan.–Mar. 1954 |
| 37685–37690 | Counsel | April–June 1954 |
| 37691–37701 | Counsel | July–Sept. 1954 |
| 37702–37718 | Counsel | Oct.–Dec. 1954 |
| 37719–37732 | Counsel | April–June 1955 |
| 37733 | Counsel | July–Sept. 1955 |

Presbyterian Materials (Continued)

| Unit Number | Publication | Date of Use |
|---|---|---|
| 37734-37746 | Counsel | April-June 1955 |
| 37747-37751 | Counsel | July-Sept. 1955 |
| 37752-37764 | Junior High Note Book | Jan.-Mar. 1953 |
| 37765-37771 | Junior High Note Book | April-June 1953 |
| 37772-37785 | Junior High Note Book | Oct.-Dec. 1953 |
| 37786-37799 | Junior High Note Book | April-June 1954 |
| 37800-37807 | Junior High Note Book | Jan.-Mar. 1955 |
| 37808-37820 | Junior High Note Book | July-Sept. 1955 |
| 37821-37842 | The One Story | Oct. 1952-Sept. 1953 |
| 37843-37865 | Opening the New Testament | Oct. 1952-Sept. 1953 |
| 37866-37883 | Fire upon the Earth | Oct. 1953-Sept. 1954 |
| 37884 | Junior High Note Book | July-Sept. 1955 |

## Scripture Press Materials Analyzed

| Unit Number | Publication | Date of Use |
|---|---|---|
| 599- 603 | Intermediate Teacher | Oct.-Dec. 1952 |
| 604 | Intermediate Teacher | Jan.-Mar. 1953 |
| 605- 621 | Intermediate Teacher | April-June 1953 |
| 622- 639 | Intermediate Teacher | Oct.-Dec. 1953 |
| 640- 641 | Intermediate Teacher | Jan.-Mar. 1954 |
| 642- 643 | Intermediate Teacher | April-June 1954 |
| 644 | Intermediate Teacher | July-Sept. 1954 |
| 645- 662 | Intermediate Teacher | Jan.-Mar. 1955 |
| 663- 664 | Intermediate Teacher | April-June 1955 |
| 665- 682 | Intermediate Teacher | July-Sept. 1955 |
| 683- 698 | Intermediate Pupil | Oct.-Dec. 1952 |
| 699- 714 | Intermediate Pupil | July-Sept. 1953 |
| 715- 730 | Intermediate Pupil | Jan.-Mar. 1954 |
| 731- 746 | Intermediate Pupil | April-June 1954 |
| 747- 762 | Intermediate Pupil | Oct.-Dec. 1954 |
| 763- 777 | Senior Teacher | Oct.-Dec. 1952 |
| 778 | Senior Teacher | April-June 1953 |
| 779- 782 | Senior Teacher | July-Sept. 1953 |
| 783- 784 | Senior Teacher | Oct.-Dec. 1953 |
| 785- 800 | Senior Teacher | Jan.-Mar. 1954 |
| 801- 816 | Senior Teacher | April-June 1954 |
| 817- 821 | Senior Teacher | July-Sept. 1954 |

Scripture Press Materials (Continued)

| Unit Number | Publication | Date of Use |
|---|---|---|
| 822– 823 | Senior Teacher | Oct.–Dec. 1954 |
| 824– 826 | Senior Teacher | Jan.–Mar. 1955 |
| 827 | Senior Teacher | April–June 1955 |
| 828– 844 | Senior Teacher | July–Sept. 1955 |
| 845– 859 | Senior Pupil | Jan.–Mar. 1953 |
| 860– 871 | Senior Pupil | April–June 1953 |
| 872 | Senior Pupil | July–Sept. 1953 |
| 873– 888 | Senior Pupil | Oct.–Dec. 1953 |
| 889 | Senior Pupil | Jan.–Mar. 1954 |
| 890 | Senior Pupil | April–June 1954 |
| 891– 904 | Senior Pupil | July–Sept. 1954 |
| 905 | Senior Pupil | Jan.–Mar. 1955 |
| 906– 918 | Senior Pupil | April–June 1955 |
| 919– 924 | Senior Pupil | July–Sept. 1955 |
| 925 | Senior Pupil | April–June 1955 |
| 926– 932 | Adult Teacher | Oct.–Dec. 1952 |
| 933 | Adult Teacher | Jan.–Mar. 1953 |
| 934– 937 | Adult Teacher | April–June 1953 |
| 938– 944 | Adult Teacher | Oct.–Dec. 1953 |
| 945– 949 | Adult Teacher | Jan.–Mar. 1954 |
| 950– 957 | Adult Teacher | April–June 1954 |
| 958– 961 | Adult Teacher | July–Sept. 1954 |
| 962– 965 | Adult Teacher | Oct.–Dec. 1954 |
| 966– 967 | Adult Teacher | Jan.–Mar. 1955 |
| 968– '969 | Adult Teacher | April–June 1955 |
| 970– 976 | Adult Teacher | July–Sept. 1955 |
| 977– 989 | Adult Pupil | Oct.–Dec. 1952 |
| 990–1002 | Adult Pupil | April–June 1953 |
| 1003–1004 | Adult Pupil | Oct.–Dec. 1953 |
| 1005–1017 | Adult Pupil | July–Sept. 1954 |
| 1018 | Adult Pupil | Oct.–Dec. 1954 |
| 1019–1031 | Adult Pupil | Jan.–Mar. 1955 |

## Unitarian Materials Analyzed

| Unit Number | Publication | Date of Use |
|---|---|---|
| 130–151 | Jesus the Carpenter's Son Intermediate Teacher | Undated |
| 152–174 | Jesus the Carpenter's Son Intermediate Pupil | Undated |

Unitarian Materials (Continued)

| Unit Number | Publication | Date of Use |
|---|---|---|
| 175–202 | The Drama of Ancient Israel Intermediate Teacher | Undated |
| 203–228 | The Drama of Ancient Israel Intermediate Pupil | Undated |
| 229–244 | The Church across the Street Intermediate Pupil | Undated |
| 245–270 | Questions That Matter Most Asked by the World's Religions Senior Pupil | Undated |
| 271–286 | Socrates Senior Pupil | Undated |
| 287–301 | Questions That Matter Most Asked by the World's Religions Senior Teacher | Undated |
| 302–312 | The Church across the Street Intermediate Teacher | Undated |
| 313–330 | Know Thyself (Guide to Socrates) Senior Teacher | Undated |
| 331–352 | Men of Prophetic Fire Senior Pupil | Undated |
| 353–363 | Refugees from War Senior Teacher | Undated |
| 364–385 | The Old Story of Salvation Senior Pupil | Undated |
| 386–401 | Today's Children and Yesterday's Heritage Adult Pupil | Undated |
| 402 | The Old Story of Salvation (last chapter) Senior Pupil | Undated |
| 403–434 | War's Unconquered Children Speak Senior Pupil | Undated |

# Appendix VI. Validity and Reliability of the Study

## Reliability of the Sample

Since most curricula were oversampled, the adequacy of the sampling process could be tested best on Missouri Synod materials, which alone conformed to the minimum selection.

The results are shown in Table 19.[1] Using the Chi-Square formula on two halves of the sample for lessons with Jewish references, a high reliability for the total sample is indicated.

By translating the Chi-Square scores into percentages, a convenient index was obtained for determining to what degree the "null hypothesis" may be accepted for any portion of corresponding halves of the sample, i.e. to what extent we may confidently assert that there is no significant difference between the samples.

The reliability of the separate <u>Analytical Categories</u> stands up very well for those categories in which the raw data was sufficiently large in each distribution column to make valid use of the Chi-Square. In all cases, the reliability of the distributions in the Analytical Categories is good to high, ranging from 30 to 80 per cent of confidence.[2] The total occurrences in each Analytical Category ranged from over 5 to 100 per cent. Since these results were obtained on two samples as small as 16.6 per cent, the over-all indication is that a 33.3 per cent sample would predict with considerable accuracy the direction of Jewish content in the Analytical Categories for the total curriculum.[3]

---

1. Below, Appendix VII.

2. The null hypothesis is usually not rejected until one has reached the 5 per cent level of confidence or below. The percentage column in Table 19, Appendix VII, shows that in the categories tested, only the totals in Cat. 7 reached as low as the 5+ level.

3. The higher the percentages in the <u>Scores</u> and <u>Totals</u> column (see Table 19, Appendix VII), the greater confidence one may place in the sampling tool.

For those Analytical Categories to which the Chi-Square formula did not apply, no statistical judgment can be made. Nevertheless, a visual comparison of the directional scores for these categories would indicate a general consistency of results as between the small samples. [4]

As might be expected, the general distributions for the two samples, including the raw data of all the analytical categories not individually subject to the Chi-Square, prove reliable. In other words, the distributions in any one-sixth sample of lessons in the Missouri Synod curriculum, if chosen by the sampling methods used in this study, would justify a prediction—within a degree of confidence of 70 per cent—that the resulting distribution and imbalance scores would accurately represent those of the total universe. The degree of predictability for the full sample is therefore very high.

A similar sampling test on the Missouri Synod's Catholic and non-Christian intergroup areas results in a similarly high predictability as to imbalances, even though the occurrence scores in the individual analytical category distributions were not, for the most part, sufficiently high in at least one cell in the distributions to apply the Chi-Square formula.

The adequacy of the variables is best judged by the sampling methods used, whereby a statistically significant number of lessons from each variable is included in the sample. [5] This resulted in oversampling of most variables. Where there were less than a statistically significant number of any given variable in the sample, all, or 100 per cent of the lessons in that variable were included. Random comparisons of the difference which such oversampling makes in the total imbalance scores proves that even a 100 per cent inclusion of variables with low unit occurrences makes no significant difference in the total results.

Clues as to the reliability of the samples are also obtained by consulting records in the files which show how the cumulative general imbalance scores for the eight intergroup areas changed with the addition of each analyzed text or portion thereof. The greatest changes came in those curricula and intergroup

---

4.  Only in one Analytical Category does the direction of the content change, i.e. Cat. 4. Yet the deviation of this score from the mean is only 1 per cent. Some of the categories (e.g. No. 6) deviate from their total imbalance scores more than do others, yet have sufficiently high raw data to denote high reliability.

5.  Cf. Table 18, Appendix VII, and other examples of variables in Tables 16 and 17.

areas where the variables eventually showed most inconsistency in either degrees or direction of orientation.  A good illustration is the comparison between the Presbyterian cumulative scores in the Catholic and Jewish areas as shown in Table 20. [6]

The variables show a higher consistency for the Jewish Group Category in Presbyterian materials than do those of other communicators. [7] However, the same communicator is relatively inconsistent in scores made in the Catholic variables.  The result is that the Jewish cumulative textual scores are quite similar throughout, while the Catholic scores vary from +15.3 to +23.4.  This observation sheds some light on the reliability scores for the 16.6 per cent sample of Missouri Synod curricula.  High reliability is obtained, even though the Jewish variable scores are highly inconsistent.  On the other hand, Missouri Synod Catholic variables are more consistent.  This observation points to multiple evidence for the over-all reliability of the sampling process.  If correlations are high on small samples in intergroup areas where variable imbalance scores are highly inconsistent, it argues for the general reliability of the larger samples.

## Validity of the Research Design

The validity of this study is partially documented by the significant findings on the curricula of the four communicators, and partially by the agreement of the verbal content with the statistical results.  The references scored in each analytical category, when looked at in the mass, hang together significantly and are helpful sources of further observations, hypotheses, and conclusions.  These data, moreover, are directly relevant to the criteria and capable of being judged by them—although not in any simple fashion.  The validity of the design may best be inferred by the reader from this fruitfulness in results.

Indirectly, judgements of validity depend upon how the research design itself was constructed and what safeguards against invalidation were built into it.  Firstly, therefore, a brief summary is given of the steps taken in setting up this project:

1. The guiding concepts (ethnocentrism—anti-ethnocentrism) were carefully defined and an elaborate critique of and rationale for them were produced.

2. Following a study of definitive works on the subject

---

6. Appendix VII.

7. Cf. Figs. 36 and 37, Appendix VIII.

and a preliminary examination of curriculum materials, the following segments of the design were formulated:

    a.  A set of <u>criteria</u> for determining the ethnocentric–anti-ethnocentric direction of published materials. [8]

    b.  Detailed and defined <u>data-gathering (analytical) categories</u>, each with a positive (for) or negative (against) pole. An attempt was made to define each category so as to be relevant to (1) the intergroup content of Protestant publications, and (2) the adopted criteria. [9]

    c.  A <u>scheme for scoring all the variables</u>, after determining, by actual examination, the variables implicit in the materials. [10]

    d.  An <u>instrument for recording the data</u> systematically so as to make them available in many combinations and refinements.

    e.  Arithmetical <u>formulas</u> for representing the data. [11]

    f.  An elaborate <u>set of rules for scoring</u>. [12]

    g.  A curriculum <u>sampling design</u>. [13]

---

8.  These were based on numerous sources, but a very critical and selective use was made primarily of Adorno <u>et al</u>., <u>The Authoritarian Personality</u>, and, later, Allport, <u>The Nature of Prejudice</u>.

9.  Cf. files for master copy "Definition of Analytical Categories with Directional Indicators," of which only a synopsis appears in the present report.

10.  These include type of manual analyzed, age group target, historical periods represented by the content, form of unit (e. g. lesson, article, story), purposes of the lesson, nature of the unit (intergroup, missions), teacher or pupil levels, and curriculum series.

11.  E. g. preoccupation, distribution, imbalance coefficients.

12.  Cf. files for monograph, <u>Rules for Scoring Statements for Their Intergroup Content</u>.

13.  To take account of all variables. For each curriculum series, a frame was made of the actual percentages of all the variables in the total curriculum to serve as a sampling guide.

3.   The categories, instruments, rules for procedure and scoring, etc. were set up after a preliminary
study of the educational texts to be used in the analysis,
and then tested on a pilot sample of materials.   This
procedure required a number of major revisions.   The
final major revision was then tested on a wide spectrum
of 60 Protestant textbooks and manuals (necessitating
some further minor internal revisions) before any con-
centrated application was made to the materials of a
single communicator.   The aid and criticism of competent persons were sought (e. g. in judging the adequacy
of the statistical design).

4.   A content analysis was then finally run on the full
samples of the curricula of the four communicators and
translated into statistical data.   Since the actual verbal-
pictorial content was also preserved and classified at
the same time as the statistical data, it is possible to
check the negative-positive scores, percentages of
kinds of content, etc., against the actual references
grouped in the files.   The major victim-oppressor categories' statistical data in this study have been verified
against the gathered verbal-pictorial content and identifying symbols.   Very few errors or irrelevancies were
discovered, and these were rectified on the statistical
data-sheets.

5.   Since the Analytical Categories are only descriptive, the content of the categories is easier to define
and less subject to the invalidation which is possible
when scoring depends upon value judgments for the
presence or absence of prejudice, the intensity of direction, or the presumed effects on the audience.

Secondly, the validity of the research design is increased by
the care with which the Analytical Categories were set up according to accepted criteria in content analysis:[14]

1.   Each category must be carefully defined, its
purpose stated, and limited to a definite area of content.

---

14.   Bernard Berelson, Content Analysis in Communication Research, was especially helpful in every state of the process of
establishing this study.

2.  Each category must be integrally related to the
E-A criteria, i.e. it must answer a main question which
the criteria suggests. [15]

3.  Each category must include all possibilities of
statements (1) made in the literature to be studied and
(2) which are relevant to the category.

4.  Each category must be so defined as to be mutually exclusive, i.e. no single content item must be
scored twice. [16]

5.  The subcategories within each category must be
directly related to each other and to the category as
defined as a whole.  (Not all specific statements scored
according to the indicators under each subcategory,
however, can be regarded as of more or less equal
weight in their intergroup implications for reasons
stated elsewhere in this report.

6.  The directional divisions within each category
are balanced; i.e. for each plus indicator there is a
corresponding minus indicator.  This inclusion of related yet contrary content makes it possible to give a
particular meaning to quantitative results, and insures
that there will be no partial, and, therefore selective
analysis.

---

15.  E.g. the ethnocentric inability to criticize oneself and one's
own groups, the tendency to idealize the social self, and the
reverse ability of the anti-ethnocentric to identify with one's
own group yet criticize it, suggests that: (1) In the intergroup
area, this ability or inability may be measured in a single Analytical Category devoted to it (Cat. 3), but also (2) In respect to
unfavorable qualities, traits, or roles attributed to other groups,
the ability to criticize one's own groups for these same qualities, traits, or roles and thus to make an inclusive break
across group lines may be translated into "self-critical: inclusive" indicators on the plus side of the portrait categories
(which measure the extent to which a communicator endows outside groups with favorably regarded or unfavorably regarded
characteristics or roles.

16.  Portions of the same statement, however, may be scored
in several categories and in several directions, because of multiple verbal content.

In the process of content analysis, an attempt was made to classify all of the relevant content in the correct categories and to check on the possible omission of relevant occurrences. Every lesson was (1) first of all, read hastily, noting such important facts as the purposes of the lesson, its general tenor, and specific intergroup statements—their direction, and ideological context; (2) the lesson was carefully analyzed then sentence by sentence, each relevant statement, phrase, or word underlined and identified by Group Category, Analytical Category, and direction, after being checked against the master definition of Analytical Categories to see whether or not the statement precisely fitted a given indicator.

One brief comment still needs to be made. Four full issues of two anti-Semitic publications were analyzed to test the ability of the design accurately to pinpoint anti-Semitism and ethnocentric correlates. The results were reassuring, inasmuch as the Jewish imbalance was −97.4, the Negro −100.0, and the International −82.0.[17]

## Reliability of the Research Design

The most important check on reliability is to determine to what extent there is agreement between two or more analysts in the application of the analytical indicators to an actual segment of material. If different investigators obtain the same results, high reliability is demonstrated.

To date, only a partial duplicate check on analysis has been attempted, largely because of the unavailability of a trained person to reanalyze part of the study. One text alone was rechecked with the aid of a secretary, who, after having done considerable collation, showed interest in attempting some analysis. She was briefly trained on five lessons, then given a Scriptural Press manual[18] of five lessons with very high and complex intergroup content relevant to all eight intergroup areas. None of the distribution cells in the Analytical Categories on so small a sample had sufficiently high occurrences to run a dependable

---

17. Catholic content, however, was not measured (one publication was edited by a Catholic, one by a Protestant). The mainline denominations in America, however, were unanimously denounced by these two groups as "duped" and "controlled" by Jews.

18. SP945−49.

Chi-Square correlation. The independent analyst showed a remarkable degree of agreement with the researcher in 84 per cent of the total raw distribution scores. The General Imbalance Score for the combined intergroup areas under Analyst A (researcher) was −16.6; under Analyst B was −17.9; with 71 and 67 score occurrences respectively. It is to be noted that Analyst B tended to score fewer categories than did Analyst A, to check the − and + columns more often, and the ± column less often. In the Jewish Intergroup Area, which occasioned a higher number of score occurrences than did other groups, the general imbalance score for A was −11.8; for B it was −12.8, a difference of 1 per cent, or a 92.2 per cent over-all agreement.[19] Distributions in 9 out of the 14 Analytical Categories scoring Jewish statements coincided precisely,[20] but the internal distributions of the remaining five categories showed some serious differences, largely due to the smallness of the sample.[21] The most serious deviations occurred in Data-Gathering Categories 4, 5, and 10.[22] A recheck of the scores for analysts A and B against the actual content of the material, however, revealed that Analyst B had some difficulty in discerning minus references in Category 4, and both minus-plus references in Categories 5 and 10. This indicates the need for special training in the meaning of these categories, and a knowledge of how to spot content relevant to their indicators.

A factor of considerable importance in Category 5 is the ability to detect a factual distortion. In order to offset the researcher's possible bias and tendency to error here, two safeguards were adopted for the entire analyzing procedure:

1. The researcher checked his initial judgments on statements which seem to contain possible negative distortions against the actual biblical text, observations

---

19. A result which because of the small number of occurrences may be taken as an indicative but not definitive figure.

20. Categories with the same scores and the same imbalances were 1, 2, 3, 8, 9, 11, 12, 13, and 14. Note that all the "Victim-Oppressor" categories are included in this list.

21. E.g. some errors consisted simply of the omission of a score or a failure to balance a score in a single lesson.

22. Codes-Prestige, Distortion-Correction, and Kinship categories respectively.

of trained scholars, qualified source books, such as reference works, encyclopaedias, and standard works accepted in a given field.

2. Statements of fact for various intergroup areas were personally checked and discussed with a number of scholars in various fields. Catholic references, if historical, were checked with Prof. Roland Bainton; if contemporary, and in doubt, with Prof. Kenneth Underwood; Jewish New Testament references with Prof. Paul W. Meyer; statements about non-Christian religions with Prof. Norvin J. Hein, etc. It is expected nevertheless, that this category will contain a high margin of error. While judgments upon them as to fact may not altogether meet with the approval of other observers, nevertheless it was necessary to include such a category in order to obtain a general picture of the relationship between actual negative distortions of fact as compared with the presence of corrective devices and factual-gathering recommendations in a given curriculum. The qualitative nature of many judgments in this category, however, still leaves it somewhat suspect. Notwithstanding, an extremely high correlation exists between the direction of the grouped imbalances of the remaining analytical categories for the interreligious in the study as a whole. This correlation seems to be almost absolute for the portrait categories. [23]

Another objective indicator of reliability is to test whether the same investigator gets consistent results (1) in different parts of the study, and (2) on the same part of the study after a time interval. The check on the reliability of the sample, already given, is therefore in part also an indicator of the reliability of results on different parts of the same study. A second analysis, one year later, on twenty-three units with high Catholic and Other-Christian content in the Presbyterian group-graded curriculum for intermediates gave an over-all agreement as between the two separate analyses of 98.1 per cent. [24] This higher agreement of the researcher with himself than with an independent analyst may have some relation to the former's

---

23. This judgment is made on visual, not statistical comparisons.

24. PR37044–37067.

greater acquaintance with the research procedures and indicators, inasmuch as some studies on the reliability of content
analysis show that the degree of agreement between analysts
corresponds to the degree of training of the analysts.

The conclusion is that the research design indicates both
high validity and reliability.

# Appendix VII. Tables

## Table 1

### Preoccupation of Protestant Teaching Materials
### with Outside Groups

(Preoccupation score given in percentage of total sample)

| Distribution of Units | Unitarian (Liberal) No. of Units | Unitarian (Liberal) % of Total | Presbyterian (Neo-orthodox) No. of Units | Presbyterian (Neo-orthodox) % of Total | Scrip. Press (Fundamentalist) No. of Units | Scrip. Press (Fundamentalist) % of Total | Mo. Synod (Conservative) No. of Units | Mo. Synod (Conservative) % of Total |
|---|---|---|---|---|---|---|---|---|
| Total sample | 305 | 100.0 | 1,084 | 100.0 | 433 | 100.0 | 482 | 100.0 |
| Non-intergroup[a] | 37 | 12.1 | 226 | 20.8 | 145 | 33.5 | 156 | 32.4 |
| Intergroup[b] | 268 | 87.9 | 858 | 79.2 | 288 | 66.5 | 326 | 67.6 |
| | | (Pre. Score) | | (Pre. Score) | | (Pre. Score) | | (Pre. Score) |
| Intergroup units: | | | | | | | | |
| Non-Christian | 63 | 20.7 | 110 | 10.1 | 93 | 21.5 | 59 | 12.2 |
| Jewish | 185 | 60.6 | 475 | 43.8 | 287 | 66.3 | 272 | 56.4 |
| Catholic | 45 | 14.8 | 200 | 18.5 | 61 | 14.1 | 63 | 13.1 |
| Other Christian | 61 | 20.0 | 200 | 18.5 | 84 | 19.4 | 62 | 12.9 |
| General | 34 | 11.1 | 260 | 24.0 | 94 | 21.7 | 128 | 26.6 |
| International | 82 | 26.9 | 347 | 32.0 | 146 | 33.7 | 69 | 14.3 |
| Other ethnic | 8 | 2.6 | 71 | 6.6 | 23 | 5.3 | 12 | 2.5 |
| Negro | 13 | 4.3 | 95 | 8.8 | 15 | 3.5 | 14 | 2.9 |
| Total | 491 | 161.0 | 1,758 | 162.2 | 803 | 185.5 | 679 | 140.9 |

a.  No mention made of other groups.

b.  One or more groups, or intergroup relations, are mentioned.

Table 2

Ideological Support for Crossing or not Crossing Group Lines as
Related to the Three Main Divisions of the Analytical Profile

(All intergroup areas are included in this table,
showing the relevance of Analytical Category 4, Codes-Prestige,
references to other Analytical Categories)

| Analytical Category | No. of References | Percentage minus Appeals | Percentage plus Appeals | Total Percentage |
|---|---|---|---|---|
| Plight (1-4) | | | | |
| Liberal | 35 | 0.0 | 44.9 | 44.9 |
| Neo-orthodox | 296 | 0.8 | 83.5 | 84.3 |
| Fundamentalist | 99 | 9.1 | 38.1 | 47.2 |
| Conservative | 48 | 7.9 | 29.9 | 37.8 |
| Portrait (5-9) | | | | |
| Liberal | 29 | 0.0 | 37.2 | 37.2 |
| Neo-orthodox | 15 | 0.0 | 4.6 | 4.6 |
| Fundamentalist | 42 | 6.7 | 13.3 | 20.0 |
| Conservative | 20 | 7.1 | 8.7 | 15.8 |
| Relationship (10-14) | | | | |
| Liberal | 14 | 0.0 | 17.9 | 17.9 |
| Neo-orthodox | 39 | 0.3 | 10.8 | 11.1 |
| Fundamentalist | 69 | 10.9 | 21.9 | 32.8 |
| Conservative | 59 | 24.4 | 22.0 | 46.4 |
| Totals[a] | | | | |
| Liberal | 78 | 0.0 | 100.0 | 100.0 |
| Neo-orthodox | 350 | 1.1 | 98.9 | 100.0 |
| Fundamentalist | 210 | 26.7 | 73.3 | 100.0 |
| Conservative | 127 | 39.4 | 60.6 | 100.0 |

a.   These totals are not to be confused with the n's in the profiles
representing Analytical Category 4, since the above percentages
refer to the number of references and not to units.  Several references often occur in each unit, and some are relevant to two or
more categories in the profile.

Table 3

Scriptural Occasions for Involving Non-Scriptural Groups

(Preoccupation and directional scores for Bible-based units in the
Negro, Catholic, and other Christian intergroup areas, illustrating
degrees to which commentary on the Bible evokes
comment upon Non-Jews)

| Communicators | No. of Biblical Units | Intergroup Areas PE Score (% of Total Units)[a] | Directional Score (Imbalance)[b] |
|---|---|---|---|
| | Negro | | |
| Liberal | 3 | 23.1 | + 75.0 |
| Neo-orthodox | 68 | 71.8 | + 95.0 |
| Fundamentalist | 13 | 86.7 | + 39.0 |
| Conservative | 11 | 78.6 | + 29.0 |
| | Catholic | | |
| Liberal | 7 | 13.3 | + 50.0 |
| Neo-orthodox | 63 | 31.5 | + 52.0 |
| Fundamentalist | 57 | 93.4 | − 54.0 |
| Conservative | 46 | 73.0 | − 86.0 |
| | Other Christian[c] | | |
| Liberal | 9 | 14.7 | + 10.0 |
| Neo-orthodox | 72 | 85.7 | + 22.0 |
| Conservative | 36 | 58.1 | − 65.0 |

a.  I. e. total period units (biblical and nonbiblical lessons, etc.)
for the intergroup area designated, e. g. Unitarian total Catholic
units are 45, of which 7, or 13.3 per cent, are biblical.

b.  For biblical units only.

c.  These data are not available for the neo-orthodox.

Table 4

The Conservative Curriculum General Imbalance for the Jewish
Intergroup Area Adjusted by Subtraction of Religious
Textbook Used in Parochial Schools

| Jewish Group Cat. | No. of Units | Directional Score − | Directional Score + | Total Cats. Scored | Imbalance $(C_I)$ − | Imbalance $(C_I)$ + | Deviation from Total Curriculum |
|---|---|---|---|---|---|---|---|
| Total curriculum | 272 | 587 | 460 | 825 | 15.4 | | |
| Parochial textbook | 15 | 53 | 41 | 69 | 17.4 | | − 2.0 |
| Adjusted total | 257 | 534 | 419 | 756 | 15.2 | | + 0.2 |

Table 5

Effect of a Single Writer in the Conservative Sunday School
Curriculum on the General Imbalance Score for the Total
Curriculum in the Jewish Intergroup Area

| Jewish Group Cat. | No. of Units | Directional Score − | Directional Score + | Total Cats. Scored | Imbalance $(C_I)$ − | Imbalance $(C_I)$ + | Deviation from Total Curriculum[a] |
|---|---|---|---|---|---|---|---|
| Total curriculum[b] | 257 | 534 | 419 | 756 | 15.2 | | |
| Writer "X" | 111 | 288 | 171 | 368 | 31.8 | | − 16.6 |
| Total curriculum less writer "X" | 146 | 246 | 248 | 388 | | 0.6 | +15.8 |

a. Adjusted to exclude single parochial school textbook.  See Table 4.

b. Ibid.

Table 6

Missouri Synod—Lutheran (Conservative):
Kinds of Negative and Positive References to the Jewish Plight,
Anti-Semitism, and Jewish Rights in Analytical Category 1

| MINUS INDICATORS Type of Negative Statements (Counter-Identification with Jewish Plight) | Frequency (No. of Units) | | PLUS INDICATORS Type of Positive Statements (Identifies with Jewish Plight) | Frequency (No. of Units) | |
|---|---|---|---|---|---|
| | No. | Total | | No. | Total |
| 1. Plight due to Jewish disobedience: A Judgment of God upon them: | | | 1. Plight due to disobedience of others: | | |
| a. For disobedience, blasphemy against God | 3 | | a. Sin of others | 1 | |
| b. For unbelief and Christ rejection | 4 | | | | |
| c. For persecution of Christians | 1 | | | | |
| d. A curse brought upon themselves | 3 | | | | |
| e. Affliction is "Just" | 1 | 12 | | | 1 |
| | | | 5. Anti-Semitism discouraged: | | |
| | | | a. Condemnation of "mass killings" perpetrated by Nazis. | 1 | |
| | | | b. Warning against disliking and condemning Jews | 1 | 2 |
| 6. Nonidentifying phraseology and content: | 2 | 2 | | | |
| Total negative indicators scored | 14 | | Total positive indicators scored | 3 | |
| Total units scored negative in Cat. 1 | 7 | | Total units scored positive in Cat. 1 | 2 | |
| Negative stress in 2.0, i.e. two minus indicators per unit scored minus in Cat. 1. | | | Positive stress is 1.5, i.e. 1 1/2 plus indicators per unit scored plus in Cat. 1. | | |

Table 7

Scripture Press (Fundamentalist):
Kinds of Negative and Positive References to the Jewish Plight,
Anti-Semitism, and Jewish Rights in Analytical Category 1

| MINUS INDICATORS | | | PLUS INDICATORS | | |
|---|---|---|---|---|---|
| Type of Negative Statements (Counter-Identification with Jewish Plight) | Frequency (No. of Units) | | Type of Positive Statements (identifies with Jewish Plight) | Frequency (No. of Units) | |
| | No. | Total | | No. | Total |
| 1. Plight due to Jewish disobedience: A judgment of God upon them: | | | 1. Plight due to disobedience of others: | | |
| a. For unfaithfulness | 5 | | a. Sin of others | 8 | |
| b. For Christ rejection | 6 | | b. Sin of Christians[a] | 5 | |
| c. For assumption of responsibility for the Crucifixion | 4 | | c. Refutation of Crucifixion charge | 2 | |
| d. Affliction is "just" | 1 | 16 | d. Unjust nature of plight | 3 | 18 |
| 2. Divine punishment upon the Jew (see no. 1 above): | | | 2. Divine providence, love, and protection for Jew in his plight: | | |
| a. Suffers without a divine purpose | 0 | | a. Suffers for a divine purpose | 3 | |
| b. God has abandoned them to their fate | 0 | | b. God preserves and is obligated to preserve the Jews | 7 | |
| c. Has rejected Israel | 0 | 0 | c. Denial that Israel is rejected; qualifications of rejection | 7 | |
| d. (Same as no. 1a, b, above) | | | d. Suffering due to mark of God on the Jews | 2 | |
| e. Annulled the covenant, or given it over to Church | 0 | | e. Due to God's faithfulness to the covenant with Israel | 2 | |
| f. Denial of any vicarious value to Jewish suffering | 1 | 1 | (For God's plan for Israel, see no. 3 below) | | 21 |

a. There are other self-critical references in lessons not scored in Cat. 1, e.g. "Have you been guilty of feeling 'superior' to anyone because he or she is a Jew? A Negro?" SP905:25.

## Table 7 (continued)

3. Solutions, mitigation
   of plight, denied or
   discouraged:
   a. Interim solutions
      implicitly denied          2
   b. Future suffering for
      Jews anticipated           3

   c. Plight seen as contin-
      uing in accordance
      with scriptural time-
      table                      6
   d. Action on behalf of
      Jews forbidden or
      discouraged                0
                                   ___
                                    11
4. Jewish rights denied          0
                                   ___
                                     0


5. Anti-Semitism approved,
   defended                      0
                                   ___
                                     0




6. Nonidentifying phrase-
   ology and context             6
                                   ___
                                     6


Total negative indicators
  scored                             34
Total units scored negative
  in Cat. 1                          17
Negative stress (relation of
  minus indicators scored to
  lessons rated minus) is 2.0,
  i.e. two negative indicators
  per lesson with a negative
  score.

3. Solutions to plight, affirmed or envisaged:
   a. Ultimate solution en-
      visaged in the resto-
      ration of Israel          22
   b. Future suffering
      shortened for Jews'
      sake                       2
   c. But end of Jewish
      sufferings is im-
      minent                     3

   d. Action on behalf of
      Jews is required of
      Christians                 4
                                   ___
                                    31
4. Jewish rights affirmed:
   a. Right to defend them-
      selves upheld              2
                                   ___
                                     2

5. Anti-Semitism con-
   demned, forbidden:
   a. Forbidden                  6
   b. Imperatives to love,
      cherish, defend
      Jews                       7
   c. Judged unchristian
      and unjust                 4
   d. All who hate, per-
      secute Jews are
      under God's curse          8
                                   ___
                                    25

6. Identifying phrase-
   ology and context            10
                                   ___
                                    10


Total positive indicators
  scored                            107
Total units scored posi-
  tive in Cat. 1                     34
Positive stress (relation
  of plus indicators scored
  to lessons rated plus) is
  3.15, i.e. an average of
  three and a fraction plus
  indicators per lesson with
  a plus score.

Table 8

Presbyterian (Neo-orthodox):
Kinds of Negative and Positive References to the Jewish Plight,
Anti-Semitism, and Jewish Rights in Analytical Category 1

| MINUS INDICATORS | | | PLUS INDICATORS | | |
|---|---|---|---|---|---|
| Type of Negative Statements (Counter-Identification with Jewish Plight) | Frequency (No. of Units) | | Type of Positive Statements (Identifies with Jewish Plight) | Frequency (No. of Units) | |
| | No. | Total | | No. | Total |
| 1. Plight due to Jewish disobedience: A judgment of God upon them: | | | 1. Plight due to disobedience of others: | | |
| a. For unfaithfulness | 0 | | a. Sin of others | 29 | |
| b. For Christ rejection | 1 | 1 | b. Sin of Christians | 12 | |
| | | | c. Refutation of Crucifixion charge | 4 | |
| | | | d. Refutation of Christ rejection | 8 | |
| | | | e. Unjust nature of plight | 10 | 63 |
| 2. Divine punishment upon the Jew (see no. 1 above) | 0 | 0 | 2. Divine providence, love, and protection for Jew in his plight: | | |
| | | | a. Suffers for a divine purpose | 6 | |
| | | | b. God preserves the Jews | 3 | |
| | | | c. Denial that Israel is rejected; qualifications of rejection | 5 | 14 |
| 3. Solutions, mitigation of plight, denied or discouraged | 0 | 0 | 3. Solutions to plight advanced: | | |
| | | | a. Ultimate solution envisaged in the reconciliation of Israel and church | 3 | |
| | | | b. Alleviation of plight a Christian duty: action on behalf of Jews required | 13 | 16 |

Table 8  (<u>continued</u>)

| | |
|---|---|
| 4.  Jewish rights denied        0 | 4.  Jewish rights affirmed: |
| |    a.  Right to freedom from discrimination, segregation, etc. explicitly affirmed — 8 |
| |    b.  Right of Jews to defend themselves, and engage in social action to gain rights — 1 |
| |    c.  Situations in which learner may consider rights — 3 |
| |    d.  Other — 3 — 15 |

| | |
|---|---|
| 5.  Anti-Semitism approved, defended        0 | 5.  Anti-Semitism condemned, forbidden: |
| |    a.  Forbidden — 8 |
| |    b.  Imperatives to seek justice for Jews — 9 |
| |    c.  Judged unchristian and unjust — 21 |
| |    d.  Those who persecute Jews under God's judgment — 3 — 41 |

| | |
|---|---|
| 6.  Nonidentifying phraseology and context        1 — 1 | 6.  Identifying phraseology and context: |
| |    a.  Plight, discrimination described — 23 |
| |    b.  Plight seen from inside — 14 |
| |    c.  Resources recommended for learning of plight — 3 — 49 |

| | |
|---|---|
| Total negative indicators scored        2 | Total positive indicators scored        198 |
| Total units scored negative in Cat. 1        2 | Total units scored positive in Cat. 1        39 |
| Negative stress (relation of minus indicators scored to lessons rated minus) is 1.0, i.e. 1 negative indicator per lesson with a negative score. | Positive stress (relation of plus indicators scored to lessons rated plus) is 5.1, i.e. 5 and a fraction plus indicators per lesson with a plus score. |

Table 9

Unitarian (Liberal):
Kinds of Negative and Positive References to the Jewish Plight,
Anti-Semitism, and Jewish Rights in Analytical Category 1

| MINUS INDICATORS Type of Negative Statements (Counter-Identification with Jewish Plight) | Frequency (No. of Units) | | PLUS INDICATORS Type of Positive Statements (Identifies with Jewish Plight) | Frequency (No. of Units) | |
|---|---|---|---|---|---|
| | No. | Total | | No. | Total |
| 1. Plight due to Jewish disobedience: A judgment of God upon them | 0 | | 1. Plight due to disobedience of others: | | |
| | | | a. Sin of others | 4 | |
| | | | b. Sin of Christians | 6 | |
| | | | c. Refutation of Crucifixion charge | 2 | 12 |
| 3. Solutions, mitigation of plight, denied or discouraged | 0 | | 3. Solutions to plight affirmed or envisaged: | | |
| | | | a. Desire to better relations; expresses hope for breaking down barriers | 3 | |
| | | | b. Possibility of solutions affirmed or assumed | 2 | |
| | | | c. Encourages suggestions for settlement (Jewish-Arab) | 5 | 10 |
| 5. Anti-Semitism approved, defended | 0 | | 5. Anti-Semitism condemned, forbidden: | | |
| | | | a. Judged inhuman, tragic, etc. | 2 | 2 |
| 6. Nonidentifying phraseology and context | 1 | 1 | 6. Identifying phraseology and context: | | |
| | | | a. Plight described | 3 | |
| | | | b. Described from the inside | 3 | |
| | | | c. Resources for study | 2 | |
| | | | d. Pictures of Jewish refugees | 1 | 9 |
| Total Negative indicators scored | 1 | | Total positive indicators scored | 33 | |
| Total units scored negative in Cat. 1 | 1 | | Total units scored positive in Cat. 1 | 25 | |
| Negative stress is 1.0, i.e. one minus indicator per lesson with a negative score. | | | Positive stress is 1.3, i.e. one plus indicator and a fraction per lesson with a positive score. | | |

Table 10

Contemporary Victim and Non-Victim Self-Portrayals in Four
Protestant Groups (Internal Distributions for Analytical Category 12,
General Group Category

| Communicator | No. of Lessons (with General Refs. in Cat. 12) | PERCENTAGE OF LESSONS | | | | |
|---|---|---|---|---|---|---|
| | | With Minus Score (Victim) (a) | With Plus-Minus Score (Both) (b) | With Plus Score (Non-Victim) (c) | Total | Imbalance |
| Liberal | 0 | 0.0 | 0.0 | 0.0 | 0.0 | — |
| Neo-orthodox | 29 | 41.4 | 37.9 | 20.7 | 100.0 | −01.8 |
| Fundamentalist | 39 | 56.4 | 30.8 | 12.8 | 100.0 | −15.8 |
| Conservative | 45 | 95.6 | 2.2 | 2.2 | 100.0 | −32.1 |
| Total | 113 | 68.2 | 21.2 | 10.6 | 100.0 | |

Table 11

Effects of the Missions Theme on the Religious Portraits
as Compared with Intergroup and Other Lessons

| Communicator | MISSIONS No. of Units | Imbalance − | Imbalance + | INTERGROUP No. of Units | Imbalance − | Imbalance + | OTHER No. of Units | Imbalance − | Imbalance + |
|---|---|---|---|---|---|---|---|---|---|
| **Liberal** | | | | | | | | | |
| Non-Chris. | 0 | | | 38 | | 76.3 | 25 | | 90.6 |
| Jewish | 0 | | | 38 | | 61.8 | 147 | | 44.6 |
| Catholic | 0 | | | 28 | | 34.6 | 17 | | 41.9 |
| Other-Chris. | 0 | | | 38 | | 55.6 | 23 | | 19.1 |
| Total | 0 | — | — | 142 | | 60.1 | 212 | | 46.8 |
| **Neo-orthodox** | | | | | | | | | |
| Non-Chris. | 14 | | 37.7 | 4 | | 70.0 | 112 | | 34.9 |
| Jewish | 4 | | 70.0 | 8 | | 81.5 | 463 | | 43.9 |
| Catholic | 4 | | 60.0 | 7 | | 3.7 | 189 | | 24.1 |
| Other-Chris. | 15 | | 100.0 | 12 | | 80.5 | 173 | | 77.8 |
| Total | 37 | | 56.3 | 31 | | 60.0 | 824 | | 43.8 |
| **Fundamentalist** | | | | | | | | | |
| Non-Chris. | 5 | 20.0 | | 3 | | 20.0 | 85 | 37.0 | |
| Jewish | 2 | | 33.3 | 2 | | 44.4 | 283 | | 7.4 |
| Catholic | 2 | 71.4 | | 1 | | 100.0 | 58 | 55.6 | |
| Other-Chris. | 2 | | 16.7 | 8 | 61.5 | | 74 | | 20.5 |
| Total | 11 | 11.9 | | 14 | 34.8 | | 500 | 1.7 | |
| **Conservative** | | | | | | | | | |
| Non-Chris. | 1 | 100.0 | | 0 | | | 58 | 57.8 | |
| Jewish | 5 | | 18.2 | 0 | | | 267 | 16.3 | |
| Catholic | 0 | | | 0 | | | 63 | 66.9 | |
| Other-Chris. | 2 | 100.0 | | 0 | | | 60 | 38.2 | |
| Total | 8 | 0.0 | | 0 | — | — | 448 | 28.7 | |

Table 11a

Effects of the Missions Theme on the Religious Portraits
and Total Curriculum, by "Content Categories"

| Communicator and Intergroup Areas | Proportion of Missionary Lessons (%) | | Proportion of Intergroup Lessons (%) | | Proportion of Other Lessons (%) | |
|---|---|---|---|---|---|---|
| | % | Imbalance | % | Imbalance | % | Imbalance |
| Liberal | | | | | | |
| Interreligious | | | 40.1 | +60.1 | 59.9 | +46.8 |
| All groups | | | 45.1 | +65.4 | 54.9 | +50.7 |
| Neo-orthodox | | | | | | |
| Interreligious | 4.1 | +56.3 | 3.5 | +60.0 | 92.4 | +43.8 |
| All groups | 7.7 | +76.4 | 6.0 | +80.0 | 86.3 | +51.0 |
| Fundamentalist | | | | | | |
| Interreligious | 2.2 | −11.9 | 2.8 | −34.8 | 95.0 | −01.7 |
| All groups | 2.3 | −10.5 | 3.0 | +08.7 | 94.7 | −00.3 |
| Conservative | | | | | | |
| Interreligious | 1.8 | 0.0 | | | 98.2 | −28.7 |
| All groups | 1.9 | +6.3 | | | 98.1 | −22.0 |

Table 12

Statements in Crucifixion References re:  Who Crucified Christ[a]

| | Liberal | | Neo-orthodox | | Fundamentalist | | Conservative | |
|---|---|---|---|---|---|---|---|---|
| Kind of Statement | No. | % | No. | % | No. | % | No. | % |
| Rome, Roman authorities, gentiles, etc. | 5 | .56 | 24 | .57 | 8 | .24 | 8 | .29 |
| The Jewish authorities, chief priests, High Priest, Sanhedrin, Sadducees, religious rulers, etc. | 0 | — | 1[b] | .02 | 1 | .03 | 2 | .07 |
| "The Jews" | 0 | — | 1 | .02 | 12 | .36 | 12 | .43 |
| "Jews and Gentiles" | 0 | — | 0 | — | 1 | .03 | 2 | .07 |
| Direct refutation of charge that Jews killed Christ | 2 | .22 | 4 | .10 | 2 | .06 | 0 | — |
| Universalization: All mankind, sinful men, etc. | 0 | — | 1 | .02 | 1 | .03 | 0 | — |
| Self-involvement: We crucified Christ, we are guilty, etc. | 0 | — | 16 | .38 | 2 | .06 | 2 | .07 |
| Other assertions: "The multitude," "the people," etc. | 0 | — | 0 | — | 2 | .06 | 0 | — |
| No mention | 2 | .22 | 9 | .22 | 10 | .30 | 8 | .29 |
| Total | 9 | 1.00 | 55 | 1.33 | 39 | 1.17 | 34 | 1.22 |
| Total units | 9 | 1.00 | 42 | 1.00 | 33[c] | 1.00 | 28[d] | 1.00 |
| Total n's examined | 185 | | 475 | | 287 | | 272 | |

Heading: NO. AND % OF UNITS IN WHICH STATEMENTS APPEAR

a.  These include statements of guilt, responsibility, and direct assertions: ". . . crucified. . . killed. . . murdered Christ."

b.  A quotation from Luke 24:20 ("our chief priests and rulers delivered him up to be condemned to death and crucified him"), in a narrative portrayal of the incident on the road to Emmaus, is given no editorial support.

c.  This figure omits several crucifixion units not analyzed at the time this chart was constructed; an examination of these units shows a similar distribution to that above.

d.  Ibid.

Table 13

Effect of Crucifixion Story on View of Jewish Plight
Indicated by Comparing "New Testament" with "Crucifixion" Absolute
Imbalances[a] for Combined Analytical Categories 1, 2, and 3

|  | Liberal Imbalance | Neo-orthodox Imbalance | Fundamentalist Imbalance | Conservative Imbalance |
|---|---|---|---|---|
| New Testament | +100.0 | + 80.8 | + 52.9 | − 85.7 |
| Crucifixion | +100.0 | +100.0 | + 25.0 | −100.0[b] |
| Directional deviation | None | + 19.2 | − 27.9 | − 14.3 |

a. Absolute imbalances ignore the number of units involved and refer
only to the relation of positive to negative scores. Do not confuse these
scores with the relative analytical imbalances in Tables 21−24.

b. Number of cells here are only 12 but include all references in the
sample classified as "Crucifixion."

Table 14

Effect of Crucifixion Story on Jewish Portrait
Indicated by Comparing "New Testament" with "Crucifixion" Absolute
Imbalances[a] for Combined Analytical Categories 5-9

|  | Liberal Imbalance | Neo-orthodox Imbalance | Fundamentalist Imbalance | Conservative Imbalance |
|---|---|---|---|---|
| New Testament | +52.7 | +34.5 | −11.6 | −55.0 |
| Crucifixion | +60.0 | +32.7 | −31.6 | −69.2 |
| Directional deviation | + 7.3 | − 1.8 | −20.0 | −14.2 |

a. Absolute imbalances ignore the number of units involved and refer only to the relation of positive to negative scores.

Table 15

Multiple Involvement of Intergroup Areas per Unit Scored

| | UNITS IN THE CURRICULA | | | INTERGROUP AREAS |
| | No. in | No. with Intergroup | No. Scored in All Inter- | No. of Groups Scored |
| Communicator | Sample | Content | group Areas | per Unit |
|---|---|---|---|---|
| Liberal | 305 | 268 | 491 | 1.8 |
| Neo-orthodox | 1084 | 858 | 1758 | 2.1 |
| Fundamentalist | 433 | 288 | 803 | 2.8 |
| Conservative | 482 | 326 | 679 | 2.1 |
| Total | 2304 | 1740 | 3731 | 2.2 |

Table 16

Sample Pattern for Presbyterian Intermediate Group Graded Curriculum
Teacher's Manual, Lessons Only

| | 1st Quarter October–December | 2d Quarter January–March | 3d Quarter April–June | 4th Quarter July–August |
|---|---|---|---|---|
| 1st Year 1952–53 | All 13 units | 2 units | 1 unit | All 13 units |
| 2d Year 1953–54 | 5 units | All 13 units | 4 units | 9 units |
| 3d Year 1954–55 | 4 units | None | All 13 units | 3 units |

Table 17

Percentage of Lessons in the Total Curriculum as Compared
to Sample, in Relation to Some Variables,
Presbyterian Intermediate Group Graded Curriculum,
Teacher's Manual

Period Category Variables

|                        | Old T. | New T. | Both | Church History | Contem-porary | Total |
|------------------------|--------|--------|------|----------------|---------------|-------|
| Universe—Total         | 28     | 77     | 3    | 39             | 9             | 156   |
| Percentage             | 17.9   | 49.4   | 1.9  | 25.0           | 5.8           | 100.0 |
| Sample—Total           | 17     | 29     | —    | 26             | 8             | 80    |
| Percentage             | 21.2   | 36.3   | —    | 32.5           | 10.0          | 100.0 |

Content Variables

|                        | Missions | Intergroup | Other | Total |
|------------------------|----------|------------|-------|-------|
| Universe—Total         | 10       | 4          | 142   | 156   |
| Percentage             | 6.4      | 2.6        | 91.0  | 100.0 |
| Sample—Total           | 10       | 3          | 67    | 80    |
| Percentage             | 12.5     | 3.8        | 83.7  | 100.0 |

Table 18

## Comparison of Sampling Percentages for the
## Curricula of Four Communicators

| | Presbyterian Units | | Unitarian Units | | Scripture Press Units | | Missouri Synod Units | |
|---|---|---|---|---|---|---|---|---|
| | No. | % | No. | % | No. | % | No. | % |
| Universe | 2523[a] | 100.0 | 319 | 100.0 | 1296 | 100.0 | 1466[b] | 100.0 |
| Sample | 1084 | 42.9 | 305 | 95.6 | 433 | 33.4 | 482 | 33.3 |

a. Oversampling due to complexity of the curriculum variables.

b. Estimate based upon best information available at time of sampling.

Table 19

Reliability of the Sampling Process, Using the Chi-Square Formula on
Two Equal Divisions of the Total Lesson Sample for the
Missouri Synod Curriculum, Jewish Group Category[a]

| | (1) Red Sample $C_I$ Score | (2) White Sample $C_I$ Score | Scores Reliability of Distribution of Raw Score[b] | | Totals Reliability of Total Occurrences of Raw Score[c] | |
|---|---|---|---|---|---|---|
| Analytical Category | | | $X^2$ | %** | $X^2$ | %** |
| 1. Rights | − 1.1 | − 1.8 | * | * | * | * |
| 2. Prej. | 0 | 0 | — | — | — | — |
| 3. Self-crit. | − 3.7 | − 0.4 | * | * | 0 | 100 |
| 4. Codes | − 1.6 | + 0.5 | * | * | 0.17010 | 60 + |
| 5. Distortion | − 8.2 | − 4.3 | * | * | 1.75316 | 10 + |
| 6. Moral | −16.9 | −12.2 | 0.5899 | 70 + | 0 | 100 |
| 7. Truth | − 3.1 | − 5.9 | 3.0977 | 30 + | 3.15528 | 5 + |
| 8. Superior | − 2.2 | − 0.5 | * | * | * | * |
| 9. Other C. | + 1.9 | − 0.9 | 0.7032 | 80 + | 0.39062 | 50 + |
| 10. Kinship | + 9.9 | +10.0 | 1.5164 | 60 + | 0.72374 | 40 + |
| 11. Host.-F. | −21.3 | −17.4 | * | * | 0.42646 | 40 + |
| 12. Host. Pres. | − 1.5 | 0.0 | * | * | * | * |
| 13. Interact. | − 0.7 | 0.0 | * | * | * | * |
| 14. Pun.-Nur. | 0.0 | 0.5 | 0.4104 | 80 + | 1.9432 | 10 + |
| Total | −17.2 | −13.4 | 0.53307 | 70 + | 0.22608 | 60 + |

a. Total sample, 33.3 per cent of universe; red and white samples, each
16.65 per cent (or 1/6th) of universe. Total sample 272 units with Jewish
mention. Red and white samples represent a selection of alternate lessons.

b. I.e. the number of −, +, and ± occurrences.

c. I.e. the total number of occurrences (add −, +, and ± scores).

*$X^2$ cannot be used where any cell in the distribution for a single analytical
category has fewer than 5 scores. Asterisks indicate that these categories
were not tested, and therefore no reliability of these particular categories
were made.

**$X^2$ is translated into percentages, or decimal proportions of confidence,
for accepting the "null hypothesis," by the use of a table listing degrees of
freedom and $X^2$ scores in cross-reference. Cf. Allen L. Edwards, Statistical Analysis (New York, Rinehardt, 1946), p. 342. $X^2$ for Scores has 2
degrees of freedom. $X^2$ for Totals has 1 degree of freedom.

Note: The $X^2$ (Chi-Square) formula tests for the same phenomenon as the
Standard Error of Proportion, but is easier to compute from raw data.
See ibid., p. 185. The $C_I$ (imbalance) scores for the two half-samples are
given in Cols. 1 and 2, making possible a visual comparison, but were not
used in the computations.

Table 20

A Comparison of Presbyterian Cumulative Imbalances (by Text)
for Catholic and Jewish Intergroup Areas

| JEWISH | | | | CATHOLIC | | | |
|---|---|---|---|---|---|---|---|
| Cumulative Imbalance | | | | Cumulative Imbalance | | | |
| 1st Manual Analyzed | 3% Sample | 16% Sample | Final Score | 1st Manual Analyzed | 3% Sample | 16% Sample | Final Score |
| +45.4 | +46.3 | +44.8 | +44.3 | +15.4 | +15.3 | +20.6 | +23.4 |

Table 21

Comparison of the Liberal New Testament and
Crucifixion Analytical Profiles for the Jewish Intergroup Area

| Analytical Category | Type of Unit | Total No. of Units[a] | Directional Score − | Directional Score + | Directional Score ± | Total Analytical Units[b] | Imbalance − | Imbalance + |
|---|---|---|---|---|---|---|---|---|
| 1 | New Testament | 47 | 0 | 2 | 0 | 2 | | .04 |
| | Crucifixion | 8 | 0 | 2 | 0 | 2 | | .25 |
| 2 | New Testament | 47 | 0 | 0 | 0 | 0 | .00 | .00 |
| | Crucifixion | 8 | 0 | 0 | 0 | 0 | .00 | .00 |
| 3 | New Testament | 47 | 0 | 1 | 0 | 1 | | .02 |
| | Crucifixion | 8 | 0 | 2 | 0 | 2 | | .25 |
| 4 | New Testament | 47 | 0 | 0 | 0 | 0 | .00 | .00 |
| | Crucifixion | 8 | 0 | 0 | 0 | 0 | .00 | .00 |
| 5 | New Testament | 47 | 0 | 32 | 0 | 32 | | .70 |
| | Crucifixion | 8 | 0 | 8 | 0 | 8 | | 1.00 |
| 6 | New Testament | 47 | 1 | 7 | 22 | 30 | | .12 |
| | Crucifixion | 8 | 0 | 1 | 3 | 4 | | .13 |
| 7 | New Testament | 47 | 1 | 1 | 3 | 5 | .00 | .00 |
| | Crucifixion | 8 | 1 | 0 | 1 | 2 | .13 | |
| 8 | New Testament | 47 | 0 | 0 | 0 | 0 | .00 | .00 |
| | Crucifixion | 8 | 0 | 1 | 0 | 1 | | .13 |
| 9 | New Testament | 47 | 2 | 13 | 11 | 26 | | .22 |
| | Crucifixion | 8 | 0 | 3 | 2 | 5 | | .38 |
| 10 | New Testament | 47 | 1 | 17 | 13 | 31 | | .33 |
| | Crucifixion | 8 | 1 | 3 | 2 | 6 | | .21 |
| 11 | New Testament | 47 | 0 | 0 | 16 | 16 | .00 | .00 |
| | Crucifixion | 8 | 1 | 1 | 7 | 9 | .00 | .00 |
| 12 | New Testament | 47 | 0 | 1 | 0 | 1 | | .02 |
| | Crucifixion | 8 | 0 | 2 | 0 | 2 | | .25 |
| 13 | New Testament | 47 | 0 | 6 | 0 | 6 | | .13 |
| | Crucifixion | 8 | 0 | 3 | 0 | 3 | | .38 |
| 14 | New Testament | 47 | 0 | 6 | 1 | 7 | | .13 |
| | Crucifixion | 8 | 0 | 2 | 0 | 2 | | .25 |
| Total | New Testament | 47 | 5 | 86 | 66 | 157 | | .52 |
| | Crucifixion | 8[c] | 3 | 28 | 15 | 46 | | .54 |

a.  "Total No. of Units" column indicates how many lessons and articles
in this sample are New Testament or Crucifixion-Mention.  Most but not
all Crucifixion units are also New Testament.

b.  "Total Analytical Units" column shows the number of New Testament
or Crucifixion units relevant to each Analytical Category.

c.  One Crucifixion-Mention unit is irrelevant to the Jewish Group Category and, because not scored directionally, is not included in this table.

Table 22

### Comparison of the Neo-orthodox New Testament and Crucifixion Analytical Profiles for the Jewish Intergroup Area

| Analytical Category | Type of Unit | Total No. of Units[a] | Directional Score − | + | ± | Total Analytical Units[b] | Imbalance − | + |
|---|---|---|---|---|---|---|---|---|
| 1 | New Testament | 285 | 1 | 11 | 1 | 13 | | .03 |
| | Crucifixion | 34 | 0 | 2 | 0 | 2 | | .06 |
| 2 | New Testament | 285 | 0 | 3 | 0 | 3 | | .01 |
| | Crucifixion | 34 | 0 | 0 | 0 | 0 | .00 | .00 |
| 3 | New Testament | 285 | 1 | 9 | 0 | 10 | | .03 |
| | Crucifixion | 34 | 0 | 1 | 0 | 1 | | .03 |
| 4 | New Testament | 285 | 0 | 18 | 1 | 19 | | .06 |
| | Crucifixion | 34 | 0 | 6 | 0 | 6 | | .18 |
| 5 | New Testament | 285 | 9 | 109 | 12 | 130 | | .33 |
| | Crucifixion | 34 | 1 | 14 | 2 | 17 | | .36 |
| 6 | New Testament | 285 | 22 | 49 | 100 | 171 | | .08 |
| | Crucifixion | 34 | 1 | 3 | 13 | 17 | | .06 |
| 7 | New Testament | 285 | 11 | 16 | 33 | 60 | | .01 |
| | Crucifixion | 34 | 1 | 0 | 5 | 6 | .03 | |
| 8 | New Testament | 285 | 0 | 1 | 0 | 1 | | .00 |
| | Crucifixion | 34 | 0 | 1 | 0 | 1 | | .03 |
| 9 | New Testament | 285 | 14 | 30 | 26 | 70 | | .05 |
| | Crucifixion | 34 | 3 | 4 | 1 | 8 | | .02 |
| 10 | New Testament | 285 | 7 | 85 | 69 | 161 | | .26 |
| | Crucifixion | 34 | 0 | 12 | 7 | 19 | | .20 |
| 11 | New Testament | 285 | 37 | 10 | 84 | 131 | .09 | |
| | Crucifixion | 34 | 6 | 2 | 26 | 34 | .11 | |
| 12 | New Testament | 285 | 0 | 1 | 0 | 1 | | .00 |
| | Crucifixion | 34 | 0 | 0 | 0 | 0 | .00 | .00 |
| 13 | New Testament | 285 | 0 | 4 | 0 | 4 | | .01 |
| | Crucifixion | 34 | 0 | 0 | 0 | 0 | .00 | .00 |
| 14 | New Testament | 285 | 5 | 43 | 17 | 65 | | .12 |
| | Crucifixion | 34 | 0 | 6 | 3 | 9 | | .18 |
| Total | New Testament | 285 | 107 | 389 | 343 | 839 | | .34 |
| | Crucifixion | 34[c] | 12 | 51 | 57 | 120 | | .33 |

a.  "Total No. of Units" column indicates how many lessons and articles in this sample are New Testament and Crucifixion-Mention.  Not all units mentioning the Crucifixion are New Testament.

b.  This column shows the number of New Testament or Crucifixion units relevant to each Analytical Category.

c.  Eight Crucifixion-Mention units are irrelevant to the Jewish Group Category and, because not scored directionally, are not included in this table.

## Table 23

### Comparison of the Fundamentalist New Testament and Crucifixion Analytical Profiles for the Jewish Intergroup Area

| Analytical Category | Type of Unit | Total No. of Units[a] | Directional Score − | + | ± | Total Analytical Units[b] | Imbalance − | + |
|---|---|---|---|---|---|---|---|---|
| 1 | New Testament | 188 | 3 | 15 | 4 | 22 | | .06 |
|   | Crucifixion | 36 | 1 | 3 | 2 | 6 | | .05 |
| 2 | New Testament | 188 | 0 | 0 | 0 | 0 | .00 | .00 |
|   | Crucifixion | 36 | 0 | 0 | 0 | 0 | .00 | .00 |
| 3 | New Testament | 188 | 2 | 8 | 2 | 12 | | .03 |
|   | Crucifixion | 36 | 2 | 3 | 1 | 6 | | .02 |
| 4 | New Testament | 188 | 0 | 14 | 9 | 23 | | .07 |
|   | Crucifixion | 36 | 1 | 3 | 1 | 5 | | .02 |
| 5 | New Testament | 188 | 31 | 22 | 13 | 66 | .03 | |
|   | Crucifixion | 36 | 9 | 7 | 6 | 22 | .04 | |
| 6 | New Testament | 188 | 42 | 22 | 72 | 136 | .09 | |
|   | Crucifixion | 36 | 18 | 0 | 17 | 35 | .50 | |
| 7 | New Testament | 188 | 29 | 21 | 21 | 71 | .03 | |
|   | Crucifixion | 36 | 8 | 2 | 11 | 21 | .15 | |
| 8 | New Testament | 188 | 1 | 3 | 0 | 4 | | .01 |
|   | Crucifixion | 36 | 1 | 1 | 0 | 2 | .00 | .00 |
| 9 | New Testament | 188 | 24 | 19 | 25 | 68 | .02 | |
|   | Crucifixion | 36 | 8 | 3 | 7 | 18 | .12 | |
| 10 | New Testament | 188 | 12 | 53 | 53 | 118 | | .20 |
|   | Crucifixion | 36 | 4 | 7 | 11 | 22 | | .07 |
| 11 | New Testament | 188 | 49 | 2 | 40 | 91 | .24 | |
|   | Crucifixion | 36 | 18 | 0 | 18 | 36 | .50 | |
| 12 | New Testament | 188 | 4 | 1 | 0 | 5 | .01 | |
|   | Crucifixion | 36 | 4 | 0 | 0 | 4 | .11 | |
| 13 | New Testament | 188 | 0 | 2 | 0 | 2 | | .01 |
|   | Crucifixion | 36 | 0 | 0 | 0 | 0 | .00 | .00 |
| 14 | New Testament | 188 | 10 | 32 | 26 | 68 | | .10 |
|   | Crucifixion | 36 | 6 | 2 | 11 | 19 | .10 | |
| Total | New Testament | 188 | 207 | 214 | 265 | 686 | | .01 |
|   | Crucifixion | 36 | 80 | 31 | 85 | 196 | .25 | |

a. This column indicates how many lessons and articles in this sample are New Testament or Crucifixion-Mention.

b. This column shows the number of New Testament or Crucifixion units relevant to each Analytical Category.

375

Table 24

Comparison of the Conservative New Testament and
Crucifixion Analytical Profiles for the Jewish Intergroup Area

| Analytical Category | Type of Unit | Total No. of Units[a] | Directional Score − | + | ± | Total Analytical Units[b] | Imbalance − | + |
|---|---|---|---|---|---|---|---|---|
| 1 | New Testament | 129 | 6 | 0 | 0 | 6 | .05 | |
| | Crucifixion | 30 | 4 | 0 | 0 | 4 | .13 | |
| 2 | New Testament | 129 | 0 | 0 | 0 | 0 | .00 | .00 |
| | Crucifixion | 30 | 0 | 0 | 0 | 0 | .00 | .00 |
| 3 | New Testament | 129 | 7 | 1 | 0 | 8 | .04 | |
| | Crucifixion | 30 | 3 | 0 | 0 | 3 | .10 | |
| 4 | New Testament | 129 | 6 | 5 | 1 | 12 | .00 | |
| | Crucifixion | 30 | 3 | 2 | 0 | 5 | .02 | |
| 5 | New Testament | 129 | 37 | 4 | 2 | 43 | .23 | |
| | Crucifixion | 30 | 12 | 0 | 1 | 13 | .40 | |
| 6 | New Testament | 129 | 54 | 8 | 30 | 92 | .33 | |
| | Crucifixion | 30 | 16 | 1 | 6 | 23 | .48 | |
| 7 | New Testament | 129 | 31 | 7 | 9 | 47 | .16 | |
| | Crucifixion | 30 | 11 | 2 | 3 | 16 | .26 | |
| 8 | New Testament | 129 | 1 | 0 | 1 | 2 | .01 | |
| | Crucifixion | 30 | 1 | 0 | 0 | 1 | .03 | |
| 9 | New Testament | 129 | 30 | 8 | 7 | 45 | .14 | |
| | Crucifixion | 30 | 9 | 1 | 2 | 12 | .24 | |
| 10 | New Testament | 129 | 19 | 20 | 20 | 59 | | .01 |
| | Crucifixion | 30 | 5 | 6 | 5 | 16 | | .02 |
| 11 | New Testament | 129 | 49 | 2 | 12 | 63 | .32 | |
| | Crucifixion | 30 | 25 | 4 | 2 | 31 | .61 | |
| 12 | New Testament | 129 | 1 | 0 | 0 | 1 | .01 | |
| | Crucifixion | 30 | 0 | 0 | 0 | 0 | .00 | .00 |
| 13 | New Testament | 129 | 1 | 0 | 0 | 1 | .01 | |
| | Crucifixion | 30 | 0 | 0 | 0 | 0 | .00 | .00 |
| 14 | New Testament | 129 | 26 | 8 | 9 | 43 | .11 | |
| | Crucifixion | 30 | 11 | 4 | 1 | 16 | .18 | |
| Total | New Testament | 129 | 268 | 63 | 91 | 422 | .49 | |
| | Crucifixion | 30 | 100 | 20 | 20 | 140 | .57 | |

a.  This column indicates how many lessons and articles in this sample
are New Testament or Crucifixion-Mention.

b.  This column shows the number of New Testament or Crucifixion units
relevant to each Analytical Category.

Table 25

Neo-orthodox Imbalance Scores for the Jewish Period Category

| Analytical Category | Old Test. − | Old Test. + | New Test. − | New Test. + | East. Church Pre-20th C. − | East. Church Pre-20th C. + | Contemporary − | Contemporary + |
|---|---|---|---|---|---|---|---|---|
| 1 | | 3.8 | | 3.2 | | 26.9 | | 31.7 |
| 2 | | 1.8 | | 1.1 | — | — | | 4.9 |
| 3 | | 1.5 | | 2.5 | | 7.7 | | 7.3 |
| 4 | | 3.7 | | 6.3 | | 7.7 | | 9.8 |
| 5 | | 62.6 | | 32.7 | 3.8 | | | 19.5 |
| 6 | | 18.1 | | 8.3 | | 3.8 | | 12.2 |
| 7 | | 11.3 | | 1.4 | | 7.7 | — | — |
| 8 | — | — | | 0.4 | — | — | — | — |
| 9 | | 20.4 | | 4.5 | 0.0 | 0.0 | | 22.0 |
| 10 | | 31.9 | | 26.2 | | 15.7 | | 48.8 |
| 11 | 1.1 | | 8.8 | | 0.0 | 0.0 | 2.4 | |
| 12 | — | — | | 0.4 | — | — | | 2.4 |
| 13 | | 0.4 | | 1.4 | — | — | | 12.2 |
| 14 | | 21.0 | | 12.3 | — | — | | 7.3 |
| Total $C_I$ | | 55.8 | | 33.6 | | 54.6 | | 87.8 |
| Total units | | 163[a] | | 285[b] | | 26 | | 41 |

---

a. These units include 40 Old Testament-New Testament combinations.

b. Ibid.

Table 26

Liberal Imbalance Scores for the Jewish Period Category

| Analytical Category | Old Test. | | New Test. | | East. Church Pre-20th C. | | Contemporary | |
|---|---|---|---|---|---|---|---|---|
| | − | + | − | + | − | + | − | + |
| 1 | | 7.8 | | 4.3 | | 66.2 | | 24.1 |
| 2 | — | — | — | — | — | — | | 3.4 |
| 3 | — | — | | 2.2 | — | — | | 2.6 |
| 4 | | 1.3 | — | — | — | — | | 5.2 |
| 5 | | 37.7 | | 69.5 | | 66.2 | | 20.0 |
| 6 | | 8.8 | | 12.3 | | 33.3 | 3.1 | |
| 7 | | 1.3 | 0.0 | 0.0 | — | — | | 2.8 |
| 8 | — | — | — | — | — | — | | 3.4 |
| 9 | | 17.9 | | 22.2 | | 33.3 | | 10.4 |
| 10 | | 16.9 | | 32.9 | | 33.3 | | 27.5 |
| 11 | 0.0 | 0.0 | 0.0 | 0.0 | — | — | | 1.8 |
| 12 | — | — | | 2.2 | — | — | | 6.9 |
| 13 | — | — | | 2.2 | — | — | | 15.5 |
| 14 | | 16.8 | | 13.0 | | 33.3 | | 13.8 |
| Total $C_I$ | | 44.2 | | 51.6 | | 72.7 | | 49.7 |
| Total units | 78[a] | | 47[b] | | 3 | | 58 | |

a.  These units include 1 Old Testament-New Testament combination.

b.  Ibid.

Table 27

Fundamentalist Imbalance Scores for the Jewish Period Category

| Analytical Category | Period Category | | | | | | | |
|---|---|---|---|---|---|---|---|---|
| | Old Test. | | New Test. | | East. Church Pre-20th C. | | Contemporary | |
| | − | + | − | + | − | + | − | + |
| 1 | | 3.3 | | 5.5 | — | — | | 60.0 |
| 2 | | 0.8 | — | — | — | — | | 20.0 |
| 3 | 0.5 | | | 2.7 | — | — | | 20.0 |
| 4 | | 4.9 | | 7.4 | — | — | | 40.0 |
| 5 | | 8.5 | 3.2 | | — | — | | 20.0 |
| 6 | | 1.9 | 8.8 | | — | — | 0.0 | 0.0 |
| 7 | | 3.8 | 3.0 | | — | — | — | — |
| 8 | 1.5 | | | 0.8 | — | — | | 20.0 |
| 9 | | 14.6 | 1.9 | | — | — | — | — |
| 10 | | 5.9 | | 19.6 | — | — | 40.0 | |
| 11 | 6.2 | | 24.4 | | — | — | — | — |
| 12 | 0.8 | | 1.3 | | — | — | — | — |
| 13 | — | — | | 1.1 | — | — | — | — |
| 14 | | 28.8 | | 10.0 | — | — | — | — |
| Total $C_I$ | | 23.3 | | 1.0 | — | — | | 58.3 |
| Total units | 129[a] | | 188[b] | | — | | 5 | |

a.  These units include 36 Old Testament-New Testament combinations.

b.  Ibid.

Table 28

Conservative Imbalance Scores for the Jewish Period Category

| Analytical Category | Old Test. − | Old Test. + | New Test. − | New Test. + | East. Church Pre-20th C. − | East. Church Pre-20th C. + | Contemporary − | Contemporary + |
|---|---|---|---|---|---|---|---|---|
| 1 | 0.0 | 0.0 | 4.7 | | — | — | — | — |
| 2 | — | — | — | — | — | — | — | — |
| 3 | 0.0 | 0.0 | 4.0 | | — | — | — | — |
| 4 | 0.5 | | 0.4 | | — | — | — | — |
| 5 | | 6.2 | 23.1 | | — | — | — | — |
| 6 | | 1.8 | 32.5 | | — | — | 30.0 | |
| 7 | | 5.4 | 15.8 | | — | — | 40.0 | |
| 8 | 1.1 | | 0.8 | | — | — | 10.0 | |
| 9 | | 15.4 | 14.1 | | — | — | 0.0 | 0.0 |
| 10 | | 26.9 | | 0.5 | — | — | 20.0 | |
| 11 | 3.0 | | 31.8 | | — | — | 30.0 | |
| 12 | 0.8 | | 0.8 | | — | — | — | — |
| 13 | — | — | 0.8 | | — | — | — | — |
| 14 | | 9.4 | 11.3 | | — | — | | 20.0 |
| Total $C_I$ | | 23.8 | 48.6 | | — | — | 61.1 | |
| Total units | 131 | | 129 | | — | | 10 | |

Table 29

Neo-orthodox Imbalance Scores for the Catholic Period Category

| Analytical Category | Biblical | | East. Church Middle Ages | | Reformation | | Pre-20th C. | | Contemporary | |
|---|---|---|---|---|---|---|---|---|---|---|
| | − | + | − | + | − | + | − | + | − | + |
| 1 | | 9.5 | — | — | | 9.5 | | 27.3 | | 4.5 |
| 2 | — | — | — | — | — | — | — | — | — | — |
| 3 | | 1.6 | 0.0 | 0.0 | | 6.9 | | 9.1 | | 1.5 |
| 4 | — | — | | 4.9 | | 2.4 | | 9.1 | | 4.5 |
| 5 | | 9.9 | | 68.8 | | 16.3 | | 27.3 | | 16.4 |
| 6 | | 12.4 | | 18.5 | 12.4 | | 0.0 | 0.0 | | 3.6 |
| 7 | 9.4 | | | 5.4 | 16.2 | | 9.1 | | 1.4 | |
| 8 | — | | — | — | — | — | — | — | — | — |
| 9 | 1.1 | | | 14.0 | 9.9 | | | 18.2 | | 6.8 |
| 10 | | 14.4 | | 34.1 | 6.0 | | | 27.3 | | 12.9 |
| 11 | 0.0 | 0.0 | 2.4 | | 28.6 | | | 18.2 | 2.3 | |
| 12 | 3.2 | | 2.4 | | 0.0 | 0.0 | — | — | 2.8 | |
| 13 | | 1.2 | | 4.9 | | 4.8 | | 9.1 | | 9.1 |
| 14 | | 1.6 | | 2.4 | 3.7 | | | 18.2 | 0.0 | 0.0 |
| Total $C_I$ | | 32.1 | | 45.1 | 9.5 | | | 58.6 | | 30.8 |
| Total units | 63 | | 41 | | 42 | | 11 | | 44 | |

Table 30

Liberal Imbalance Scores for the Catholic Period Category

| | Period Category | | | | | | | | | |
|---|---|---|---|---|---|---|---|---|---|---|
| Analytical Category | Biblical − | Biblical + | East. Church Middle Ages − | East. Church Middle Ages + | Reformation − | Reformation + | Pre-20th C. − | Pre-20th C. + | Contemporary − | Contemporary + |
| 1 | — | — | — | — | — | — | — | — | | 3.4 |
| 2 | — | — | — | — | — | — | — | — | — | — |
| 3 | — | — | — | — | 0.0 | 0.0 | — | — | — | — |
| 4 | — | — | — | — | | 20.0 | — | — | | 6.9 |
| 5 | | 28.6 | — | — | | 40.0 | 33.3 | | | 32.0 |
| 6 | 0.0 | 0.0 | — | — | 20.0 | | 33.3 | | | 22.3 |
| 7 | — | — | — | — | 0.0 | 0.0 | — | — | 0.0 | 0.0 |
| 8 | — | — | — | — | — | — | — | — | — | — |
| 9 | 0.0 | 0.0 | — | — | 0.0 | 0.0 | | 33.3 | | 4.8 |
| 10 | | 14.3 | — | — | 0.0 | 0.0 | 0.0 | 0.0 | | 9.0 |
| 11 | — | — | — | — | 0.0 | 0.0 | — | — | — | — |
| 12 | | 14.3 | — | — | — | — | — | — | | 6.9 |
| 13 | | 14.3 | — | — | — | — | — | — | | 20.7 |
| 14 | — | — | — | — | | 20.0 | — | — | | 10.3 |
| Total $C_I$ | | 50.0 | — | — | | 9.4 | 20.0 | | | 58.1 |
| Total units | 7 | | — | | 5 | | 3 | | 29 | |

Table 31

Fundamentalist Imbalance Scores for the Catholic Period Category

| Analytical Category | Biblical | | East. Church Middle Ages | | Reformation | | Pre-20th C. | | Contemporary | |
|---|---|---|---|---|---|---|---|---|---|---|
| | − | + | − | + | − | + | − | + | − | + |
| 1 | — | — | — | — | — | — | — | — | | 33.3 |
| 2 | — | — | — | — | — | — | — | — | — | — |
| 3 | | 3.5 | — | — | — | — | — | — | | 33.3 |
| 4 | | 3.5 | — | — | — | — | — | — | | 33.3 |
| 5 | 11.1 | | — | — | — | — | — | — | 33.3 | |
| 6 | 32.8 | | — | — | — | — | — | — | 66.7 | |
| 7 | 28.4 | | — | — | — | — | — | — | — | — |
| 8 | — | — | — | — | — | — | — | — | — | — |
| 9 | 2.5 | | — | — | — | — | — | — | 66.7 | |
| 10 | 2.5 | | — | — | — | — | — | — | 33.3 | |
| 11 | 10.5 | | — | — | — | — | — | — | — | — |
| 12 | 21.1 | | — | — | — | — | — | — | 33.3 | |
| 13 | 1.8 | | — | — | — | — | — | — | — | — |
| 14 | | 2.3 | — | — | — | — | — | — | — | — |
| Total $C_I$ | 54.0 | | — | — | — | — | — | — | 40.0 | |
| Total units | 57 | | — | | — | | — | | 3 | |

Table 32

Conservative Imbalance Scores for the Catholic Period Category

| | Period Category | | | | | | | | | |
|---|---|---|---|---|---|---|---|---|---|---|
| Analytical Category | Biblical − | Biblical + | East. Church Middle Ages − | East. Church Middle Ages + | Reformation − | Reformation + | Pre-20th C. − | Pre-20th C. + | Contemporary − | Contemporary + |
| 1 | — | — | — | — | — | — | — | — | — | — |
| 2 | — | — | — | — | — | | — | — | — | — |
| 3 | | 2.2 | — | — | | 16.7 | — | — | — | — |
| 4 | | 4.3 | — | — | — | — | — | — | 14.3 | |
| 5 | 15.2 | | — | — | | 11.1 | — | — | — | — |
| 6 | 39.1 | | — | — | 16.7 | | — | — | 0.0 | 0.0 |
| 7 | 58.7 | | — | — | 83.3 | | — | — | 85.7 | |
| 8 | — | — | — | — | — | — | — | — | — | — |
| 9 | 15.2 | | — | — | 33.3 | | — | — | 42.8 | |
| 10 | 1.4 | | — | — | 0.0 | 0.0 | — | — | | 14.3 |
| 11 | 15.2 | | — | — | 13.4 | | — | — | — | — |
| 12 | 6.5 | | — | — | — | — | — | — | — | — |
| 13 | — | — | — | — | — | — | — | — | — | — |
| 14 | 2.2 | | — | — | 83.3 | | — | — | 14.3 | |
| Total $C_I$ | 86.1 | | — | — | 33.3 | | — | — | 55.6 | |
| Total units | 46 | | — | | 6 | | — | | 7 | |

# Appendix VIII. Figures

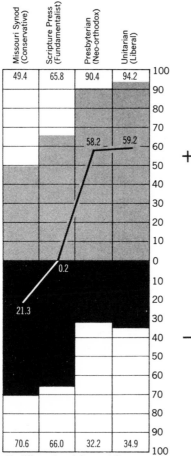

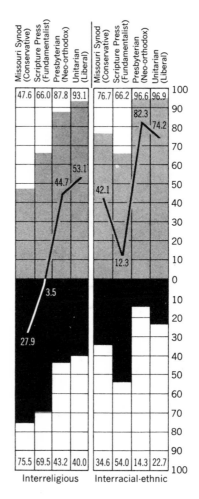

Fig. 1. General Distribution and Imbalance Scores for Four Publishers, Showing Their Respective Intergroup Orientations. (All the group category general scores are grouped indiscriminately in this graph.)

Fig. 2. Breakdown of General Distribution and Imbalance Scores into (1) Interreligious and (2) Interracial-Ethnic Areas. Interreligious scores: Non-Christian, Jewish, Catholic, and Other Christian group categories. Interracial-ethnic scores: Negro, Other Ethnic, and International group categories.

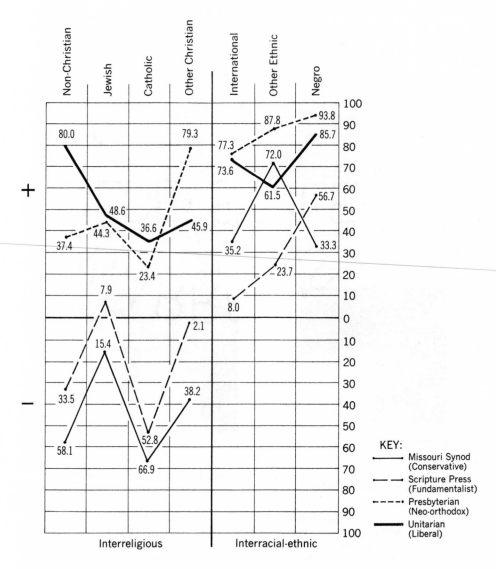

Fig. 3. Comparison of Imbalances in the Interreligious and Interracial-Ethnic Areas, Based on General Scores for Seven Intergroup Areas. (The general group category is omitted, inasmuch as it embraces uneven mixtures of both religious and racial references.) This graph is abstracted from Figs. 34 and 35, which show the negative and positive distributions.

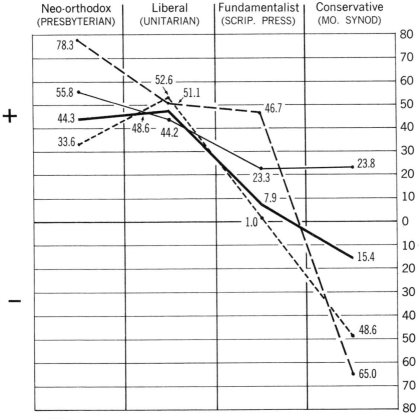

KEY:

●————● Old Testament

●------● New Testament

●— —● Non-Biblical

━━━━ Total

Fig. 4.  Orientation toward Jews and Judaism in Biblical and Nonbiblical Units.  (Based on imbalance scores only.)

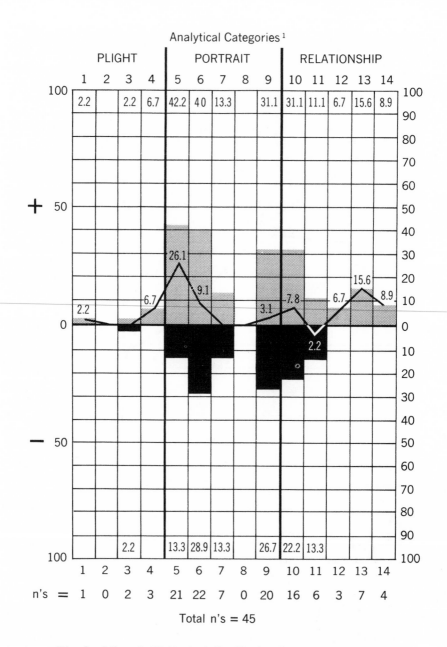

Fig. 5. Liberal (Unitarian) Profile for Catholic Group, Showing Relative Distributions and Imbalances. Over-all orientation is +36.6. For definition of these categories see Appendix
II. For explanation of the scores, consult Appendixes I and III.

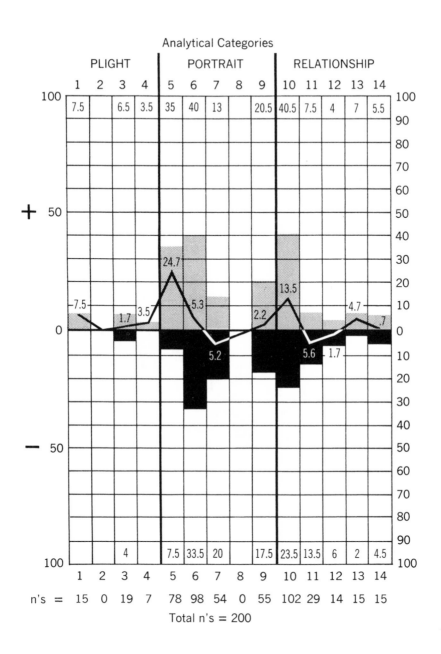

Analytical Categories

| | PLIGHT | | | | PORTRAIT | | | | | RELATIONSHIP | | | | |
|---|---|---|---|---|---|---|---|---|---|---|---|---|---|---|
| | 1 | 2 | 3 | 4 | 5 | 6 | 7 | 8 | 9 | 10 | 11 | 12 | 13 | 14 |
| (top) | 7.5 | | 6.5 | 3.5 | 35 | 40 | 13 | | 20.5 | 40.5 | 7.5 | 4 | 7 | 5.5 |
| (bottom) | | | 4 | | 7.5 | 33.5 | 20 | | 17.5 | 23.5 | 13.5 | 6 | 2 | 4.5 |

| | 1 | 2 | 3 | 4 | 5 | 6 | 7 | 8 | 9 | 10 | 11 | 12 | 13 | 14 |
|---|---|---|---|---|---|---|---|---|---|---|---|---|---|---|
| n's = | 15 | 0 | 19 | 7 | 78 | 98 | 54 | 0 | 55 | 102 | 29 | 14 | 15 | 15 |

Total n's = 200

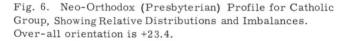

Fig. 6.  Neo-Orthodox (Presbyterian) Profile for Catholic
Group, Showing Relative Distributions and Imbalances.
Over-all orientation is +23.4.

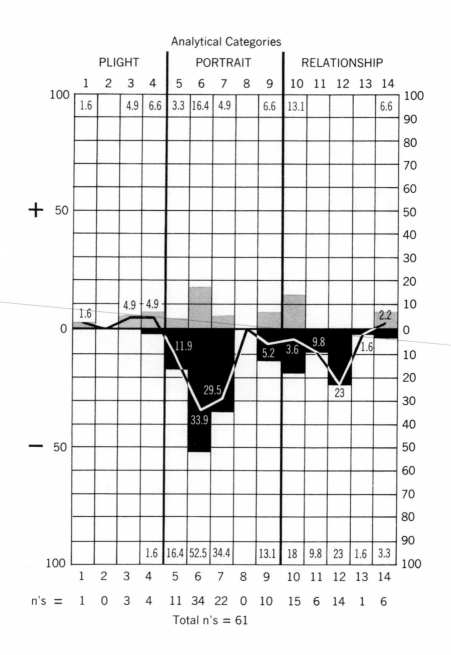

Fig. 7. Fundamentalist (Scripture Press) Profile for Catholic Group, Showing Relative Distributions and Imbalances. Over-all orientation is −52.8.

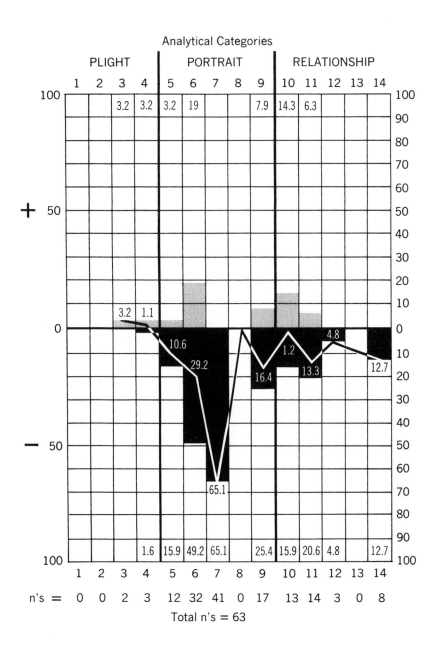

Fig. 8. Conservative (Lutheran—Missouri Synod) Profile for Catholic Group, Showing Relative Distributions and Imbalances. Over-all orientation is −66.9.

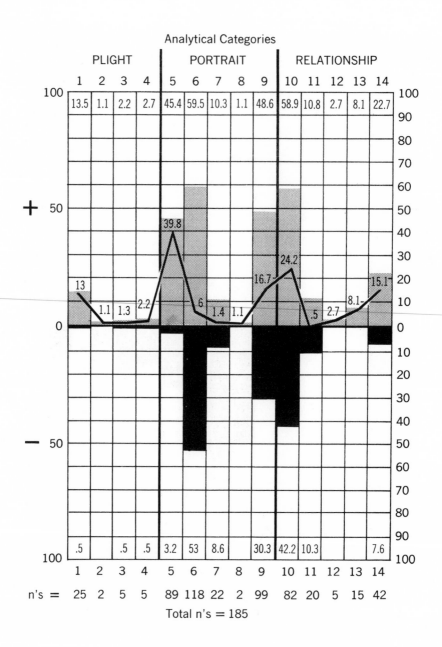

Fig. 9. Liberal (Unitarian) Profile for Jewish Group, Showing
Relative Distributions and Imbalances. Over-all orientation is
+48.6.

392

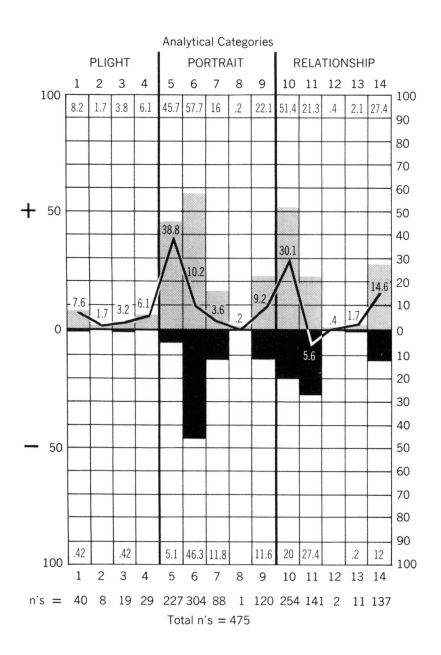

Fig. 10. Neo-Orthodox (Presbyterian) Profile for Jewish
Group, Showing Relative Distributions and Imbalances. Over-
all orientation is +44.3.

393

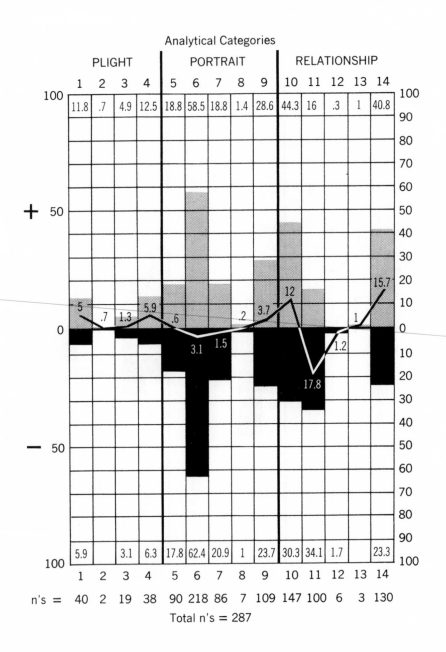

Analytical Categories

| | PLIGHT | | | | PORTRAIT | | | | | RELATIONSHIP | | | | |
|---|---|---|---|---|---|---|---|---|---|---|---|---|---|---|
| | 1 | 2 | 3 | 4 | 5 | 6 | 7 | 8 | 9 | 10 | 11 | 12 | 13 | 14 |
| 100 | 11.8 | .7 | 4.9 | 12.5 | 18.8 | 58.5 | 18.8 | 1.4 | 28.6 | 44.3 | 16 | .3 | 1 | 40.8 |

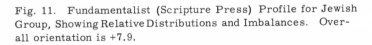

| | 1 | 2 | 3 | 4 | 5 | 6 | 7 | 8 | 9 | 10 | 11 | 12 | 13 | 14 |
|---|---|---|---|---|---|---|---|---|---|---|---|---|---|---|
| 100 | 5.9 | | 3.1 | 6.3 | 17.8 | 62.4 | 20.9 | 1 | 23.7 | 30.3 | 34.1 | 1.7 | | 23.3 |

n's =  40  2  19  38  90  218  86  7  109  147  100  6  3  130

Total n's = 287

Fig. 11. Fundamentalist (Scripture Press) Profile for Jewish Group, Showing Relative Distributions and Imbalances. Overall orientation is +7.9.

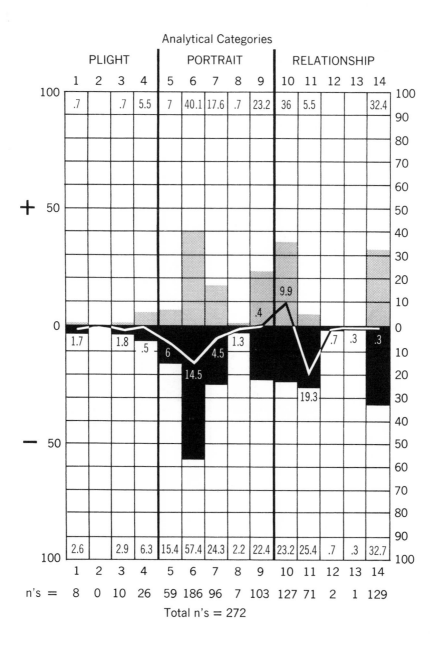

Fig. 12. Conservative (Lutheran—Missouri Synod) Profile for Jewish Group, Showing Relative Distributions and Imbalances. Over-all orientation is −15.4.

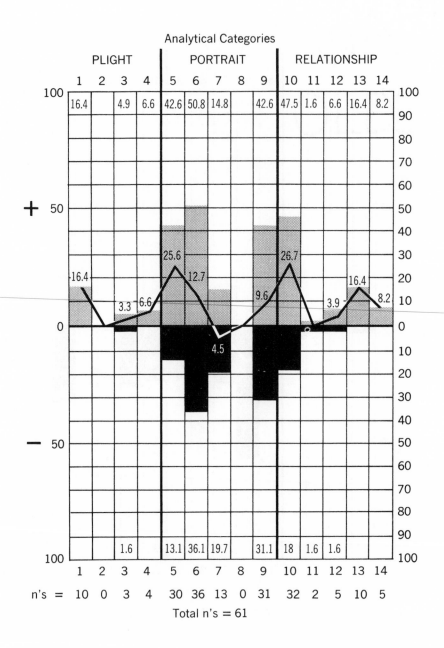

Fig. 13. Liberal (Unitarian) Profile for Other-Christian
Groups, Showing Relative Distributions and Imbalances. Over-
all orientation is +45.9.

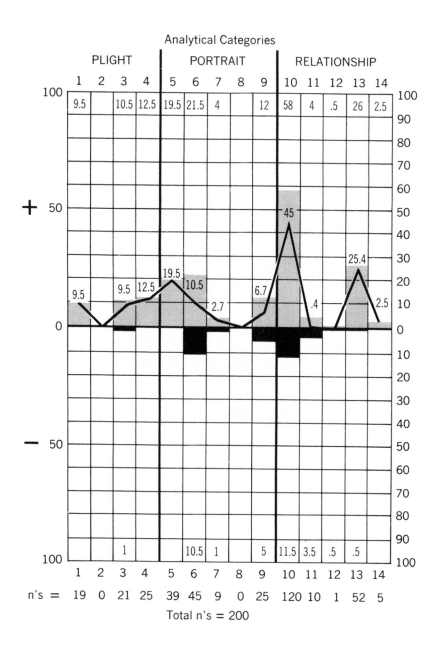

Fig. 14. Neo-Orthodox (Presbyterian) Profile for Other-Christian Groups, Showing Relative Distributions and Imbalances. Over-all orientation is +79.3.

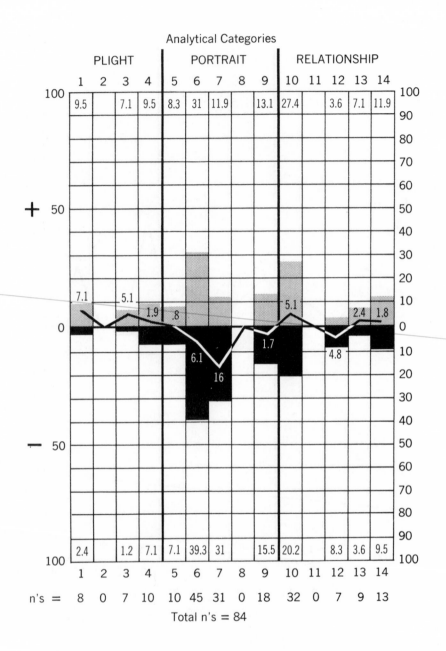

Fig. 15. Fundamentalist (Scripture Press) Profile for Other-Christian Groups, Showing Relative Distributions and Imbalances. Over-all orientation is −2.1.

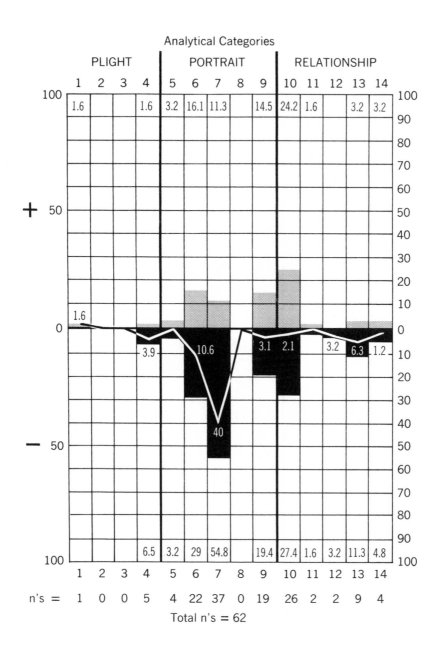

Analytical Categories

Fig. 16. Conservative (Lutheran—Missouri Synod) Profile for Other-Christian Groups, Showing Relative Distributions and Imbalances. Over-all orientation is −38.2.

399

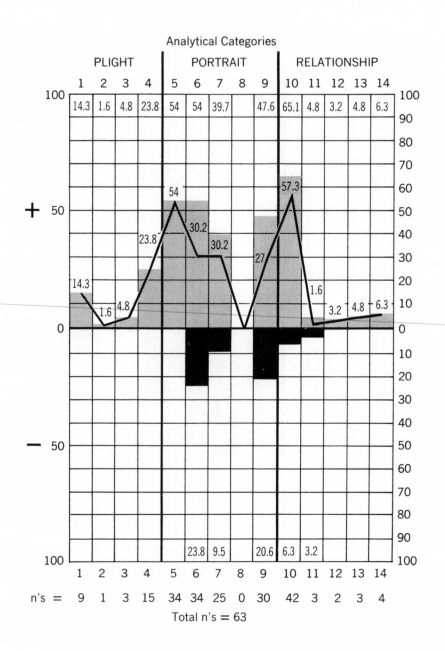

Fig. 17. Liberal (Unitarian) Profile for Non-Christian
Groups, Showing Relative Distributions and Imbalances.
Over-all orientation is +80.

400

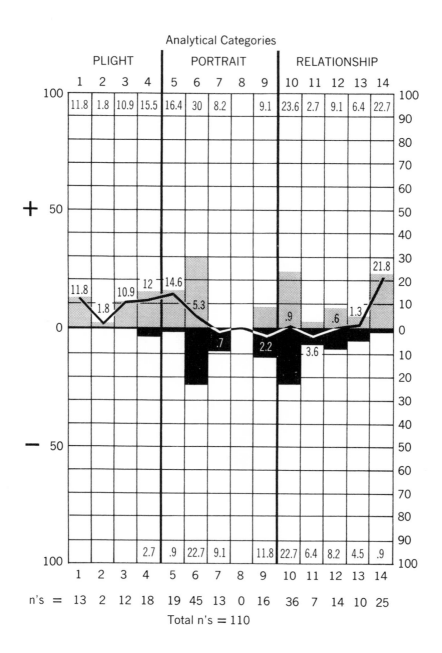

Analytical Categories

| | PLIGHT | | | | PORTRAIT | | | | | RELATIONSHIP | | | | |
|---|---|---|---|---|---|---|---|---|---|---|---|---|---|---|
| | 1 | 2 | 3 | 4 | 5 | 6 | 7 | 8 | 9 | 10 | 11 | 12 | 13 | 14 |

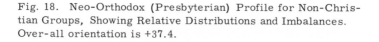

n's =   13   2   12   18    19   45   13   0   16    36   7   14   10   25

Total n's = 110

Fig. 18. Neo-Orthodox (Presbyterian) Profile for Non-Christian Groups, Showing Relative Distributions and Imbalances. Over-all orientation is +37.4.

401

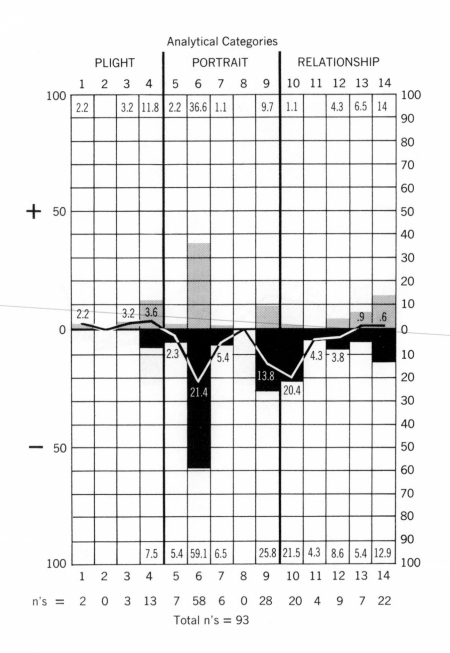

Fig. 19. Fundamentalist (Scripture Press) Profile for Non-Christian Groups, Showing Relative Distributions and Imbalances. Over-all orientation is −33.5.

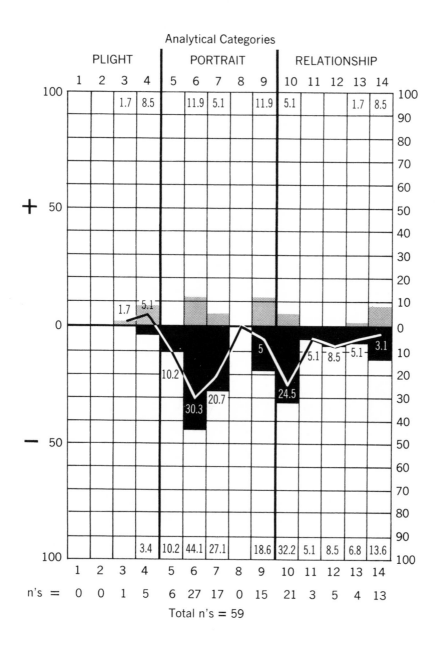

Fig. 20.  Conservative (Lutheran—Missouri Synod) Profile
for Non-Christian Groups, Showing Relative Distributions and
Imbalances.  Over-all orientation is −58.1.

403

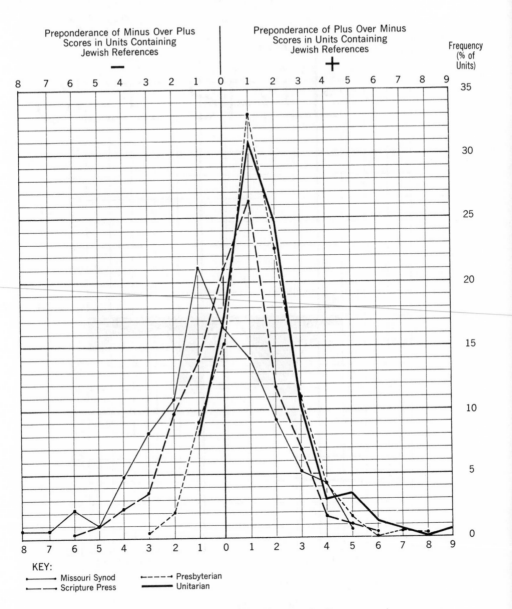

KEY:
•——• Missouri Synod          •——-—• Presbyterian
•——— Scripture Press         ▬▬▬ Unitarian

Fig. 21. Ambiguities and Anti-Ethnocentric Resources in Curriculum Writing, Showing Negative and Positive Ranges and Frequencies of Plus or Minus Overages of Scores per Lesson for Jewish Content Only. Each lesson was rated separately for its plus and minus scores. Overages were determined by subtracting the lesser figure from the greater (e.g. 3 plus scores from 6 minus scores per lesson equals −3).

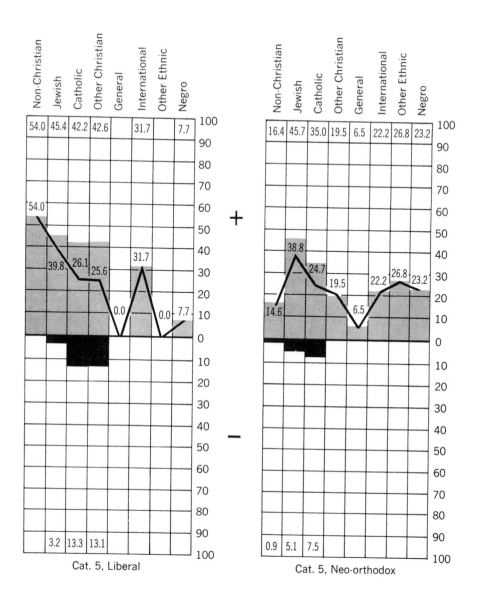

Fig. 22. Analytical Imbalances for Category 5, Showing Extent
of Distortions and Corrections for Eight Intergroup Areas
(Unitarian and Presbyterian). (For definition of this category
see Appendix II. In order to see this and Figs. 23 to 33 in their
proper contexts, consult the profiles for Figs. 5 to 20, above in
this Appendix.)

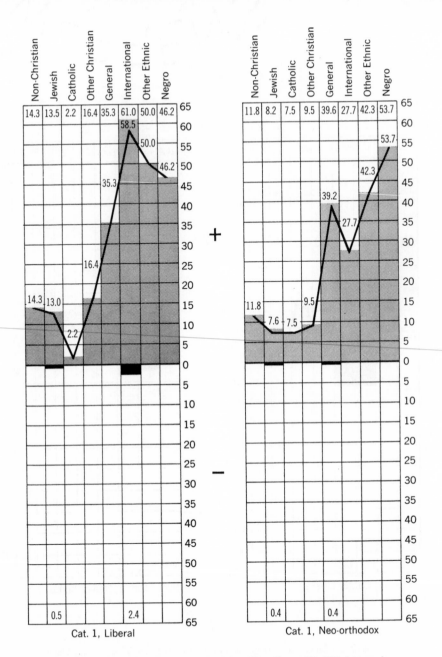

| Non-Christian | Jewish | Catholic | Other Christian | General | International | Other Ethnic | Negro |
|---|---|---|---|---|---|---|---|
| 14.3 | 13.5 | 2.2 | 16.4 | 35.3 | 61.0 | 50.0 | 46.2 |

Cat. 1, Liberal

| Non-Christian | Jewish | Catholic | Other Christian | General | International | Other Ethnic | Negro |
|---|---|---|---|---|---|---|---|
| 11.8 | 8.2 | 7.5 | 9.5 | 39.6 | 27.7 | 42.3 | 53.7 |

Cat. 1, Neo-orthodox

Fig. 23.  Identification and Nonidentification with Plights and
Rights of Outside Groups as Shown in the Analytical Distribu-
tions and Imbalances for Category 1 (Unitarian and Presby-
terian).  (For definition of this category see Appendix II.)
These graphs are abstracts from the profiles, including
Figs. 5–20.

406

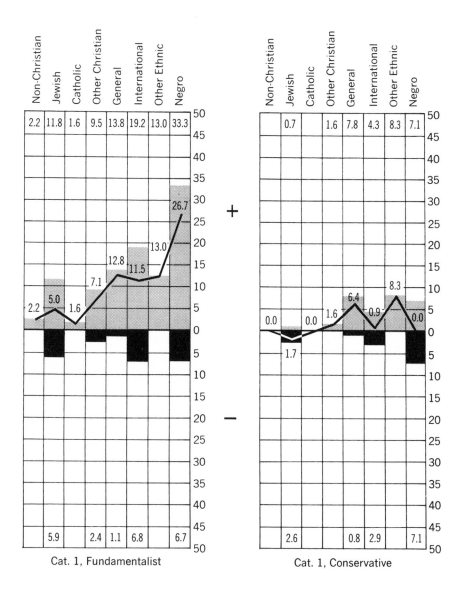

Fig. 24. Identification and Nonidentification with Plights and Rights of Outside Groups as Shown in the Analytical Distribution and Imbalances for Category 1 (Scripture Press and Missouri Synod). (For definition of this category see Appendix II.) These graphs are abstracts from the profiles, including Figs. 5–20.

407

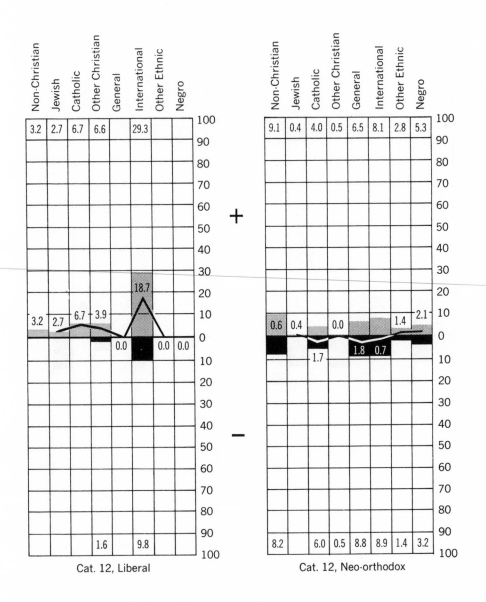

Fig. 25. The Contemporary Self-Image as Victim and Non-victim: Analytical Distributions and Imbalances for Category 12 (Unitarian and Presbyterian). (For definition of this category see Appendix II.)

408

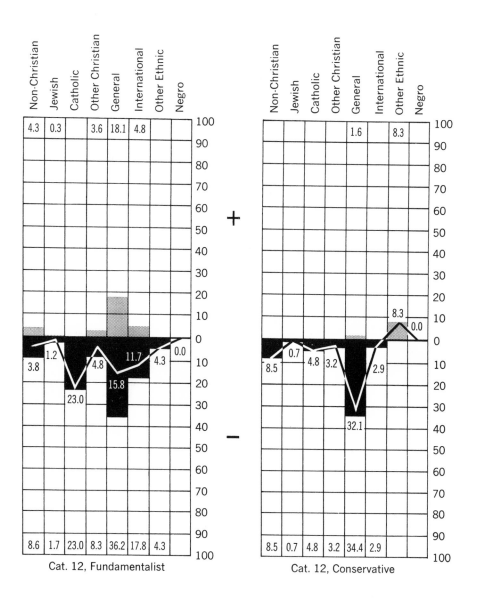

Fig. 26. The Contemporary Self-Image as Victim and Non-victim: Analytical Distributions and Imbalances for Category 12 (Scripture Press and Missouri Synod). (For definition of this category see Appendix II.)

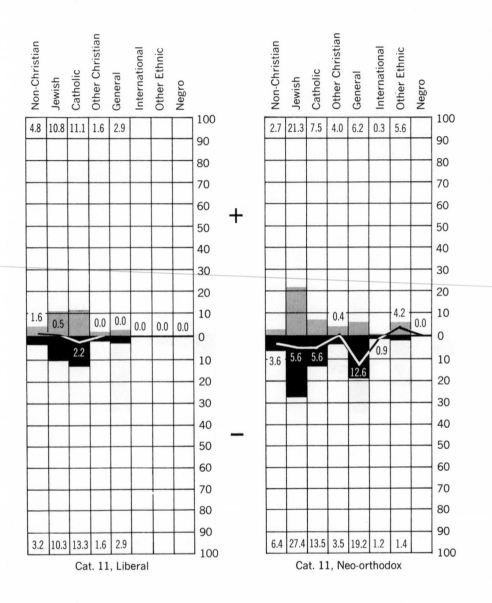

Fig. 27. The Past Other-Image as Oppressor, Represented by
the Analytical Distributions and Imbalances for Category 11
(Unitarian and Presbyterian). (For definition of this category
see Appendix II.)

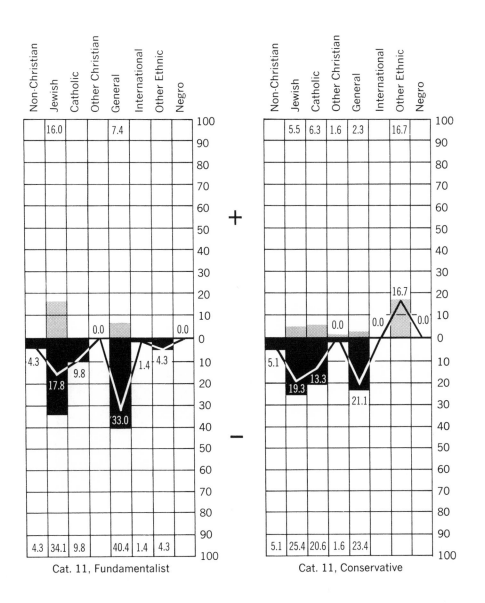

Fig. 28. The Past Other-Image as Oppressor, Represented by the Analytical Distributions and Imbalances for Category 11 (Scripture Press and Missouri Synod). (For definition of this category see Appendix II.)

411

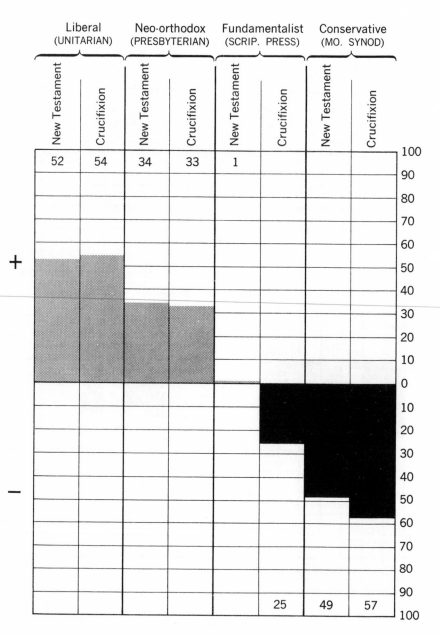

Fig. 29. New Testament Lessons Compared Directionally with
Lessons on the Crucifixion as to Jewish Content. Imbalance
scores for the Jewish group category were obtained for lessons
which mention or deal with the Crucifixion story and compared
with scores for the New Testament. (Note: Scores for New
Testament do not exclude Crucifixion units.)

412

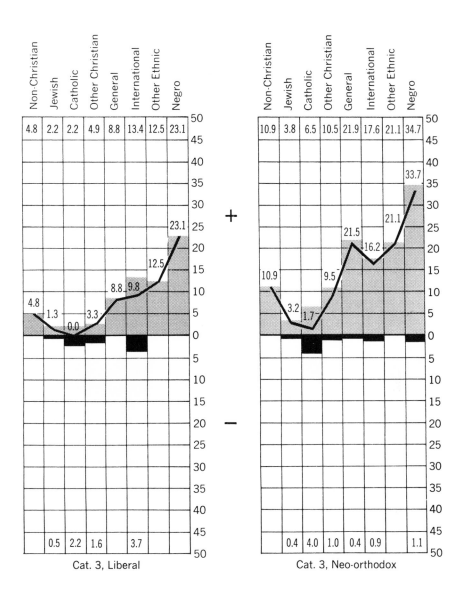

Fig. 30. Ability to Engage in Intergroup Self-Criticism, Shown by the Distributions and Imbalances for Category 3 (Unitarian and Presbyterian). (For definition of this category see Appendix II.)

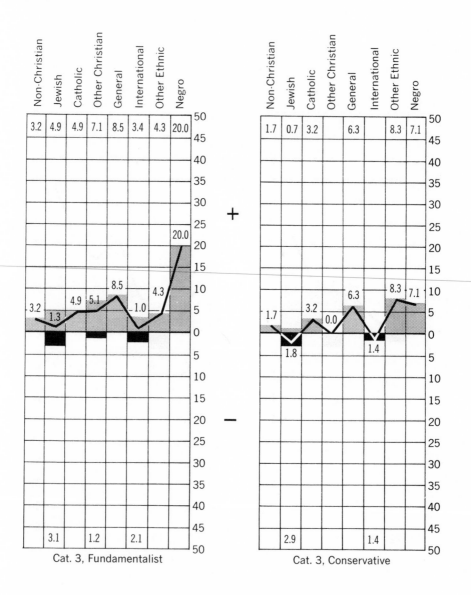

Fig. 31. Ability to Engage in Intergroup Self-Criticism, Shown
by the Distributions and Imbalances for Category 3 (Scripture
Press and Missouri Synod). (For definition of this category see
Appendix II.)

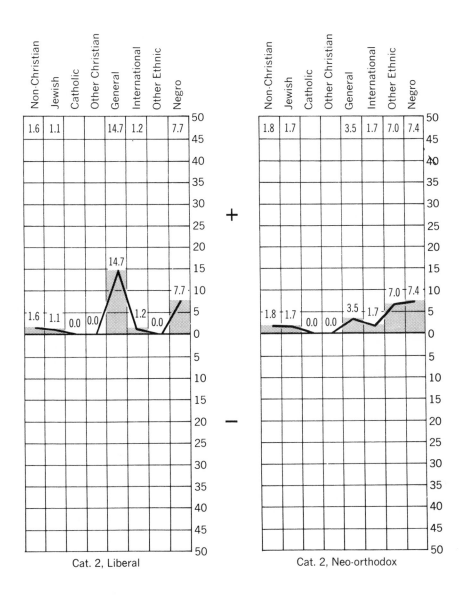

Fig. 32. Indirect Self-Criticism, Shown by the Distributions and Imbalances for Category 2 (Unitarian and Presbyterian). (For definition of this category see Appendix II.)

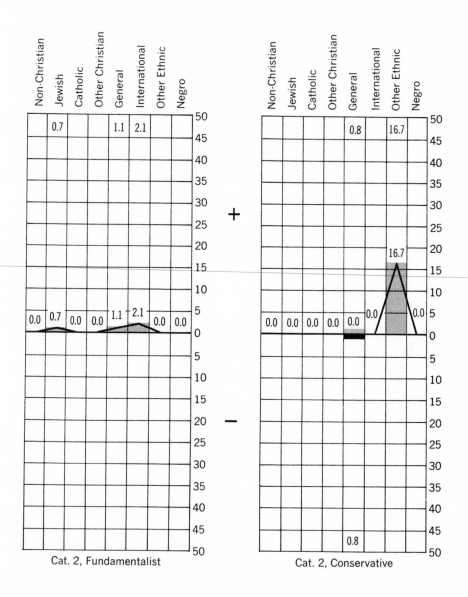

Fig. 33. Indirect Self-Criticism, Shown by the Distributions and Imbalances for Category 2 (Scripture Press and Missouri Synod). (For definition of this category see Appendix II.)

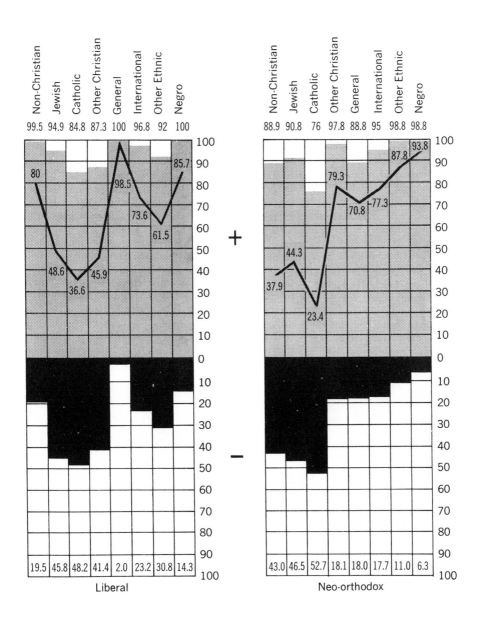

Fig. 34. Orientation of Liberal and Neo-Orthodox Curricula
to Outside Groups: General Distribution and Imbalance Scores
by Intergroup Areas.

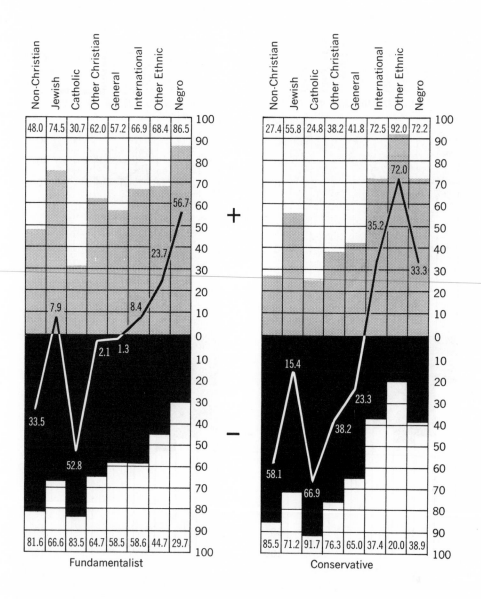

Fig. 35.  Orientation of Fundamentalist and Conservative Curricula to Outside Groups: General Distribution and Imbalance
Scores by Intergroup Areas.

418

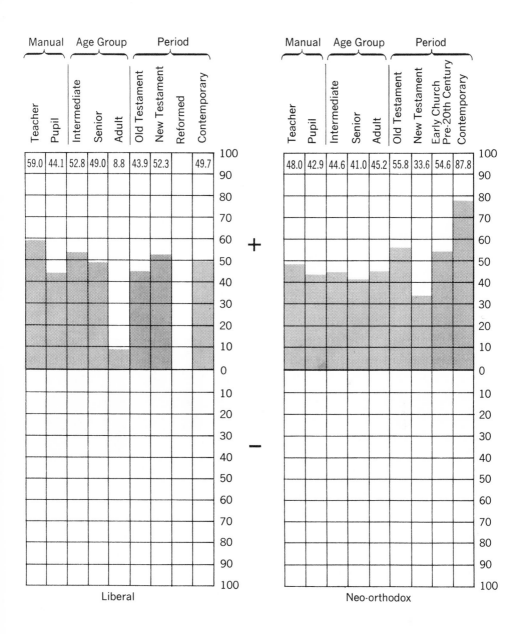

Fig. 36.  Some Liberal and Neo-Orthodox Variables, Jewish
References.  Imbalances only are shown.

419

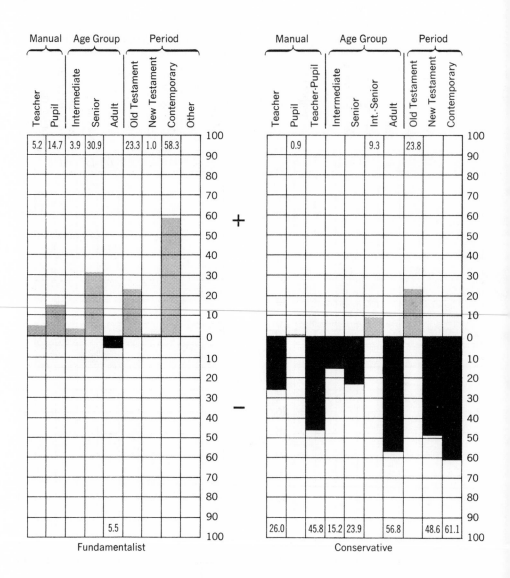

Fig. 37. Some Fundamentalist and Conservative Variables,
Jewish References. Imbalances only are shown.

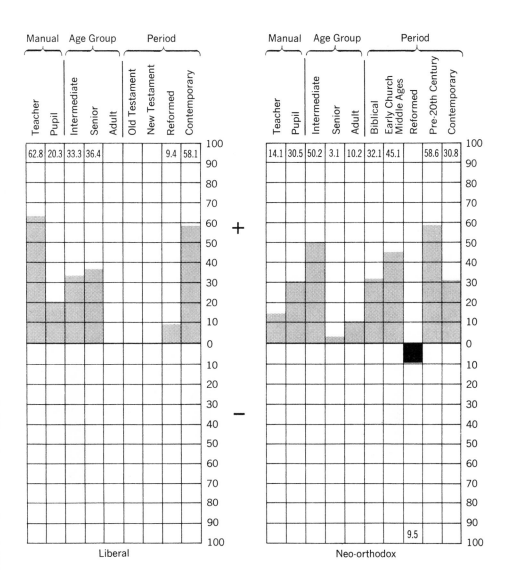

| Manual | | Age Group | | | Period | | | | | | Manual | | Age Group | | | Period | | | | | |
|---|---|---|---|---|---|---|---|---|---|---|---|---|---|---|---|---|---|---|---|---|---|
| Teacher | Pupil | Intermediate | Senior | Adult | Old Testament | New Testament | Reformed | Contemporary | | | Teacher | Pupil | Intermediate | Senior | Adult | Biblical | Early Church Middle Ages | Reformed | Pre-20th Century | Contemporary | |
| 62.8 | 20.3 | 33.3 | 36.4 | | | | 9.4 | 58.1 | | | 14.1 | 30.5 | 50.2 | 3.1 | 10.2 | 32.1 | 45.1 | | 58.6 | 30.8 | |

Liberal                                    Neo-orthodox

Fig. 38. Some Liberal and Neo-Orthodox Variables, Catholic Scores. Imbalances only are shown.

421

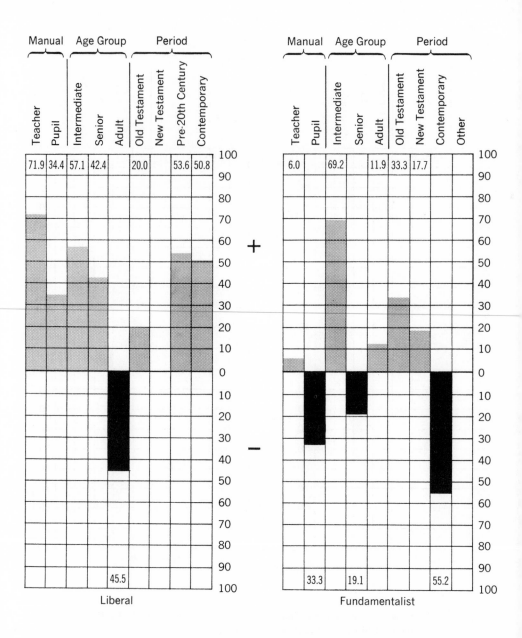

Fig. 39. Some Liberal and Fundamentalist Variables, Orientations to Other Christians. Imbalances only are shown.

# Bibliography

## Christian Social Theory for Intergroup Relations

Bainton, R. H., The Travail of Religious Liberty, Philadelphia, Westminster Press, 1951.

Henry, Carl F. H., The Uneasy Conscience of Modern Fundamentalism, Grand Rapids, Eerdman, 1947.

Loane, Marcus L., Makers of Religious Freedom in the Seventeenth Century, Grand Rapids, Eerdman, 1961.

Miegge, Giovanni, Religious Liberty, New York, Association Press, 1957.

Niebuhr, H. Richard, Christ and Culture, New York, Harper, 1951.

Niebuhr, Reinhold, "Democratic Toleration and the Groups of the Community," Chapter 4 of The Children of Light and the Children of Darkness, New York, Scribner's, 1944.

O'Connell, David Arthur, Christian Liberty, Westminster, Maryland, Newman Press, 1952.

Petry, Ray C., Christian Eschatology and Social Thought, New York, Abingdon Press, 1956.

Ramsey, Paul, "A Theology of Social Action," Social Action, 12 (1946), 4–34.

Scarlett, William, ed., The Christian Demand for Social Justice, New York, New American Library, 1949.

Smith, Timothy L., Revivalism and Social Reform, New York, Abingdon Press, 1957.

Spann, J. Richard, The Church and Social Responsibility, New York, Abingdon Press, 1953.

Troeltsch, Ernst, The Social Teachings of the Christian Churches, trans. Olive Wyon, 2 vols. New York, Macmillan, 1931.

Wright, George Ernest, The Biblical Doctrine of Man in Society, London, SCM Press, 1954.

## General Works on Intergroup Relations

Adorno, T. W., et al., The Authoritarian Personality, New York, Harper, 1950.

Allport, Gordon W., The Nature of Prejudice, Cambridge, Mass., Addison-Wesley, 1954.

American Council on Education, Intergroup Relations in Teaching Materials, Report of the Committee on the Study of Teaching Materials in Intergroup Relations, Washington, American Council on Education, 1949.

Clark, Kenneth B., Prejudice and Your Child, Boston, Beacon Press, 1955.

Clinchy, E. R., All in the Name of God, New York, John Pay, 1934.

Cushman, Robert E., Civil Liberties in the United States, Ithaca, Cornell University Press, 1946.

Dance, E. H., History without Bias? London, Council of Christians and Jews, 1954.

Dean, John P., and Rosen, Alex, A Manual of Intergroup Relations, Chicago, University of Chicago Press, 1955.

Eakin, Mildred Moody, and Eakin, Frank, Sunday School Fights Prejudice, New York, Macmillan, 1953.

Elliott, John H., Building Bridges between Groups That Differ, New York, National Conference of Christians and Jews, n. d.

Gittler, Joseph B., Understanding Minority Groups, New York, Wiley, 1956.

Hirsh, Selma, The Fears Men Live By, New York, Harper, 1956.

Maher, Trafford P., Olson, Bernhard E., Weinryb, Bernard D., "Intergroup Relations in Religious Textbooks," a symposium, Religious Education (March–April 1960), 109–38.

Myers, Gustavus, History of Bigotry in the United States, New York, Random House, 1943.

Pope, Liston, "Religion and the Class Structure," Annals of the American Academy of Political and Social Science, 256 (1948), 84–91.

Quillan, I. James, Textbook Improvement and International Understanding, Washington, the American Council on Education, n. d.

Schermerhorn, Richard A., These Our People, Boston, Heath, 1949.

Simpson, George E., and Yinger, J. Milton, Racial and Cultural Minorities: An Analysis of Prejudice and Discrimination, New York, Harper, 1953.

Williams, Robin M., Jr., The Reduction of Intergroup Tensions, New York, Social Science Research Council, 1947.

Yinger, Milton J., Religion, Society and the Individual, New York, Macmillan, 1957.

Non-Christian

Addison, James T., The Christian Approach to the Moslem, New York, Columbia University Press, 1942.

Appasamy, A. J., The Gospel and India's Heritage, London, S. P. C. K., 1942.

Arnold, T. W., The Legacy of Islam, Oxford, Clarendon Press, 1931.

Ashby, Philip H., The Conflict of Religions, New York, Scribner's, 1955.

Bloom, Alfred, "A Basis for the Comparison of Religion: Christianity and Buddhism," Journal of Bible and Religion, 24 (1956), 269-74.

Das, Bhagavan, The Essential Unity of All Religions, 2d ed. Wheaton, Illinois, Theosophical Press, 1947.

Devanandan, Paul David, "The Christian Attitude and Approach to Non-Christian Religions," International Review of Missions, 41 (1952), 177-84.

Dewick, E. C., The Christian Attitude toward Other Religions, Cambridge, England, Cambridge University Press, 1953.

Dorman, Harry Gaylord, Toward Understanding Islam, New York, Teachers College, Columbia University, 1948.

Faris, Nabih Amin, ed., The Arab Heritage, Princeton, Princeton University Press, 1944.

Fleming, D. J., Ethical Issues Confronting World Christians, New York, The International Missionary Council, 1935.

Hamilton, Clarence, Buddhism: A Religion of Infinite Compassion: Selections from Buddhist Literature, New York, Liberal Arts Press, 1952.

Harrison, M. H., Hindu Monism and Pluralism, New York, Oxford University Press, 1932.

Heiler, F., "How Can Christian and Non-Christian Co-operate?" Hibbert Journal, 52 (1954), 107-18.

Hocking, William E., Living Religions and a World Faith, New York, Macmillan, 1940.

Hogg, A. G., The Christian Message to the Hindu, London, SCM Press, 1947.

Joad, C. E. M., Counter Attack from the East, London, George Allen and Unwin, 1933.

Kraemer, Hendrik, The Christian Message in a Non-Christian World, New York, published for the International Missionary Council by Harper, 1938.

Martin, J. A., Jr., "Role of Christianity in the Meeting of East and West," Journal of Religion, 14 (1950), 367-80.

Müller, F. Max, ed., The Sacred Books of the East, Oxford, Clarendon Press, 1897-1901.

Nilsson, U. P., "Universal Religion," trans. M. Block, Review of Religion, 17 (1952), 5-10.

Paton, D., Christian Missions and the Judgment of God, London, SCM Press, 1953.                              .

Perry, Edmund, The Gospel in Dispute, New York, Doubleday, 1958.

Ross, Floyd H., Addressed to Christians: Isolationism vs. World Community, New York, Harper, 1950.

—— The Meaning of Life in Hinduism and Buddhism, Boston, Beacon Press, 1953.

Soper, Edmund Davison, The Inevitable Choice, Nashville and New York, Abingdon Press, 1957.

—— The Philosophy of the Christian World Mission, New York and Nashville, Abingdon Press, 1943.

Streeter, Burnett Hillman, The Buddha and the Christ, London, Macmillan, 1932.

Suzuki, D. T., The Essence of Buddhism, Pasadena, California, P. D. and Ione Perkins, 1947.

—— Mysticism: Christian and Buddhist, New York, Harper, 1957.

Titus, Murray T., The Young Moslem Looks at Life, New York, Friendship Press, 1937.

## Jewish

Abrahams, Israel, Studies in Pharisaism and the Gospels, 2 vols. Cambridge, Cambridge University Press, 1917, 1924.

Ackerman, Nathan W., and Jahoda, Marie, Anti-Semitism and Emotional Disorder, New York, Harper, 1950.

Agus, Jacob B., Guideposts in Modern Judaism, New York, Block, 1954.

Allis, Oswald T., Prophecy and the Church, Philadelphia, the Presbyterian and Reformed Publishing Co., 1945.

Bacon, Alexander Samuel, The Illegal Trial of Christ, Annville, Pennsylvania, Press of Journal Publishing Co., 1908.

Baeck, Leo, The Pharisees and Other Essays, New York, Schocken Books, 1947.

Berger, E., The Jewish Dilemma, New York, Devon-Adair, 1945.

Berkhof, H., "Three Divisions in the Life of the Church,"
  Ecumenical Review, 6 (1954), 138–46.
Bernstein, Peretz, Jew-Hate as a Sociological Problem, trans.
  David Saraph, New York, Philosophical Library, 1951.
Braude, William G., Jewish Proselyting, Vol. 6, Providence,
  Brown University, 1940.
Brookes, James H., Israel and the Church, New York, Fleming
  H. Revell, n. d.
Brown, Heywood, and Britt, George, Christians Only, New
  York, Vanguard Press, 1931.
Cohon, Samuel S., "The Place of Jesus in the Religious Life
  of His Day," Journal of Biblical Literature, 48 (1929),
  82–108.
Daube, David, The New Testament and Rabbinic Judaism,
  London, Athlone Press, 1956.
Davies, William D., Paul and Rabbinic Judaism, London,
  S. P. C. K., 1948.
Easton, Burton Scott, Early Christianity: The Purpose of Acts,
  and Other Papers, ed. Frederick C. Grant, Greenwich, Con-
  necticut, Seabury Press, 1954.
Echkardt, A. Roy, Christianity and the Children of Israel,
  New York, King's Crown Press, 1948.
Ehrenberg, H. P., "Rediscovery of the Jew in Christianity,"
  International Review of Missions, 33 (1944), 400–06.
Enelow, Hyman G., A Jewish View of Jesus, New York, Block,
  1931.
Filson, Floyd V., The New Testament against Its Environment,
  London, SCM Press, 1950.
Finch, Rowland George, The Synagogue Lectionary and the
  New Testament, London, S. P. C. K., 1939.
Foakes-Jackson, F. J., The Acts of the Apostles, New York
  and London, Harper, 1931.
Friedländer, Michael, The Jewish Religion, London, Shapiro,
  Vallentine, 1922.
Friedman, M. S., "Martin Buber and Christian Thought,"
  Review of Religion, 18 (1953), 31–43.
Glanville, Reginald, God and the Jews, London, Epworth
  Press, 1947.
Goldstein, Morris, Jesus in the Jewish Tradition, New York,
  Macmillan, 1950.
Graeber, I., and Britt, S. H., Jews in a Gentile World: The
  Problem of Anti-Semitism, New York, Macmillan, 1942.

Grayzel, Solomon, The Church and the Jews in the XIIIth
    Century, Philadelphia, Dropsie College, 1933.
Guignebert, C. A. H., The Jewish World in the Time of Jesus,
    trans. S. H. Hooke, part of The History of Civilization,
    ed. C. K. Ogden, London, Kegan Paul, Trench, Trubner,
    1939.
Hedenquist, Göte, ed., The Church and the Jewish People,
    London, Edinburgh House Press, 1954.
—— "Bringing the Gospel to the Jews," Ecumenical Review, 7
    (1955), 232–37.
Helfgott, Benjamin W., The Doctrine of Election in Tannaitic
    Literature, New York, King's Crown Press, 1954.
Herberg, Will, Protestant, Catholic, Jew: An Essay in Amer-
    ican Religious Sociology, New York, Doubleday, 1955.
—— review of "Christianity and Anti-Semitism," by N. Berdyaev
    New Republic, 133 (August 22, 1955), 20.
Herford, Robert Travers, Judaism in the New Testament
    Period, London, Lindsey Press, 1928.
—— The Pharisees, New York, Macmillan, 1924.
—— What the World Owes to the Pharisees, London, George
    Allen and Unwin, 1919.
Hoenig, Sidney Benjamin, The Great Sanhedrin, Philadelphia,
    Dropsie College, 1953.
Isaac, Jules, Has Anti-Semitism Roots in Christianity? New
    York, N. C. C. J., 1961.
Jasper, G., "State of Israel and Christendom," International
    Review of Missions, 40 (1951), 313–21.
Jocz, J., The Jewish People and Jesus Christ, London,
    S. P. C. K., 1949.
—— "Jewish-Christian Controversy Concerning Israel," Inter-
    national Review of Missions, 37 (1948), 382–92.
Johnson, F. Ernest, "The Jewish Question as an Ecumenical
    Problem," Ecumenical Review, 7 (1955), 225–31.
Johnson, Willard, "The Crucifixion and Anti-Semitism," re-
    print from the National Jewish Monthly, distributed by the
    National Conference of Christians and Jews.
Johnston, G., "The Church and Israel: Continuity and Discon-
    tinuity in the New Testament Doctrine of the Church,"
    Journal of Religion, 34 (1954), 26–36.
Kagan, Henry Enoch, Changing the Attitude of Christian to-
    ward Jew, New York, Columbia University Press, 1952.
Kallen, Horace M., "Of Them Which Say They Are Jews," and

Other Essays on the Jewish Struggle, ed. Judah Pilch, New York, Bloch, 1954.

Kertzer, Morris N., What Is a Jew? New York, World, 1953.

Kilpatrick, G. D., The Trial of Jesus, London, Oxford University Press, 1952.

Klausner, Joseph, From Jesus to Paul, trans. William F. Stinespring, New York, Macmillan, 1943.

—— Jesus of Nazareth: His Life, Times, and Teaching, trans. Herbert Danby, New York, Macmillan, 1945.

—— The Messianic Idea in İsrael, from Its Beginning to the Completion of the Mishnah, trans. W. F. Stinespring, New York, Macmillan, 1955.

Knight, G. A. F., "Our Truncated Faith," International Review of Missions, 33 (1944), 167–73.

Levertoff, Olga, The Wailing Wall, New York, Morehouse, 1937.

Levison, Nahum, Jewish Background of Christianity, Edinburgh, T. and T. Clark, 1932.

Lewis, Abram Herbert, Paganism Surviving in Christianity, New York, Putnam's, 1892.

Loewe, H., ed., Judaism and Christianity, Vol. 2 of The Contact of Pharisaism with Other Cultures, New York, Macmillan, 1937.

Lovsky, F., "Christian-Jewish Relations: Some French Points of View," International Review of Missions, 44 (1955), 274–91.

Lowenthal, Leo, and Guterman, Norbert, Prophets of Deceit: A Study of the Techniques of the American Agitator, New York, Harper, 1949.

Mace, David R., Hebrew Marriage, London, Epworth Press, 1953.

Marcus, Jacob R., The Jew in the Medieval World, Cincinnati, Union of American Hebrew Congregations, 1938.

Marcus, R., "The Pharisees in the Light of Modern Scholarship," Journal of Religion, 32 (1952), 153–64.

Moehlman, C. H., The Christian-Jewish Tragedy: A Study in Religious Prejudice, Rochester, Hart, 1933.

Montefiore, C. G., The Old Testament and After, London, Macmillan, 1923.

—— Rabbinic Literature and Gospel Teachings, London, Macmillan, 1930.

—— The Synoptic Gospels, ed. C. G. Montefiore, 2 vols.

London, Macmillan, 1927.

Moore, George Foot, Judaism in the First Centuries of the Christian Era: The Age of the Tannaim, 3 vols. Cambridge, Mass., Harvard University Press, 1927–30.

Neumann, F., "Christian Love and the Jews," International Review of Missions, 44 (1955), 264–73.

Oesterley, William O. E., The Jewish Background of the Christian Liturgy, Oxford, Clarendon Press, 1925.

Oesterreicher, John M., The Apostolate to the Jews: A Catholic View of the Mission to the Jews, New York, America Press, 1948.

Olson, Bernhard E., "Christian Education and the Image of the Pharisees," Religious Education, 55 (1960), 410–17.

Palliere, Aime, The Unknown Sactuary, New York, Bloch, 1928.

Parkes, James W., The Conflict of the Church and the Synagogue, London, Soncino, 1934.

—— The Jewish Problem in the Modern World, New York and London, Oxford University Press, 1946.

—— Judaism and Christianity, Chicago, University of Chicago Press, 1948.

Roth, Cecil, The Jewish Contributions to Civilization, New York, Harper, 1940.

Runes, Dagobert David, The Hebrew Impact on Western Civilization, New York, Philosophical Library, 1951.

Schoeps, H. J., "Religious Bridge between Jew and Christian: Shall We Recognize Two Covenants?" trans. R. Manheim, Commentary, 9 (1950), 129–32. For discussion, cf. Vol. 9 (1950), 383–84.

Schonfeld, Solomon, The Universal Bible, Being the Pentateucha Texts at First Addressed to All Nations (Torat B'nei Noach— Teaching for the Sons of Noah), London, Sidgwick and Jackson, 1955.

Sittler, J., "The Abiding Concern of the Church for the Jewish People," Ecumenical Review, 7 (1955), 221–24.

Sparks, H. F. D., The Old Testament in the Christian Church, London, SCM Press, 1944.

Steinberg, M., A Partisan Guide to the Jewish Problem, Indianapolis and New York, Bobbs-Merrill, 1945.

Stewart, Roy A., Rabbinic Theology, Edinburgh, Oliver and Boyd, 1961.

Tasker, R. V. G., The Old Testament in the New, 2d ed. rev., London, SCM Press, 1954.

Tillich, Paul, "Faith in the Jewish-Christian Tradition,"
    Christendom, 7 (1942), 518-26.
—— "The Meaning of Anti-Semitism," Radical Religion, 4
    (1938), 34-36.
Trachtenberg, Joshua, The Devil and the Jews, New Haven,
    Yale University Press, 1943.
Trattner, Ernest R., Understanding the Talmud, New York,
    Nelson, 1955.
Walker, Thomas, The Teaching of Jesus and the Jewish Teach-
    ing of His Age, London, Allen and Unwin, 1923.
Weigall, Arthur, The Paganism in Our Christianity, New York
    and London, Putnam's, 1928.
Williams, Arthur Lukyn, A Manual of Christian Evidences for
    Jewish People, Vol. 1, London, S.P.C.K., 1919.
Winter, Paul, On the Trial of Jesus, Berlin, Walter de Gruyter,
    1961.
Wright, George Ernest, The Challenge of Israel's Faith, Chi-
    cago, University of Chicago Press, 1944.
—— God Who Acts, London, SCM Press, 1952.
—— "The Old Testament, A Bulwark of the Church against
    Paganism," International Review of Missions, 40 (1951),
    265-76.
Zeitlin, Solomon, Who Crucified Jesus? New York and London,
    Harper, 1942.

Roman Catholic

Bainton, Roland H., The Reformation of the Sixteenth Century,
    Boston, Beacon Press, 1952.
Barrett, E. Boyd, While Peter Sleeps, New York, I. Wash-
    burn, 1930.
Beesley, Thomas Quinn, "What It Means to Marry a Protestant,"
    Forum, 82 (1929), 226-30.
Black, Algernon D., If I Marry Outside My Religion, New York,
    the Public Affairs Committee, 1954.
Blanshard, Paul, American Freedom and Catholic Power,
    Boston, Beacon Press, 1949.
—— Communism, Democracy and Catholic Power, Boston,
    Beacon Press, 1951.
Boehmer, Heinrich, The Jesuits, trans. Paul Zeller Strodach,
    Philadelphia, Castle Press, 1928.
Catholic Faith: A Catechism, Book 3, Washington, Catholic
    University of America Press, 1938.

Catholicism in America: A Symposium, editors of Commonweal,
    New York, Harcourt, Brace, 1954.
Congar, Yves M. J., The Catholic Church and the Race Question,
    Paris, UNESCO, 1953.
Cowan, Wayne H. et al., Facing Protestant–Roman Catholic
    Tensions, New York, Association Press, 1960.
Elderkin, George W., The Roman Catholic Problem, New York,
    Vantage Press, 1954.
Gurian, Waldemar, The Catholic Church in World Affairs,
    Notre Dame, University of Notre Dame Press, 1954.
Herberg, Will, Protestant, Catholic, Jew: An Essay in Amer-
    ican Religious Sociology, New York, Doubleday, 1955.
Hughes, Philip, A Popular History of the Catholic Church, New
    York, Macmillan, 1947.
Johnson, Frederick A., Christ and Catholicism, New York,
    Vantage Press, 1954.
Kane, John J., Catholic-Protestant Conflicts in America, Chi-
    cato, Regnery, 1955.
Knox, Ronald A., The Belief of Catholics, New York and Lon-
    don, Harper, 1927.
Lamb, George, trans., Tolerance and the Catholic: A Sym-
    posium, New York, Sheed and Ward, 1955.
Landis, Benson Y., "Protestants and Catholics," Commonweal,
    42 (July 27, 1945), 356–58.
Maycock, A. L., The Inquisition, London, Constable, 1926.
Maynard, Theodore, The Catholic Church and the American
    Idea, New York, Appleton-Century-Crofts, 1953.
McKnight, John P., The Papacy: A New Appraisal, New York,
    Rinehart, 1952.
Miller, William, "A Catholic Plan for a New Social Order,"
    Social Action, 17 (February 15, 1951), 3–43.
Niebuhr, H. Richard, "Issues between Catholics and Protes-
    tants in Midcentury," a symposium, Religion in Life, 23
    (1954), 199 ff.
O'Neill, J. M., Catholics in Controversy, New York, McMullen
    Books, 1954.
Peers, Edgar A., Spain, the Church and the Orders, London,
    Eyre and Spottiswood, 1939.
Pelikan, Jaroslav, The Riddle of Roman Catholicism, New
    York and Nashville, Abingdon Press, 1959.
Rafton, Harold R., The Roman Catholic Church and Democracy:
    The Teachings of Pope Leo XIII, Boston, Beacon Press,
    1951.

Reynolds, Arthur G., What's the Difference? Protestant and
    Roman Catholic Beliefs Compared, Toronto, Commission
    on the Christian Faith, 1954.
Scharper, Philip, ed., American Catholics: A Protestant-
    Jewish View, New York, Sheed and Ward, 1959.
Silcox, Claris E., and Fisher, Galen M., Catholics, Jews and
    Protestants, New York, Harper, 1934.
Smalley, Beryl, The Study of the Bible in the Middle Ages,
    New York, Philosophical Library, 1952.
Smith, G. D., ed., The Teaching of the Catholic Church,
    Vol. 1, New York, Macmillan, 1949.
Stokes, Anson Phelps, Church and State in the United States,
    New York, Harper, 1950.
Stuber, Stanley I., Primer on Roman Catholicism for Protes-
    tants, New York, Association Press, 1953.
Tavard, George H., The Catholic Approach to Protestantism,
    New York, Harper, 1955.
Tillich, Paul, "The Permanent Significance of the Catholic
    Church for Protestantism," Protestant Digest, 3 (1941),
    23-31.
Underwood, Kenneth Wilson, Protestant and Catholic:
    Religious and Social Interaction in an Industrial Community,
    Boston, Beacon Press, 1957.
Verrill, A. Hyatt, The Inquisition, New York, Appleton, 1931.
Wood, Leland Foster, If I Marry a Roman Catholic, Chicago,
    National Council of the Churches of Christ in the U.S.A.,
    1945.

Other Christian

Bilheimer, Robert S., The Quest for Christian Unity, New York,
    Association Press, 1952.
Clark, Elmer T., The Small Sects in America, New York,
    Abingdon Press, 1949.
Forster, Walter O., Zion on the Mississippi, Saint Louis, Con-
    cordia, 1953.
Fry, C. Luther, The U.S. Looks at Its Churches, New York,
    Institute of Social and Religious Research, 1930.
Mayer, Frederick E., The Religious Bodies of America, Saint
    Louis, Concordia, 1954.
Mead, Frank S., Handbook of Denominations in the United
    States, New York, Abingdon-Cokesbury Press, 1951.
Nichols, James Hastings, Democracy and the Churches, Phila-
    delphia, Westminster Press, 1951.

—— *Primer for Protestants*, New York, Association Press, 1947

Niebuhr, H. Richard, *Social Sources of Denominationalism*, New York, Holt, 1929.

Ryrie, Charles Caldwell, *The Premillennial Faith*, New York, Loizeaux Brothers, 1953.

Stuber, Stanley I., *How We Got Our Denominations*, New York, Association Press, 1949.

Tate, Edward Mowbray, *Church School Curricula and Education for Protestant Unity*, New York, private printing, 1932.

Wentz, Addel Ross, *A Basic History of Lutheranism in America*, Philadelphia, Muhlenberg Press, 1955.

Wolseley, R. E., "The Church Press: Bulwark of Denominational Sovereignty," *Christendom*, 11 (1946), 490–500.

Wright, Conrad, *The Beginnings of Unitarianism in America*, Boston, Starr King Press, 1955.

Younger, George, "Protestant Piety and the Right Wing," *Social Action*, 17 (May 15, 1951), 5–35.


## Negro

Bowen, Trevor, *Divine White Right: A Study of Race Segregation and Interracial Cooperation in Religious Organizations and Institutions in the United States*, New York, Harper, 1934.

Brown, Ina Corinne, *The Story of the American Negro*, rev. ed. New York, Friendship Press, 1950.

Culver, Dwight W., *Negro Segregation in the Methodist Church*, New Haven, Yale University Press, 1953.

Gallagher, Buell G., *Color and Conscience*, New York, Harper, 1946.

Loescher, F. S., *The Protestant Church and the Negro*, New York, Association Press, 1948.

Mays, Benjamin E., *Seeking to Be a Christian in Race Relations*, New York, Friendship Press, 1946.

—— and Nicholson, Joseph W., *The Negro's Church*, New York, Institute of Social and Religious Research, 1933.

McGurk, Frank C. J., "A Scientist's Report on Race Differences," *United States News & World Report*, 41 (September 21, 1956), 92–96.

Myrdal, Gunnar, *An American Dilemma*, 2 vols. New York and London, Harper, 1944.

Niebuhr, Reinhold, "Christian Faith and the Race Problem,"

Christianity and Society, 11 (1945), 21–24.

Pope, Liston, The Kingdom beyond Caste, New York, Friendship Press, 1957.

Richardson, Harry, Dark Glory: A Picture of the Church among Negroes in the Rural South, New York, Friendship Press, 1947.

Wentzel, Fred D., Epistle to White Christians, Philadelphia, Christian Education Press, 1948.

# Index

The tables and graphs appearing on pages 351–422 have not been indexed.